The Destined Hour

Also by George Feifer

TO DANCE: THE AUTOBIOGRAPHY OF VALERY PANOV

MOSCOW FAREWELL

OUR MOTHERLAND AND OTHER VENTURES IN RUSSIAN REPORTAGE

THE GIRL FROM PETROVKA

SOLZHENITSYN

MESSAGE FROM MOSCOW

JUSTICE IN MOSCOW

BARBARA and BARRY ROSEN
with GEORGE FEIFER

The Destined Hour

The Hostage Crisis
and One Family's Ordeal

DOUBLEDAY & COMPANY, INC.
GARDEN CITY, NEW YORK
1982

Library of Congress Cataloging in Publication Data

Rosen, Barbara and Barry with George Feifer.
The Destined Hour.

Includes index.
1. Iran Hostage Crisis, 1979–1981—Personal narratives.
2. Rosen, Barbara.   3. Rosen, Barry.
I. Rosen, Barry.   II. Feifer, George.   III. Title.
E183.8.I55R66   955′.054
AACR2

BOOK DESIGN BY BENTE HAMANN

ISBN: 0-385-17895-6
Library of Congress Catalog Card Number 81–43857

First Edition

For Sarah, Abraham, Lillian, and John

AUTHORS' NOTE

The names of several Iranians who appear in the book
have been changed for their protection.

Think not, O King! thy sceptre or thy power
One moment can arrest the destined hour.

—Abol Qasem Ferdowsi,
author of *The Book of Kings,*
the Iranian national epic.

FOREWORD

I first saw Barry Rosen standing out from the hoopla that otherwise filled a television screen. It was the day after the fifty-two American hostages in Iran had returned to America, provoking an extraordinary outpouring of national rejoicing and admiration. Barry was answering journalists' questions with what I would soon discover is characteristic modesty and astuteness. Even more than that, I liked the quickness of his mind and the twinkle in his eyes. The celebrated four hundred and forty-four days had weakened his health more than outsiders suspected. But he had reserves for quips—as well as for yet more curiosity about Iran, a country he had loved and which had caused him unusual pain.

When we met in person several weeks later, a trail of cheering schoolboys was following him as he walked to his in-laws' house in Brooklyn. He stopped to talk with them in an easy, nonpatronizing voice. Despite his recent ordeal and his thirty-six years, Barry was full of boyishness himself, especially in his shy smile and his eagerness. When the boys returned to their stickball game, he continued walking and soon passed the tired elementary school his wife, Barbara, had attended. "HAPPINESS IS BARRY!" proclaimed a large sign in the windows of the school's upper floor. The subject of that loving declaration tried to distract my attention from it.

His fame, red-hot then, has cooled little. Just because so much was made of the fifty-two hostages, especially of their publicity-saturated return in the winter of 1981, many assumed he would be forgotten quickly—in keeping with the new American pattern of the "instant personality," whose moment of celebrity leaves him an instant has-been. That is not Barry, partly because he abhors being a celebrity. When strangers stop him on the street, as they still do long after his return, his blushing smile covers a wince. He does not want to spoil people's pleasure in shaking his hand, or offend their patriotism. At the same time, he insists the affection for him is misplaced. It makes him dishonest, he feels, because it derives from false assumptions about his conduct as a hostage. Whatever he says about himself, this modesty is one of the very factors that make him admirable.

"You can't tell people not to greet you; that's a reflection of something open and generous in the American character," he told me. "But I can try to keep it at the 'Welcome home' level and not let them make me more than I am. Because I don't want to fool myself or encourage them to fool themselves. Hero worship is all wrong in my case—and the last thing we need, especially since none of the fundamental problems of dealing with Iran have been faced."

Since he speaks with this directness in public, the public has had good time to become disenchanted. In fact, it continues to be drawn to him.

"Hey, Barry! Aren't you Barry . . . er, Rubin?" asks a large man in a shiny suit as we walk in mid-Manhattan. "You did a great job out there in I-ran. How are things shaping up for ya now?" Having exchanged views with the hearty man, Barry leaves him beaming, then turns to me, beaming himself. "They're beginning to mix me up," he says happily. "It's 'Rubin' now. Soon they'll forget Rosen altogether."

Everything I learned during the preparation of this book convinced me this hope is genuine. References to his bravery—in the press and in official citations, as on the street—embarrass him particularly. In all the time we spent together during the past year, he stressed nothing more than his conviction that he was not a hero in any sense.

"Being a prisoner is almost wholly a passive experience," he kept telling me. "There's nothing heroic in the daily routine of confinement —and if some prisoners do manage to acquit themselves bravely, that didn't apply to me. I barely squeaked through with a passing grade. So many people insist on making me more than I was."

What he was referring to in his constant warning against heroics will reveal itself in the pages that follow. I hope it will be just as clear that severe demands on himself largely explain his mediocre rating of his own conduct. The fastidious Barry always looks perfectly turned out, even after a night of work. He is a hard self-taskmaster who instinctively criticizes rather than excuses himself for deviation from high expectations of his own performance. From my own work in Soviet affairs, I know that after he was appointed chief of the Voice of America's Uzbek service in 1974, he made it one of the best of the services broadcasting to the Soviet Union. (He majored in Persian-Iranian studies and minored in Central Asia as a graduate student, which led to his appointment.)

This account begins with his return to Iran in November 1978 as the American Embassy's Press Attaché. Seven months later, his immediate superior wrote that "Mr. Rosen quickly established himself as one of the most knowledgeable Americans on the Iran scene at the Embassy. . . . His presence here has been extraordinarily beneficial. . . . Even the most rabid anti-American publications made time for Rosen. His command of the language, his deep knowledge of Persian history and culture, made him a welcomed participant in frank discussions about the US-Iran relationship. My only regret is that he was not assigned here a year or two earlier."

His special knowledge of Iran helped make him a crucial figure in the Embassy as the situation grew increasingly hazardous for Americans. The affection for the country that nourished this knowledge is so deep that he is continuing his studies about it—as Columbia University's first Presidential Fellow—despite his hostage experience.

All that, however, makes him sound too somber. Had I met him at a gathering, knowing nothing about him, I would have taken him for a man-about-town. He loves to eat, travel, watch baseball, and especially to joke. There is no trace of the pedant, or even of the bureaucrat, in him. In this sense, Barry Rosen is a regular guy who happened to volunteer for the Peace Corps in Iran, happened to go to graduate school when he returned, happened to take a government job afterward, and happened to be assigned to Tehran at the crucial time in its relationship with America.

*

Barbara Rosen is even more the regular girl, and just as easy to come to know. If speaking of her grace before her intelligence sounds patronizing, that is what impresses one first about her—as it impressed Barry when he first laid intrigued eyes on her. A Brooklyn housewife waiting to join Barry in Tehran when the American Embassy was seized, she swiftly became one of the hostage wives most sought after for comments and television interviews. I was abroad throughout the period of her public appearances, but my American friends who followed the domestic side of the crisis spoke of the unaffected manner that enhanced her beauty. The screen did not mislead them.

They also commended the appeal of her common sense, natural wisdom, and candor—and if anything, they underestimated those qualities. She had received a master's degree in education from Brooklyn College but had had no formal training in foreign affairs. Nevertheless, her analytical powers quickly became apparent. Barbara is given to the kinds of solutions that might actually work, rather than merely to wave the flag or enhance the reputation of the proposer. Even in the tensest moments, she didn't bleat or panic but talked forthright good sense, and not only because she had, through Barry, an acute perception of Iran and Iranians.

What my friends did not suspect—because Barbara hid it so well—was that she felt great conflict about her appearances. The public saw her as a television "natural." She saw herself—and more important, Barry—as a victim of the celebrity craze. Trying to use the publicity more than it used her, she smiled at the lens. It was a revelation to me that strong self-control kept her from shouting outrage to many people behind it.

When not making an appearance, she is the strong, silent type. Her blush shows less visibly than Barry's, thanks to her darker complexion. She is also more serene by nature, less driven to achieve and perfect. Despite this difference, the couple have much in common. They share a great need to talk to one another, truly talk—about everything. Even by American standards, both are powerfully devoted to their children.

More than anything, Barry and Barbara share a need to be honest and frank about what they see and experience. That largely explains their affinity, despite different backgrounds. It is the strength of the relationship, the "secret" that makes their marriage work. They seem unable to answer any question with less than the whole truth, especially to one another.

What distinguished our working sessions is the quality least possible to convey secondhand. It is candor. Neither made any attempt to prettify their sentiments, to deny selfish and otherwise embarrassing thoughts that alternated with the noble. Their stories gave me many insights into life in Iran and America. I was drawn to them even more as persons for their uncommonly "straight" selves.

Although less embarrassed about celebrity status than Barry, Barbara too tries to disassociate herself from show-business publicity she feels is undeserved. Her nervousness at writing her acceptance speech for the Mother of the Year award came more from her conviction that it ought not to have gone to her than from concern about sentences and paragraphs, which by then had become fluent. She used the occasion to remind the audience of the mothers who had been widowed by the death of eight servicemen in the attempt to rescue the hostages, in April 1980: mothers who had been forgotten in the fanfare about the return of the hostages. For Barry, learning of those deaths was the most depressing moment of his captivity. He promised himself to discharge his obligation to the surviving families—and he is keeping that promise by campaigning to raise money through the Simons Fund, for college educations for the seventeen fatherless children.

For reasons she will explain, Barbara had serious doubts whether to accept that award. She and Barry together had even graver doubts whether to write this book. Just because they had become symbols of the crisis, they very much wanted to set the record straight, for they feel that the symbolism—the intentional and unintentional distortion of the truth through media magnification and craving for melodrama —is part of the very problem that helped produce tragedy in Iran.

They are unusual people, especially for their willingness to blame themselves as much as anyone else for shortcomings. Even if they had not been cast in leading roles in contemporary history, I would have felt lucky to enjoy their frequent company.

George Feifer
Sharon, Connecticut
April 1982

I had forgotten the smells. Herbs and spices scented the air, summoning pungent memories. For a moment, I wondered whether I valued the country for itself or because I knew it well enough to consider it "mine." Even the pervasive odor of sweat and stale clothes was flavored with intoxicating nostalgia.

All the types were there in the airport, especially men in baggy suit jackets and stubble who outwardly resembled heavies in television films. I thought of what a shame it was—and how potentially dangerous—that so many Americans, brought up to react to this "sinister-foreign" appearance, had no opportunity to know the charm and generosity underneath. The scruffy man who changed money in his little booth was nibbling at a sweet, raw onion. Putting aside his dinner of a stew called *khoresht,* he received me with the typical blend of deference and dignity that made most passing encounters in Iran a pleasure. Despite stiff jet lag and the detachment I supposed I needed for my new position, I gave in to a moment of relief that so little had changed. These were the people I had come to understand and cherish.

But this couldn't be Iran without ambiguity. I also sensed so much had changed that I might just as well be visiting a new country as returning to the one of the best years of my youth.

In those Peace Corps years my tendency to idealize, together with my infatuation with Iranian manners and poetry, made me much too romantic about the country to observe it objectively. Even then, however, I knew Iran was sloppy, disorganized, and almost comically concerned with putting on a good show: with making up its face and saving it, whatever the situation and consequences. But ten years ago the airport was far from the shambles I saw now. The people were much less tense. Something more drastic had happened than the reports and confidential cables I'd been studying the past year had prepared me for.

I called my new boss. Jack Shellenberger, the Public Affairs Officer, apologized that he could not meet me because of the 9 P.M. curfew. "Try to make it to a hotel as quickly as possible. I'll see you in the morning." But since when did Iranians take any form of deadline seriously? Why was everyone rushing to evacuate the airport before the curfew?

My driver scrambled with the best of them. First we observed the rituals, as if the urgency had suddenly evaporated and he had all week to bargain. "You speak Farsi just like" (he reached for an extravagant compliment) "an Iranian. You know the score, sir, so I'll make you a very attractive offer, an excellent price." The old court language of Iran, Farsi eventually became the national tongue. Mine was in fact adequate but still rusty, even after a review course in Washington.

The beaming driver helped settle me in his bumpy back seat. Having had me with proper leisure, he raced his taxi toward Eisenhower Avenue until the ancient Peykan threatened to rattle apart. Hammer marks of homemade repairs dotted its fenders in the pattern of bracelets from the bazaar. All Tehran drivers become maniacs behind the wheel, but my new protector, who grew increasingly anxious about the hour, was a species of speeder I hadn't previously encountered. We were still on the outskirts. Suddenly he ripped his gears to pieces, screeched to a stop, jumped out, and relieved himself on his hubcap.

But he was no less eager than any Iranian I'd known to establish a personal rapport, to be hospitable, to *make me feel comfortable and happy*. This must not be a mere business relationship, with the distance and possible nastiness that implied, but something genuine—because personal. When we had sped off again, he turned around in his seat every few minutes to offer his artless smile with doses of genuine concern. "How're you doing?" His hand clasped my knee in a gesture of reassurance. He was worried that the long flight had taken a lot out of me: I looked pale. "Please don't be upset. I'll get you there with not one little problem. I hope you are feeling fine." A little less ardor on his part for lifting his eyes off the road to delve deeply into mine would have made me feel even finer.

Water flowed down open courses called jubes on the shoulders of the streets. This too prompted the happiness of recognition, together with memories of beguiling medieval towns where jubes were for washing food and clothes. But it also prompted more questions. Vast amounts of money spent for royal pleasure and for the latest, most elaborate military equipment. Vast amounts of publicity about—and in Washington, belief in—the Shah's modernization. But not enough hold on reality or concern with ordinary lives to replace jubes with closed sewers.

The driver revealed the gaps in his teeth without embarrassment as he settled his eyes on me again. When we passed the massive, mosque-like monument erected by the Shah in honor of the Shah, my own eyes blinked at the look of Tehran's major arteries. The November bleakness that gave a gloomy chill to the smog was nothing new in the capital. What depressed me was the touch of doom in the air. Something more than tanks patrolling the streets and ransacked Western banks announced that the Shah's rule was crumbling. Windows of Western airline offices, Westernized businesses, theaters that showed Western films were shattered. The crowds that had done the smashing were clearly angrier and the Shah's control more precarious than I had imagined. I wanted to give him the benefit of the doubt in these first minutes back, but in my bones I already knew he could not last much longer.

"Yes, many offices are burned," said the driver, as if reading my thoughts. "The ones that were involved with the West, especially with America." He turned around again and squeezed my hand. "This is not the Iran you knew. You have returned at the worst possible time for you."

We raced down Shahreza Avenue, past more signs the Shah had erected to himself, or permitted others to erect. The driver braked at a corner and waited, with noisy impatience, for a red light to change. Something was unpleasantly familiar about that particular intersection. Oh yes: In 1969 I had been in an accident there.

Then too I was in a taxi waiting for the green, when someone hit us sharply from behind. The blow stunned me more than the timid driver. We knew there was going to be trouble as soon as we looked around. The other car was a large Mercedes.

The plump man who extracted himself from behind his wheel was the equal of his machine. He began intimidating my driver even before waddling up to grab his trembling neck. "I'm going to send you behind bars. Get this straight from the beginning: I'm a retired military officer." Still puffing and bellowing—and smoothing his sleek suit at the same time—he told a passing policeman that he was going to arrest the driver because he had backed into his car. "I was stopped there for the light. That idiot was one hundred percent wrong!"

When I told the policeman who I was and what I had seen, the Mercedes man's fury rose to a new pitch. When I said I wanted to sign a statement in the police station, the veins in his neck gorged. At the station he continued to rip at the driver while trying to intimidate me, too, with the threat that he knew—he drew a breath to help himself establish the importance of his next phrase—the chief of the National Police Force. It happened that one of my odd jobs was giving English lessons to that particular General. I knew the country well enough to play his game, and began by asking for a telephone.

"Whom do you want to call?" asked the desk officer.

"I want to call General Mobassir."

The slight pause in the room was punctuated by looks of disbelief.

"But the General won't be in his office at this hour," was the best anyone could think to reply.

"Naturally not. I have his home number."

The expressions of disbelief hardened but were shaded with apprehension on the unlikely chance I wasn't bluffing. The desk officer dialed the number for me. The receiver was swiftly replaced onto the cradle when a servant answered "General Mobassir's residence." While the Mercedes man shuddered in defeat, I signed my statement and shook the bewildered taxi driver's hand. The bully was still white when I left.

The forgotten episode came back as we waited for the light, this time without incident. It pulled together features I liked least about Iranian life: the arrogance of the Shah's nouveaux riches; the insecurity about how to behave with strangers that often instinctively led to attempts at domination; the vast importance of *parti,* a friend in the right place. But to me the Mercedes man had represented a nasty *element* in society, whereas now all society seemed nastier. The taxi driver's warning—Westerners must be very careful now; this is not the old Iran—was more ominous than the isolated bullying I had known well enough nine years before.

But it was a few minutes past nine o'clock and no punishment had come for violating the curfew. The driver helped me with my luggage, warmly wished me well, and rushed off. I had managed to get a room in a hotel on one of the main avenues, minutes from our U. S. International Communication Agency offices. The price in rials indicated runaway inflation, but the television set in the lobby spoke of something worse. A group of Iranian singers and dancers were performing as if life were joyous in the deeply strained country, as if everything were normal in the now deserted streets. Falseness stilted their movements. Something eerie lurked in broadcasting that kind of show at this kind of time.

Less hungry for food than for contact with the gentle country I had known, I settled myself in the dining room and ordered a glass of Iranian tea. "Sorry," said the waiter as I visualized the samovar. "We have only Lipton's." I asked for "little stones," my favorite Iranian bread among the scores of nourishing, rich-flavored varieties. The long, flat whole wheat loaf is baked on *sangak* ("little stones"), whose indentations remain in the delicious crust. "Sorry," said the waiter. "We have only white toast."

From my room I telephoned a close friend of my Peace Corps days. The concept and institution of *parti* was central not only to the Mercedes man but to Iranian life in general. With the rapidly deteriorating political situation, my friend Farhad was delighted to have what he supposed would be "a hand" in the American Embassy. Even without this, I believed he was happy to hear from me; ten years ago we had seen much of each other, and he knew how fond I was of him. But after we talked for a time, he lowered his voice. "You made a terrible mistake by coming back," he mumbled.

How differently I had imagined my return! How much I had wanted Barbara to be with me, how many outings and days I had planned for showing her this land's beauty and delicacy! It was almost eleven o'clock here, going on three in the afternoon in New York. I'd been alone a great deal in my adult life—by choice, the better to explore. But I hadn't wanted to return to Tehran alone. The idea discouraged me, and I'd protested before giving in to warnings not to take my family at this time.

Still, something depressed me more now than Barbara's absence. The thought of how hard it was in Washington to feel the pulse of Iran, even when reported by competent observers, blotted out my personal disappointment and my image of Barbara and the children at their late Sunday lunch that minute. The feeling of urgency and of imminent danger, even of panic, was vastly greater here than anything conveyed by the press or the cables I'd studied.

Loneliness intensified my fatigue after the twenty-four-hour trip. Finally I got up to try to locate the source of light that was flooding the room, keeping me awake. I opened the curtain. Below me, surrounding the hotel, a new wall was being built. This, too—walls around everything—was central to Iranian attitudes and life, reflecting the people's deep insecurity about themselves, their desire for privacy, and their intense devotion to their families. But this wall was in fact a steel fence, reflecting a new need to protect Westerners from whatever was building up against them. And the light was coming from an American tank. It was manned by Iranian troops in full battle gear. I couldn't sleep.

During most of my Peace Corps period I taught English at the National Police Academy, a supposed equivalent to a university. The chief of my department was as typical an Iranian official as I ever met. Major Afshar was a generally agreeable man whose uniform was lightly armored in gold braid. Our central conflict was over the language-learning gear supplied by one of Washington's more enlightened aid programs. The equipment was excellent. The Major would not let me use it.

After proper rituals of greeting and welcome, visiting delegations were taken, with as much haste as would not appear unseemly, to the language lab's elaborate booths, handsome tape recorders, and extensive tape library. This gleaming proof of How Progressive We Are, How Modern Are Our Ways, was produced for Iranian senators and foreign visitors alike. It was an expression of the same delicate modesty that inspired the Shah to identify himself as the King of Kings and Light of the Aryans. The Major, with his yards of gold lanyards, was a peacock in the land of the Peacock Throne. When the visitors left, the language lab was polished by the chief cleaner and locked. It was extremely important to the Major; showing it off was high among his professional functions. Despite my arguing and badgering, it was not to be used for anything so unimportant as language instruction.

"Let me at least use the library books," I pleaded. "Let the students take them home."

"They'll lose them," he countered.

"The books were sent here for *use*."

"You don't like me. You don't come in to drink tea with me."

"You're not letting me do *my job*."

Gradually I accepted that my grievance was relatively insignificant. Two Peace Corps friends encountered much more discouragement in the orphanage of a remote town where they worked. Perhaps just because Iranians lavish such attention and effort on their families, orphans are considered less than normal and have a very difficult time. It was briefly relieved for my friends' charges when dignitaries visited, just before which the orphanage officials would hurry to the bazaar for clothes, blankets, and toys. The children dared not touch anything during the inspection. The goodies were rushed back to the bazaar on the heels of the departing dignitaries.

Although such stories helped put the Major's notion of duty in a wider context, the betrayal of the job I had to do, that good old American attitude, remained hard to swallow.

"You don't like me," he complained the last time at the touching little party he, the students, and the staff gave me when I left. I didn't dislike him, but for all the knowledge I'd acquired about the workings of Iranian society, the look of the locked, empty language lab kept me from warming to him personally. And he was as sensitive to this as indifferent to his graduates' real skills. It is almost fair to say that personal relationships—friendship, trust, mutual esteem, mutual back scratching—are everything in Iran. The Major's job was part of the outer, official life that he and everyone like him regarded as raw material to mine and manipulate for enriching his inner life of family and friends.

Learning a foreign language was also part of the outer life, therefore taken seriously only by the exceptional. This was one of the better-equipped educational institutions. I had only sixty-odd students in my class, all dressed in khaki tunics with orange epaulets and boots so heavy that a trip to the blackboard sounded like a royal salute. Arriving in the morning, I would be treated to an embarrassingly formal welcome. Many cadets were my age—twenty-three—and some officers were considerably older. Some would soon be off for study in the States. No matter how many times I asked, none would sit down until I sat. But deference was one thing, learning quite another.

Like almost all Iranian students, mine had been raised in education by catechism. The teacher says a phrase and the class repeats it in mumbled chorus. At best, this led to a spewing back of what few understood.

The drive to repeat word for word what the teacher said was like the power of a stampeding herd. The most eager students would memorize fifty textbook pages but were panicked by a request to rearrange a sentence or an attempt to coax a reply to a question not explicitly answered in the text. The nearly palpable fear of saying the "wrong" thing produced a related fear of independent thinking. The inner shakiness of the strutting cadets was in direct proportion to their polishing of their uniforms and their images of themselves as clever, cool, and impervious to disapproval.

People who knew it all and actually grasped little were of course murder to teach. My favorite method was acting out scenes, such as buying something in a shop or going to a theater. The soon-to-be officers almost choked with embarrassment when asked to play their little roles. Losing face is more devastating to Iranians than any other nationality I know. Surely it comes from a deep national lack of self-confidence: a fundamental insecurity I came to feel had grown mostly from the country's constant overrunning by Turkic and Mongol occupiers. It was one of the oldest civilizations, with many splendid cultural achievements in which deep pride could justifiably be taken. But invaders looted and subjugated, and Iranians learned to swagger to hide their humiliation. Yet more humbling concessions extracted by the British and Russians within the last century hardly helped.

The sense of self was so fragile that how to protect, pamper, and nourish it often took up more time than tackling a job for its own sake. *Ab-e ru*, literally "the water of one's face," was more cherished in most situations than working effectively or acquiring knowledge. One had to *appear* to perform one's job well, even if failure to admit a mistake would cause an industrial accident. One had to *seem* superbly knowledgeable, even if this required ludicrous faking and fabrication. Criticism by an outsider was catastrophic, and in acting out unrehearsed scenes with words that hadn't been memorized, my students perceived a terrible threat. They feared nothing so much as losing their dignity, as letting their public pose of smart, tough, "with-it" officers slip to reveal something vulnerable. Sometimes I refused to translate the words I used in my own little scenes. This drove them crazy. Was I trying to force them to make fools of themselves?

Being made a fool of was *failing*, and one could not, *must* not fail. Examinations were taken accordingly. I would move the students from their accustomed seats to the far corners of the room. As they gave up their usual places, anxiety intensified until it could almost be heard. It bears repeating that no one was afraid of not learning English. A puncture in the self-inflated image of easy, self-assured competence was what was feared.

"I expect you all to demonstrate your honor in taking this examination," I would say in my most solemn Farsi—which was the devil to pronounce on top of my inward laughter. "When I return, I assume everyone will be in precisely the position he occupies now. And that each of you will honor me by honoring himself, together with the purpose of our work." Then I would leave for a glass of tea.

My colleague, an Iranian lieutenant, would urge me to stay in the room in order to exercise at least some control over the "cheat fest," as we called it. But I was impatient to enjoy myself at tea with him, anticipating the hilarious moment of return to the classroom. On the way back I would cough, clear my throat, and bang on corridor doors —but no amount of advance warning sufficed. I would open the door slowly to a scene of desperation and panic. Cadets bounced off the walls and each other in their race to return from the seats next to their regular cheating partners to the ones I'd assigned them.

When the scrambling finally stopped, a collective "Phew" went up, after which students would begin looking up to catch my eye and show me, with great earnestness, how hard they were working. Most were still huffing with the exertion of their race.

When the time came for handing in the papers, I could have formulated the excuses myself. "I just wasn't able to study last night; it's never happened before." "You asked just the wrong questions; I knew all the others." "My mother would love to have you over to a delicious lunch tomorrow." The most heavily trafficked approach from the outer world to the inner was the stomach. That is to say, Iranians constantly tried to proffer food to switch relationships from official to *personal,* which they could manage. If I had accepted all the invitations to Mama's lunch or the school cafeteria, if I had even slightly encouraged the bearing of little snacks to my desk—an ice cream or a tea, a little dish of romaine lettuce and lemon—I would have become as bloated as an emir.

*

The catch was the attractiveness of the "inner" life. In time I stopped taking the cheating seriously, for this was impossible after living in Iranian society. Its virtues and pleasures lay elsewhere, as I discovered to my increasing pleasure.

The feeling for the Iranian psyche I was acquiring made me reluctant to impose on my students the guilt and shame of being public failures. If this meant departing from my strict standards of honesty, I found comfort in reminding myself that I was "broadening my horizons" by doing as the Iranians did. If I taught less to my students than I'd resolved when I started, the compensation was in learning what the Iranians taught *me,* which was at least as important as my English lessons. This too involved the inner life.

The cadets were the kind who, when visiting America as officers, dropped in on my mother with thoughtful gifts and without telling anyone—because they knew how much this would please me and they felt an obligation to *my* family. On a personal level, their warmth and capacity to give of themselves made me glow. Once I recognized how different the cultural context was, I came to feel that the cheating, like the goldbricking and the colossal wastage of time and resources, wasn't what it first appeared to be. There were exceptions, of course. But to the extent that generalization about any people is valid, it is important to say that Iranians did not see these things as serious faults. They gave preference to other values. And after a year or more with them, I couldn't be certain that the American perspective and standards were higher or better.

My opposite number in the Academy, the boyish-looking Lieutenant who urged me not to leave the classroom during examinations, was several years older than I. Short and slim, he revealed a splendid set of teeth with his quick, frequent smile. Slightly oriental features betrayed his ancestry, which was orginally from a Turkic tribe in the South of Iran. Unlike many men his age, he did not carry a pocket mirror, but he did check himself carefully in front of almost every mirror he passed. In his great concern for how he looked, Farhad Mardoni was thoroughly Iranian.

Concern for friends' well-being—their physical comfort and state of mind—is an equally strong national characteristic. Iranians' urge to make personal intimate contact put off many Westerners, even those who had lived in the country for some time. A new acquaintance straightens your tie, brushes the dandruff from your shoulders, cups his hands on your thigh as you sit and talk. One way or another, he pushes himself inside the barriers Westerners draw around their persons, then *touches* with his body or attention. Americans in particular were intimidated by these gestures of familiarity—which Iranians craved as a way of shifting the relationship from that of the awkward, potentially dangerous outer world to the safety and warmth of the inner.

Farhad made this transition on the morning I was introduced to him in Major Afshar's office, not by inquiring why I was so bald so young, as did many Iranians in their reaching out for chumminess, but by looking at me as if I were both a long-lost friend and a man who deserved the highest respect. His eyes announced that he had no interest in competition, but that he wanted to care for me, almost take me in as part of his family. When we left for our own office, Farhad immediately called for the "tea boy" (a pockmarked man of forty) and ordered tea with the ever-present cookies called "bisqueet." By this time I knew his welcome was part of the complex forms of etiquette called *ta'arof,* a crucial element in Iranian relationships and society. Although it was *de rigueur,* Farhad made me feel as if I were terribly important to him: that my comfort and happiness were the most interesting and significant matters he would encounter all day. He pulled our chairs closer. We didn't so much talk as draw together.

Nothing differs more among Iranians and Americans than their sense of time. The Iranian attitude is most pronounced in the countryside, where the sky and ageless mountains—now denuded and bleak —impart an awareness of more-permanent things. The serenity in the villages is enormously soothing. But even most Tehran residents feel they have endless amounts of time. Not to give it to a friend, therefore, and even a new acquaintance, is both a grave insult and an incomprehensible twisting of values. What normal person would rush off on an outer-world matter when hours could be spent talking—and fussing—about sentiments and feelings? It is the difference between a Sunday picnic and lunch at McDonald's.

Summer and winter, the Iranian lunch break is four hours long. Farhad often invited me home with him: a gesture of greater than ordinary hospitality, since Iranians in his position were not encouraged to fraternize even with their staunch American allies. We would walk the three blocks to his small, sparsely furnished apartment, past drab, massive Qasr Prison, which was back to back with the Academy, past the enormous lines of relatives waiting to bring food to inmates, past several dead ends as colorful as the one in which I lived. Sometimes other academy friends would join us, but I was just as happy when we went alone.

Farhad had recently been married. Before this, he would plague me with the standard questions about Western women. One word of confirmation from me would have turned the spark in his eye into a roaring fire. Are they really so incredibly *easy?* Could I fix him up with one? Would a guy like him be able to bed her the first evening— do they all really just lie down? Iranian men's image of Western women was as good a demonstration as any that their misconceptions about Western life in general was the equal of Western misconceptions about theirs. It was drawn almost exclusively from Western films and television, which electrified them with curiosity and lust. I hardly knew a young man who did not pant over his daydream of meeting a woman from Rome or Los Angeles—and sleeping with her pronto. Even the most Westernized among them—Western on the surface, as this attitude revealed—insisted that their brides, the Iranian women they would marry, had to be virgins. Despite devotion to macho talk and poses, or because of it, young Iranian men were simultaneously baffled and frightened by sex. The handsome, dapper Farhad had never been to bed with a woman before he was married, apart from two prostitutes. He turned scarlet when I finally introduced him to a recently arrived American girl. Stuttering miserably, he all but lost command of his ordinarily fluent English, of which he was very proud.

His new wife, the daughter of a small importer of cooking oils, was less than beautiful and very shy. While Parvin was finishing her several stews of celery, eggplant, and tangy chicken stuffed with rice, we would stuff ourselves with the varied nuts, fruits, and sweetmeats she had set out for us. As leisurely and deliciously as we ate, several hours would remain before we were due back, at four o'clock, in the Academy. Farhad fetched two sleeping mats from the corner of the nearly bare living room and rolled them down. Parvin rested in the other of the two rooms. Farhad had to see to my comfort, which meant not leaving me alone.

"Pajamas" is an Iranian word meaning "clothes for the legs." Farhad produced a stack for me to choose from. He himself was delighted to get out of his suit, which was for the impersonal world outside the walls, and into his own pajamas, the Iranian domestic costume. But we never changed in one another's presence. When we went swimming, he hid himself to get undressed.

Unless I protested, he would actually tuck me in with a hand-sewn quilt in graceful ancient patterns. We would sleep or doze until Parvin brought a cup of tea at three-thirty. Such togetherness took some getting used to. After this, doing without was a deprivation.

*

Thanks partly to his ethnic origin, Farhad was even more deferential to his superiors than the average young officer. Major Afshar browbeat him constantly, transferring some of his irritation at my pressing for use of the library and paper supplies to a safer target than a foreigner. Farhad bowed, scraped, and held his job because his English was too good to sacrifice.

But even his conduct derived less from intimidation than from *ta'arof*. Its rules evolved in order to give people one met the dignity they deserved, which was done partly by showing one knew one's place in relation to them. Three people making together for a room calculated with computer-like speed and accuracy who should pass first, second, and third through the door.

(Although I had learned that the guest—especially when foreign—was often given the honor of passage before people of even the highest rank, I tried to allow my elders to pass before me. When my resistance was determined, I might be gently but firmly propelled through the door.)

Sitting in a room brought more rules into play. The closer to the host one was placed the greater his importance; the nearer to the door the greater the courtesy to those in the "elevated" center. A motion to rise that slightly moved the chair against the floor was an almost mandatory sign of respect for anyone who entered. A little bow with a mumbled "How are you?" had to follow.

A palm against your chest indicated humility: You knew you were less important than the person you were signaling to. Although it could become plastic, a hand held there with an attempt at genuine interest in the other person was a pleasant gesture to give and receive. Whatever you were engaged in later, when seated, you turned every ten minutes or so to the people nearest you and asked how they were feeling. It did not matter that you hadn't been talking to them. Your gesture showed that you were nevertheless thinking about them and did not forget this civility.

People kept getting up, pivoting to others, bowing slightly, and reseating themselves. Largish rooms sometimes resembled the Swiss toy with an organ and popping-up puppets. Leaving rooms involved matching ceremony. Just as you had tried not to show the soles of your feet when sitting, you were now careful not to reveal your disrespectful rear. You avoided this by backing to the door, keeping your courteous countenance on those still in the room.

One morning, I was asked to partake of *kalapache* by the just-promoted Colonel Afshar. A foreigner was to consider himself highly honored by an invitation to this traditional breakfast occasion. *Kalapache* was the eager consumption of the head and hoofs of a sheep. Orange juice poured upon the head made the placid eyes glisten. Picking at my portion stretched my resolution to "go native" to its limit.

I was seated in a place of honor, near the beaming Colonel himself. For some reason he dismissed a lieutenant from his presence.

Half crouching with respect, the young officer backed toward the door until he collided with a coffee table and fell flat. He got up, begged forgiveness, and slinked the rest of the way to his exit, holding a salute. No one looked. *Ta'arof* was rarely laughed at. But despite such excesses, I took pleasure in many of the little ceremonies. They seemed to enhance the self-respect of everyone involved. Or perhaps they merely appealed to my liking for neatness.

In any case, *ta'arof* too had its limits. It never operated at bus stops, which were left to shoving chaos. When a photograph was about to be taken, no one stopped for courtesies before thrusting in. Guests advancing on a buffet dinner more resembled a crowd at a sale than a people raised with elaborate social customs. *Ta'arof* had apparently not been extended to modern institutions and situations, and the result could be anarchy. I sensed that Iranians functioned best under the guidance and restraints of a code. Without it, many seemed at a loss how to react. When authority broke down or did not cover a situation, people seemed to switch personalities so they could dive in and secure their share of what was going in the free-for-all. Iranians themselves seemed to recognize their need for the rules and customs of an established order. The historical instability of the political system, which sometimes collapsed into terrifying disorder, surely sharpened this need.

✸

The premarital physical distance between Farhad and Parvin fit a general pattern. My Iranian girl friend and I did not even hold hands in public. She was a highly educated, uninhibited young woman, but we waited for intimacy until she came to America, to which I'd returned first. Social pressures were simply too great in Iran. Any suspicion about her would have caused her entire family great distress.

Treatment of the moon in Iranian poetry—and the native love of white skin—made her name, "Moon Face," especially intriguing in Farsi. Her eyes were so extraordinary that I subjected myself to the full formalities with her parents, without whose approval I could not have seen her.

Mahru lived in a thoroughly middle-class district. As I approached it, the streets were bordered more and more solidly by walls that completely blocked off each house. It was like walking the passageways of a maze. Only the pavement's dusty asphalt was available to the public.

Once again I felt how strong the Iranian craving was for privacy and emotional security against the threatening outside. One never knew what lay behind the high barriers of stone or mud brick, but it was impossible not to sense the general awkwardness with outsiders that put them there. The conviction that the only people to trust are oneself and one's family lies deep in the Iranian psyche. Traveling around the country, I came across homesteads near lonely roads in the middle of the desert. They were of course entirely walled off.

In this upwardly mobile quarter, other reasons might also have applied. Nearer to the address Mahru had provided, it struck me that walls might be an expression of selfishness as well as a need for protection. Most Iranians appeared to have a weakly developed sense of obligation to what might be called the civic community. I knew that exquisite gardens lay behind many of those walls. If a traveler somehow entered, he would receive the traditionally lavish hospitality. But the family felt no compulsion to share their greenery and other treasures with those who remained outside.

Mahru's parents served me tea. Their small talk was full of the usual concern for my comfort and peace of mind. In this case, the careful feeling out of the unknown and possibly dangerous stranger, that accompanied their ritual phrases had an immediate purpose. After an hour of delicate tea and talk, they laid down the rules for Mahru, who hadn't yet appeared. We could walk together within half a kilometer of the house. I could buy her an ice cream. We had two hours, and could not hold hands.

The second time, we were permitted to go to the movies. The lecture about their daughter's reputation was just as long. Yet, relative to most middle-class families, this was a modern one. Many daughters were as guarded and chaperoned as the standard jokes about these things. Among the images that stuck in my mind's eye was of beautiful university students wearing Carnaby Street's miniskirts under their chadors. The drab black sometimes separated just enough for a peek —and the wearer winked. I craftily arranged to meet one of these temptations. Her brother came along.

The usual communication with a middle-class girl took place during what Iranians called a "rende-vu," a few snatched minutes at a preselected movie theater. Virginity was so important that families of even the most progressive urban bridegrooms would insist on medical inspections, and enough sober Iranians talked about surgeons who specialized in stitching together hymens on the eve of marriages to make the point about the fixation, even if no such doctors actually existed.

The national history having shaped the national psyche, the latter deserved to be as complex as the former was long. Some of the people, some of the time, reveled in eating, drinking, ribaldry, and sex. Iran's ancient religion encouraged "the good life," and pleasure-loving streaks ran like veins through the marble of Iranian Islamic conviction. But at the turn of the twentieth century, Iranian women hardly left home. In the late 1960s, when I was feeling my way by trial and sometimes mortifying error, some moved about almost freely, and a hard core of Tehranis under fifty wore dresses rather than the chador.

However, you were not supposed to address one on the street. In cities, talking to a woman not escorted by a husband you knew was an intolerable sexual implication—and if obviously not that, then a slur on her dignity. If the wife wasn't with the husband, you did not send your regards. To avoid other implications, you did not mention her at all, except in rare circumstances and the most elevated language. There are two words for "wife." As luck had it, I picked the wrong one at first—and was excused only because I was a foreigner.

Under the Shah's pushing and prodding, urban middle-class women had recently made substantial progress in opportunities to get an education and pursue a career. Yet most were still confined by traditional restraints. I knew dozens of smart Tehran men who, in their Madison Avenue suits and with their Sorbonne or Oxford educations, looked and talked like cosmopolitan Westerners. But their attitudes about domestic arrangements remained deeply Middle Eastern. "I'm going to marry an Iranian girl," they would confide, often immediately after grinning and flushing through detailed questions about Western women in bed. "And if I can't find the one I want, my mother will find her for me."

Arranged marriages remained an everyday reality, even among the educated. A mother who spied a likely-looking girl for her son might follow her home (it went without saying that single women, even in their thirties, lived at home) and introduce herself to the mother: the start of a lengthy, complex process of acquaintanceship and negotiation between the families, whose first meetings would probably take place without the prospective husband and wife.

Naturally, there were exceptions. "Westernitis," signifying the feverish experimentation with Western things and ways—often the cheapest glitter—was one of the most popular words of the 1960s. Although this begat more jeans, rock records, and rotten television than changes in social attitudes, Iranians, with the encouragement of the Shah's grasping for F-5 jets, gobbled down a bit of everything. And of course they were not so pure before the promiscuous hunger for gadgets and styles to need corrupting entirely from the outside. Male students occasionally found female students, or nonstudents, willing to risk public disgrace. But apart from the obnoxiously rich, who flaunted themselves and their nighttime carousing, everyone was extremely private about sexual liaisons. If for this reason they were less rare than they seemed, the students' panting misinformation made plain that they were only slightly less rare.

This dead end for passion usually ended at a house of prostitution. Establishments abounded in the larger cities, usually within a particular district. The several blocks in south Tehran given over chiefly to the booming business were thick with policemen and surrounded by a wall. The madame produced her objects—which is how everyone regarded the girls—for the customers' selection. A modern short story called "Under the Red Light," which treated prostitutes as human beings, constituted a revolution.

※

The extraordinary thing was that with all these restrictions—with the double-standard emphasis on being seen to be "good" by prying neighbors—Iranian women somehow managed to be both feminine and dignified. Those who led something of their own lives had to be tough in order to overcome the tripled difficulties of asserting themselves. But most retained their lyrical and poetic qualities. They seemed more genuine, on average, than the men, and often more genuinely educated and creative. No doubt this had something to do with their liberation from men's time-wasting compulsion to demonstrate their superiority.

For the counterpart to the women's struggle to be themselves despite the obstacles and handicaps was the men's struggle to show themselves as more masculine than they were. Spending so much time in each other's company while the women were largely locked away, most developed almost inevitable odd notions, and fear, of women. Islam was less responsible than a distortion of it. Man was the master in pre-Islamic society; woman was his draft animal and concubine. The Prophet Mohammed wanted to give women more stature and respect—which was the original purpose of purdah: seclusion and the veil. It was hoped a woman so protected would no longer be regarded as a piece of property.

The manipulations of this—the harem, the banishment of women from all public life and view—came later, when men in power found them convenient. Although institutionalized in the medieval period, women's relegation to separateness and to the house is not inherent in Islam.

Meanwhile, the effect on men is deeper and broader than their pinching female flesh in the street and awkwardness with women as persons. For all their powerful, genuine love of their daughters, Iranian families blatantly favor and spoil their sons. Boys will carry on the all-important family—which is why many girls, who will be leaving soon, are almost written off at adolescence. A large percentage of the spoiled boys grow up into spoiled, irresponsible men. Their pampered egos are dangerously fragile.

The opposite side of the coin is the companionship men enjoy with men: friendships so deep and strong that the same word should not be used for those between American men. They are raised together. Those who grow up on the same street or graduate from the same school are linked by mutual obligations as strong as a secret society's. When one is in trouble, he can count on real financial and emotional support from the others. When another achieves a significant economic or political position, his old friends consider him their *parti:* their patron in power.

Iranian life is interlaced with these relationships. In a small village outside Tehran, soldiers with automatic rifles link pinkies as they walk across a bridge. At dinner in the city an Iranian dentist sits so close to a recently introduced American that he almost encompasses him. He talks directly into the American's mouth, breathing out the fragrance of the raw onions he rarely fails to eat with meat. Trained to protect himself against odors and intimacy, the American draws back. But the dentist follows, and the dance to close and open the distance continues throughout the meal.

The Iranian picks a loose thread from the other's shirt. "You have a pimple under your chin," he observes consolingly. "Is that why you didn't shave today?" He wants to find out who the American is, and what he thinks. He is driven to touch, emotionally as well as physically.

Finally the American understands. When Iranian men first put their arms in mine, I tried to squirm free rather than respond. But when my discomfort diminished enough for acceptance of such gestures, I realized they were expressions of kinship. Some men simulated intimacy for advantage or gain. A few *used* me to lay hands on something American. But most radiated genuine affection and concern, from which it was hard to return to the inhibited, deodorized blandness of so many American relationships. I learned most of what I know about male friendship in Iran. Somehow it was like going home to an earlier, richer period of human closeness.

Tehran was surely less ugly fifty years before, when it started its messy growth from a little village. By 1968, the smog-ridden sprawl lacked shape or sense. But it was beguiling. I liked it from the first day.

The sun was setting. In the island that separated the airport highway's two roadways, block after block of blankets were anchored by people and samovars, with plates of kebab and rice squeezed in between. Friday was the general day off in the Muslim world. Thousands of tightly entwined families were picnicking in the treasured strip of green.

In the evening, I visited the glorious garden of a hotel in the hills just north of the city. An old man was watering individual leaves with incredible care. The spur to Iranians cherishing each flower and lovingly nurturing each square meter of green was the overwhelming bleakness of the countryside, especially the denuded Elburz Mountains. Even knowing nothing about this desolate vastness, I fell under the garden's spell. My severe nervousness about committing myself to a totally strange land dissolved. Its serenity was as moving as its perfect order.

The violent contrasts also appealed to me immediately. Very little was in perfect order outside the walls of the garden and the hotel, a creation of the Shah's father. But although I saw little beauty during my first drives in the city, there was something exciting and evocative in the very disorder. The streets were alive with men hawking nuts, magazines, pomegranate juice, knife-sharpening—singsonging their appeals and joined by mothers begging with their swaddled children in their arms. (I soon learned that the blood the beggars displayed—to make their appearance more pitiful—was from self-inflicted scratches.) I wanted to find out why these humble sights captivated me. It was as if they weren't new to me, despite their very "foreign" appearance, but scenes from my ancestry.

Although the life of a Peace Corps volunteer was full of adventure and joy, it could also be desolate. It was sometimes overpoweringly lonely in the most direct sense: You were alone in a distant, very different land, with no buddies to call, no code words like "Ebbets Field" to toss off for wrapping up in the comfort of shared associations. "What am I doing here?" was all I could think to repeat to myself in the grip of this mood. "Why don't I drop this crazy test of myself and *go home* [to the girl I'd been seeing through most of college]?" The Corps gave you hundreds of books about Iran. If you wanted, you could spend the free time of your full two years reading in your room. On days I felt sorry for myself—for the strain of speaking Farsi and practicing *ta'arof* instead of flopping in a chair with an old friend, for the seeming impossibility of meeting an Iranian girl I could *talk* to—I was tempted to surrender to my loneliness by doing just that. But while I could, I wanted to learn by doing rather than reading. I forced myself to go out and mingle. I would visit my new friends. If not up to that, I'd give myself the pleasure of a very long walk, which was my favorite way of looking around and learning.

My little apartment was on the edge of southern Tehran, the old part of the city. Even there, where native life was lived much more than in the modern sections, people became much more rushed and much less "Iranian" than in the villages from which they came. Yet the daily routine retained a powerful flavor. I loved the sounds of the streets. The rich—which included almost all resident and visiting Americans—lived largely in the northern sector, where street life was feeble. My district nourished it. A public bathhouse stood on the avenue where my dead-end street joined it. Cleanliness was most prescribed for Friday, the old Islamic market day. On Thursday mornings mothers would enter with swarms of mud-caked children, emerging in the afternoon with gleaming angels. On my afternoons off I went to enjoy the steam and hard scrubbing. I would walk back the hundred yards to my apartment as if on air, and sleep until evening.

On my street itself, a man would be hawking delicious sweetened beets he had cooked on his charcoal stove. When the iceman came, I'd lug my block from his cart and up my stairs, dripping with sweat from the heat. The quilt maker separated his cotton threads with an ancient contraption. At first I took its "plunk plunk plunk" for the song of an exotic stringed instrument. Boys were constantly pushing through the crowds with their trays of kebab and spicy chicken broth. Cries of stall operators and peddlers blended with recorded prayer calls from the local mosque.

"*Naft! Naft!*" went one of the most singsong calls. It was from the kerosene man, who roamed the streets with big cans in an old wheelbarrow. In winter everyone but the rich kept warm by huddling over little stoves. *Naft*, the standard fuel, played an important part in contemporary Iranian life.

I had once done some work on a contemporary Iranian writer named Sadeq Chubak. In a story called "*Nafti*," "The Kerosene Man," a poor village servant girl secretly observes the kerosene man who services the house in which she works. Her life is so bleak that she falls in love from afar. Visiting an important shrine not far from Tehran, she ties the traditional snip of cotton on the bars of the saint's tomb in hope that her fervent dream will be heard: marriage to the *nafti*. The profound relief that the holy outing gives her builds to a kind of ecstacy. After the rattling bus takes her home, the *nafti*, who is already married and knows nothing of her hopes, fills the stoves with kerosene and leaves. . . . Chubak's work—about the feelings of ill-treated animals and prostitutes, about the unhappy sides of Iranian life in general—differed markedly from classical Iranian literature, but I liked it no less for that.

My own *nafti* filled my can twice a week. He always refused my offer of tea, indicating that he was unworthy as he was; his clothes were too dirty. . . . When I gave him money, he bowed gracefully and held his hands to his chest in a gesture of gratitude. Then he would reach out to take the rials so as not to come near me in his clothes. He remained in his bow to avoid imposing on me by looking in my face.

The lowest of the low in his own society, the *nafti* nevertheless acquired a kind of nobility in his performance of the forms of Iranian etiquette. It lent an importance and a human dimension to our little meeting that made it far more gratifying to both sides than the comparable transaction in the West. He had time for the rituals. I sensed the pleasure he took in them. To avoid giving the offense of showing his rear, the *nafti* backed out the door with as much dignity as the richest residents of northern Tehran.

More *ta'arof*. Here more even than higher in society, Iranians' sense of proportion enchanted me. I loved their respect for the little courtesies and symbols that enriched daily life. The onion seller, in his little round cap and balloon trousers, took his lunch break in my dead-end street. Spreading a tattered blanket directly on the street, he would set out his bread, onions, and yogurt. But he never failed to first place a rose in a chipped glass of water and stand it in the middle of the blanket.

I lived on the top floor of a three-story apartment house that jumbled Eastern and Western architecture. The mishmash was surrounded by a mud-brick wall in the typical state of disintegration. Eggplant, mutton, and mint, saffron, and other herbs provided the usual aroma in the corridors. The smell of cooking oil mixed with the smell of Diesel oil from passing cars and trucks. In spring and autumn there was also an amazingly sweet scent from wild flowers that sprang up after every rain.

The smell and taste of dust were also pervasive, in case anyone forgot that Tehran had grown, and was still growing, out of the desert. It was strongest on my rooftop. A dome of smoke rose almost constantly from a brickworks in the sister city of Rey, one of the oldest in Iran—from which Tehran had grown. When the smog lifted, stars shone brilliantly, as if the desert had never been disturbed.

From May to October, I usually slept on the roof. The partial panorama of lights from there came to me as a call to explore. On weekends I sometimes walked from morning until evening, yet never tired of it. The city was in my blood.

Sometimes I went to the main post office, in downtown Tehran. The early-twentieth-century building looked like a railway station crossed with an armory. It featured columns, cupolas, turrets, metal lions, splashes of pre-Islamic architecture, pompous European influences, brownish brick, turquoise decorations, seven-color tiles called *haft rangi, everything* that could be stuck on. I came to see it as an accurate reflection of the incredible bureaucracy jammed inside. One functionary of course sent any poor petitioner who reached him to another —after treating him to a suitable wait. The second official passed him on to a third, who directed him to the fourth; and the zombie-like wandering from one to the next took place in a network of corridors cleverly designed to confuse and confound the public. Hundreds crowded into the largest halls and spent the day there, not bothering to run the maze. Everything I had read about the notorious Indian civil service made it seem miraculously efficient by comparison. The Iranian version was devoted to fighting the public, chiefly in order to fleece it. Some of my trips were to collect a package from Brooklyn. In the tradition of the bazaar, the customs officers demanded outlandish fees—seventy-five dollars for a shirt that had cost twelve in Macy's— and waited for me to begin the bargaining. (I was better off when the package contained something to split, since they graciously accepted half in most cases.) After wasting the better part of a day reaching the right office, I was a dead pigeon. "Keep it, you've won," I said. When I summoned up the energy to engage in trading, I left the building exhausted and broke.

South Tehran's twisting streets were a much friendlier maze. The walk I took most would begin on Lalezar-e Now, not far from my building. I often had dinner there, in one of the restaurants interspersed with the Iranian equivalent of burlesque theaters. Stew, eggplant, tomato, pickles, and much delicious bread for fifty cents. Vodka for washing it down on rich days was easily available. Although Islamic traditionalists campaigned for abstinence, many Iranians felt little need to hide their enjoyment of alcohol.

Ferdowsi Square featured a striking statue of Abol Qasem Ferdowsi, the national poet. I had made the happy discovery that Iran erected almost no statues to military heroes, reserving this honor chiefly for cultural figures. Ferdowsi Street, the largest center for carpets and handicrafts, led from Ferdowsi Square. On the way to the British and the Turkish embassies, it teemed with large and small shops, many owned by Jews and Armenians. It was like a longer, more colorful Delancey Street at the turn of the century. Every kind of carpet, every conceivable article and artifact were on sale somewhere in the dusty, bursting shops. Every kind of currency, but especially dollars, was sought by the horde of money changers.

An urge to read the street and shop signs largely prompted my study of Farsi—a difficult language at first, but one with which I was beginning to be comfortable. Tehran University's Farsi-for-foreigners courses seemed slightly artificial, so I'd enrolled, with the help of Farhad, in evening classes of something called "The War Against Illiteracy": the sole foreigner in a freezing room crammed with a potpourri of Iranian types, from teenaged welders to septuagenarian tea boys. Now the language was fun. In pockets of this quarter, as in most of the entire country apart from northern Tehran's foreign colonies, one might as well be on another planet without it. I memorized phrases from the day's newspaper as I walked. Crossing the jammed streets, jumping over jubes, I imagined I was blending in.

To practice the spoken language I stopped in shops that took my fancy. This also provided training in the arts of making polite conversation and buying. It was impossible to put a foot inside a door without inaugurating a colloquy—initially, of course, about anything but business. It was equally impossible to examine a little hand-painted box or mirror decorated with traditional birds and flowers without raising the curtain on the song and dance of the bargaining process.

"You like the little nightingale?" asked the charming owner of a little shop in his ill-fitting serge and collarless shirt.

I did like it. Against the hardness and roughness of much of Iranian life, the nightingale's beauty that is celebrated in so much poetry and art seems to shine in a spotlight. In my lonely hours, I had painted the walls of my own little room with roses and nightingales, and from then on kept my scrutinizing landlord at the door. This one in the shop was delicately stylized. Its muted greens, oranges, and browns evoked the Iranian landscape at its happiest. I decided to see if I could afford it—but by trying something different this time.

One learned not to compliment the possessions of one's Iranian friends *too* highly. The radio had recently broadcast a little spoof about a man's first visit to an acquaintance's family. Having effused throughout his tour of the house, he was presented with everything, including wallets, deed, and wife.

"You are right to admire the little nightingale," the shopkeeper persisted. "Your taste is impeccable."

"I do think it is very beautiful," I answered, instead of the usual "It's not what I want" for bargaining.

"How much, my friend, do you think it's worth?"

"I don't have the slightest idea. I just admire it tremendously."

The shopkeeper was one of those who made an art of looking shabby. He studied me for a moment. "*Pish kesh,*" he said with great warmth. "It's yours. Because you speak like a nightingale."

"You are much too kind, sir. The nightingale is truly beautiful, and it will always remind me of your matching gesture." I quickly conjured up the most elaborate way of giving thanks in Farsi. "All I can say is, I am your sacrifice."

I walked into the street with my "present." My friend would have pursued me even more quickly if not for his shock. When it seemed he might actually have a heart attack, I turned back with a smiling suggestion that *ta'arof* should not be given unless truly felt. He was so flustered that he charged me the equivalent of a few dollars for the nightingale, half of what it must have been worth.

*

Squabbles between outraged enemies added to the noise of the streets. Many were caused by dented fenders and alleged insults to wives. When a dispute of this kind loomed or *namus* (the all-important family pride), seemed challenged, the response was immediate. The men leaped from their cars, usually led by the one who knew he had caused the trouble. (Any admission of responsibility was a fatal blow to *namus*.) While dukes went up, off came the encumbrance of sandal-like shoes. Fists trembled with eagerness to smash the offender's insolent face—and almost never did. It was a *show* of prowess, a ritualized display of determination to kill for the human territory called honor. Even at these times, when the practiced charm of the bazaar and the home had suddenly switched to a menacing thrust, the Iranian urge to ornament everything, as an astute observer recently put it, transformed the combat into a dance.

Everyone knew the partners were not going to fight. When they had attracted a worthy crowd and demonstrated their willingness to go to the limit, intermediaries materialized. Restrained by them—while venting supposedly bitter anger at the restraint—the vindicated pair slowly pulled back, still hissing furious warnings. The final withdrawal was swift; the fists often opened for handshakes.

Although Iranians' anxiety and awkwardness with each other in the "outer" world resulted in constant use of intimidation there, it rarely strayed from the script. The instinctive approach to settling disputes was a threat, but in the sense that offended individuals controlled themselves from carrying them out, Iranian society seemed much less violent than American, where people blustered *and* shot. Iranian streets were safe. Violent crimes were usually prompted by passion and committed with knives. Burglary, not mugging, was the favored professional crime, and of course every respectable second-story man had to have at least one helper for his ladder. The wags had it that frequent tea breaks and *ta'arof*—should the burglar or the helper go first through the window?—reduced efficiency to the general level even in this line of work.

SAVAK, the security police, was a separate matter. But many ordinary policemen went about on bicycles, whistling to each other while they checked doors and windows. They did not wear guns. One reason Iran appealed to me was that I saw so few of them.

*

There was no hurry to reach my destination. Not to rush had become one of the few luxuries. Time wasn't money.

Finally I approached the main entrance to the bazaar. Traffic there was like an explosion in slow motion. Pot salesmen, broom salesmen, mechanics, men with gas burners and refrigerators on their backs pushed in every direction. A little caravan of donkeys bearing sacks of wheat and nuts tried to force through. Boys delivering bread on bicycles had more success. The delicious loaves were stacked five feet high and the boys sang at the top of their lungs to hear themselves above the babel.

Half the crowd seemed to be sinking, for the bazaar itself lay underground. I made my way in through a little gulley. Light entered through large overhead openings spaced about a hundred feet apart. But a dusky atmosphere prevailed; many areas were cold and dank even in summer.

Not that I visited nearly all the areas, no matter how many times I explored. The bazaar was the largest in the Middle East, therefore probably the world. The immense city within a city was composed of incalculable passageways twisting and turning like a gargantuan snake. Together, the trails and tunnels were many miles long. Here and there a passage broke ground, coming up into a square flanked by yet more stalls and shops, and in one place, the Royal Mosque. But the vast majority started and ended in the bowels of the city. I doubted if anyone knew the exact dimensions or circumference of the whole. From the outside, the labyrinth couldn't be seen. On the inside it was too irregular and amorphous for precise measurement.

The bazaar was as much seediness, commercial morals, and plain dirt as the "romance" of the Middle East. Traffic beggared description. Quilt makers, silversmiths, tanners, yogurt peddlers, sellers of dates, and sellers of tools, ancient weapons, coins, trinkets, religious artifacts, trays of kebab, glasses of tea . . . sellers of seemingly everything mingled and jostled. Bales of cotton caromed off carcasses of lamb. Traffic simultaneously went off in, and converged from, all directions. More donkeys tried to get through, their owners shouting, "Watch out!" to everyone. A tourist who allowed one of the fantastic sights to engross him while forgetting to keep an eye peeled in all directions might easily emerge a cripple.

If he emerged at all. I used to picture someone who knew no Farsi getting lost and perishing in the immense cavern, his futile shouts of "Help, I want to get out of here!" in a Western language echoing off the stone walls. But the walls also provided comfort. Little niches with cups tied to a chain served as sanctuaries of water and of faith for travelers. Pictures of the saints that decorated the niches were multiple symbolism, for the death of Hossein, the seventh-century grandson of Mohammed whose martyrdom provided the emotional source of Shi'ite Islam, happened when he was denied water, the great essential, at a time of need. Snippets and threads of cotton were tied to these little shrines in hope of remembrance by the saint pictured there. It was not that Islam was never far away from daily life; it was an integral part of that life.

Most of the stalls and shops selling religious materials were clustered together. Food produce was concentrated in other areas, as were carpets and rugs. Although Ferdowsi Street seemed to have a world monopoly on Persian rugs, an even greater supply was displayed here, with hundreds hanging around each stall.

The main jewelry section was partly above ground on a kind of veranda near the Royal Mosque. Partly because I loved the superbly handcrafted agate rings, partly to create some business in the bazaar, I decided to have a ring made. In the booth I chose after hours of touring the jewelry-making section, three male generations in their underwear were tapping away on dazzlingly intricate pieces of metalwork.

The father in charge was delighted and patient. He helped me find a craftsman to carve the sides of the ring in my design of the typical nightingales-and-roses theme. He brought me to a gem cutter who would work on the inscription I wanted. It was a line of Sa'di, one of the most famous bards of thirteenth-century Shiraz, city of gardens and poetry. "The People of Adam Belong to Each Other, and Their Creation Is of One Essence" rhymes gracefully in Farsi. This is how I felt in the Iran of 1968. Acquiring insight into a very different way of life was deeply gratifying. But it was more than that. Despite the spells of overpowering loneliness, I was very happy.

When I went to pick up the ring two weeks later, the man in the booth lovingly unwrapped its protective cloth. The work looked even better than I'd hoped. My birds and flowers seemed alive in the gold. Farhad pointed out that my new habit of talking with my hands had developed because I was so proud of the ring.

I of course took it with me in August 1969—by boat through the Caspian Sea. It would be almost ten years before I saw the country again, rushing from the airport to beat the 9 P.M. curfew.

A girl friend pressured me to go to a publicity party to launch the jumbo jet in 1971. The affair took place aboard a plane parked at Kennedy Airport, about ten miles from our house. Barry likes to say he was "smitten" by his first sight of me from the other end of the cabin, and quickly hatched a ploy. I didn't notice him until he came up and spoke.

"Is that an Iranian blouse you're wearing?"

It was an Indian blouse, but there was something appealing, because it was unusual, in the question. We talked for several minutes. He seemed a pleasant person, and asked very politely for my telephone number. I gave it to him, but hesitantly.

Robert Redford looks never meant anything to me. I wouldn't notice a crooked nose if I was able to exchange ideas with its owner. I didn't want to see Barry, not because he didn't bowl me over but because I was "recovering from a broken heart" and didn't want to think about dating. I *wouldn't* have seen him if my mother hadn't refused to fib again. I told her to say I wasn't home the three or four times Barry called the following weekend.

Barry told me he wanted very much to meet me again but everything had a limit. He'd made up his mind to make one, final try. This time my mother handed me the telephone and said I'd have to tell my own stories.

I had taken a summer job in a Manhattan office while waiting to start teaching for the first time, in September. Barry was so pleasant again on the phone that I said I'd see him after work one day. His place was midtown, off seedy Ninth Avenue. The brownstone looked no cleaner than the neighboring buildings, but Barry had made his tiny apartment pretty and interesting—for example by painting a decrepit bathroom with rainbows. He obviously cared about his surroundings and had the imagination to decorate them. There were walls of books—and, of course, a beautiful Persian carpet.

Two years before, I'd been formally engaged. It was the big thing in my life until the first affair—from which I was recovering when Barry appeared. My former fiancé was one of my cousin's best friends —which helped get us going under my mother's powerful eye.

It started when I was sixteen. Even then the macho type put me off. Joe was a kind, considerate boy who came to our house every Sunday. After four years of this—me never looking at another boy—we agreed to announce our engagement. I told him that everyone else I knew was getting a two-carat ring, which I too had to have. Joe answered that he couldn't possibly afford anything like that. "I don't care if you can afford it. It's what I want."

I also wanted the reception in the swank Terrace on the Park, with the right band, the right flowers, the right everything. The display would have cost over five thousand dollars in 1969 prices. "Joe, I don't care what you can manage. That's what all my friends are getting."

The ring was bought. The contract for the fancy ballroom was signed. Barbara got everything Barbara exacted—but wasn't happy. A week before the tragedy was scheduled, she asked herself why she had made her childish demands. It dawned on her before the wedding day that if she truly wanted Joe, she would never have resorted to extortion for trinkets.

Barry was a living opposite to Doing What the Others Do, at least the others I knew. By the time we met, when the memory of what I had done to Joe made me squirm, I think I knew what I truly wanted. Barry was a graduate student at Columbia University, with just enough money to squeeze through by working at a collection of odd jobs. (The synagogue for which he ran a children's recreation center fired him when he married out of the faith.)

We covered half of Manhattan on foot that first evening. We ate, of all things, delicious Cuban-Chinese food in a broken-down diner, where the waiters joined us. We shouted to each other over the subway squeals on the ride back to my house in Brooklyn. I had a marvelous time.

After we married, Barry's mother liked to confirm how lucky I was and to assure me that I fell in love with her boy because he was so cute. "No, because he has a beautiful brain," I always answered. His intelligence and sensitivity attracted me from the first—and continued to attract me.

We talked our heads off from the moment I knocked at his door. He knew so many interesting things! He *did* so many interesting things! I grew to love him, even want him, for the way he thought and expressed himself. He was the teacher, I was the student. He knew so much more than I did, and also how to share it: that was the turn-on.

Barry was not only more entertaining than any man I'd known but also more idealistic and principled. A story he told about his childhood revealed more about him than even he seemed to realize. When he was nine years old, an older tough threatened to beat him up unless he shoplifted a toy for him from a Woolworth's on Pitkin Avenue. Barry gave in, then bawled miserably the entire twenty minutes home. He ran into his mother's skirt. "Please, God, *please*. I didn't mean it," he sobbed—and it took his mother a long time to convince him that retribution for sin wasn't on its way. Barry laughed at his naïveté when he told me the story, remembering how seriously he had once taken the Ten Commandments. His point was that he had lost all his religious faith, but I sensed that his deep childhood commitment to moral good still dominated him. It now emerged in his concern for doing the right thing with other people and other countries, and the way he could be upset by nastiness and evil.

But none of this explains why I found him so easy to talk to, which is something different. For some reason, I could tell him everything I felt and thought. I had never known a man like that, never *wanted* to discuss everything with the men I did know. I used to call him and talk for hours.

It was a grinding hour between my house in Brooklyn and his place, on Manhattan's West Side. We spent almost as much time that year on the subway as on the telephone. We had met in June. By the end of the summer, Barry and I were very good friends. We were no more than that because I knew that *he* knew that becoming lovers would make it terribly serious for us both—and he waited for a long time for me to be certain. It might sound odd that I was more impatient than he, but I was also grateful. He was a better, broader, more understanding friend than I'd ever had. High school classmates sometimes bumped into me and asked what I had in common with that arty, New York intellectual, as they saw him. In a way, we had everything in common—because we talked about everything.

He described his father with touching affection and his mother with concern and a little sadness. When he took me to meet them, I saw how much "family" meant to him. His father loved life and got on with everyone. He joked that I was much too pretty to be a spaghetti bender and accepted me immediately, at least on the surface. His mother seemed to have more trouble coping, and she had a list of complaints to prove that someone, or something, was persecuting her. She probed with questions about my religion. Was it to become involved with Catholic girls, she asked herself, that she had sacrificed everything for her boys, raised them in a spotless Orthodox home and sent them to a yeshiva? Others had not kept a kosher home, never sent their sons to a yeshiva—yet they married nice Jewish girls. "Why is it always *my* children? Why am *I* always the one sent the troubles and the heartaches?"

Barry had told me beautiful things about an Iranian girl he'd loved. I tried to hint to his mother that I might be a relatively mild disgrace and problem compared to a Muslim lady sitting at her table. I dropped the subject when I saw she wasn't amused.

My family was twenty times larger than his. They all used my parents' house, the one I grew up in, as a kind of social club, partly because my grandparents lived with us. After Barry came for Christmas the first time, he kept referring to it as a banquet hall: About fifty people were squeezed into the little living room. Most of the clan—several dozen uncles, aunts and cousins—would grow to love him in a few years, but started with raised eyebrows and warnings. Mixed marriages bring lots of problems, they implied. How would we raise our children? But I was supposed to be the one with the higher education and the wisdom, so they left me to my own decisions.

Since it was up to me, I spent all my free time with the person I liked best. Time was scarce because as well as teaching I was getting a master's degree in education, and Barry was working very hard at graduate studies in Iranian history and culture. On weekends, we went to plays in Greenwich Village and Central Park. We sat near any fountain we could find, and he described the jubes in Iranian villages, of which the running water reminded him. This went with Iranian films, Iranian exhibitions, and even a comical attempt to try to teach me Farsi: He was a bit of a Persian freak. When we went to dinner with his Iranian friends, they seemed startled at his knowledge of obscure tribes and kings. He even straightened out the confusion for some of them between Persia and Iran. Iran derives from "land of the Aryans"; Iranians were known to the West as Persians ever since the ancient Greeks first came into contact with "Persis," the province of Pars.

But this didn't close him to other interests. We covered Manhattan on foot while he opened the world to me. The best was his putting me in touch not only with what he knew but also with my own thoughts. He had a way of getting me to verbalize many I'd had before but hadn't been able to express. Sometimes I didn't even have to say these things. He simply understood and said I was communicating very well because my eyes were an open book.

Before Barry, I had been in limbo. It was nearly impossible to find common ground with "my kind": John Travoltas in the making, with their old high school talk about cars and sports. Yet I couldn't quite find my place when I went looking for other interests in Manhattan. Barry was my answer for compatibility. He was tender and romantic. He'd kiss me on street corners, whisper how sexy I was—and love it when I told him he mustn't. He knew how to hold me—mentally, since we still weren't lovers.

Barry let me decide when I didn't want to put that off any longer. As when we talked, he was wonderfully sensitive to my feelings, and brought out what I had to give. This was in the fall, months after we had met.

His father died in February, immediately after a heart attack. It was a hard blow to Barry, who adored his father and felt very close to him. My own father was warming to Barry by this time. That night, he called from Brooklyn to offer to drive Barry back to his parents' house, which was also in Brooklyn. I was there when my father arrived, at midnight.

Several days later, my mother stared me in the face. "Are you and Barry sleeping together?" she demanded. I could never lie to her. She was too honest herself. When we were young, she used to say that whoever lied had a pimple on his tongue, and she always knew anyway. This time I didn't answer, but my face gave me away.

"Will you never learn your lesson?" she shouted. This was a reference to my previous affair, which had hurt her badly. "What kind of person have I raised?" She was *very* angry.

When she had something against me as a schoolgirl, I couldn't concentrate on anything, couldn't excuse or forgive myself. She was a hard person when she believed I had sinned. If she didn't want me to do something, I almost always didn't. But I also couldn't function, because she was the person who gave me what I liked best about myself. Now it was worse. She refused to sit at the table with me—and I stopped eating, because I didn't want to interfere with her meals. And also because I'd immediately lost my appetite.

It went on for a month. Barry needed comforting after the loss of his father, but he was the one who gave the comfort when he saw how I looked. My mother wouldn't speak to him either—until he confronted her one day.

"What are you doing to your own daughter?" he said. "Don't you see how you're destroying her, making her actually sick?" A loud argument followed. Barry left as distressed as when his father had died.

I was sleeping a lot too, probably to escape the conflict. That afternoon, my mother came into my room and hugged me as I lay in bed. I hugged her back very hard. "Thank God this is over," I thought. "Now we can get on with our lives." But getting on meant moving forward. My mother's reaction actually propelled us toward marriage, because it seemed the natural next step.

The wedding was scheduled for July. In between, Barry and I continued visiting bookstores, art galleries, and theater bars. I realized that he was driven in his quiet way. It was more than loving to walk his legs off. He hated restraints. One way or another, he had to be on the move.

The marriage could only be in our old Brooklyn house, where the clan gathered for every holiday. Everything else was up for argument. By this time both families were resigned to the inevitable, but both kept fighting for their own. To make it a little more Jewish here, a little more Catholic there. . . .

From a compromise on a Unitarian minister to perform the ceremony, we gradually shifted—meaning I was pushed—to a rabbi. But I insisted that if a rabbi presided, the reception be Italian-style: strictly non-kosher. My mother suggested consulting one of my uncles, who owned a catering business.

"Uncle Dominic, how about catering my wedding?"

"Love to, Barbara. What would you like to have?"

I barely began with sausage and peppers when he interrupted to announce that he was a kosher caterer! "My partner's Jewish, honey. We work a lot with the local temple." Uncle Dominic could lose his license for violating the dietary laws, so we ended with a kosher reception despite my best intentions.

On the other hand, I also had to tone down some of the Catholic campaigning. The ceremony was planned for the front yard, the large reception for the rear, with a stage for the band. I was to appear from my grandmother's door and walk through a little archway. On the great morning, the lawn was still unmowed and the yard was a shambles of unrigged tents and tables. An Italian florist was busy decorating the archway—in white crosses. I talked him out of that particular pattern. Come what would, I wasn't going to upset Barry on our wedding day—but I couldn't stop his mother feeling upset if something disturbed her. Those crosses would have done more than that.

I couldn't stop my own mother, either. When my father had the tents rigged, she climbed one of our tallest trees and hung a cross on a big branch. In more than one way, it was a heavy cross. "That rabbi may be marrying you," she said from over our heads, "but Jesus is going to be above him." Then she marched inside to dress, and reappeared with a slightly lighter cross on a chain around her neck.

"Ma, do you have to wear that?" I almost pleaded.

"Yes, I have to wear *that*." I knew that tone better than my name. It declared that nothing I said would have the slightest effect on her.

The rivalry continued even during the ceremony—which, of course, had to raise new conflicts. At Catholic weddings the groom waits for the bride with his best man. The Jewish way is for the parents to be there too—and Barry's mother stood firm at the altar despite the terms of the truce we'd worked out earlier, which would have kept her seated. Three times, people went out to remind her. "Here Comes the Bride" was playing, but the bride wasn't coming, because at the last moment I felt I couldn't take any more chipping away at things. Finally, someone pushed me out of the door and through the archway.

My first whisper to Barry was to ask him to make his mother abide by the compromise. At last she sat down—in my father's seat. After cleaning up the yard like ten men that morning, he perched on a damp stoop while his daughter was married.

The rabbi had noticed everything. He dwelled heavily on the need for toleration. Above all, good marriages need understanding and sensitivity to other people's feelings, he said. It was no academic sermon. Maybe some of the guests on the fringe hadn't felt the tension, but this day of days had far too much of it for me.

The rabbi's words kept coming back to me during the following years. Barry and I shared so much—we felt so naturally good together —that our religious troubles seemed like a cold rather than anything permanent. I discovered that Italians and Jews shared a lot, especially in outgoingness and love of family. Barry and I in particular had even more in common, which is really what made us click. Religion was the only barrier. It didn't melt away after the marriage.

When Alexander was born, Barry insisted on a briss, the full religious ceremony for circumcision. After my weeping and pleading, he knew how much that hurt me. When Ariana came, he took her to a temple to have her blessed with his grandmother's Hebrew name, which I didn't even know. Discussing the potential problems as a single woman, I was convinced they wouldn't matter. That was easy to believe *before*. My ideas began changing as soon as I became pregnant. Whatever I'd thought earlier, this was my flesh and blood, something I *felt*.

Although not religious, Barry wouldn't even color me an Easter egg after I'd made authentic Hanukkah and Passover dinners for him and his family. His worst was enrolling me for religious instruction. I happened to get the mail one day and was almost knocked down by the appointment card. We had our first fight when Barry came home; an angry, terrible exchange. If I wasn't a good Catholic, I couldn't have been a better Jew, because I couldn't fake these things. I was what I was, and if he loved and respected that, why was he so determined to change me, without even asking?

I went to the conversion class—streaming with tears. I sat there with such misery on my face that Barry didn't ask me to go a second time. Later he started buying me Easter eggs—beautiful, hand-painted ones from the Smithsonian Institution. After the first few years our Christmas trees no longer seared him. I doubted he'd ever buy one himself—but eventually he did. To some extent he learned that give-and-take has to be mutual, even in this. I did the trees myself, trying to make them ecumenical. My decorations were mostly birds, with no star on top—just to bring seasonal cheer into the house.

It was less religious beliefs I was trying to defend than my sense of fairness, and maybe my pride. "You wait!" I used to tell him. "The children will marry obstinate Catholics one day, who will pressure them—then we'll see how you feel." Eventually he laughed. He was so understanding and considerate in almost everything else. I always knew I needed someone different because I was slightly "odd": My thoughts and wants didn't fit in with my surroundings. Barry's special qualities more than compensated for our sporadic religious troubles.

The International Communication Agency was essentially a reorganized United States Information Agency. Of the staff of about ninety who served in Tehran in 1978, thirteen were Americans and the rest Iranian secretaries, printers, artists, and special assistants in publishing and cultural affairs. The English-teaching section had been damaged by a bomb ten months before. Our offices, which were still intact, occupied a six-story building on Saba Street, off one of northern Tehran's main thoroughfares. The first thing I noticed about the faceless brick structure was the absence of any identifying sign or nameplate. Then I was struck by the elaborate security measures at the entrance. Both features, of course, derived from the same apprehension.

Embassy staff meetings were held five days a week at 9 A.M. From the earlier conference in our own office, I would make my way the mile or so to the embassy compound with Jack Shellenberger, the Public Affairs Officer. The Chevrolets at our disposal were protected by bullet-proof glass and equipped with two-way radios, whose antennas passing Tehranis might associate with SAVAK, the Shah's detested secret police. When we had time, I pressed Jack to walk instead of ride.

Besides, walking was still my favorite way of observing. When Jack was otherwise occupied, I went alone.

Again I was struck both by what had changed in Iranian life and what had remained the same. Skirmishes over traffic mishaps and alleged insults erupted just as I remembered them, and the deeply aggrieved parties made the expected display of challenge and threat without crossing the line to physical violence. Yet even this ritualized defense of personal pride seemed to put menace into the air. Street manners had clearly deteriorated, probably because people were tenser.

No wonder: Parts of Tehran were almost under occupation. The main thoroughfare leading from ICA to the Embassy was Takht-e Jamshid, the city's tawdry former Fifth Avenue. A troop carrier stood at the intersection of Pahlavi, its machine gun at the ready and pointed up the city's only nearly elegant, tree-lined avenue.

Shortly before I arrived in Tehran, the Shah had instituted martial law and installed a military government in reaction to the severe riots whose wreckage I saw on my ride from the airport. The Shah then tried to form a coalition government, approaching mostly elderly men of various parties that he himself had decimated in the 1950s and 1960s, when he was consolidating his power. They all realized there was little hope of saving the monarchy without the cooperation of the leader of the opposition, then in exile near Paris—who categorically refused even to see any appointee of the Shah. Still casting about with increasing desperation, the Shah, however, would not transfer power to a regency council. No public figure would risk playing his old game of granting concessions until he felt strong enough to grab them back. All his attempts to shore up his rule with moderate politicians had so far come to nothing.

Meanwhile, troop carriers roamed the city. The most prominent was parked almost permanently at the major intersection of Takht-e Jamshid and Pahlavi, at the edge of the richer northern districts. Nervous soldiers in the back of the vehicle scanned the streets from under their helmets but never seemed able to spot snipers before they were fired on. When shots rang out, the soldiers chased off in their direction—while anti-Shah demonstrators quickly materialized at the crossroads they had just vacated.

The modern, slightly bunker-like main offices of the National Iranian Oil Company, the state monopoly, were halfway to the Embassy. Workers striking in the fields in protest against the regime were drying up the flow of oil, and clerical staff were trying to support them. As I passed the large building, windows in the upper stories opened and armfuls of documents, letter files, and computer readouts were tossed out like wastepaper. In happier times the deluge might have been mistaken for confetti. As it was floating down, army trucks sped to the building. Squads of soldiers raced inside while others sealed off the street. Before the soldiers could seize the paper throwers, they were being pelted by ashtrays and typewriter rollers thrown from windows of lesser oil buildings across the street.

In a moment, the soldiers opened fire, sometimes joined by units of the National Police. When bullets began ricocheting off walls near my head, I ran into an alley for refuge and huddled on the ground with half a dozen Iranians. While they were muttering about the crazy turns life had taken, I thought of the reassuring tone of so much of the American press, which still treated the Shah as supreme. This was portrayed as mere minor trouble for the military government.

The embassy compound occupied twenty-seven acres of prime Tehran real estate near the very center of the "better" business district. It included warehouses and service buildings, a cooperative store, and the Ambassador's residence, set in lush gardens. The Chancery, which housed the most important offices, was the working hub.

Staff meetings were held in the Chancery's Conference Room, which was called "the Bubble." Around the table, heavy plexiglass formed a "secure room" within the room. An electric current running through the glass supposedly foiled bugging equipment.

Ambassador William Sullivan chaired the meetings, which were attended by the Embassy's section chiefs—political, economic, military, agricultural, security, and other—and by several observers, including myself, often to help handle the press briefings. The Ambassador's mellow voice suited his distinguished appearance.

"Good morning. I gather the shouting, shooting, and blackouts continue. No water in our quarter. . . . Any good news?"

The good news for the day was the safe arrival of a shipment of dogfood for the pets of embassy personnel. Among the bad news was the identification of our ICA building as CIA headquarters by antiregime activists at the University. Not for the first time, the Ambassador commented on the inspired thinking in Washington that had conceived the name International Communication Agency. This gave us new initials that every teenaged anti-American prophet in the world could reveal to mobs as confirmation that we were spies and worse.

Reports between the good and the bad indicated that Americans were leaving Iran in droves. A voluntary evacuation had been recommended on December 8, a few days earlier. Well over half the dependents of embassy staff—who originally numbered about a thousand, including dependents of military personnel—had flown home. The private American community of businessmen, technicians, and others had once numbered almost forty thousand. A slightly smaller percentage of their dependents had also left during the past week.

Everyone knew the military forces were the key to Iran's future. There was still some hope that whatever happened to the Shah, they could be saved, guaranteeing the country's integrity, including protection for American installations, radar posts, and other strategic interests. The assistant chief of the Military Advisory Assistance Program sustained this hope for the meeting, reporting that the Army was "very much in place, but cold, bored, and wondering what it's all about."

In a way, what it was all about was a Shi'ite Muslim cleric in Paris, Ruhollah Khomeini, who had been exiled in 1964, after his opposition, among other things, to the Shah's granting immunity from criminal prosecution to American military personnel stationed in Iran. Khomeini was an ayatollah, an honor bestowed by the consensus of religious leaders and confirmed by popular approval upon highly learned, respected mullahs. Although the Muslim clergy had no organized hierarchy, the title ayatollah, literally "sign of God," was the highest acclaim. Less fallible than temporal leaders, they could appeal on doctrinal matters over the heads of rulers, thus involving themselves in the political process.

Khomeini was totally, implacably opposed to the Shah. The official line was that he was a retrograde cleric, exiled for opposition to the Shah's land reform. The reality was that the Ayatollah despised and detested the Shah for a combination of personal, political, and religious reasons which coalesced in scornful, ridiculing charges that

the Shah was not a true Iranian and that his subservience to America
had corrupted the Iranian and Islamic way of life.

In the late-nineteenth century, Shi'ite clergymen living abroad
joined Westernized intellectuals in bitterly opposing concessions to
British monopolists. Their distribution of "bulletins" on Islamic law,
together with attacks against Western perversion of Iranian and
Islamic tradition, helped topple pre-Pahlavi monarchs who favored
Western penetration. Khomeini's message was remarkably similar in
thrust and emotional appeal but delivered by more effective means.
Cassettes of his sermons and stern instructions circulated throughout
the country like water through its jubes.

In his attitude to the regime he was on the radical end of the spectrum of ayatollahs, a significant minority of whom did not believe the
Shah must be destroyed; some compromise was possible if the King of
Kings would become a constitutional monarch. But Khomeini's passionate appeal to Islamic consciousness, which for centuries had been
the spine of Iranian nationalism, ignited many kinds of smoldering dis-
content. In the jammed stalls and shops of Tehran's bazaar, tapes of
his fierce denunciations of the Shah drew crowds side by side with
tapes of *Grease.* Maybe this incongruity—Kentucky Fried Chicken
outlets doing heavy business during some of the angriest rioting—
helped prevent many Americans from recognizing the gravity of the
threat of revolution. Or it was hope for the Shah, or lack of contact
with "ordinary" Iranians. In any case, the Ayatollah's immensely powerful grip on the dreams of millions of Iranians wasn't made clear to
the staff meeting. The Political Officer reported that "the cassette
business" was booming although "Khomeini makes no sense in Paris
and makes no sense here."

From what I observed while moving around the city, Khomeini
made all too much sense with Tehranis. But first there was the question of the Army—which wasn't fully in place, as reported, but starting to wobble and defect. Walking back to ICA from the Embassy, I
passed the circle of tanks and troop carriers that protected the
unidentified Israeli Mission. Young people strolled up to the troops to
place carnations in the barrels of their machine guns and rifles, while
the soldiers laughed and joked with them. This was hardly a disciplined army. Although gloomy enough, the staff meeting seemed to
me not to fully reflect the potential for military breakdown, which
would put power in the streets.

✻

During my Peace Corps period, the range between Muslim
believers and nonbelievers seemed naturally wide. Villagers and recent arrivals to city slums spent hours in ritual ablutions and daily
prayers, while Tehran's elite made a point of denigrating "backward"
Islam, which had undermined the greatness of ancient, pre-Islamic

Iran and kept the country poor. Still, the mean struck me as distinctly more believing than the American one. Perhaps it is more accurate to say that Islam, which wove itself into everything from cooking to banking, was more a part of daily life than Western Christianity and Judaism. In any case, the religious quotient in Iranian society had taken a quantum leap since 1968.

This was surely not because vast new numbers had found faith in the intervening ten years. Shi'ite Islam in Iran was as much a nationalistic as a spiritual phenomenon. The cement in the formation of the nation-state in the sixteenth century, it remained the people's primary link to the nation, above dynasties and everything else. Especially in crises, their loyalty went instinctively to the mosque.

While the Shah's touted economic boom provided jobs, consumer goods, and the hope of comfort, Islamic identification was blurred. But a major recession that began in 1976 brought great hardship and disillusionment to millions. While modernization promised general development and a sense of direction, Islamic concepts of justice receded. But the great mass of Iranians, including even many of the new middle class, had perceived that modernity did not bring well-being, especially modernity in the forms of the Shah's dreaded secret police and colossal expenditure on American arms while poverty persisted and millions of uprooted villagers languished. As the regime's major props were seen to crumble, despair and anger soared, and people sought guidance, solace, and a sense of identity in their roots—and in justice, which, in the Iranian mind, is closely connected to punishment of the wicked.

They also sought revenge partly to avoid confronting their own attraction for Western temptations while they glittered. Again and again in Iranian history the country seemed subject to more foreign influences than its culture could absorb. A rejection was building up, as of a transplanted organ that had toxified the blood. No matter how much and how freely Iranians had borrowed from it, a growing number were convinced the secular West was irredeemably ill.

The "detour" to that secular West, especially to the Shah's "coconspirators" in Western capitals, was seen as a betrayal of their most sacred ideals and traditions, rather than as a mistaken turn. Never mind that the Islam in which they now sought salvation was all things to all people, from religious zealots to human-rights groups; or that it contained as much wishful thinking as historical truth. Its allure was all the greater for its vagueness. For more and more people, it was the common-denominator cure-all, especially since the Shah himself, in his insecurity and intolerance, had eliminated all viable secular alternatives.

Everything that had gone wrong was associated with the imperial family and their real and imagined excesses. Only Islam could provide everything needed to correct and heal. The Shah looked resplendent on the covers of Western magazines, but it was to the mullahs, in their traditional garb, that most people turned for a way out—even to those mullahs who had rejected good Western influences as well as bad when they challenged their authority.

*

The ninth and tenth days of Moharram, a month of mourning commemorating the martyrdom of Mohammed's grandson Hossein, are the holiest days of the Shi'ite Islamic calendar. It is a time of high-pitched lamentation, when grief spills out for Hossein's cruel death. An absolute distinction between good and evil, saints and Satan, is central to Shi'ite Islam, and nothing is more beloved than the martyr whose agony helps Iranians release their sorrow for their own oppression and suffering. This is most clearly expressed in passion plays that are avidly watched, especially by less-educated believers. In 1968 I saw one depicting Hossein's pain as he approached death. The makeshift stage was near the center of Tehran's red-light district. A circle of prostitutes wept openly. Like so many others, they deeply identified with the martyr.

The ninth day of Moharram was Hossein's agony; the tenth day, Hossein's death. In 1978, they fell on the tenth and the eleventh of December. Those two days, I worked at the Embassy's information center, which had been advising the American community of where demonstrations were expected and where shooting had erupted. We urged callers to remain home until the end of the religious holiday. Many Westerners in the city feared the procession would work up from religious fervor to violence that might threaten foreigners and even topple the regime.

When my shift ended, I left the Embassy for a look. This exploring in possibly dangerous places did not delight the Ambassador, but I did not want to rely on reports of the Embassy's Iranian observers. The young army officer who had asked to go along was the only other Westerner I saw on the streets. Otherwise they spilled over with millions of determined, confident demonstrators.

They were demonstrating political opposition at least as much as religious observance. It was now less the passion plays that interested them than the opportunity to associate themselves with "the resistance." Newly politicized women in black chadors covering everything but the eyes and nose participated in the processions; formerly they had been onlookers. The processions themselves were without chains and flagellation, for the emphasis was elsewhere. This was underlined when a military helicopter flew overhead and almost every fist spontaneously went into the air against it while antiregime cadences rang out.

Above all, the discipline and coordination were impressive. Food was distributed from trucks, ambulances waited for emergencies, and coins were handed out for people to invite their friends by telephone to join the crowds. It seemed so well controlled that I felt safe throughout miles of walking, even though I was recognizable as a foreigner and people looked straight at me while pronouncing the now-ritual slogans of hatred. Even the chanting of "Death to the Puppet Shah!" was orchestrated and seemed matched to the obscene references to President Carter scrawled in paint over walls. This would seem to spell inevitable overthrow to any authoritarian regime unwilling either to grant great concessions or use mass terror.

The following morning, the Embassy was palpably relieved. For days before the holiday, Western analysts had predicted a great confrontation. If the Shah survived it, they felt, he would have passed another "the worst." The expected clash had not taken place, but only because the mullahs and their secular allies had complete control over the demonstrators—and because the military government had relinquished its authority over the entire southern part of the city, where the main processions took place. That had been the arrangement negotiated with the government: "No violence if we police our own."

In the north, especially on the roads leading to the sumptuous Niavaran Palace, tanks and guard posts stood everywhere. I could not drive for more than a few minutes without encountering a blockade where special permits—in addition to my charmed identity card from the Foreign Ministry—had to be shown. But the south had been temporarily handed over to the opposition. I saw not a single policeman or soldier where they were ordinarily concentrated. It was an unpublicized partial surrender. When President Carter renewed American support for the Shah the next day and stressed that "the predictions of disaster that came from some sources have not been realized at all," I remembered how weak my grasp of the situation had been when I was in Washington.

*

Mohammed Reza Pahlavi succeeded his father, who abdicated under Allied pressure for siding with the Germans during World War II despite his official neutrality. Reza Shah's outwardly impressive army, which he had been building for fifteen years, crumbled almost at the sight of British and Soviet expeditionary forces. The Allies needed Iran for its oil fields and as the principal land route for delivering Lend-Lease supplies to the Soviet Union.

Mohammed Reza was twenty-two years old at his accession. Throughout the war he remained essentially an instrument of Allied control. When the British departed in 1946, and the last of the Russians later withdrew under stiff U.S. pressure, he began what was essentially the start of his reign, cautiously, without apparent antiparliamentarian or even antidemocratic tendencies. People used to tell me that his strapping, authoritarian father, the former General of the Russian-trained Cossack Brigade, inspired fear with a glance. Especially in the tall shadow of this first Pahlavi, the short young Shah, who had had a sickly childhood, did not seem powerful. Farhad liked to say that the succession should have passed to Mohammed Reza's twin sister, Ashraf. The father and twins used to sit under a palace tree. Many painted a picture of Ashraf entranced by her father's talk of how to rule in the patriarchal Persian tradition—which the Shah also identified with Atatürk, his hero. Sitting slightly apart from the other two, Mohammed Reza would read poetry on these occasions.

Several assassination attempts seemed to intimidate him, but remarkable survivals—one bullet pierced his face in 1949—nourished a mysticism in him that grew and grew. He came to believe that his destiny was to rule and to transform Iran, which commingled with a drive to exhibit that he was no weakling, but genuinely majestic.

The events of 1953 were a crucial turning point precisely because he had so little influence on them. Mohammed Mossadeq, the popular Prime Minister, had upset him, chiefly by nationalizing the Anglo-Iranian Oil Company. A failed attempt to remove Mossadeq so frightened the Shah that he left the country. In the widespread dissatisfaction with Mossadeq that followed loss of oil money and near economic collapse, a CIA maneuver helped restore the Shah to power.

From then on, he was Iran in American eyes. Within three years, Iran was the beneficiary of our largest aid program. All our plans and hopes were pinned to him—while he seemed haunted by the memory of his near impotence in 1953. He developed a fascination for guns and tanks. Fearing all opposition, he coopted or squeezed what he did not destroy. He had been shown to be so weak that he had to demonstrate strength in all his policies, whether well- or ill-conceived.

He announced that he would not be crowned until he had made Iran a modern nation. It was not for him to be king of a poor, backward country. By my first Peace Corps year he had become strong enough to crown himself in a display that would have satisfied the most ravenous ego. Tehran's mud walls were whitewashed for the occasion, while the city's beggars were removed by the truckload. The wide assortment of people around me on the parade route seemed to enjoy the ostentation for the Shah, for Iran, and for themselves. But I was introduced to the underside of the pageantry and the tempting economic takeoff when Major Afshar, of the Police Academy, summoned me to his office. The "charges" against me were using the Shah's name without his full title and commenting to someone that his display of grandeur seemed out of proportion to daily life. The Major grimly warned me never again to mention His Majesty's name without "that highest respect and deference which he commands." My shakiness during the rest of the day gave me a taste of what Pahlavi rule meant to Iranians.

Shortly after this, I happened to witness a shock force of National Police invade Tehran University during a student strike. The troops clubbed viciously and indiscriminately, keeping at it after blood was bubbling on the faces of young women as well as young men. Although the country as a whole was orderly, ruthless force kept beating into silence small outbursts of opposition—and abroad, where Iranian students could not be beaten, anti-Shah groups were laying down organizational roots. I had too little experience of authoritarian regimes to measure the desire for the Shah's promised good life against the strikes, imprisonments, and unspoken tension. But cracks in his rule struck me as much as its strengths. There was outlet only for praise and gratitude. I doubted such a regime could last.

The Shah had hardly introduced brutality into Iranian life. Bastinado, breaking the bones of the soles with clubs, was an old Iranian tradition. The founder of the dynasty that preceded the Pahlavis made a mound of the twenty thousand eyes he had had gouged from residents of a city that had protected the last heir of the former line. But the Shah's instrument of repression contained detested new elements, and these grew to grotesque proportions, even in a time of supposed peace and prosperity.

He had founded SAVAK, the State Intelligence and Security Organization, in 1957. American advisers and technology helped make it strong beyond its years. Its effect on the nation transcended arguments of whether it imprisoned, tortured, and killed a hundred thousand Iranians, as some estimated, or five times that, as others insisted. Beyond individual tragedies and even mass horrors, the pervasive fear it spread destroyed confidence in the security of the "inner life," which had been taken for granted. People worrying whether their cousin, best friend, or brother might be reporting on them cast a pall far beyond the houses of torture. Like a serpent, the centralized agency secretly snaked through Iranian life.

Allied occupation and Soviet grasping during the Shah's first years of rule apparently traumatized him. But his response to all questions about SAVAK and suppression of opposition in terms of evil enemies, especially communists, was absurd even to those fully aware of communist intentions and methods. The General whom I taught English was one of the regime's experts on the Marxist threat. If the adviser's reasoning reflected the advised's as closely as one would assume, the regime's anticommunism bordered on mania. General Mobassir usually received me in pajamas. His vast library of Marxism-Leninism was decorated by swords and pictures of the Shah. He would sit me down there and talk nonsense about the Red menace, never suspecting that nationalist Islam would soon be the inspiration for the strongest opposition. (Incidentally, the General obtained my services free, since private lessons for him were not supposed to be in my Peace Corps assignment.)

Surely the Shah's personal insecurity helped explain his reliance on SAVAK. The same insecurity fed his urge to flaunt everything from medals to showcase atomic power plants as proof of his greatness. Most Iranian men I knew in the 1960s were fond of showing off, and many took vicarious pride in his displays. It was when they became almost obsessive that popular disgust spread. Celebrations in 1971 of the two thousand five hundredth anniversary of the Iranian monarchy, intended to mark Iran's supposed step into the circle of great powers, were a hundred-million-dollar offering to the vanity of His Royal Majesty, King of Kings, Light of the Aryans, Commander-in-Chief of the Royal Armed Forces—who was incessantly referred to with those titles and more. Each guest was fed on food imported from Maxim's and elsewhere, on dinnerware of equivalent luxury, to a value that approached the country's annual per capita income.

Although intelligent, the punctilious monarch let his grandiose notions of himself and his mission sweep him away from his always feeble contact with ordinary folk. Perhaps he did not know the full extent of corruption involving many near him, including members of the Royal Family. It was enormous. Tractors locked up in barns for sale and other misuses of foreign aid that AID people told me about were little pranks, almost expected in the Third World, compared to the big profits. Day after day I would see scenes of wretched, seemingly unchangeable poverty in southern Tehran and provincial cities, while television broadcasts of the Shah's activities would linger on a kind of Hollywood glitter and opulence among his entourage. Knowing the right people—who had to be near the source of power at the Palace— led to the making of fortunes, especially by middlemen for arms purchases and subcontractors for large Western firms. As the gap widened between rich and poor, splashy spending of parts of those fortunes offended traditional society and the general public. While entertaining Western readers, extravagances of the court and friends of the court built native resentment into outrage.

The Shah wasn't responsible for the insecurity about themselves that fueled Iranians' spurts of self-obsession, nor for their sometimes frantic searching for a national identity. Somewhere he meant well, surely believing that his Westernization was the answer to Iran's major problems. But that Westernization was often myth and show. Never mind that the two-party system he twice instituted had the governing party and the so-called opposition jigging together to his tune. Even some of the celebrated highway construction was a minor disaster. The goal was to widen every town's main road, whatever the cost to traditional ways and architecture. (They were renamed Pahlavi, of course, and where previous monuments and statuary had honored only great contributions to Iran's culture, the new boulevards were decorated by obelisks to the Shah and his father.) The broadening of Pahlavi Avenue in the city of Kashan was so destructive that I myself felt a little outraged during my first visit. Houses with masterful craftsmanship in classical patterns had been cut in half. When the popular mood turned, such symbols of the loss of old graces helped reinforce the perception of the Shah as flouting everything sacred to proclaim his own glory. The breakdown of the old "corporate" structure—of craft guilds, tribal prerogatives and village groupings—was associated with loss of a sense of responsibility for decent behavior, all attributed to the central government's "usurpation" of proper authority.

If the race to progress had been as well conceived as publicized, the inevitable resentment of its price might not have swelled into vast disillusionment with Western ways. But its grave flaws were probably inevitable under the Shah's advisers and cronies. Surface was the only thing: glamour items of technology and billions of dollars' worth of sophisticated arms to make the Shah feel stronger. More attention went to the electronic veneer than to the agricultural infrastructure or the social foundation. Heavy spending raised popular expectations enormously but largely benefited the privileged, who formed links with importers, entrepreneurs, and speculators when they themselves didn't go into business.

During my third-class travels in the countryside, promises to become a new West Germany by the year 2000 seemed more like delirium than mere bluff. The peasants' lives were scarcely touched; many had been ruined by the importation of huge quantities of foreign food. Only outsiders who hadn't seen the mainstream of national life could pronounce "modernization" with a straight face, for it could have been called a grab bag for the elite just as well. When recession struck, in 1976, austerity measures—while purchases of vast armories of military hardware continued—burst the confidence of all, apart from the Shah's closest supporters. He was blamed for the severe disruptions of Islamic family and cultural patterns—caused especially by rapid migration from squeezed villages to wretched "tin towns"—that now seemed to have been suffered in vain. Despair over their lot and confusion by the city's alien ways took people of the slums, who would have been the Shah's supporters if modernization had given them a fairer cut, to the mullahs for comfort.

In the end, the Shah was despised not because he violated Western concepts of good government but because he exceeded Iranian notions of what was fair for a monarch to stake out for himself—and to do to others while taking it. His hunger for personal attention persisted throughout everything. Professors told me about their yearly summons to His Majesty to discuss how the University might be improved—"but he wanted only flattery, never any real discussion of problems and possibilities." Just before I arrived in November, he appeared on television to tell the nation that he had "heard your message." Although this was the day after serious rioting, it may not have been too late even then. But he probably provoked more anger on the defensive than when he "commanded," as his pronouncements were obligatorily labeled. He seemed to grasp that resorting to all the force at his command might keep him on his throne but ensure that his teenaged son, to whom he had resolved to pass the succession, would never sit there. He used enough force to kill and outrage, then backed off—while the opposition gained new momentum. Demonstrators were shot, a forty-day mourning period followed, a new demonstration was held to honor the martyrs of the last one, and the cycle continued. His isolation and paranoia deepened. He waited for American guidance, then felt embittered because one Washington faction urged him to exert more force and another was convinced that would only seal his doom. Having made the country his personal corporation, he was frozen with indecision just as his enemies grew in numbers, confidence, and ability to act.

*

Christmas in Iran was not celebrated except among the small Christian minorities and Western residents. This one seemed more like the approach of civil war than a holiday season. Guerrilla-style disruptions occurred almost daily in Tehran. Felled trees and burning buses paralyzed the capital's traffic for hours by blocking main streets. Struck banks closed for lack of cash. Small businesses were folding, and in the kingdom of oil wealth, heating fuel had become as scarce as gasoline.

The authorities promised it would not happen, but night after night workers operating the national power grid shut off the electricity. Unseen activists defied the curfew to appear on rooftops and cry, "God is great, death to the Shah, Khomeini is our leader!" through megaphones. In the city's eerie blackness, small groups dashed along the streets to exhort people to join the holy war against the enemies of Islam.

It was no accident that power went off at eight-thirty, minutes after the start of the television news. General Azhari, the military government's Prime Minister, would be silenced just as he was working into his explanation of the troubles and promises of improvement. His appeals for an end of the strikes and a return to order had no chance.

When the screen went blank, I would fumble for my dinner. Sometimes it was too dark to find candles. Being alone had become almost natural, and when I needed company, I switched on my tape recorder and talked to Barbara on a cassette the American Post Office would deliver in less than a week. My main items of domestic news were what I was cooking at the moment and the temperature of my tea. The day's problems at the office would sometimes follow, which would lead into a wrap-up of the current political situation. "And now," I would proudly announce, "for the revolutionary top ten in Tehran today." For my hits I would record classical Iranian music for sitars and flutes instead of the imitative, inferior Iranian rock 'n' roll.

Barbara said my amateur jumble made her laugh and kept her spirits up. It did even better for me in that depressing darkness.

◦

Ten days before my arrival, Ambassador Sullivan had sent a crucial cable, entitled "Thinking the Unthinkable," to Secretary of State Cyrus Vance. The Ambassador foresaw that if Iran's military government and martial law failed to contain the growing turmoil quickly, the Shah—this was the unthinkable prospect for America—would not survive. The "eyes only" communication went directly to the Secretary of State, probably unseen by anyone else in the Embassy.

No doubt in an attempt to avoid defeatism, the Ambassador did not stop his staff from sending their own cables to Washington, many of which were far more optimistic during the late fall and early winter. But by early January, Tehran was bursting with speculation about the Shah's rumored plans to go abroad, and Mr. Sullivan began to reveal the full extent of his pessimism at the Embassy's morning conferences.

"Since our last meeting," he said in his controlled voice, "the situation has become, let us admit, dicier. I saw H.I.M. [His Imperial Majesty] yesterday. He looks like someone hit him on the nose. The bruise is inside. . . . He's all hands out, seeking something to hold onto. . . . A lot depends on the military. . . . The Shah will depart. He thinks it'll be a brief outing. I'm not so sure."

The Palace announced the Shah's "brief outing" as a holiday. He could certainly have used one. He looked exhausted and depressed; no one knew that he was also seriously ill. But very few Iranians believed this was a holiday from which he would return. Nine tenths of the nation received the news that he was about to leave as a proclamation of victory—even though the Shah did not officially admit defeat, maintaining that his government would continue functioning in his name until his unspecified homecoming. It was an extremely impressive triumph by essentially unarmed protestors over a powerfully militarized, intensely controlled state.

The Shah left for Egypt the morning of January 16. Following a kind of news blackout until his plane took off, a short announcement was made as if he were going on one of his skiing trips. Tehran leaped for joy. Within minutes, celebrants thronged the avenues near the ICA offices.

Partly in precaution in case someone decided to pelt the building, we left before the end of the working day. The streets were still so packed with singing, shouting, arm-waving men and women that our minibus could not get through. Newspapers were thrust to the sky and against our windows. "THE SHAH IS GONE!" proclaimed the largest headline I'd ever seen in Iran. Its grammar was even more striking.

Until now, "The Shah" was always plural; "they" commanded, "they" received visiting dignitaries. Now *he* had left the country: an ordinary mortal; but the implications, coming hours after his departure, were startling. I almost felt sorry for the now pathetic figure. Perhaps he hadn't relied on bullets during his final weeks because he was afraid —or was still waiting for Washington to save the throne, possibly by arranging negotiations with Khomeini. In any case, he accepted that the end was the end, instead of unleashing slaughter.

Not everyone rejoiced. While the Shah had sobbed at the airport, one of the officers in his entourage kissed his boot. But our ICA contingent was surrounded by nothing less than national thanksgiving. In the old tradition of supreme celebration, people were passing around trays of cakes and sweets that local shopkeepers had spontaneously provided. Rolls of crepe paper (and toilet-paper substitutes) were tossed into the air and attached to windshields. Instead of our obviously American van being assaulted, as we had anticipated, we were ignored by the rapturous throng. I could hardly believe that this moment, which I'd long considered inevitable, was actually here. Week by week, year by year, Mohammed Reza Pahlavi had alienated more and more people in almost every segment of society, but the festive din told me I hadn't fully appreciated how much hatred he had generated.

The inclusion of America in that hatred worried me most. This was not the first time Iranians, with their fear of invasion and intervention, perceived the devil in "anti-Islamic" influences. Pointing to foreign corruption made it easier to live with native weakness, in this case decades of passivity and collaboration with the Shah's despotism. To many, America was as evil as Islam was good, and we had made enough mistakes to make the symbolism seem like logic to the national majority.

Horns honked. Windshield wipers carrying photographs of Khomeini swished in rhythm. Celebrants displayed bank notes with the Shah's portrait cut out of them; others carried mullahs on their shoulders. And the "Now it's America's turn" slogan occasionally sounded around us. The glue in the varied forces that joined to bring down the Shah was the perception of him—all the more powerful for being simple and less than half true—as a violator of Iranian-Islamic values in the service of Washington masters.

The human traffic stalled our minibus for an hour. I half expected it to be lifted up and carried off. Two weeks before, the Shah had replaced his military government with a civilian one headed by Prime Minister Shahpur Bakhtiar, an honorable man who had been jailed six times for opposing the Shah's policies. A Sorbonne graduate, Bakhtiar had been a leader of an opposition coalition emasculated by the Shah. A year earlier he might have had a chance. The Shah could have abdicated in favor of the Crown Prince; a regency council might have established new machinery of government; some sort of continuity might have been maintained. Now I was certain it was too late for leadership from anyone identified with Western democracy and parliamentarianism.

For all his credentials, Bakhtiar could not appeal to a people who had surged this high and wide. His constituency was tiny pockets of educated liberals. It was not the Prime Minister whom the crowd saw as their liberator, but the cleric in Paris whose image they carried in thousands. As we waited in an impassable boulevard, our driver reached under his seat and produced his own stack of photographs of the solemn Khomeini. This surprised us, but less than it should have. We unrolled the portraits against our windows, and our protectively decorated Chevrolet finally got through. Being Iranian, the driver might have laid in a stock of Khomeini cards to hedge his bets—but I doubted it. It was largely the exile's day, and if the Army would not allow him to return, civil war was probably inevitable. This was the next question everyone asked: Would the Army stay loyal to the Prime Minister of a finished Shah, even if he had agreed to serve only on condition that His Royal Majesty leave?

I once did some work on Pakistani politics in the 1960s. A mullah seemed to be emerging as the most popular alternative to a succession of civilian and military governments. He had supposedly devised a constitutional system based wholly on the Koran, the Traditions of Mohammed, and Islamic law. How could a politician propose such rigidity in the twentieth century? How could a people embrace it? Research at Columbia and McGill University's Islamic Institute helped me understand the appeal of the Pakistani cleric—and of Ruhollah Khomeini, whom he remarkably resembled.

Throughout the chaotic winter, "mullah" still conjured up something obscurantist or invidious to most Westerners. "Black-robed mullah" remained a trigger phrase in the American press. Those who used it would not resort to "black-clothed priests" or "yarmulked rabbis," but the Islamic clergy, like Islam itself, was considered dark, irrational, and threatening—almost a natural enemy.

The great mass of Iranians, by contrast, regarded their clergy as confidants and benefactors. Although the nouveaux riches mocked them, villagers and the urban poor turned to them for solace, understanding, and help during emergencies. There were degenerate, backward, and corrupt mullahs, of course. But their popular image was of simple friends.

Apart from being more learned—which was how they became mullahs—they differed very little from laymen. They were not celibate and belonged to no hierarchy in the Western sense. They lived with their people, on their offerings. "Clergy" is actually misleading, since mullahs are scholars, teachers, interpreters of Islamic law, administrators of charity, and wise men.

Like any other group, they split into factions on some issues and united on others. In general they played politics and defended their own. But this was less significant now than their relative independence. Although the Shah had a coterie of his own well-paid mullahs, the great majority were supported by religious taxes and property endowments—and were not allied to the state. As the Shah's system began to collapse, only the clergy, which had always stood apart, remained essentially intact.

This enhanced their prestige. More came from their traditional concern, despite individual lapses, with good and evil, waywardness and justice. When everything official seemed corrupted, the mullahs were the only institution to offer a moral alternative.

They had self-interested conflicts with the Shah. Some fought his land reforms in the early 1960s, because the mosques controlled large tracts. Others were jailed later. But as a whole, they opposed the Shah for what they perceived as his wrongs to their people, especially his undermining of Islamic values by the introduction of Western ones.

Introduction of alien values was particularly resented because the memory of perverting foreign domination was kept raw by the Iranians' inclination to see themselves as victims. Indeed, this was partly what distinguished Iranian Islam from the larger body from which it broke away. And one of the cardinal features of Shi'ite Islam, which suited the national character and helped assuage self-pity for suffering as "losers," was the intense concentration on the bitter injustice visited upon the martyred saints.

The amazing proliferation in town and country of shrines to those saints—and to their sons and grandsons—could serve as landmarks to the national psyche. It was millions of personal hurts. Almost every Iranian carries within him a heightened sensitivity to injustice. Outside Paris, Ruhollah Khomeini returned again and again and again to the Shah's injustices against the people. His slow, seemingly inexorable voice began to reverberate deep in people's feelings and thoughts.

His words themselves were anything but yielding. Even while still in Iran, he, almost alone among the high clergy, was totally uncompromising. He gave expression to strains deep in Shi'ite Islam and even pre-Islamic Iran. Good was good, the Shah utterly evil. There was no meeting point.

"We have lived under a military government for fifty years. The Iranian people will resist until their last drop of blood. . . . Our nation will not tolerate puppets and agents of foreigners. The time for them is gone. I invite the nation to continue its struggle."

The simplicity of his lessons acquired ever greater appeal. His long exile gave him an aura of purity. And he was politic enough to speak in generalities and make alliances with groups—intellectuals, moderates, secular nationals, leftist guerrillas—that would not ordinarily see salvation in a man who preached that every problem could be resolved with application of Islamic law and custom. He attracted the wide spectrum of oppositionists chiefly with promises that he would be no more than the moral force in the reborn society and would not concern himself with daily political and social issues. An Islamic republic would be free.

"Imam" is both "saint" and "spiritual leader" in Farsi. I began to hear "Imam Khomeini" shortly after my return. It was not clear to me in which sense it was used, because, I felt, it was unclear to Iranians themselves. But it was perfectly clear that this seventy-nine-year-old son and grandson of ayatollahs with the seemingly scowling countenance and hypnotic eyes was cherished by more and more Iranians, who referred to him in a term of simple endearment and respect. The fervor for him derived from a combination of personal admiration and belief that he had shown them how to restore their dignity and self-respect. Here was *the right way* at last: the old, honest, shining way.

It was no more improbable to see the solution in fundamentalist Islam than for Americans to see it in fundamentalist Christianity. And if our country came to a dead end, would not the Moral Majority's adherents swell to a hundred million?

*

After the Shah's departure, on January 16, Khomeini's return was almost inevitable. He delayed chiefly out of concern whether the Army, if it continued to support Bakhtiar, would physically stop him. Peering toward Paris, the country held its breath for two weeks. Airports were closed, supposedly for safety reasons. But would the Imam be coming today? Tomorrow?

When he ended his fifteen-year exile, on February 1, I doubted whether more people had ever been packed on the streets of any other city at any other time. His twelve-mile route from the airport to the cemetery where "martyrs to the revolution" were buried—some of the thousands killed by the Shah's forces—was a cheering, adoring, ecstatic mass. For the first time in my life, I actually saw a sea of humanity.

"How does it feel?" I was asked. "What are your emotions?" These queries came from a New York *Post* editor who had called me from his office to request a "blow-by-blow" description of the arrival. My chief emotion at that moment was slight astonishment at his presumption. As a press attaché I tried to supply what factual information I could for reporters, but there was hardly time or reason to serve as one for a cheeky newspaper fond of shallow questions.

I returned to images of the stupendous throng on the office television set. Suddenly the picture went blank and a formal portrait of the Shah appeared while the imperial national anthem was struck up. A minute after this apparently final gesture by a group of the Shah's supporters, television service ceased completely and I went downstairs to continue observing the spectacle.

The forest of placards matched the number of near-delirious welcomers. Gigantic canvases, some of them two stories high, had been hand-painted with portraits of the uncompromising Ayatollah. From Saba Street I made my way south toward the main crossroads, where the Shah's troop carriers used to be parked. Trapped in flesh, it took me twenty minutes to negotiate a short block. Khomeini was scheduled to pass there within an hour, but the crowds had long delayed him; worshipers climbing on his van blocked the driver's view from the windows. The irony struck me while hundreds of thousands surrounding me waited as if their lives were about to be transformed from agony to bliss: I was standing on the corner of Pahlavi and Shahreza streets, named in honor of the old dynasty, to see the man who had brought it down.

Trying to set straight my own thoughts about the great change, I made an effort not to be caught up in Khomeini's charisma. The harder task was not to judge through my American eyes.

Islamic Iranian dynasties were much less long-lived, therefore less strongly rooted than Western ones. They came and went with those who seized power. The Pahlavis came when General Reza Khan, of the Cossack Brigade, marched into Tehran. (He took the name Pahlavi, a symbol of pre-Islamic glory—and of his own distaste for what he saw as the subsequent tarnishing—when he crowned himself, in 1925.) Still, the institution itself of monarchy had legitimacy, if only because its history was so long, with no republican experience to introduce a notion of alternative ways of rule. Classical Iranian poetry was full of tales of kings and kingship, which fixed themselves in the national consciousness.

If Mohammed Reza had been able to be a constitutional monarch, surely this would have provided the most propitious framework for Iran's stability and development. By this time in the twentieth century the advantages of reform and evolution seemed obvious. Revolutions are terribly risky. Once their momentum has started, they are very hard to stop. When power surges to the streets, the last word usually goes to the bully with the biggest fist or largest gun. New revolutionary leaders so often seem to learn little except to become even more intolerant than the old.

The Shah's belief that Iranians needed discipline from above because they had so little within them was rooted in a certain reality. Iranian individualism sometimes bordered on anarchy. Without direction, the natural inclination is more to seek personal advantage than to cooperate. But how to develop the needed self-discipline without corresponding scope for responsibility? In any case, the Shah had violated so many limits that he ended by encouraging not cooperation but rebellion growing from nearly total alienation.

He was unable to reign without repressing, and perhaps no one could; it might have been in the nature of things that apart from a brief interval, the constitutional monarchy established in 1906 was never more than a paper solution. I believed the Shah had a chance in the early 1960s, but instead of taking it, he retreated to his pomp and military power, and Washington, nervous about oil and Moscow, stopped pressing him to reform. During his last ten years, he presided over an unhealthy, destructive regime. He made it impossible for Iranians to express themselves or even be themselves.

Khomeini's van still had not arrived at the crossroads. I had no idea of who he really was and what he would bring. In all my official dealings with the Iranian, American, and European press, I followed

Washington's guidance so faithfully that journalists called me a "hard ass." But the people needed to breathe. The country needed a change, and I welcomed it. In this limited sense, I, too, was a revolutionary. I truly hoped a peaceful transition could be worked out and that after today's rapture—five years after—Iranians would feel they had found their way.

*

There was time for a quick visit with some old friends that evening. I happily took along Barbara's Hanukkah gifts, which had been misplaced for months in the mail, for their children.

When teaching in the Police Academy lost its satisfaction, I sought extra work. Friends told me about O.R.T., the Organization for Rehabiliation through Training, an international Jewish agency for improving vocational skills. My days-off job there was teaching English to nurses and medical technicians in a hospital on the boundary of the Jewish ghetto, which began near an entrance to the bazaar.

It was a nondescript district of small shops and low mud-brick houses inhabited chiefly by the poorer Jews, many in transit from the provinces to the middle class in northern Tehran. There were junk dealers, quilt makers, kosher butchers, violinists who played for weddings, and flocks of tailors who cut down suit jackets for younger brothers. It was a ghetto without walls, where Muslims lived too. Apart from a small, hidden synagogue, it scarcely differed in appearance from the rest of southern Tehran.

I met many Jewish families through the hospital, but had known the friends I was going to visit independently, from my first week in Iran. "Baba," as I called the husband—"Papa" in Farsi—was a pharmacist. "Maman" was a housewife. Their two teenaged daughters, whom I had taught English but who ended by working on my Farsi, were high school pupils. They were all extremely hospitable, moderately religious, politically and emotionally conservative: as close as any Jewish family I knew to the "typical" one. They fed me as they fed themselves: copiously, and with frequent laughter.

Much of the Jewish community was now caught in the agonizing dilemma of whether to stay or to emigrate. As in Germany in the 1930s, most Jews considered themselves totally loyal and beyond suspicion by any rational new leader; but just because the Nazi example was so fresh, some campaigned for "escape." Others disputed that, leading to distressing fights among relatives and old friends.

*

When I arrived, in the early evening, the Imam was resting at a religious school in southern Tehran, and the family was tense and glum. Their apartment was almost empty except for beds. They had sold nearly all their furniture, including most of the family heirlooms.

Light rectangles where mirrors and photographs had hung made the wallpaper look dirty.

Iran's recognized non-Muslim minorities—Christians, Jews, Zorastrians—constituted about 2 percent of the population. They felt relatively secure under the Shah, and with good reason. Even the Baha'is, who were not recognized as a legitimate religion—because they were considered not People of the Book but heretics of Shi'ite Islam—felt protected from popular hatred. Some undeclared Baha'is occupied high positions, for the Shah seemed to sense that his minorities would serve him more loyally than many Muslims.

The Jews in particular felt grateful to the Shah. Many accepted that much had gone wrong with his rule in general but not with their own conditions. After the formation of Israel, it could have been much more difficult than it actually was to be Jewish in this Muslim country. In fact, some Jews were apprehensive and almost all were careful. I heard anti-Semitic remarks from highly educated professional people and from taxi drivers, and anti-Israel sentiment was considerable despite—or partly thanks to—the Shah's good relations with Tel-Aviv. Very few Jews advertised themselves as such. Especially in Tehran, however, they were able to observe all aspects of Jewish custom and ritual without interference, and they had no doubt whom to thank for this. "His Royal Highness is our Cyrus the Great," said the rabbi at a Rosh Hashanah service I attended.

There was no need to ask the family why they had sold their furniture. They had made up their minds as soon as it was clear the Shah was leaving, when I was last able to see them. In the meantime they had obviously found the resolve to emigrate.

"But Khomeini gave specific guarantees about the Jews last week," I reminded them. "And the Chief Rabbi met him at the airport this morning. Maybe everything will be all right."

With my identity card of the almost magical powers of diplomatic immunity and American strength in my pocket, I could not press further and suggest that their fears might be exaggerated. Perhaps they weren't; no outsider so handsomely protected could make a judgment about others' security. In his pronouncements in exile, Khomeini's intractable devotion to Islam had sometimes crossed the border into anti-Semitism. Railing against Jews, Zionists, and imperialists, perhaps he himself could not distinguish between Israel and Judaism. In any case, the family did not want to hear more of our old kind of political discussion. Minoo, one of the daughters, served as spokeswoman.

"We have to go," she said quietly. "There will be no more life for Jews in this country. We will never again be able to hold our heads up."

When they arrived from Brooklyn, Barbara's choice of Hanukkah gifts for the family had made me proud of her. Now, in the circumstances, they seemed superfluous and even silly, and I wondered whether to give them. Baba's seventy-three-year-old father would not be going, because he did not feel up to it and did not want to leave the ancestral graves. He sat in the corner, wearing a yarmulke and fingering his beads. Most of the Jews I would see in the coming weeks were either eager to start a new life, like Minoo, or felt trapped and finished, like her grandfather. As Khomeini had promised, he totally reversed Iranian policy toward Israel, broadcasting this by having the new Provisional Government receive members of the Palestine Liberation Organization as the first foreign delegation. The PLO proceeded to take occupation of the old Israeli Mission, which the Jewish middle class took as a grave warning. They felt no trust whatever either in Khomeini's assurances of religious toleration or his ability to control anti-Semitic groups that might decide to act on their own.

❖

Much of my ICA work—supervising publication of our magazine in Farsi about American culture and politics, arranging meetings between Iranian and visiting American journalists—had collapsed even before the Shah's departure. Now I spent most of my time helping with Ambassador Sullivan's almost daily news conferences and in my own "crisis" briefings of the American and foreign press. Everyone who remained in the Embassy now dealt much more closely with politics, especially the skeleton staff involved with the press.

I also tried to establish firmer contact with the Iranian press, which was one of the chief reasons for my assignment in Tehran: ICA's relations had been largely with Western, especially English-speaking, correspondents. But Iranian journalists were on strike when I arrived—and when they returned to work, I continued to meet editors and reporters largely outside their offices. With the great uncertainty about who and what would follow the Shah, few people wanted to be identified with Americans.

On January 29, the editor in chief of one of the country's three major newspapers met me in a kebab house. I arrived early and waited at a table under stained-glass windows. For the first time in weeks I breathed the atmosphere of the "old" Iran.

Since severe rioting had begun in November, most Americans understandably remained home as much as possible. No one could blame them for taking little pleasure in native life. Few, however, had taken much pleasure before.

Although the Foreign Service was more open than Americans as a whole to "strange" ways of life, the majority preferred the American colony: commissary, movie theater, and a scattering of other outposts with suburbia's comforts and cultural interests. Shortly after I arrived, one of my superiors revealed himself as a member of this group. In two years he had sent a hundred weighty cables to Washington but had hardly set foot in the real Iran. I persuaded him to come with me to a tea house just north of Tehran, where the view of the mountains alone had to calm and gladden an open mind. Clean running water in the jubes sounded like a touch of spring on the freakishly warm afternoon. The serenity was overwhelming. We took off our shoes, stretched out on small platforms called *takhts* and watched the picturesque assortment of townspeople crossing the central square. It was clear why *takht* was also Persian for "throne." These were particularly elevated in the sense of affording relaxation. The smell of bread baking in a nearby oven seemed to bring with it a respect for the important things in life. My companion tried to relax for a moment but simply couldn't enjoy himself in this haven.

Perhaps it was the native faces, which spoke of lifetimes of hard work and hard wear. Some of the men had shaved heads; most were unkempt. A gentleman in an ancient suit jacket behind us was playing with his beads. My superior actually shuddered: The local color seemed to offend him. Although slightly more tense than the average Foreign Service officer, he also may have been more open. Even the best of disheveled Iran—and the Middle East in general—simply didn't appeal to most Americans.

*

But my grasp of Iranian attitudes might now have been no better. Waiting in the lazy warmth of the kebab house that shut out the agitation of the streets, I realized that Iran's old ability to combine emotions would surely endure through much more critical times than these. Pressed by the revolution's demands, I had no time to see events through the corrective perspective of daily life—no time, for example, to take part in the poetry games I used to play with my Iranian friends. The task was to begin a classical line with the last letter of the last line recited by the person before you.

> A tree whose quality is bitterness,
>> If it should be uptaken by the root
> And planted in the soil of Paradise,
>> Even there would produce a bitter fruit.

> The blossom which adorns the hedge
>> And dry reeds at river's edge
> Alike await the blow,
>> The cold, uncompromising steel
> Which we shall wake at last to feel.

> Love is where the glory falls
>> of thy face: on convent walls
> Or on tavern floors the same
>> Unextinguishable flame.

Those warm, graceful evenings were no doubt being enjoyed all over Tehran even now, if only as a refuge. The least literate Iranian knew so much poetry that I felt ashamed for my education. Exquisite verses afforded genuine pleasure, release, and even a sense of freedom to almost all Iranians.

And the glory of the old cities and shrines remained as calming and uplifting as the delicacy of the poetry. The bus ride from Tehran to Shiraz was seventeen hours. Just when you believed you would never arrive, you swung down into a valley and your breath was taken away. The entrance to the city is a massive arch tiled in blue. Just beyond it stands a statue of Sa'di, the thirteenth-century poet whose line about humanity being of one essence I carried on my ring. The city itself is carefully planned, orderly in a gentle way, and filled with evidence of taste for the literary arts and gardens. The most superb is the garden of Bagh-e Eram, featuring groves of a rare pine tree above flowing water. One of the most beautiful mosques was named after a beloved Iranian leader who refused to call himself King and kept himself open to the people, without a grasping, arrogant bureaucracy.

Not returning to such places or even spending "ordinary" days with Iranian friends, I knew I was not reporting fully on Iran. Even in political upheaval, a country is not its politics. Much more remains the same than changes, especially in Iran, whose history is so long and shared experiences so strong that *fundamental* attitudes seem unchanging. But I had no time. Everyone apart from the revolutionaries hoped things would settle down now—and if they did, I promised myself to get my bearings with some days in the cultural and social "background" that no political event can truly revolutionize.

❖

Editorship of the prominent newspaper *Ettela'at* provided a high place in the Shah's establishment. A handsome, well-dressed man in his fifties, Abbas Javid looked the part. He knew more change was inevitable but clearly feared radical change—for the country and for himself. Perhaps he was as eager as I to open channels of communication that might have a moderating effect.

He shook my hand with the traditional little bow and inquiries about my health. Serious talk began with less than the customary preliminaries and continued throughout the leisurely meal. Javid was almost unrelievedly gloomy. No matter how much hope the Carter administration had for Bakhtiar, he said, he could not last as Prime Minister, let alone as a leader who could save Iran from chaos and anti-American excess. Bakhtiar had far too little support, especially since Khomeini had refused to negotiate with him on the ground that he was the Shah's appointee and puppet.

Farhad had used to ask why "you" had killed President Kennedy and Dr. Martin Luther King. In those tragedies as well as everything else, he took me as a representative of all America. He also refused to believe that the assassinations were not the work of a conspiracy of American leaders, in this case directed by Lyndon Johnson, the supposed beneficiary. "I do not know if Machiavelli has been translated into Iranian," wrote an American recently who had lived for fifteen years in Iran. "But it would be superfluous to do so, for his subject is one in which Iranians need no instruction." In fact, medieval Iranians wrote "mirrors for kings," texts that established them as mentors in statecraft and political maneuvering.

Although far more worldly, the editor of *Ettela'at* reflected the same outlook. Bright as he was, he assumed Jimmy Carter "could not have let the Shah fall" unless as part of his calculations. Washington surely had an *overall plan,* he thought—or hoped, or dreamed. In his unwillingness to accept that America did not have the wisdom and power to control events, he was representative of most moderates—and perhaps of the Shah, too, who had waited and waited.

But if Washington did not act, the future would be bleak. Javid predicted that Khomeini "would soon return from Paris, would remain inflexible when he did, and would reveal himself as a new autocrat." He described the exile as rigid and vacant of ideas: an authoritarian by nature who would, among other things, quickly put an end to all press freedom. Pressure by Tehran clerics to feature Khomeini and Islam in the newspapers, he said, almost made him nostalgic for the good old days of SAVAK's "more gentlemanly, more Persian-like" pressure to glorify the Shah. These clerics made clear to him that as victors in the revolutionary movement, they deserved first billing and the last word.

That same afternoon, *Ettela'at* was to publish an interview its Paris correspondent had had with Khomeini. Confidentially, Javid called him "a person living in darkness" whose taking upon himself to decide what deserved prohibition as "against the national interest" would lead to political as well as press tyranny. He foresaw Khomeini exercising direct control of a new government, not retiring, as he had hinted and many expected, to lofty moral leadership. Yet despite all this, Javid hoped the military would not try to oppose Khomeini, for this would only fracture the entire social structure, causing far more bloodshed than until now.

I cabled a summary of Javid's comments to the several Washington offices to which I normally reported but tried not to take his predictions at face value. A year earlier, while he was still prominent in the Shah's establishment, *Ettela'at* had run a government-sponsored attack on Khomeini as a faithless dupe of the British, an invention that helped make religious groupings the leaders of the opposition, rather than discrediting the Ayatollah. Still, I had to admit he had talked with much astuteness and sense. Would Khomeini truly retire to the holy city of Qom? No one really knew what he was made of.

*

Several days later I gave up any thought of having Barbara with me during the foreseeable future. The Embassy ordered all dependents of staff to leave. This was called a "temporary" measure, but it was mandatory. Dependents in the private American community were urged very strongly to go home too.

As Javid predicted, pressure for Bakhtiar's removal intensified. Massive demonstrations against him at Tehran University were ferociously countered by troops, who killed several dozen students and wounded hundreds. Two days later I walked to the University. Its atmosphere could not have been more different from when I had studied there, in 1968. Then little protests were almost instantly crushed. This first Iranian university, which the Shah's father had established to educate an elite for service to the country and dynasty, had become an outpost of resistance to every remnant of Pahlavi rule, including, of course, Bakhtiar. It encompassed the entire spectrum of opposition, from extreme Trotskyite to extreme clerical, with a hodgepodge of parties and factions in between.

From the government's point of view, the University was totally out of control. From any neutral viewpoint, it had ceased to be an institution of learning. Muslim packs led by mullahs were marching one way, the Marxist Feda'iyan guerrillas another, and Muslim leftists—the militant Mojahedin—a third. Every square foot was a revolutionary pulpit. Young women and men, including clerics, were hawking a dozen varieties of leaflets and pamphlets, and the main bulletin board reminded me of Peking's famous poster wall. Most of the posters here ridiculed the Shah and praised Khomeini in one way or another; some described how to make a Molotov cocktail, others how to use an automatic G-3 rifle. Even the communists were represented in the form of the newly reemerged Tudeh party, which, after the Shah's severe repression of it, seemed to have come from under the wall.

No soldiers or police were about: They would not risk it, even—or especially—in the presence of groups who trumpeted the need for an armed struggle. The authorities' control was exerted in safer places. A bulletin board on my way to the campus was filled with announcements of forthcoming assemblies, demonstrations, and marches by the various groups. While I was trying to take mental notes, something sharp pricked my back. I turned around to an Iranian soldier with a bayonet, ordering me—whom he obviously took as a nosy Iranian—to move on.

Evidence of suppression of the demonstration at the University itself was still fresh. After a look at the University mosque, painted over with antiregime signs, I walked to the adjacent square. Bloodied scraps of notepaper and newspaper blew about on the asphalt near smoke-blackened buildings. Dried stains on the ground itself were marked by wreaths and photographs of youths. HERE DIED A MARTYR FOR THE REVOLUTION, read the signs.

Yet the authorities were not determined or strong enough to stop a gruesome exposé of their work: a sickeningly brutal slide presentation in the Fine Arts Auditorium. Estimates of the number of people killed by the Shah's repression during the revolutionary period varied very widely, but the vast area of smashed flesh shown in the auditorium made numbers almost irrelevant. Even without the religious implications for Iranian Muslims, the "show" of victims—"martyrs"—made a devastating impression. Photographs of broken faces and mutilated bodies filled the screen, and filled the hushed audience with anguish. An hour was all I could take. By this time, much of the audience was sobbing. The most heartbreaking scenes were the sacrifice of children. Children with missing limbs, children shot indiscriminately, children throwing stones at soldiers and being mowed down by automatic fire . . . it was one of those times I wondered why the revolutionaries had been so relatively *non*-violent so far.

*

How did America get into this? Why were we supporting a regime that used American arms against its own children? The American presence in Iran began with the idealism of missionaries, educators, and advisers. Governmental involvement can be said to have started in World War II—when we, as anti-imperialists, assumed the essentially generous role of guarantor of Iranian independence against British and Russian designs. What went wrong?

For one thing, it was our nearly total identification of the country with the Shah. Hours after dissidents were arrested for demonstrating against him on December 31, 1977, President Carter declared at a New Year's Eve dinner in Tehran that "Iran, because of the great leadership of the Shah, is an island of stability in one of the more troubled areas of the world." The Shah was his host at that magnificent dinner. The President, or his advisers, knew of the resentment against the Shah, which by now had grown very strong. They couldn't take it seriously, could not feel its importance, because to them, the Shah, not sentiment in homes and on streets, was Iran.

(The ironies of that New Year's celebration grew heavier month by month. Quoting the Sa'di poem whose line I'd taken for the inscription on my ring, the President's speech stressed the powerful ties between Iran and America. Nothing is more prized than friendship, said Mr. Carter; no other country is closer to the United States. The Shah spoke of an Iranian tradition according to which a guest's first visit in th New Year is an augury of the entire year.)

As late as 1977, much of the opposition was decidedly moderate, attacking not the Shah but corruption, torture, and lack of rule of law. Encouraged by President Carter's championing of human rights, they took positions intended to please the United States, and the Shah, too, seemed to cooperate—by, for one thing, improving conditions of well-known prisoners. But when he tested the human rights policy by arresting a liberal, socially progressive ayatollah, Washington scarcely took notice, while it agreed to increase military cooperation yet further and announced the forthcoming visit by President Carter, cutting the ground from moderates they had encouraged.

The assumption that Iran could not manage as a modern state without the Shah went hand in glove with our eagerness to believe his myths and half-truths. He held America in his spell—and not only those who knew little about the country: Despite all I had seen, I, too, sometimes found myself awed by the imperious man's "strength." This strength had become an illusion years before President Carter's encomium, even before President Nixon's unqualified embrace; but we all live largely by illusions. This one, of a firm but fair friend bestowing civilization upon a superstitious people, was particularly attractive.

Naturally, it was *our* civilization we believed the enlightened monarch was introducing there. We had thin contact with what is known as "the broad masses." Least of all did the mullahs and the bazaar merchants—two important leadership groups—strike us as reliable or representative of what we wanted. It was far easier to identify with the Shah and his advisers, who spoke English and knew Western ways. This small elite provided our picture of the country, and little was done to get a feel for the Iran beyond and below it. Much misunderstanding was allowed to fester in the darkness of cultural differences.

However, this is hardly unique to Iran. I doubt that it would have led to tragedy if not for Iran's place in our foreign policy. Soviet expansionism frightened not only the Shah, of course, but most of Washington—and with good cause. Soon after the start of the Cold War, Iran was seen as a bulwark of our defensive line: a consideration that gradually overwhelmed all others. The Persian Gulf, with its crucial oil, fit into a global strategy derived chiefly from the need to contain communism. Trusted in his own anticommunism, the Shah became our gendarme for the unstable region, and for much of the Middle East.

During most administrations, Washington hoped to restrain the Shah's appetite for military power and to influence him to make reforms. But by helping restore him to power, in 1953, we committed ourselves—and became his captives to a degree. In the panic of the Vietnam War, our pressure for reform virtually ceased. In 1972, President Nixon and Henry Kissinger arranged permission for the Shah to buy almost any nonnuclear weapon he wanted with his oil revenues, which were on the verge of soaring. By this time idealism was not nearly so predominant in American motivation: Arms sales, high technology, and other business deals, especially of massive oil consortiums with immense profits, made fortunes for Americans with contacts, while the Department of Commerce served almost as a salesman for exporters. Official American pressure against suppression of opposition ceased until our worldwide interest in human rights that began in 1977 (not directed specifically toward Iran and, in any case, probably too late). Our tutelage of SAVAK, which the average Iranian student in particular considered a major fact in his political life, affected popular opinion much more than the belated human-rights policy that President Carter began.

Essentially, Americans swallowed the Shah's explanation that his enemies were never better than communists or other "troublemakers." I hope historians will speculate on how closely the insecure monarch's preoccupying anticommunism matched our own, and how the degree to which this fixation—as opposed to the reality of Soviet expansionism—determined our policy. Whatever the mixture, it turned out to be disastrous for us. Not for the first time, America helped bring about one of the things it most feared.

No doubt debates about who "lost" Iran, our "island of stability," will go on for years. The irony is that the kind of person most likely to make that charge was the kind most responsible for the failure of our policy. Our sharply unbalanced view of Iran as an anticommunist bastion helped obscure political and social realities there. By seeing the country almost entirely through the prism of Soviet threat and subversion, we ignored *what was important to Iranians themselves,* thereby weakening resistance to that threat. We simply could not see that the danger to most Iranians had become the Shah, not the Politburo. The very concentration on the danger from Moscow, which was much more *our* worry than an Iranian one, kept us from thinking about working for the kind of reform that might have prevented the Shah's collapse. Billions of dollars of American military equipment could not shore up a policy flawed in one of its central pillars. Our anticommunism produced weakness, not strength.

Did it matter that our most serious mistakes did not derive from evil intent or even from selfishness? I had seen enough of the world to conclude, rather than simply trust, that America is instinctively more generous and democratic than most countries. It was not just our industrial power but also a vision that entitled us—when we were not being ignorant or silly—to leadership in foreign affairs. Europe sometimes laughed at our "childish" ideals, but where would we all be without them? Less cynical, or experienced, than Europeans, we did not naturally think of power politics or spheres of influence, but of freedom, human rights, and general decency. Our naïveté occasionally crossed the line to foolishness. In the name, or illusion, of doing good, we had bombed and brutalized in Vietnam. But at least we *tried* to do the right thing. We were genuinely not interested in grabbing other parts of the world. We often acted on principles for their own sake—which secretly sustained the hopes and ideals of many who scoffed at us. At the risk of sounding like one of the naïve Americans, I felt that our foreign policy was more motivated by idealism than any other I knew.

The great shame was that this ensured neither clear vision nor sensible policies. That most Americans believed we were "doing good" in Iran did not alter the fact that our friend the Shah had thousands of Iranians tortured and killed, that although we loved our own children and would never knowingly kill others', the weapons that ripped apart the children I saw on the slides were of our manufacture. Just because we are so little interested in foreign affairs, our potential for mistakes is increased. Just because we know our hearts are in the right place, we operate on faith, which makes us less likely to correct our mistakes until they become glaring or bloody enough to break through our self-centered innocence or self-righteousness.

Khomeini's charge that we were "the head of the imperialist snake" struck most Americans as proof of his fanaticism. It came to strike most Iranians as proof that he understood them—and us. For all our instinctive anti-imperialism, there was a reason why we—even more than the British and the Russians, whom we started battling for Iran's sake—came to be seen as the cruelest imperialists. Perhaps some of this was inevitable. America provokes much envy and criticism when it deserves better; that is the price of being a symbol from which hundreds of millions expect more elevated conduct than they would dream of seeking in their own governments. But in the case of Iran, it had to be acknowledged that much of the emotion *was* deserved; it *did* have a basis in fact. America had badly confused its priorities.

Four days after arriving, the Ayatollah appointed Mehdi Bazargan, a seventy-year-old engineer, religious layman, and human rights activist long jailed for opposition to the Shah, as Prime Minister of his "shadow government." With Khomeini's immense authority growing even greater, everyone realized it would soon be the real government unless the rapidly disintegrating Army staged a coup.

As soon as Washington realized how potentially disastrous the situation had become, preventing the military from splitting or falling apart became one of its chief objectives. It alone could save Iran from full revolution and possible anarchy. The Administration exerted its now puny influence to have the military support Bakhtiar.

But the General Staff knew the Army was in no condition to support anyone except Khomeini's appointee. Troops and junior officers were defecting, and there were hints of larger rebellion unless allegiance was shifted from the supposedly official government to Bazargan's, now called the Provisional Revolutionary Government.

The issue was decided on February 9, when air force cadets and technicians mutinied at two major Tehran bases and were joined by local residents. The only force eager to restore order—the old order—was a segment of the Imperial Guards. They were mauled when they failed to put down the revolt: a defeat that most made clear the Army's impotence and the consistent misreading by the White House of the entire revolutionary situation.

From our vantage point in the Embassy, it seemed that the President repeatedly preferred Zbigniew Brzezinski's advice to sounder counsel. First the Shah was encouraged to use more force; then Bakhtiar was supported when there was no hope for him; later, *in extremis,* an attempt to resort to a military coup was made when the military was dissolving. The futile hopes for "rescue" and determined backing of men who could not save anything followed from inability to accept the depth and passion of hatred of the Shah, a national revulsion that found an outlet in support for Khomeini.

After the revolt at the air bases, the military's neutrality was inevitable. Two days later, on February 11, I heard it announced on my radio at home. One could hardly leave one's house, because the ever-earlier curfew was now set in the early afternoon, and in any case, embassy security instructed us to remain indoors.

I was at home again when Jack Shellenberger called to say the ICA building had been ransacked. Our staff had melted to a fraction of its former size and there was little work for the Iranians still on the payroll. Embassy security instructed Jack, several others, and me not to appear at the Embassy now, but if our skeleton crew was to resume operations, temporary space would be found for us within the compound.

The Army's elimination as a political force spelled the end of Bakhtiar, who resigned on that same February 11, and fled, eventually to Paris, after months of hiding. Newspapers featured photographs of his last meal as Prime Minister sitting untouched on the table, for he had departed.

It was now open season on the Shah's backers, including the once vaunted Imperial Guards. Their barracks and armory were several blocks from the house where I was staying because heating oil for my own was impossible to find. That evening, rockets lit up the sky. From my window I watched tracer bullets ripping into the barracks and armory, followed by explosions inside. Although I couldn't determine the identity of the attackers—who turned out to be a collection of leftist guerrillas—their purpose was clear. While they were taking their revenge, I telephoned Barbara to tell her I was safe, then found myself giving her a running description of the battle. I had to share my excitement at witnessing this grim finale.

"Please don't take chances, Barry. Are you really all right?"

"Of course I am. Send over some gefilte fish."

"Why can't you be serious?"

"It's been awfully serious all week. Remember Greece?"

"I don't have to say how much Zander talks about you."

"Jack has sent most of the others back. Honestly, I still can't say when I'll be seeing you."

The rocket firing continued most of the night. The telephone went dead at six o'clock in the morning. The last thing I heard was a faint request by Christopher Snow, Director of the Iran-America Society, asking me to hurry to his house. Chris was a colleague and friend; I might have gone to his place anyway for a working telephone. Being without contact just then was frightening.

I left immediately. Waves of men, including many teenagers, were descending on the smoking barracks and armory. Some raced past on Japanese scooters and in pickup trucks, with bands of exultant youths in the rear pumping their fists in triumph. A smaller stream, pushing against the current and almost literally armed to the teeth with weapons they had taken from the armory, were showing them off like trophies more valued for themselves than instruments of change for good. One gleeful boy could not have been more than twelve years old. A heavy combat helmet flopped on his head, a knife and an army pistol were tucked into opposite sides of his belt, and he was carrying a new pair of marching boots in his outstretched hand. The sight of these items prompted some of those going the other way to break into a trot for their share.

My fear came mostly from the men who were trying to find out how to operate their weapons. Getting shot by accident appealed to me even less than getting shot by zealously anti-Western kids. Unable to decide whether to push on or slink back, I tried to become part of the walls that surrounded the houses. But the stream of runners and vehicles didn't stop; I had to make up my mind.

I felt some relief after inching off the street that was serving as the main route to the armory. Too soon: A band was approaching, waving its guns. I wasn't aware that I was watching what would become known as *the* revolution in the revolutionary interval that had started with the Shah's toppling: the day during which power shifted from the Army to the civilians with guns. But I did realize that something crucial was changing. Until now, the revolutionary forces had taken remarkably little blood. They had managed to topple the second-most-modern military machine the Middle East (after Israel) virtually unarmed. I wondered what would happen now that some of the most active and angry protestors were grabbing hundreds of thousands of weapons. I also wondered whether I was going to make it past the several dozen impassioned men ahead. "God is great, Khomeini is our Leader," they screamed, seemingly convinced that all normal restraints on them had been lifted together with fear of the Army. They were *the victors,* and would now proceed to have their way.

My detour had taken me within a few minutes of my own house, which I'd had no opportunity to check during the past week. The gate had been forced. The front door was broken open. I took a deep breath and went in. No one was downstairs, but the looting had obviously been recent, maybe wasn't even completed. I crept up the stairway. Upstairs, what hadn't been taken was strewn on the floor, but there was no one there either. Although everything of material value —television, radio, carpets, clothing—was gone, the photographs of Barbara and the children were untouched. I took them with me.

❖

Chris Snow and I swore to each other that our "Boy, am I glad to see *you*" clichés had never been more genuine. I spent the rest of the day on his telephone. The following morning, we ventured to check what had happened to the headquarters of the U. S. Military Advisory Assistance Group, which adjoined the Iranian Armory. Turning a corner just short of the site, we encountered a striking girl of about twenty and her slightly older male companion. They jammed their rifles into us as if we were captured enemy agents. To keep calm while they searched our pockets, I tried to concentrate on a banner at the entrance to our military offices, which I could see with a corner of my eye. "This is now the property of the Revolution," it read in Farsi.

The girl's rifle dug into my back. She did all the talking, in a metallic voice.

"Who are you? What are you doing here?"

I said we were American diplomats.

"Go back," she commanded. "If you keep on in the same direction, you will be shot. If you try to return, we won't even ask questions."

We were relieved that she hadn't shot on the spot. Walking back, we passed a block that had been occupied largely by departed Americans. All that remained of families that had spent years in the country were bank statements and checkbooks littering the sidewalks near the houses.

Power had definitely shifted; public retribution began that evening. General Nematollah Nassiri, head of SAVAK until a few months before, was displayed on television in a final appearance before being shot. His head was bandaged. It seemed clear that beatings which included the larynx were responsible for his barely audible voice. "I am totally ignorant of the things you are telling me about," he half whispered and half croaked to a questioner, the father of four guerrillas who, he charged, had been tortured and killed in prison. I despised Nassiri and what he and SAVAK had done but couldn't stomach the grisly ritual he was forced to perform. Whether or not someone surely responsible for the torture and killing of thousands deserved this punishment wasn't for me to answer. I only knew I couldn't watch.

The next day was February 14. Jack Shellenberger and I went to the Embassy early in the morning. After the ransacking we had no office, but wanted to read our missed cable traffic and were told we could go to work if we chose. Not wanting to be seen anywhere near an American car, we rode up front in the jalopy of Jack's driver, an amazingly ramshackle Peykan. The Deputy Chief of Mission, the Embassy's second-in-command, told Jack to order me to stop putting myself in danger by wandering around the city. The paradox was that the Embassy itself was invaded and seized less than two hours after we arrived.

We never established exactly what group or groups the invaders belonged to, although the best guess was Marxist guerrillas called "Feda'iyan-e Khalq," or "Those who would sacrifice themselves for the People." They might have included some of the horde I had seen returning from the armory with stolen arms. There seemed to be more than a hundred of them, mostly young, all with automatic weapons. Some analysts believed they were encouraged by an unofficial Soviet radio station which suggested that SAVAK officers had taken refuge in the Embassy.

It was a long day. Ambassador Sullivan behaved with great dignity and decisiveness, but that didn't soothe the fierce anger of the young men in beards and khaki. They had apparently come for revenge, or perhaps in fear of a counterrevolution, and we hoped their jumpiness wouldn't extend to their trigger fingers. In late afternoon we were freed by the intervention of Bazargan's Deputy Prime Minister, but I suspected, even after apologies from the government, that the inspiration for the seizure came from the same people who ended our seven hours of being locked in a vault, lined against walls, and saying our good-byes to the world. For a few hours, especially while the militants pushed through the marines' tear gas and stormed our cable refuge, we expected a second St. Valentine's Day massacre.

When the negotiations ended and the invaders seemed to have left, most of the staff went, under the protection of the government's "liberators," to the restaurant on the embassy compound. Convinced that was among the least safe places in the city, Jack and I obtained authorization to leave and look around. We peeked out the back gate, checked for snipers on the nearly deserted street, and made our way to a larger avenue, to look for a taxi. The passenger already riding in the one that stopped was a middle-aged woman in a chador, to whom I spoke Farsi. She talked heatedly about "the heroic deed" at the Embassy. "I have nothing against Americans as people," she allowed. "But their government and the Shah are responsible for all the wrongs we have suffered. Both must be punished."

I asked the driver to stop at a newspaper kiosk. AMERICAN EMBASSY FALLS! read the major headline. A group of ICA's Iranian employees who had gathered at Jack's house hugged and kissed us in obvious joy that we were alive. But, almost without exception, conversations I overheard of ordinary Tehranis the following days echoed the conviction of the taxi passenger.

The revolution was essentially the passing of power from the Army, where it was believed to lie, to the people who seized weapons. It was not The People, but diverse groups inspired by common hatred and temporarily united by common purpose. Their success was so quick and relatively easy that the new Provisional Government, which wanted to maintain a working relationship with the United States, had no means to exert control over them.

Guns were the crucial factor. Prime Minister Bazargan's plea for their return was ignored. Had the Imam put all his authority behind him, the government might have grown stronger. But although Bazargan was his appointee, Khomeini seemed to regard him as a caretaker for keeping the essential wheels of government turning while more fundamental questions could be sorted out. Khomeini's revolutionary vision gave greater support to radical mullahs hoping to establish an Islamic state in which they would exercise power directly as policy makers and administrators. Only unification of church and state, they felt, could undo the evil of the Pahlavis and ensure it stayed undone. One of the Islamic scholars executed by Reza Shah had put this attitude concisely: "Our religion is our politics, our politics are our religion," he had said. Since then, the lessons these mullahs learned from the "evil" of the regime of the just-deposed son hardened their conviction.

But many who had worked for the revolution, from guerrillas to moderates, shrank from the thought of a theocratic state, and Khomeini did not want to "lose" them. While ambiguity and uncertainty persisted, no group would surrender its weapons. On the contrary, most sought more of them for use in the power struggle that seemed increasingly likely as the anti-Shah alliance lost its raison d'être. The partial anarchy resembled a nineteenth-century time of brigand bands and pervasive insecurity. Outside the major cities, too, much of Iran was controlled by Islamic militia groups and local volunteers.

Still heavily armed, the revolutionary guerrillas, both Islamic and secular, now regarded each other as potential enemies. Out of this jumble grew a network of Islamic "committees"—"komitehs"—that gave their allegiance not to the Bazargan government but to a parallel hierarchy. The komitehs took over most police and civil-service functions in much of the country. To the extent that local law and order existed at all, it was in their hands: the same that hunted supporters of the old regime and brought them to revolutionary courts. Although Bazargan was known as a genuinely religious Muslim, he was essentially a conservative statesman of the old style: not nearly radical enough for a whole range of groups that believed the revolution was *their* victory.

Central Tehran was no exception to the new rule of local rather than national law and order. After the Embassy's seizure, furniture and fixtures lay strewn about, the most striking of which was a bust of Abraham Lincoln lying on its side. A bullet hole in the bulletproof glass at the marine entrance drew attention to itself, and the smell of tear gas lingered in the carpets for months. With this on the inside, no less than three groups set to work offering protection for the compound. One was assigned to the Ambassador. The second, a rag-tag collection of former air-force cadets, patrolled the compound's east and south walls. The third stayed on after participating in our "liberation" on the afternoon of February 14.

This third band, which called itself a komiteh, soon prevailed, assuming responsibility for the security of the entire compound. It was not responsibility in the sense of discharging an obligation to normal higher authority. Although our new guards numbered fewer than fifteen men, the Bazargan government apparently lacked the power, and perhaps also the will, to take control of them. Embassy staff meetings kept taking up the question of how to rid us of our "protectors," or at least guarantee that they be subordinate to some governmental authority; and the government kept giving us assurance that this would soon be taken care of. Failure to do it illustrated as well as anything else the Provisional Government's inability to function throughout the country. They procrastinated, drifted, and made speeches while the young man in charge of our guards ran a fiefdom of his own.

He was an enterprising bully named Masha'allah. "Masha'allah"— "what God wills" is usually uttered in awe or consolation after a blessed event or a disaster. From the rear, the lumbering former butcher reminded me of a sumo wrestler. When he turned around, his heavy mustache and unshaven jowls were even more intimidating, even apart from the revolver in his belt. Good as he was at banter, intimidation was his strongest suit. His brother helped, and his people, all of whom carried rifles or automatic pistols, jumped to his command. But when a decisive job needed doing, he liked to handle it himself.

Arriving for work one morning, one of my technicians, a politically simple man who helped with the transmitters and teletype machines, failed to nod in recognition of the War Lord. "Who are you?" Masha'allah demanded. "Who are *you* to ask me who *I* am?" my man answered. "I'm working for Mr. Rosen." Masha'allah dragged him from his car without another word and manhandled him badly before I could reach them. God help me, I thought, if I said the wrong thing in my own Embassy.

Protection of the compound was made more difficult by the weakness of our internal arrangements. To say it was totally insecure would be to leave out the substantial improvements made after the February seizure—steel doors at entrances, steel window boxes filled with sand to stop sniper fire, iron bars on all windows—and the farcical elements in the arrangements. Despite an elaborate new buzzer system to keep out intruders, the chain wrapped around the main gate would not have stopped a bicycle thief. Our hired Iranian guards in new uniforms we supplied could not have safeguarded a barrel of kerosene in an emergency. As Ambassador Sullivan had earlier cabled Washington, security remained a major problem. Even if and when the marine guard would be up to full strength at twenty-four men, he cautioned, it could not hope to fend off the kind of attack made in February—which some event, such as a visit by the Shah to the States, might trigger.

If another assault were launched, everything would depend on Masha'allah's komiteh, whose protection was a mixed blessing. They did provide it in some ways. The city as a whole was so torn by conflicting authority that traveling without protectors was a serious risk. Especially on trips to the airport, "our" komiteh's guns and identity cards, supposedly issued by the Central Komiteh, were very useful at roadblocks. Although it felt odd to rely on such a coterie, sad experience taught us that our diplomatic papers were much less helpful. "Martial Law" in particular, as some of the non-Farsi speaking officers dubbed the corpulent butcher, carried much more weight in several ways. Whatever the legal rights and wrongs, when Iranian strangers confronted each other in "outer" life, not covered by friendship or ta'arof, the one able to muster most intimidation often prevailed. When Masha'allah charged representatives of militia groups and other komitehs, he got a response. I sometimes felt relieved and even grateful for his escorting company despite my feelings about him personally, and despite the bizarreness of the Embassy's dependence on a man not brilliantly versed in diplomatic affairs.

The price for his protection was being partial prisoners—*his*—in our own Embassy. When his men smashed embassy cars and vans in games of chicken, we could do nothing. (They adored racing the vehicles around the compound and hitting trees as often as one another.) When he chose the buyers in the sale of cars and furniture left by departed Americans, we were equally powerless, even though we knew he was collecting a "commission" on the turnover. On top of other humiliations, there was ample evidence that he was appropriating goods from the Embassy co-op, and the War Lord's spoils probably extended to dismantling equipment and picking through our warehouse. "I don't want to hear that 'protector's' name again," sighed the Deputy Chief of Mission at a staff meeting. But he could not dislodge him. Many feared that if he did, our "diplomatic immunity" might easily become even more vulnerable.

*

Jack Shellenberger was almost Masha'allah's opposite: a handsome, subtle, extremely well-read man who developed a keen feeling for Iran through his sensitivity and devotion to duty. Since the seizure, when we believed we were about to die together, our relationship grew from high professional respect to matching personal fondness. We spent many hours together on evenings and weekends, sometimes leaving directly from work. I showed him "my" places in Tehran from the Peace Corps days; he introduced me to a wide range of reading I would have missed. For me, he was the closest approximation of family in Iran, and I felt a growing bond to him, the kind that made us both at ease even during silent hours when we worked or read.

Eager to set up our ICA activities again, to whatever extent it might be possible to operate now, Jack and I asked to move to a likely building we found a few minutes' walk from the Embassy. Washington's refusal of permission for this, on the ground that we would be secure only *inside* the compound, seemed to us to reveal that the desk officers did not comprehend the extent to which the Embassy had lost control of its freedom of action. It was natural that they failed to understand this; the situation was too extraordinary to believe without being seen.

With hindsight it would be clear to everyone that the Embassy should have shut down, rather than try to continue operating under its demeaning conditions. This was discussed among the officers, of course. After the February seizure, I personally told ICA and State Department officials that the Embassy should close until the Provisional Government produced believable evidence that they could guarantee our safety. In time, however, I, too, accepted the reasons for attempting to maintain relations with the new authorities, no matter how trying our conditions, and despite even the Embassy's humiliation. Iran's oil still seemed crucial to the West. Its seven hundred thousand barrels per day in 1979 was only 4 percent of U.S. consumption, but it was supplying 9 percent of West Germany's imports, 20 percent of Great Britain's, and 18 percent of Japan's. Perhaps our electronic listening posts for missile tests near the Soviet border would not be permanently shut down, and in any case, the Soviet border and the country's role in our global strategy remained important, no matter how overemphasized it had been. It was still essential to protect the Strait of Hormuz, and we hoped to rebuild a political and military relationship preserving a moderate, pro-Western outlook. In general, it seemed less final—and easier, in a way—not to make the difficult decision to close the door.

We very much wanted to establish working relations with the new regime—specifically Bazargan, who struck us as decent, although already undercut by Khomeini's recent criticism of him as "weak and given to Western influences." Closing an Embassy is not only a grave diplomatic step—an admission of defeat that also cuts oneself off—but also a large housekeeping nuisance. As long as hope exists, keeping things going has a momentum of its own. What would happen to the commissary and other American facilities if we left? What would happen to countless business contracts, and even to the evacuated embassy officers' goods and effects? Such seemingly trivial questions were raised alongside strategic ones, and the usual personal considerations were mixed with these large and petty reasons. Washington policy makers whose strategy relied on eventual accommodation with the Provisional Government had a personal stake in not seeing that policy fail.

One high official who questioned "negative" reporting had visited Iran in the autumn to see for himself. The better to observe firsthand, he passed himself off as a member of the Senegalese Embassy and was taken to the great Friday prayer meeting at Tehran University. Either unaware of what he was saying or frightened of discovery, he repeated, *"Marg bar Amrika,"* "Death to America," with the best of them.

What we did do was reduce the embassy staff still further. After the seizure, our own was cut in half; we were now four American ICA officers. The Embassy as a whole was now served by forty-odd civilian and military personnel, down from well over a thousand. Jack Shellenberger was also very good at disposing of files that might be lost in another incident—but this, too, was not as easy as it might have appeared. Although no one liked files, records, and other bureaucratic impedimenta, it was the devil to work without them.

The overall plan was to stay out of Iranian domestic politics and try to be seen staying out. The Embassy accepted that we must attempt not to fuel any smoldering resentment and that the surest way to fail in this would be to somehow help the reviled Shah. The general assumption was that after his stays in Egypt and Morocco he would go to California, perhaps to the estate of Walter Annenberg, the businessman and former ambassador to Britain.

In early March, Washington asked Ambassador Sullivan's advice about whether to admit the Shah to the States. The Ambassador and others strongly urged that permission not be granted. My opinion was harsher: that we should permit no member of the Pahlavi family not already there to enter. "If you do decide to let him in," I told the same high official involved with making policy about Iran, "please let me know a day in advance—so I can make a dash for the airport."

But on this question there seemed to be no divergence between the people at the Iran desks in Washington and those in the field.

The Iranian Jewish community was far from homogenous. It included rich and poor, radicals and ultraconservatives. Shortly after the revolution, several organizations of mainly young Jews on the far left marched and appeared on television in loud support of Khomeini and his anti-Zionism. This intensified the foreboding of the mainstream and the elders.

Some ten thousand people, roughly 15 percent of the Jewish population, had left by the consummation of the revolution, in mid-February. Many of the families I knew best went with them, most to the United States. The exodus slowed sharply after that, largely because the Embassy had abandoned its visa service. Security could not be guaranteed in the visa building, which was outside the compound and had been ransacked repeatedly.

On May 9, a powerful industrialist and friend of the Shah named Habib Elghanian was shot for "ties to Israel and Zionism." The new leaders had executed at least two hundred persons by then, including seven "putrid vestiges of the old regime" with Elghanian. He was the first known Jew, and his fate vastly increased the Jewish community's fear. Nervous rumors circulated that other Jews being held on unspecified charges also faced death.

Cables from Washington multiplied in proportion. Increasingly distraught American Jews—and Israeli citizens who also turned to Washington—were anxious for information about friends and relatives from whom they had heard nothing. Several other members of our shrunken embassy staff knew some Jewish Tehranis, but none more than I. In the absence of communication with the elders, I was asked to establish contact if possible, discreetly using my friends to arrange a meeting.

Several days later I was taken to meet the Chief Rabbi. His very modest office was near the synagogue in central Tehran. "Let's go somewhere else," he said slowly when I arrived.

It was a poor district of locksmiths and shabby groceries. When I began to say something, he put his finger to his lips. We walked in silence, he looking over his shoulder so often that I became uneasy.

Rabbi Shofat was a short man with a small white beard. Without his black suit and hat, which seemed straight from prewar Europe, I would have mistaken him for a bazaar merchant. Perhaps because he could have been one of my grandfather's friends, I liked him immediately.

At last we entered a darkish building, climbed many flights of stairs, and ended in a small room in the rear. Rabbi Shofat told an old man that we were not to be disturbed, but an even older woman in a kerchief quickly delivered two glasses of tea. When the rabbi drank his glass, his weariness seemed to ease somewhat. "Now we can talk," he said.

He had been as eager to make contact with the Embassy as we with him. When he convinced himself that he could trust me, he began an account of what was disturbing him. The previous day he had led a delegation of Jews to talk to the Imam. Khomeini's assurance that no campaign was underway against their people had been given in a way that only increased the delegation's fears. "If you are good and not Zionists, no harm will come to you," he pronounced. A mullah in his entourage added that a list had been compiled of some five thousand Jews who would be prohibited from emigrating.

The rabbi's weariness again seemed to overwhelm him. He was working day and night to somehow get Jewish Iranians out of the country and into Europe, Israel, and America. He continued about the pressures that were squeezing the Jewish community toward possible disaster, then broke down and wept. I put my arm around him, brushing away my own tears.

Even in the rabbi's outpouring of distress, we had no evidence of an official anti-Jewish campaign as such. The minority that were suffering, and would go on to suffer horribly, were the Baha'is, who were murdered and mutilated, their property confiscated, their sacred shrines demolished. If not encouraging these atrocities against the "heretics from Islam," the new government seemed to be making little effort to stop them. Compared to the Baha'is, Jews and other minorities were still physically safe. But neighbors had broken down the door of a small carpet vendor I knew and told him to "get out; you dirty Jews brought all our troubles." I realized how presumptuous I had been even to consider urging my Jewish friends to stay. Those who took the droning, occasionally impassioned attacks on Israel and Zionism as indirect menace were fearing more than fear alone.

Radio, press, and television identified Iran's evil enemies and root cause of its domestic problems as "United States imperialism, Israel, and Zionism." Two Tehran synagogues I had visited were almost empty. One of the posters I most often passed in the street was fashioned in the classic Persian miniature style. It depicted Khomeini as a victorious Moses, pointing to such lines from the Koran as "In that day, their excuses will not profit those who did injustice." The broken devil pharaoh beneath him was the Shah, with a shattered sword and Pahlavi crown—and hanging onto the coattails of imperialism: Uncle Sam with a British vest and a Star of David, not identified as Jewish or Israeli. Khomeini's Delphic ambiguity in never openly differentiating between Zionism and Judaism thickened a fog in which anti-Jewish threats merged with the other revolutionary resentments and hatreds.

When I asked what the United States might do to help, the rabbi focused on visas. He knew why almost none were being issued, but pleaded for any possible exceptions. He embraced me and saw me to the door, and I tried to put my emotions in place during the heavy walk back to the Embassy.

Charles Naas, Deputy Chief of Mission, transmitted the rabbi's request to Washington that no official American plea or intervention be made on behalf of the Jewish community. That would only worsen the situation, the rabbi had told me. That made sense to the Deputy Chief, whose reports from others tended to agree. Two days later the Senate passed a resolution sponsored by Senator Jacob Javits, of New York. It expressed "abhorrence" at Iran's "summary executions without due process." Not mentioning Jews specifically, the resolution was couched in terms of human rights in general, as if they had not been violated by a multiple of hundreds during the Shah's thirty-seven-year rule, when the Senate voiced no such concern. I had no answer to the dilemma of whether to speak out about violations of human rights in other countries or to try to encourage restraint through unpublished diplomatic influence. Both approaches had advantages and risks. Not to cry out at some point when lives were unjustly taken or endangered was a violation of my own nature—but every case, it seemed to me, required individual consideration.

That Iran's "revolutionary justice" merited criticism was wholly true but no solution to a complex issue. No doubt the Senate resolution gave its sponsors and supporters the satisfaction of taking righteous action, but what might it actually accomplish? At the least, human rights policy should have been consistent. The long silence about SAVAK's crimes ought to have made interested parties in Washington and elsewhere cautious about issuing condemnations now. Even without Senator Javits' personal involvement—his wife had worked for the Shah's Iran Air—the Senate's appeal might have been expected to seem tainted to Iran's revolutionary authorities.

In fact, it enraged them even more than I feared. William Sullivan had left Tehran in April, officially for consultations, although few expected this Ambassador, originally appointed to the Shah's court, to return. The immediate official reaction to the Senate resolution was notification to Washington to postpone sending a new ambassador, with warnings about the countries' future relations in general. The surge of anti-Americanism throughout Iran made all that came before seem mild and abstract by comparison. "Our relations with the United States are the relations of . . . the plundered with the plunderer," declared the Imam. "What need have we of the United States?" An infuriated press, always eager to pounce on scapegoats for explanation of why the revolution seemed to be bringing as many troubles as gains, railed at what it called American interference in Iran's internal affairs and attempts to frustrate the revolution and humiliate the

Iranian people, in the old pattern. The damage to the Jewish community feared by the rabbi was exceeded by the wider harm caused by the well-intentioned Senate action.

Amid the din of anti-American rhetoric, senior embassy officials shook their heads over ignorance of foreign realities which spawned resolutions that rang nobly to domestic audiences but sounded like hypocrisy or worse in the countries for which they were supposedly intended. "How long will it take?" wondered a colleague I admired, "for American editorialists, congressmen, people with only a minimal understanding of world events, to learn that the color of truth is gray, that to condemn is too late, that not to recognize one's own past failings can be ruinous?"

Perhaps we could do nothing about failings under the Shah just because the revolution cherished them as an explanation for everything, attributing to us so much that was Iranian fault more than American. It was the old tendency to see all troubles coming from foreign incursions and foreign domination. But I had hoped a modus vivendi might be worked out, if slowly and painfully, as the pent-up forces released by the revolution dissipated themselves. The chances of that now seemed far slimmer.

An American correspondent wanted to talk to me about the situation after Elghanian's execution. We left my office for a grassy knoll on the grounds looking down on the main gate, which seemed serene in the absence of demonstrators. The correspondent mentioned that political officers he had already interviewed were basically reassuring: Iran was "clearly moving toward postrevolutionary stability" in which Iranian-American relations would probably be normalized. I, too, was optimistic for the long run. I still believed, or wanted to, that the two countries had a natural relationship. But first, I had to say, there would be severe problems. We were so close to the Shah that we were tarred by the same brush. "Somehow," I concluded, "we are going to have to pay."

A few days later, massive anti-American demonstrations erupted in many places in the country. When the Tehran contingent, a hundred thousand strong, marched down Takht-e Jamshid, a group broke away just outside the main gate. Like urban commandoes, they climbed the wall, ripped down the American flag, and tore it to pieces. This incident joined half a dozen others on the Deputy Chief of Mission's list, including even the "requisition" of surplus furniture stored in an unoccupied American residence, to take up with the Iranian Foreign Ministry. These were mentioned at the morning staff meeting, which the same Deputy Chief, Charles Naas, now chaired. As usual, embassy security—and the behavior of our protector—were also discussed.

"What on earth was it last night?" Charles asked Colonel Leland

("Jumper") Holland, the Army Attaché, whose ability to get along with Masha'allah helped greatly with security.

"Masha'allah claims the cook's brother is a communist," explained Jumper. "He decided to question him."

"No, I mean the shooting at 3 A.M."

"That was a mix-up. Our protector's night patrol was off schedule, so the brethren thought it was an unfriendly."

"Anyone hurt?"

"The driver went into a tree. The car is pretty well messed up."

Other officers present went on to report about the evening's two executions, loss of informants to report on the chaos in oil production, two American oil technicians who claimed to be held hostage by worker demands, and an anti-American tirade on television (which was followed by a Mickey Rooney film).

We had to laugh despite the seriousness of everything, or because of it. When the compound was invaded and the flag ripped apart, groups of Iranian sentries, apparently appointed to keep order in the demonstration, stopped the "commandoes" from further damage. If not for them, Masha'allah and his men could not have prevented the Embassy from being overrun.

Our Brooklyn house, the former servants' quarters of an estate that once stretched from Van Sicklen Street, where we lived, to what became the Verazzano Bridge, was more than a hundred years old when my parents bought it, in 1953. It was more like an old bathrobe than anything to wear in public. The ground floor, where most of my memories accumulated, had a porch, living room, dining room, and kitchen, no room with any more quiet or order than another. People coming and going used them all as comfortably as those who lived there. More than anything, what set it apart from other lower-middle-class houses nearby was a stone wall surrounding the yard. What set *us* four children apart from the others we knew was my mother's restrictions on stepping outside the wall.

My elementary school was directly across the street. The wall made the house a kind of family reservation; after school, my brothers, my sister, and I remained within the compound unless we had permission to leave for something specific. Being enclosed became a state of mind. When my younger brother was old enough for his first pair of shoes, my mother took him to shop for them. He couldn't remember ever having been beyond the wall and cried hysterically when he passed through the gate.

Quite enough set me apart, even without the wall. Since that part of Brooklyn was populated largely by southern Italians, most of the girls in my school were quite short. As tall as the boys, I stuck out unmistakably. Even my name was different. My father, a former construction laborer, is Ukrainian. Bogutski, my surname, sounds Jewish —which is what I was usually taken for, since Jews were the other major ethnic group in the neighborhood.

Many of the neighborhood girls had little interest in school; their future lay in early marriage and motherhood. My mother had different ideas for *her* children and pushed us gently but firmly toward the cultural and academic pursuits she would have wanted for herself. While she prepared dinner and we sat around the dining room table, she carefully supervised our homework, finishing with hard questions.

My mother's strictness was probably inherited from *her* mother, who raised her offspring on the tough Lower East Side. My grandmother kept her children from becoming involved in street crime. My mother's equally sharp eye kept us in line. Friends were welcome to play with us under her supervision in the compound, but we were never allowed out for the local pastime of "hanging out" on street corners and in candy shops.

We had religious instruction every Wednesday and attended children's mass every Sunday, walking home through streets smelling of tomato sauce and baking bread. Confession was every Saturday, but there was precious little to confess. The rage in junior high school was for nylon stockings, makeup, and miniskirts. I couldn't even wear the stockings—and certainly couldn't shave my legs. "Keep your mind on the school work, not the opposite sex," we were admonished. I was not permitted to date until Joe appeared, when I was sixteen years old—and I didn't dream of trying to trick my mother about where I was. Anyway, she couldn't be tricked. The negative side of this was progressing from feeling different to feeling I didn't belong in any social group. I had little in common with most of my early-childhood friends. Neither did I belong with the Jewish girls, whose uniform was bobby sox and loafers. They had some of the same interests, but their social lives were directed by their parents, who were as happy to keep us separate as mine.

The positive side was my perception of myself as someone supposed to do more in life than get married and raise children. This preparation for "productive" adulthood came together with insistence that we remain children well into adolescence. We believed in Santa Claus long after others laughed at the idea. That was largely in submission to my mother's hopes for us—and her will. "Don't believe in him," she warned, "and see how many presents you get."

I imagined myself a link between the fairy tales we were told and the reality my mother was trying to train us for. Most of my family teasingly called me "Princess"—which I put down to my height. I was dressed in white and fussed over, not with presents but with a tone of voice that hinted I was "special." After I began doing well in school, much was expected of me, and I began to expect it of myself.

There was no reason to cling to the fantasy when I grew up. Although going to college was an achievement in my family, it obviously made me no princess. Eventually I got a pleasant job teaching school in Brooklyn, but no glass slippers or crown came with the appointment. Still, something inside me waited for my "future." I never talked about it. I was a reluctant talker in general about my feelings, especially outside the family—and sometimes within the family too, which felt I had become too "liberal," thanks largely to the various revolutions of the 1960s. But the expectation lingered. It was as though I had been promised a palace—if I remained a good girl and worked hard.

*

Barry could only be a partial fulfillment of the expectation, because I never thought of myself as a housewife. When we married, he had two more years as a graduate student and we lived mostly on my teacher's salary—which I liked. Although we worked together in the house, I enjoyed being the breadwinner. I stopped working when I was about to have Alexander, but knew I'd go back one day, although probably not to teaching: With my own children to raise, I did not want to spend all my "child energy" in school. Motherhood could not be my sole role. The notion that I should be doing something more demanding continued to nag me gently, even though I had no idea what my real calling was supposed to be.

Barry understood this, but I suspected he felt it was part of my failure to grow up fully, thanks to my mother's continued "domination" of me, as he put it. He sometimes said I had never quite cut the umbilical cord and therefore expected someone else to produce or provide something wonderful for me. I wasn't sure about that but always maintained that my mother treated me as an adult since our marriage. I didn't feel dominated.

This was part of a larger disagreement between us—but not a painful or constant one—about my attachment to my family. He was devoted to his warm, colorful mother, but compared to my family, his was so small that it was hard to call it by the same name. There was no need for the least pretending with the crowd that filled the house much of the time. You could sit down and talk—or not, if you weren't in the mood.

I loved that atmosphere. We had a barbecue in the yard every Memorial Day and every Fourth of July, with softball games among the cousins. Christmas dinner was always at our house because my grandparents lived with us; now my grandmother is alone in a tiny "suite" of her own since my grandfather died, in 1966. The first time Barry came for Christmas Eve dinner, we were still "courting," and officially platonic. Roughly thirty-five people, an average number, were squeezed in at the tables. Italians don't eat meat then, so his plate was piled with calamari, scungilli, and other "strange Italian" things he'd never tasted. To make him comfortable, two of my louder uncles chipped in with some good-natured Jewish jokes. Barry winced a bit at their obviousness, but I think he had the hardest time adjusting to the "mass of humanity" aspect. After being raised in a small family, and being something of a loner, it was a little overwhelming.

I happened to be truly friendly with all my cousins, and loved the closeness we felt. One of the things I disliked about moving to Washington—and about the idea of being a Foreign Service wife—was depriving our children of relatives seen daily. I believe the extended, not the nuclear, family contributes most to children's healthy development.

I tried to return to Brooklyn as many weekends as I could, whereas Barry preferred staying in Washington by ourselves. This was one of our more serious disagreements. He's the type who needs privacy which was one thing never available in the old house: With so many people there, you couldn't find a place to sit down and read without being interrupted by questions and comments. To me this seemed a small price for the emotional benefits of an extended family. Not having one, Barry didn't know what he was missing. But I think he was learning it was not a major conflict, just the almost inevitable preference for the familiar. It faded because he usually gave in to my wish to spend time at the Brooklyn house. By the third Christmas he was in the thick of the joking and laughing—and loved it.

When William Sullivan left Tehran in April, his last words to me at his good-bye party urged me to leave too. "I just don't think a Jewish officer should subject himself to the potential consequences," he told me privately. I stayed largely because I believed I might be able to establish useful contacts with the rapidly revolutionizing press, and perhaps even with people close to the clerics.

My other reasons for staying were more selfish. One was to deal with the growing urge to go home. Since that seemed slightly dishonorable, I had to demonstrate my moral fiber. Besides, it was more exciting to be in the thick of things in Tehran. To keep myself from thinking too much about the family, I tried to concentrate on my "public" reasons: my duty as one of the Embassy's "old hands" who had a chance to make the contacts and do the reporting we needed.

In early May I saw an old friend, a foreign-desk editor for *Kayhan,* Iran's largest daily newspaper. Although he was soon removed, I knew another important journalist there and eventually managed to meet the editor in chief. A former minister in the Provisional Government, he was new to the post, having just taken over after an assault on the old editorial board by clerics and printers demanding more radical support of Khomeini. The first editorial under the new board, entitled "A Purge at *Kayhan,*" apologized to the Imam and the nation for not being revolutionary enough. That afternoon, Khomeini told a delegation from the newspaper that "the nation wants a paper which conforms to its voice, and if they are going to write in support of criminals and traitors, it cannot belong to us."

The editor's office had elements of a circus and a bazaar. A dozen people were waiting to see him, a dozen interrupted, a dozen listened openly to our conversation. The editor answered telephone calls on a wide range of professional and personal subjects. We were served tea, but the kindly man, who obviously took his duties and his obligations to his staff very seriously, hardly had time to sip his. Still, he tried his best to answer my questions fully and, it seemed to me, honestly.

The publisher, a former bazaar merchant close to Khomeini, joined us. If nothing else, our talk revealed a clear divergence between him and the editor, which was repeated throughout most of the press. It was principally the difference between the professionalism of the editor, who had many of the proper revolutionary attitudes and credentials but nevertheless responded as a newspaperman, and the politics of the publisher, who obviously cared more about ideology than newspapers.

The old editorial board, of more than a hundred members, had been fired. It was expected that less than half, those who "formally pledged to uphold the Islamic revolution," would be rehired. The publisher assured me that he had compiled a file on all former members and knew "exactly which individuals had betrayed the revolution." The editor, who revealed a scholarly bent and sharply greater interest in maintaining journalistic standards than in investigating his staff's loyalty, was concerned about the strict new press law that apparently was coming. According to rumors of the past month, it would be enacted soon. The editor said he intended to publish criticism of the bill, which he believed would lead to "strangulation not unlike that of the old regime." The requirement that the Ministry of National Guidance know the exact political stance of each newspaper's management was "unbelievable, and none of the government's business."

The publisher stopped a comment in mid-sentence, for he had something more important to attend to: A Sudanese delegation had arrived at his office for noon prayers. The publisher asked to be excused, quickly prepared himself with ritual ablutions, and invited the delegation into a new prayer sanctuary adjoining his office. Between interruptions from his staff and other supplicants, the editor and I continued talking for a time. His concern about the press law turned out to be fully justified: It would be passed in August, and in much the form he feared.

I passed on to Washington what I had learned in my *Kayhan* visits, which led to nothing that could be considered influence. I was slightly more successful with a few other papers, even managing to provide information for a few stories and to correct some faulty facts and startling misinterpretations in others. Several moderate editors confessed they feared a revolution that would go on to completely merge the state with the mullahs' interpretation of Islam. They even hinted that American help in preventing this would be appreciated, but I could think of nothing useful.

Most of the radical press refused to believe that Washington was not planning, or plotting, to restore American "control" of Iran. But a few editors saw me—if only to denounce imperialism and explain why the United States could never be trusted. *Ta'arof* was almost always extended first. When I entered an office, I would be greeted graciously and offered tea. The attacks and accusations came when the meeting shifted from its personal to its business phase. As long as I'd known them, Iranians liked having two on their side when something difficult or nasty was likely to arise. Now I was outnumbered four or five to one, and their team did its best to keep me from getting a word in.

*

Our own press corps in Iran had expanded markedly in numbers but little in quality. The revolution had become a big news story. Flocks of reporters flew into Tehran, of whom few wrote with much perception—or concern—about the country's deepest social and political currents.

Television correspondents who were personalities seemed the least solid. They would be dispatched from Europe at a moment's notice, establish themselves in the Intercontinental Hotel or the Royal Hilton, and ask for a ten-minute "overview" ("Barry, what's making the Iranians so heavy?") before interviewing the Ambassador and filming their often shallow story.

During the Shah's reign, much American reporting from Iran was rewritten palace press releases. Bullied if they sought information elsewhere, many reporters relied almost entirely on interviews with his fawning ministers and skillful press people. I wish I had a dime for every standardized summing up of the country in terms of the Shah's imaginative modernization that was delivering a backward people from the sixteenth to the twentieth century. After the revolution, little changed with respect to initiative in establishing a broad range of sources or interest in tackling fundamental issues. By concentrating on the "action"—the Kurdish War, street battles, and anti-Americanism—without exploring causes, most American reporters continued to give a superficial or misleading picture.

Iran did not fit easy patterns, and Americans did not easily circulate in so different a culture. They tended to observe from a self-centered perspective: to see the revolution primarily as an attack upon the West, rather than as a revolt against repression. The Ministry of National Guidance did its best to ensure this by treating American reporters as state agents. Seemingly unable to accept that our government could not control our press, ministry officials turned their outrage on the Embassy when they read weak and slanted stories. But I was disappointed at how many of those stories appeared with concentration on the secondary. Was the revolution primarily about institutionalizing the veil and prohibiting rock music?

The Shah had had an excellent press in America because so many journalists saw their stories through his eyes and encountered no other. The mullahs now had a very bad press, perhaps because they seemed too alien and sinister. But the larger question, which would affect crises in other countries too, was the quality of our reporting and the great concern, especially in the electronic media, with image. The exceptions stood out all the more against the background of predictable and mediocre reporting. Several major newspapers, news magazines, and one of the wire services were represented by inquisitive, totally independent reporters, some of whom paid the price for their excellence by being expelled. Apart from this, the record in Iran was distinctly mixed.

•

The day came when I needed relief from Tehran, at least for an hour. I took Jack Shellenberger to the splendid hotel I visited on my first day in Iran, where the old gardener lovingly watered every leaf. It provided no respite. As if to symbolize past corruption, it had been converted into a gambling casino for the Shah's new class of flaunting rich, then "cleansed" by the revolution. Ripped-out slot machines, wires exposed like feeble roots, lay in rows along the dirty floor. As if to symbolize revolutionary damage to good in the process of eradicating a former regime's bad, the garden was in disarray and the hotel was decaying. It was sorry evidence of the difficulty of stopping at a happy medium—when a country started with resentment and revenge.

Back in Tehran, a pervasive insecurity dampened normal reactions to spring. The economy was severely disrupted; workers' committees still controlled many industries; garbage heaps piled high alongside muddy roadways. And the government made no noticeable headway in assuming control over local komitehs. They patrolled the roadblocks and decided which cars to stop: often embassy ones, which were carefully searched for weapons. Most were polite when they stopped cars I was riding in and took me into custody; some showed me *ta'arof*, handing me a cup of tea with one hand while their other clutched a rifle. Nevertheless they conducted their searches and asked their questions as men convinced that power naturally belongs to them. Being removed from one's car and held at a local komiteh headquarters for three hours one day provided no immunity against its happening the next. My diplomatic passport might as well have been a canceled bankbook, and complaints to the Foreign Ministry changed nothing. I learned later that one komiteh "delegation" went to my house to check on my identity.

After the looting of the house, I spent almost all my limited time there half holed up in what would have been Barbara's and my bedroom. One night I heard a small convoy of vehicles stopping at a house almost opposite. I opened the window to see an armed detachment springing from cars and trucks, scaling the gate, and pounding on the door. Screams rang out from inside. Soon a man was led out of the house and into one of the cars, which sped off. It was unfair to call the revolution a fraud because of such incidents, but they tightened the pit of my stomach. Who was that man, and what chance did he have for a fair hearing?

We knew perfectly well who Reza Amini was: an Iranian of very wide contacts among the old press and bureaucracy who had served as an embassy adviser for almost thirty years. Early in my assignment, he took me under his wing and we spent hours discussing cultural, political, and social issues. Although the extremely well dressed Reza bore a striking physical resemblance to the Shah, he was moderate and broad-minded as well as consistently dignified. He considered emigrating when his middle-class world crumbled around him, but could not force himself to leave Iran.

When he called me early one April evening, his voice was the first thing about him I'd ever known to go askew. "Barry, people are banging on my door. From the revolutionary prosecutor's office. They want me to go with them. Don't say anything to anyone yet, but I'm rather worried." When I called back later, his house had been searched and his documents, including an American immigrant visa, had been confiscated when they took him away. His wife believed he stood accused of meeting with prominent figures in the old regime, but several Iranian newspapermen had told me he was considered a collaborator for serving the American Embassy.

The truth was that Reza, who foresaw what was coming, consistently advised trying to moderate the Shah's rule. He even made his peace with what might be called "revolutionary excesses," believing they were an inevitable reaction to the former regime's despotism. The Embassy immediately launched a campaign to find out where he was being held and on what charges. I joined a small team that kept calling every official we could think of who might help secure his release. Power was so fragmented that we were not certain who held Reza, let alone what awaited him.

The danger was real and immediate. Prisons were so full of "antirevolutionaries" that no room remained for petty criminals. The Revolutionary Prosecutor General revealed that Qasr Prison, the one adjoining the Police Academy (of my Peace Corps days), held almost fourteen hundred men at the time of Reza's arrest and up to two thousand by late May.

Although the revolutionary dispensers of justice were still far behind SAVAK in efficiency of repression, their mock trials with virtual absence of defense disturbed us all. Even (or especially) if deserved, sentences should have followed genuine legal procedures, where guilt easily would have been established. But Ayatollah Khalkhali, the "hanging judge," boasted of his victims, and the executions looked more and more like cruelty, rather than legal punishment.

Those who defended them claimed the public demand for revenge was too strong to thwart. If not satisfied—if the people were not assured that justice would be done to the old oppressors—it would build into a demand for much more ferocious retribution. The flaw in this argument was the visible pleasure taken in the killings. While members of the audiences screamed at the accused during the "trials," a gloat went up in the new high places, and the following morning's newspapers featured grisly pictures of corpses.

Together with SAVAK's former commander, whose repelling performance I had watched on television, leading generals made up the first group executed, on February 15. Since then, revolutionary courts had dispatched roughly five hundred people. Because the Shah's judges were pronounced tainted and "not familiar with Islamic law," trials were not conducted under the old legal system. The Provisional Government had no control over many revolutionary courts, which informed the nominal judicial authorities of executions after they had been carried out. These courts often accused defendants of nothing more specific than "warring against God" and "corruption on earth." They gave the accused literally two minutes to reply before sentencing and almost immediately shooting them.

I hoped these atrocities did not make nonsense of my belief in Iranian society's essential nonviolence. They were happening on the revolution's fringe, or its leading edge, and we had to keep in mind at that time that in numbers killed, Iran was still a less violent country than it had been under the Shah. Still, our worry was growing that the new regime might become no better than the old; perhaps even worse. The opportunity to stop a revolution after it has destroyed detested old practices and before it starts destroying its own new ideals is generally over before most people realize the line has been crossed. By then, that moment may have already passed in Iran.

The revolution was making itself look worse than what preceded it not because it was worse but because its violations of human rights were less sophisticated and more publicized than SAVAK's. At least to the West, the executions conveyed an image of the Iranian revolutionary as a vicious fanatic. More important, it was giving many Iranian moderates and liberals who had supported Khomeini serious second thoughts. For me, recognition that it was still *relatively* nonviolent as revolutions go—especially revolutions spawned in genuine popular hatred of the old—was much less comforting after the arrest of people I knew. Reza Amini was not an abstraction or even a trend, but a man I deeply respected and admired. I was sorry to be so personal about an issue that deserved reflection in the widest historical and sociological context; but if something worse happened to him—if I opened the morning newspaper to see a photograph of *his* body lying in a pool of blood—I did not think I would be able to discuss the revolution with much objectivity.

But wasn't this what happened to friends and relatives of the Shah's countless victims?

❁

Walks weren't enough; I jogged as much as I could to relieve the tension. My route took me from Jack Shellenberger's house, where I was living mostly for company, past armed members of local komitehs who stared at my sky-blue jogging suit as though it were human plumage. I changed direction and followed the clean jubes of northern Tehran, which became filthy with garbage and worse by the time they reached the south. Would the revolution get to tackling that?

I also felt an urge to see Iranian friends, not for information but for something personal, perhaps to look for ways to hold on to "my" country as it threatened to slip away. Anyone who has lived through a revolution will understand why I lost contact with Farhad. Police officers were now in danger, even if they had been far from wrongdoing. I had to wait to hear from him—and did not.

The Iranian I saw most of now, who was distinctly more intellectual than Farhad, had been educated partly in the States. It would have been wrong to use that verb about a large proportion of Iranians who had studied in American universities. They were not *educated* there, at least not in the Western sense, but acquired engineering, accounting, medical, and other skills. Education as the acquisition of broad-mindedness and tolerance eluded them, which was one reason young people who had studied in America went to the vanguard of the uncompromising and intolerant, as well as the radical. Their American-acquired skills made them better-prepared enemies than sympathizers.

My friend Hamid was too intelligent and sensitive to fully fit this category, although his grudge against American "imperialism" was as strong as anyone's. He had intended to return to law school in the States but became so caught up in the revolution that he took a job as reporter for the *Ettela'at* chain, where he acquired many inside clues about the otherwise murky governmental maneuvering. He shared them as generously as his personal and political feelings. We walked together for hours and ate in modest restaurants (where vodka was still being served under the table, despite the revolutionary prohibition against alcohol). Hamid was open, outgoing, and more genuinely interested in my family than many Brooklyn friends who actually knew Barbara and the children. I liked him very much.

We happened to spend an afternoon together in the Lar Valley, north of Tehran, shortly after Reza Amini was taken. The Shah had spent some of his last days in Iran at his skiing lodge there. When Hamid and I picnicked alongside the gushing stream, tribesmen were milking sheep and the mountains glittered in the spring sun, but we couldn't stop talking about the executions.

"You and your *habeas corpus*," he said. "You don't understand; this is something we *must go through,* because the old regime was so cruel and rotten."

"How many revolutions have gone through the same 'purging' and came out worse?"

"That can't happen in Iran. You still don't understand Islam or what the revolution is about, what we must do to finish it."

"I thought the revolution was about due process, pluralism, regional autonomy—that's what everybody I knew said he was fighting for. The most fundamental civil rights are being sacrificed for Khomeini's 'Unity of the Word.' You're a law student and you're for that?"

"It has to happen. The first priority is destroying the old regime so it can never rise again. You can thank the Shah for the 'excess,' as you call it. If he hadn't been what he was—and if America hadn't helped him—there would have been other ways."

In my arguments with Hamid I stressed that once a revolutionary movement makes exceptions in the law for dealing with "evil men," the door is open for abuse of others. I might have added that even the prosecutors and judges now seeing to the killing were in danger, since revolutions tended to devour themselves. Yet the situation was less simple. Abuses had abounded, after all, under a "modernizing," Westernizing regime that pretended to strictly observe legal norms. And the great majority of Iranians—this, too, deserves repeating—were utterly convinced that justice was being done to torturers and killers of children.

In any case, the number of executions noticeably declined now, if only because almost three quarters of the Shah's senior officer corps had been killed, together with many ministers of previous governments who had not fled the country. In mid-July, Khomeini declared partial amnesty for all who had worked for the Shah's government, apart from SAVAK and military officers accused of torture and murder. Although scattered "free-lance" courts continued to try and punish, the national fury seemed to have spent itself.

That coincided with what we took as a softening of anger toward America. Badly overworked and exasperated, Charles Naas, to whom embassy leadership had passed after Ambassador Sullivan's departure, left in June. His replacement was a new Chargé d'Affaires, Bruce Laingen, whose mission was to normalize embassy routine as much as possible and restore confidence to the depleted, demoralized, and lonely (familyless) staff.

Although the Embassy's social calendar had been reduced severely, we of course held our traditional Fourth of July reception. To our surprise, several ministers of the Provisional Government attended, along with some journalists I had invited from the leftist and Islamic press. We interpreted their willingness to make this gesture as a hopeful sign.

Even before Bruce Laingen's arrival, Jack Shellenberger and I had been trying to arrange an interview for the Embassy's chief officer, one that would allow him to put forward the American point of view on essential matters. This was unusually difficult, because Pars, the semiofficial news agency I was dealing with, feared retribution in case the American viewpoint touched on "sensitive" issues, and the agency, as its managing director admitted to me, would be accused of "being too friendly" to Washington. But prolonged negotiations about questions and ground rules did lead to an interview of our new Chargé in his office in early August. Some of his forthright answers about United States intentions in the Middle East and hoped-for friendliness with Iran in particular were deleted. But after more protracted negotiations, other answers were published in every major newspaper. We took this as another promising sign. Although Bruce was concerned that the deletions and watering down much reduced the impact of his answers, I felt that after our long silence in the face of savage attacks on America and wild distortions of its policies, the statement alone of our wish for good relations was worthwhile. At last we seemed to be emerging from our bunker. We were encouraged enough to devise a strategy for "building conceptual bridges" to Shi'ite Islam.

Then our hopes since February were answered: Masha'allah was removed. A detachment of armed Revolutionary Guards appeared at the compound very early on the morning of August 12. They searched grimly for Masha'allah. Negotiations followed; for an hour or so we thought the intimidating "Martial Law" would win the newcomers over—or even arrest them as he had done with previous groups determined to take over from him. Finally shouts and gunfire were heard. At nine-thirty, Masha'allah and his men were driven off in buses. (A few months later I saw him at the airport, looking more prosperous than ever.)

This event was even more auspicious than earlier ones. We now luxuriated under protection of Revolutionary Guards, who had acted, we were told, under orders of the Prime Minister and the Foreign Minister, in coordination with the Central Komiteh. The Foreign Ministry even declared that "the Iranian Government is responsible" for the U.S. and other embassies. The chain of command and lines of authority were still fuzzy, but the Embassy's mood improved still further when we learned that fifteen uniformed policemen, directly responsible to the government, would soon further protect the compound.

A quick start was made removing Masha'allah's sandbags at the gates and other homemade fortifications so the Embassy might look— and, we hoped, act—more like itself.

Two weeks later I telephoned the wife of Reza Amini. I had almost stopped calling her. It was depressing to keep asking whether she had any news of Reza, embarrassing to acknowledge American impotence in this matter. I had used every contact I could think of in and out of the press to find out about him. The Embassy raised his imprisonment at every possible meeting with the Provisional Government, and the State Department exerted all its influence on the Iranian Chargé d'Affaires in Washington. It became a kind of test case for Iranian-American relations in general, a barometer of the Embassy's mood.

Now came great news: Reza's wife confirmed that the name I'd read in that morning's list of amnestied prisoners was his. Reza himself felt he could not meet me now. More than this, he had lost hope for the revolution—understandably, after imprisonment—and planned to emigrate if he was permitted. In prison he had been accused of being a CIA spy. But his release is what mattered at that moment. With Masha'allah gone and Reza free, the Embassy was actually cheerful for the first time since I could remember—at least in offices of the relatively few of the staff who had known Reza before he was taken.

Jack Shellenberger often said that if he wanted to remain in Iran for anything, it was to greet a liberated Reza. After struggling with this for five months with great dedication—on top of his usual sense of personal responsibility for the well-being of every American and Iranian he worked with—he had been transferred to a new post in Canada a few days before. Good-byes were difficult for us both. Part of him wanted to stay, not only for Reza but because he felt he had an obligation to continue, having been through so much during his tour. On the other hand, the two years had left him extremely tired. Like me, he tried to be optimistic despite serious worries about security—more serious than ever for him, just because he would no longer share the pressure. "You'll be okay as long as the Shah stays out of the States," he said. "I'll see you in a few months, when you get home."

Jack's replacement took up the work of trying to restore some of ICA's normal functions. The Iran-America Society had reopened and was gearing up for the fall term of English courses. It had indications that thousands of students intended to register.

The visa problem seemed also to be resolving itself. After our ransacked visa office was closed, the Embassy said it would not reopen planned new facilities on the compound until Masha'allah was removed and adequate security guaranteed. The Provisional Government seemed eager to break this logjam, if only to give itself a safety valve by letting some of the most disgruntled and unhappy leave. Shortly after Masha'allah's unceremonious exit, the new visa office—in the converted compound restaurant—reopened indeed, and the number of student and emergency visas that had been issued in the interim jumped dramatically.

Iranian ability to combine seemingly incongruous matters showed itself immediately. While much of the press kept up its anti-American lashings, the crush for visas grew immense, bringing with it bribes for places in line, a black market in the numbered tickets we distributed to try to introduce some order, and payoffs to policemen supposedly responsible for keeping things neat. Thousands of the same kind of young people—perhaps the very same young people who at other times shouted, "God is great, death to America," stood impatiently in line, in great hope of studying in the reviled United States. The *Kayhan* I passed around at a morning staff meeting nicely summed up the schizophrenia: A cartoon strip showed a man on a soapbox railing ever more vehemently against America. In the final square he telephones our consul to whisper, "Is my visa ready yet?" This was no creation of a cartoonist's imagination. One of the journalists I saw who was most dedicated to the Islamic revolution was the editor of the National Iranian Radio and Television magazine. After a particularly contentious conversation one day, he took me out of the hearing of his colleagues to whisper a private question: Psst, could I get him a nice fellowship to an American university?

The line grew longer and longer, even when we were issuing hundreds of visas a day. (More and more Jews joined it; by the end of the year more than 30 percent of the Jewish population would be gone.) At the same time, Americans had begun returning to Iran. Businessmen were encouraged at least to try to clean up their affairs. After discussions, a procedure for delivery of spare parts for Iran's American-made military equipment had been agreed upon, and items paid for by the old regime began arriving. I was working on a plan to set up an exchange between theological seminaries in Iran and America. To us it all seemed part of a difficult but promising period of restoring at least a semblance of normal relations.

The Embassy recognized that much of the new leadership suspected Washington did not really accept the changes in the country and believed it was biding its time for a return of some form of Pahlavi rule or its equivalent. It also recognized that the new leadership was determined to demonstrate total independence of United States influence. Both friend and foe of America looked back at our previous involvement in Iran as excessive and we realized we now had to maintain a low profile, with emphasis on strict noninvolvement. This is what we did, in hope that if we kept at it with enough patience and tact, a breakthrough would occur, possibly with ayatollahs more moderate than Khomeini. We were badly mistaken.

*

Perhaps our summer optimism derived mostly from failure to detect underlying realities. Perhaps we were less at fault than events we could not have predicted. In any case, hope began to crumble before it had fully crystallized.

Even while it prevailed and U.S.-Iranian relations seemed to be mending, hazardous currents were flowing. It was a time of great domestic tension, in which Khomeini and the radical clerics were attempting, in a loosely organized way, to impose their almost fundamentalist concept of an Islamic state upon the country. A new constitution being prepared by moderates and liberals envisioned a pluralistic society with government essentially on democratic, Western lines, although under moral guidance of the clerics. The radical mullahs perceived this as more than a threat to their plans for a theocratic state. They regarded any separation of mosque and state as heresy—the very kind responsible, in the broadest sense, for the country's "fall" under the Shah.

Battle lines that had been fudged during the anti-Shah alliance were now plainly visible. The radical mullahs applied influence, intimidation, and violence to eliminate their former allies as a political force. Their crackdown on everyone who seemed in opposition included even moderate ayatollahs who believed their duty was to counsel and inspire, not to govern.

Other domestic difficulties were growing graver. The most unsettling was striving for autonomy by the country's ethnic minorities, most visibly the Kurds, some of whom were in armed rebellion. Under pressure of "Islamic unity" imposed by Khomeini's adherents, Iran showed signs of splitting apart. This only intensified the radical mullahs' efforts to tighten up, which now extended to a kind of witch-hunt against the "enemies." The Islamic Republican Party, which was most closely identified with Khomeini, resorted to use of mobs and thugs who called themselves members of "The Party of God." They smashed demonstrations and offices with fervor, carrying on a venerable Iranian political method in which legal associations of the "brave" and "manly" degenerated from preservers of public morality into bands of toughs. Their principal targets were secular nationalist parties, religious parties and associations under moderate ayatollahs, leftist groups, and assorted figures in the civil service and in Bazargan's Provisional Government. I myself saw a Party of God squad helping Revolutionary Guards force Muslim guerrillas, members of the Mojahedin-e Khalq, from a hospital that served as their local headquarters.

On August 7, Revolutionary Guards closed *Ayandegan*, the most respected secular newspaper, which was left of center in outlook and high in journalistic standards. Although it had backed the revolution wholeheartedly, it was no supporter of a theocratic state. The Imam encouraged the stifling of nonclerical voices. "We gave you freedom but you plunged yourselves into prostitution," he said in a highly publicized speech. "We gave you freedom but your pens condemned, plotted against, sought to ruin our realm . . . we do not need intellectuals, those intellectuals." Within two weeks, more than twenty newspapers of which the radical mullahs did not approve had been shut down, many after arrests and beatings of editorial staffs.

A member of the editorial board of *Ayandegan* called me frequently during the grim period of closings, sometimes while I watched carloads of armed men patrolling the street past my window, or on their way to another "job." I had invited him to our July Fourth reception, at which he talked to me, as usual, of the need for an independent

Iran, free of American domination and able to exercise its own personality. Now he dreamed of refuge in the States. Altering his voice, he informed me that he was moving daily, from one hiding place to another. Several hours before our carefully planned meeting, he called again to say he couldn't come. I never heard from him again.

Foreign journalists were expelled not only because they might directly influence the great battle for control of the country but also because their reporting on the domestic crackdown and the bloody Kurdish rebellion was seen as a "fabricated" attack on the revolution. Correspondents of the Los Angeles *Times*, the New York *Times*, NBC, and the Associated Press were ordered to leave. The BBC, which the Shah had accused of being one of the most powerful instruments of his downfall, would follow; the number expelled would reach eighteen. The Revolutionary Council, secret executive of the radical mullahs and like-minded members of the Provisional Government, decreed new regulations for the foreign press in mid-August. From that time, foreign journalists would be held criminally responsible for "any report appearing in their media against the Islamic Revolution or the Government and People of Iran, and will be prosecuted in Iran and in international courts." When I went to the Ministry of National Guidance for clarification of this puzzling warning and to inquire why an American correspondent had just been expelled, the Deputy Minister for the Foreign Press motioned me from in front of his desk to a chair at his side. "Come sit beside me, not so far away," he invited in the old Iranian way. After tea, he opened a desk drawer and pointed to a jumble of papers. "I have evidence," he said quietly, "that the correspondent was an agent of your imperialist CIA." He quickly closed the drawer. "That is enough," he concluded. "His expulsion is an internal Iranian matter."

Violence begat violence. Groups who were under attack, or felt they would be, responded by sabotaging railways, blowing up bridges, and assassinating high radical mullahs. No one knew exactly whom the assassins represented; they might even have included vengeful loyalists to the Shah or fundamentalist Muslims who rejected the mullahs' leadership. But Khomeini identified the instigators: mercenaries in the service of the CIA. "Those who pose as leftists and who think they are supporting the people are agents of the United States," he explained, calling on his followers to "break the pens and tongues" of American lackeys. Khomeini was not a military commander giving battle orders. He apparently did not involve himself in details but worked in keeping with the Islamic legal principle of consensus of leading figures and advisers. But whether or not he genuinely feared that American involvement threatened to reinstate the old forms of oppression, his general pronouncements served as a guide to action for millions.

Press reports of American atrocities followed quickly. The newspa-

per of the Islamic Republican Party led the field in attributing otherwise unexplained disruptions—of which there were many, thanks to
the increasing dissension in the country—to American saboteurs. "U.S.
Plotting Anew Against Islam and Iran," ran one headline in early October. The paper accused the United States of having prepared a
strike plan devised by the CIA in coordination with Israeli and Egyp-
tian security services. "American Mercenaries in Bukan Kill a Revolutionary Guard and Take a Baker Hostage," read another headline.

"U.S. Agents in Revolutionary Guard Clothing Disarm the Local
Populace in Kermanshah," disclosed a third newspaper. The text, in
common with others, suggested a secret hand had plotted the divi-
siveness in Iran to pave the way for America's return to power.
Another headline informed: "U.S. Plotting to Crush Revolutionary
Clergy." A photograph of a Revolutionary Guard burned to black in
some encounter was captioned with an explanation that this was the
work of CIA mercenaries.

Even without this spate of invention, astute Iranians, especially politicians, knew enough about survival to avoid contact with the Embassy. We were building bridges, but only to secondary—and reckless
—men such as those who attended our Independence Day reception
and the slightly larger group who received me in their offices. For
months, ICA had been trying to establish a relationship with National
Iranian Radio and Television, which was the vehicle for some of the
most fervent anti-American stories. I finally met the editor of that
vital establishment's magazine, the man who had whispered a request
for a visa. But no one in the Embassy was able to see the chief of
N.I.R.T., Sadeq Ghotbzadeh, who would soon become Foreign Minister.

It would be too neat to say that everyone clever enough, or close
enough to Khomeini, to know the important trends, sensed he should
avoid us; and that everyone naïve enough to see us fell, in part because he was tainted by the contact. But there was an element of
truth in this simplification. Although Bruce Laingen talked with Ayatollah Beheshti, head of the Islamic Republican Party, and explor-
atory contact was made with a few of the Revolutionary Council, we
rarely got to see the people who mattered. Even when we did, there
was no understanding behind the occasional personal cordiality. Resentment, suspicion, and fear kept us in different worlds.

Through all this, Prime Minister Bazargan's government remained
as weak as ever. Accusations that it was trying to normalize relations
with the United States made it no stronger. Most people in Washington who made decisions about Iran put all their marbles on Bazargan,
an understandable move from afar, since his wish to deal with
America in an acceptable way seemed the only solution to the chaos
and anti-Americanism. Even Bazargan's Foreign Minister told Secretary of State Cyrus Vance in October that "we cannot tolerate your

attitudes of the past": a difficult declaration for any American statesman to work with. In any case, Bazargan alone had little influence.
His "old-fashioned" attachment to notions of recognizable order
needed to run a modern state and his belief that no foreign power
was to blame for many of Iran's internal problems made him cut an
inferior figure in the jockeying for power and for Khomeini's favor.

This jockeying and infighting was often based, in the old Iranian
pattern, on grudges and drives for personal gain, nourished and
dressed up by political goals. Much of it was conducted in nasty
ways. Former editors who still saw me told stories of ugly machinations behind the cloak of religious purity; they resembled the worst of
the monarchy's intrigues. In a way, playing up to anti-American sentiment was the worst of the worst—and one of the best ways to claw
ahead. I asked people I trusted what we might do in this situation.
Some now wanted America to somehow put an end to the new intrigues. Iran, they said, needed help in turning back toward what had
seemed possible in the early days of the revolution, in restoring dignity to the country's public life. As the butt of attacks even when we
did nothing, this seemed to me self-deceptive and a little pathetic. All
we could do was wait.

*

No one could say what waiting would have led to if not for a disastrous decision by President Carter. From time to time during the
Shah's nine months abroad, the State Department continued to query
the Embassy about the probable reaction if he were admitted to the
United States. Over the summer the question was put specifically in
terms of possible danger to the Embassy. Chargé Laingen answered
in confidential cables to Washington whose contents I did not know.*
But it was impossible not to sense the nearly unanimous opinion of
other officers that almost nothing could be worse for Iranian-
American relations than the Shah's admission.

I wasn't proud of sharing this opinion. To turn our back on a former ally, no matter what mistakes he had made, would be more hu-
miliating to us than to him. Having had our friendship when those
mistakes were made, he deserved it more, not less, now, when he was
at least partially paying for them. More than a standard of behavior
was at stake. Other leaders might not want to associate themselves
with a power that appeared to cast off former partners like ballast
when the going got rough.

Despite many strong reasons for preserving our dignity by welcom-
ing the Shah, I was utterly opposed to it. Having failed so often to

* Iranian radicals later captured the Embassy's copies of these cables and made
them public. They indicated that in July, Laingen believed the United States
should eventually admit the Shah, but to give refuge to him then "would almost
certainly trigger massive demonstrations against our Embassy," with no assurance
this would not escalate to assault.

recognize the power of symbols to Iranians—and the significance in particular of the Shah as the symbol of evil—to do so again would announce that we understood nothing about the revolution. Those who bruited the possibility probably didn't understand that admission would be a seemingly calculated insult to almost an entire nation. Sooner or later we had to acknowledge that our support of the Shah had been badly conceived and managed. In short, we had to let go of him; preserving our honor at this stage with otherwise expected hospitality simply cost too much hatred. The risk also was too great. If we *had* to receive him, that should wait until Iran's new leaders felt more secure about themselves. While they were fighting among themselves to shape the country's basic structure, the issue of the Shah could be exploited in ways we could not predict.

But no one asked my opinion officially—or, as far as I knew, the opinion of other officers with substantial service in the country. Embassies provide information for decisions that are made, and must be, in Washington. It was nothing new or unusual that we were presented with a fait accompli.

I stood in for John Graves, Jack Shellenberger's replacement, at the staff meeting on the morning of October 22. Bruce Laingen said he would have to leave the meeting early for urgent talks with Provisional Government officials; we should carry on without him, discussing embassy security. He then set aside ordinary procedure for what he called an important item of information. The Shah, he said, would arrive in New York later that day for medical treatment.

Total silence followed. In time it was broken by a faint groan. Faces literally went white. I put my hands over my own face and had a good think—not about policy or professional duties but about how much I wanted to go home.

The State Department's press guidance, which I was to use for answering questions of Iranian journalists, did not mention the campaign for the Shah's admission by David Rockefeller, Henry Kissinger, and other admirers. It stressed the overriding humanitarian reason—specifically the need to treat his lymph cancer—and his undertaking to engage in no political activity during his stay. Apparently the Shah's illness was much graver than it appeared from the State Department announcement. By keeping it secret for years, the Shah probably prolonged American support; knowing it was dealing with a cancer patient would surely have prompted Washington to consider more seriously what might follow his rule. Later it was learned that President Carter had operated on inaccurate information: It was *not* medically necessary to treat the Shah in the United States, since perfectly adequate facilities were available elsewhere.

The President could operate only on mixed signals and flawed guarantees. On three separate occasions, Prime Minister Bazargan and his Foreign Minister, Ibrahim Yazdi, assured Chargé Laingen that the

Embassy would be protected, even though they had warned of the popular reaction. We already had the new police detachment in the compound, and Revolutionary Guards were to be posted outside.

Whatever the details of how it was made, I thought it a disastrous decision.

Officers attending the staff meeting were instructed to inform staff in person, not by telephone. We were to review security procedures with them, and I remembered repeated briefings by the chief security officer: the marine contingent was there to check on security violations and aid in any necessary destruction of confidential material, not to battle invaders; our job in case of serious trouble was to retire to a secure area to wait for help from the Provisional Government.

I picked up my new two-way radio and gathered the two other ICA officers, ending my little presentation with a confession of how eager I was to see Barbara. This would happen in a month or two, when my tour would end.

＊

While the Shah underwent tests at New York Hospital, I was charged with reporting on media reaction, with special attention to the medical explanation. Demands for return of "the criminal Shah" to justice in Iran were almost immediate, accompanied by criticism of the Provisional Government for not securing his quick extradition. One newspaper revealed that lymphoma is a form of cancer to which Iranians were not susceptible; the Americans' fraudulent medical excuse was cover for political maneuvering with the Shah. Explicitly or otherwise, such articles played on Iranians' fear of his restoration to power, with all the associated oppression.

A few days later, I went to see a new Director of the Foreign Press Section of the Ministry of National Guidance. Our talk turned into a harangue about American imperialism and CIA "undermining" of Iran. "How can we begin to establish some understanding," he stormed, "when your country is harboring that criminal?" The moral of his story about SAVAK's torture of his nephew was that "we can't have normal relations until you send that killer back to Iran." My attempt to return to the question of possible readmission to Iran of American correspondents was not very fruitful.

Yet press outrage was less explosive than we had anticipated. Reaction was *relatively* controlled; I exchanged congratulations with other embassy officers over our seeming safe passage through the crisis we had feared perhaps more than any other. At a press gathering a week after the Shah's entry, the direct superior of the man I'd just seen at the Ministry of National Guidance assured me that Moscow would spare nothing to take advantage of Iranian resentment of the Shah's reception by America. In general, he said, the Soviet threat was much more worrisome to the country than the Shah's American connection.

My counterpart in the Soviet Embassy, who never failed to break into any dance he thought I might be enjoying with a prominent Iranian official, hurried over and begged to disagree. As usual, he chided me for American attempts to "sabotage the revolution of the Iranian people." I countered that Soviet propaganda served only to inflame Iranians with fanciful reports of supposed American activities. He answered that in view of the American record with the Shah, nothing fanciful was necessary. The Russian record in Iran was far worse, as I easily pointed out to him.

The Soviet press officer had no idea what a relief it was to play the old Cold War shouting match—here conducted in the most diplomatic language—instead, for a moment, of worrying about the new challenge to our foreign policy that had been ebbing and flowing during the year since I had arrived in Tehran.

*

Eid-e Qurban, the Muslim holiday that commemorates Abraham's willingness to sacrifice his son to God, fell on November 1. As a token of this, sheep were sacrificed throughout the Islamic world. Supposedly outlawed in the 1930s, the tradition of the camel kill also survived in a few Iranian towns.

On one Eid-e Qurban during my Peace Corps years, I'd gone south by bus to Kashan, which was on an ancient trade route traveled by camel caravans. The camel to be sacrificed there was led past low, mud-brick houses, then along a route of extraordinarily twisting streets to the bazaar and the mosque in the center of town. Decorated with colorful plumes and scraps of mirror set in his black robes, the animal was a blinding sight in the mid-morning sun.

Finally the procession reached a pit the size of a football field in an open tract on the edge of town. Several thousand family groups picnicking along the lip might have come for a happy outing. A wave of excitement washed over them when the camel entered the pit. While two men held her, a third produced a long knife and quickly severed the main artery in her neck. Blood rushed out as if from a hydrant, pumping the crowd's excitement even higher. The camel screamed. Women and children rushed past police and into the pit to observe the rhythmic torrents of blood. The camel slowly became too weak to stand. Still screaming, she sank to her knees, then, after another interval, keeled over completely. Before she was fully dead, the crowd was swarming over her to cut up the body.

I had to admit to myself that Iranians probably had a bloodthirsty streak, after all. But when my revulsion wore off, I gradually realized that there had been much more ritual than brutality. Excited as it was, the crowd never became vicious or fanatic. After all, animal sacrifices were nothing new to my own ancestors. The overriding impression at the end of the "camel kill" day was not violence but participation in an ancient ceremony. Especially the town poor, who could not afford to sacrifice a sheep, let alone a camel, seemed gratified to have taken part in something so traditional—which also provided meat, for it all went to them.

My memories of that extraordinary day, which seemed to take me close to the Iranian soul, were mixed with hope that it foretold peace. Surely the Iranian people derived satisfaction from all the ritual chanting and killing. Maybe it had been justified and necessary, like some national tradition. Maybe it was out of the system.

On Eid-e Qurban in 1979, I went south again, this time to the city of Isfahan, which is like a fabled oasis in the desert. Seventeenth-century Iranians called it "half the world," because they could not picture a more beautiful place. I could imagine how it affected Europeans of the time, who suddenly came upon its glory after traveling for empty, desolate days. It is the city of turquoise mosques, one more magnificent than the other. The Friday Mosque, the most historically important, is an example of Iranian architecture from the tenth to the nineteenth centuries: To glorify themselves together with God, dynasties over nine hundred years added to and rebuilt it.

Kathryn Koob, a recently arrived ICA colleague who had taken over as Director of the Iran-America Society, wanted company and help in extracting a society for English-language teaching from a group of seventy-five Isfahan University students who had seized it, in order, as they promised, to distribute its assets to the oppressed and underprivileged. Our task was to persuade local authorities to return the property to the Society, its legal owner.

The trip promised respite from Tehran and a chance to soak up some history, and perhaps perspective, in a living museum I hadn't visited in ten years. It was also a way to snatch a few days of comparative rest at government expense—we unashamedly stayed at the best hotel—and to avoid a large demonstration scheduled for outside the Embassy on the day we left.

As foreigners, we were given seats of honor in the bus, directly behind the driver. We listened to reports about the demonstration on his radio. Close to a million people were said to be taking part, but Revolutionary Guards representing the Provisional Government stopped them from marching on the Embassy. This was enough for a weekend of relief. I also had the pleasure of finding a lost Iranian boy the age of my own Alexander and returning him to his parents, who were charming as well as grateful. But Isfahan was not as I remembered. Either it had lost its shine or I the last of my illusions.

Living apart from Barry was nothing new. We had spent a third of our married life that way, most of it when he was in Washington with Voice of America and I remained in Brooklyn to become tenured as a New York City teacher, which required another full year. The following year, I was pregnant with Alexander and stayed in Brooklyn too, on the grounds—or excuse, because I didn't love Washington—that it was senseless to look for a job, knowing I'd quit when the baby arrived. (I *had* to work somewhere; we were saving to buy a house.) Barry came up or I went down to Washington every weekend. So it wasn't separation as such that was difficult now, but separation abroad—especially while he was in Iran.

It took a series of events to keep me from going. Originally we were scheduled to leave for Tehran together in early summer 1978 but delayed departing so I could give birth to our second child in Brooklyn. Being at my mother's house would solve the problem of who would look after Alexander while I was in the hospital. The new baby was due in early September, but almost two weeks passed after the date without a sign of labor.

Finally mild cramps began early one morning. Alexander's birth had been difficult, so I thought there was plenty of time. Barry promised to take the first plane up from Washington. My father left to attend to a quick errand, promising to return quickly. I settled down to a long labor.

A few minutes later I was certain it would be extremely short. Contractions were frequent and intense.

"Mom, the baby's coming."

"Relax, Barbara. Your father will be back in five minutes and get you to the hospital."

"I'm not sure we have five minutes."

"Don't be silly, Barbara. Please try to stop screaming. You're scaring Alexander."

I stuffed a pillow into my mouth, taking it out every few minutes to assure her she would be a grandmother again very soon.

"Barbara, keep the pillow in for Alexander's sake."

By this time, an aunt and cousin who lived on the next block had arrived and I persuaded Alexander to go downstairs to play with them. Then I tried again to convince my mother that we had no more time. She looked and gave in to fleeting panic. "Oh, my God, what am I going to do? The baby *is* coming!"

My cousin ran down the street to look for my father's car. My aunt got the doctor on the telephone and screamed questions too fast for time to hear the answers. My mother gripped my hands to give me strength, while the baby made one of the fastest first appearances on record.

"What is it, Mom?"

"A girl, darling."

"You're sure? Check again." Barry and I had followed the advice of a book called *Your Baby's Sex: Now You Can Choose.* We very much wanted a girl; maybe it wasn't mumbo jumbo. But my cousin had dashed back into the room. Her husband had recently been with her in the delivery room and mistakenly proclaimed, "It's a boy!" when the doctor held up *their* newborn. In his eagerness for a son, he had confused the umbilical cord with something else. My mother checked again to make certain we avoided that particular muddle.

Meanwhile, I was trying to locate something in a book about natural childbirth that was on my night table. "Here it is: Pick up the baby with her head down and try to get the mucus out of her mouth." That worked well enough, but not the next step, putting the baby on my stomach. The umbilical cord wasn't long enough.

The answer was to cut the cord, which was one of the next prescribed steps anyway. My mother couldn't bring herself to do it. By then, her friends from the school across the street had begun to crowd into the room, together with Lucky, our bark-at-everything dog. Sanitary conditions were not quite up to standard.

Emergency medics cut the cord when they arrived, but I wouldn't let them carry me downstairs. On my own power I freshened up and showed little Ariana to Alexander and my grandmother. When we arrived at the hospital, our obstetrician was making himself useful by directing traffic. Ariana was placed in isolation, because she was "unsanitary," but she was back home with me in perfect health in little more than a day. I decided if I had another child, it would be at home, rather than in an impersonal hospital.

Ariana was born on September 21. As the situation in Iran had been growing more tense throughout the summer, Barry's superiors in Washington had kept changing their minds about whether it would be wise for the children and me to accompany him. After the way Ariana was born, we decided to delay the move to Tehran another six weeks, until she was given medical clearance.

Then cables from the Embassy in Tehran warned of danger and urged us to delay for several more weeks; and when anti-American sentiment appeared to be growing, rather than softening, the Iran Desk in Washington finally pressed Barry to go alone. That was mid-November.

It was hard for him to leave without his family. He was badly torn: not wanting to subject the children and me to danger, yet eager for me to share his Iran with him. Iranian children used to follow him on the streets of Tehran like the Pied Piper, and he took time to make friends with them. Now he wanted his own children with him. And he wanted me to share the experiences in which he delighted there. After all the years of describing and explaining, his disappointment was severe.

In general, I am less emotional than Barry. That is partly because he expresses his feelings better than I, partly because I control mine more than he; but the main reason is that Barry actually feels more deeply. My instinct, except with the children, is to push on with what needs doing while trying to minimize problems, mine and others'. When people tell Barry their troubles, he empathizes and suffers. Even reading affects him deeply, and this vulnerability to feelings was one reason he took his decision to go without us so badly.

It was his romantic side that hurt. People liked Barry, for he was a charming host and guest in Washington social life. But he was dreaming of showing the children and me one of the Iranian gardens he had used to describe. Or taking me to a remote settlement over the mountains where the old ways, especially of almost family-like bond between villager and traveler, were preserved. That was his equivalent of a tropical island.

The outing he described most vividly began with a day-long ride in a rickety old bus shared with farmers and farm animals. Finally you arrive at Soltaniyeh, the fourteenth-century capital of Mongol Iran, now almost a ghost town, with thousands of screaming crows. All that remains is the huge mausoleum built by a Mongol ruler whose entire life was devoted to a magnificent obsession: bringing the bodies of martyred Imams Ali and Hossein to Soltaniyeh to be buried with him. For that he built an astounding building, decorated fabulously with turquoise tile and surrounded by a forest of minarets. The Mongol hoped the bodies of the two symbols of Shi'ite Islam would make it a place of pilgrimage, therefore an important center. But he was unable to obtain the bodies, and the capital became an empty one, like the driving ambition of his life—and in a way, as Barry said, like the Iranian expectation of the return of the Twelfth Imam after more than a thousand years, and avenging of the martyrs' deaths. Barry's understanding of the Iranian psyche heightened the dramatic effect of this ancient mosque, with its combination of dazzling beauty and forlorn abandonment in desolate countryside. He felt as though he were discovering a half-forgotten kingdom.

His first letters from Tehran were full of regret. His job was exciting and he was happy to be back—but not with his family "broken." "I hope perhaps in one more month things will clear up and all will be right with the world—meaning *you'll* be here," he wrote. "I miss all of you very much and—forgive the repetitiveness—it's the only thing I think about in this empty house. Sometimes I imagine by the time I see Alexander and Ariana, they'll be in college."

But he knew I was worried about the children and even slightly relieved not to go. And despite our promises to ourselves that I'd be flying over *next* week or the week after that, the situation steadily worsened. Three months after his return, clinching proof came that it had been wiser to stay home.

On February 14, a band of more than a hundred leftists attacked and seized the Embassy in Tehran. Not many Americans knew about the episode, because it was overshadowed by the murder the same day of the American Ambassador in Afghanistan. But most who did know called it the most shocking example so far of the Iranian revolution's raging anti-Americanism—and an equally unnerving example of America's inability to protect its diplomatic people.

The State Department gave Barry its Award for Valor for his coolness and bravery that day. The citation stated: "Mr. Rosen displayed remarkable poise, courage and good judgment in a situation which could easily have cost American lives. . . . Throughout the ordeal, Mr. Rosen conducted himself in a highly commendable and professional manner, and by his actions contributed to the safety and well-being of his Foreign Service colleagues."

What happened was that a band of young extremists raked the Embassy with heavy machine-gun and other automatic-weapon fire, then stormed it, shouting threats to kill the "Yankees." Bullets had been ricocheting off the second-floor communications vault, where about forty embassy personnel had taken refuge. Some began to pray; others swallowed confidential documents. Barry and others took out photographs of their families to say good-bye.

Although the Press Attaché didn't usually involve himself in political activity, Ambassador Sullivan ordered Barry, with his Farsi, to surrender the Embassy when hope of protecting it ran out. The invaders raced up the corridor, waving guns like terrorists and looking wild-eyed enough to shoot the first thing in sight. Barry stepped out to deal with them, and for the next 2½ hours talked himself hoarse, partly with a running translation for the Ambassador, so no one would be shot out of misunderstanding between captors and captives. He also had a spray of gun barrels in his face with threats to kill him unless he opened the safe in each office, which he didn't. By the time the Embassy was rescued—by guards probably sent in by the Iranian Government—he had put in a day's work as a genuine hero.

In my parents' house, in Brooklyn, I was entertaining and happened to switch on the radio when my guests left in the early afternoon. There wasn't time to worry about Barry, because the first newscast I heard announced the incident had ended without casualty. (It was then approaching midnight in Tehran.) When the State Department called later in the afternoon to confirm this, my mother and I were on our way to a shopping errand in Manhattan. As our elevated train passed a Jewish cemetery, one tombstone acted like a magnet on my eyes. The name on its face was Rosen.

The funny feeling that gave me lasted until Barry telephoned from Tehran the next day. He knew better than anyone that my premonitions often came true, no matter how ridiculous that sounded: In the middle of the night almost a year before, we discussed the old question of whether I should go to Tehran. "Barry, maybe there'll be such a bad earthquake that *you* won't be asked to go." Three weeks later, a disastrous earthquake in a northeastern province killed thousands of people. A month or so later, when the Shah still appeared unshakable, I said he might not be asked to go because "maybe there'll be a revolution there."

"Please," said Barry. "No more predictions about Iran."

November 4 dawned a drizzly day that prompted daydreams of Florida with Barbara. It was Sunday, a normal workday in Iran. The embassy staff numbered about eighty now, up from the forty of the early months after the revolution. Many of the additions were on temporary duty; some were assigned to help businessmen who had returned to complete contracts. We did not consider that the beginning of resumption of heavy involvement in the country.

Back in my office from Isfahan, I first checked the press to prepare our report for the morning staff meeting. Most newspapers provided their readers with times and routes of major demonstrations. Apparently nothing anti-American was scheduled for the day. There were just the usual relevant items to summarize for Washington, which on that day were few: no unusually strident charges or complaints against America.

My cable drafted, I took a telephone call from a magazine called *Message of Peace,* based in the holy city of Qom. The journal had a strong anti-Western bias, but the call informed me that I was expected in Qom to discuss the possibility of exchanging Islamic and Christian theological students between Iran and America. Then I pondered how to fulfill a directive from a more exalted ICA officer. He *had* to be exalted—and isolated—in order to have devised this particular project: a blueprint of Iran's current power structure. At my level this seemed like a request to photograph air. Washington naturally wanted outlines and diagrams, but the situation remained so amorphous and fluid that few Iranians themselves had a clear idea of who reported to whom and who was responsible for what. The new order's most characteristic trait still seemed to me that there *was* no power structure. Power was largely up for grabs among the clergy, various revolutionary organs, and street mobs unleashed for specific jobs.

Our ICA offices were now in a small building fifty yards directly inside the Embassy's main gate. Takht-e Jamshid, the street outside the gate, had been renamed Taleghani, in honor of a recently dead progressive ayatollah. At ten o'clock or so, the sidewalks and roadway began to fill up with demonstrators, slowly at first, then with a surge. When their noise grew more clamorous than usual, I got up from my typing and went into my secretary's office for a better view. Several dozen young men and women sporting plastic-covered pictures of the Imam on their chests were visible through the gate. The boys wore old suit jackets over turtleneck sweaters; many of the girls were in black chadors or kerchiefs. Both sexes were in their late teens and early twenties: a collection of types who took their anti-Americanism very seriously.

"God is great!"

"Long live Khomeini!"

Although they seemed no more worked up than earlier protestors, something held me at my secretary's desk, watching the swelling cluster. Suddenly there were not several dozen but several hundred demonstrators. Then twice that or more. No better trained or disciplined than ever, our crew of embassy guards—those we ourselves had hired—were overwhelmed by the new arrivals.

"God is great!"

"Long live Khomeini!"

"Death to America!"

Just as suddenly, a handful of seemingly designated men started climbing over the gates. Their scrambling appeared both preposterous and utterly natural, as if fated. Some had pistols and lead pipes. Another cut the chain with a large bolt cutter. With the gate flung open, a roar of triumph sounded and a rush of demonstrators, more than we'd seen, poured in like a flood of frenzy. The Embassy's defenses had been breached in seconds.

Thick clubs waved in the air, mingling with portraits of Khomeini held high like icons. The rush was now a tidal wave of field jackets, mustaches, sweat, and grimaces of hatred. The roar had become an unholy howl—but for some reason I couldn't yet react seriously. "There goes my great report on the so-called power structure," I smirked to myself. "And there goes Iran. I bet we close the Embassy by tomorrow."

Even though the gate remained wide open, some of the fist-waving men kept demonstrating their valor by climbing over the wall. A hundred bodies were now inside the compound, twitching with menace, lining up in a kind of battle order. A lieutenant of the National Police Force—in whose Academy I had taught—skipped up to embrace the scruffy invaders. The Revolutionary Guards who had taken over as our protectors from Masha'allah had been stationed outside the compound; I could picture them joining the invaders. The game was up. I felt a certain relief at that, mixed with the excitement of observing a historic moment.

When "shock troops" had captured the Embassy nine months before and marched us out of the vault where we had taken refuge, we assumed we were about to be shot in our own blinding tear gas. When they grabbed my beard and ordered me to open safes whose combinations I didn't know, I believed the end was very near. As much as anything else, the invaders' inexperience made me apprehensive. They were so frightened by what they were doing and so amazed by their ease in penetrating the imperialist monsters' outpost that they made themselves doubly dangerous through nervousness.

More experienced this time, they also seemed more determined—which, curiously, boded better for our safety than during the previous invasion. I was less worried about getting shot thanks to somebody's jumpiness.

The fifty yards that separated us from the main gate seemed to shrink to ten. We were right on top of the action and totally cut off, since the Chancery was several minutes' run away. The first detachment of boys and girls—I refused to think of them as men and women—rushed directly for our outer door, which I had naturally locked and barred. I instructed my secretary not to open it for anyone, then ran into my own office to search for classified materials that might not have been locked away in the Chancery with the others. The unsettling sounds of my colleagues being routed from nearby offices penetrated the walls while I was searching. Together with their Iranian employees, they were being driven to the Commercial Library in a nearby wing. The "Death to America" chanting was now so violent that its vibrations almost shook my floor.

As I was rushing through the papers in my last desk drawer, the scrape of the bar being removed from my secretary's door stiffened the hairs on my neck. "Mary, what are you doing?" I screamed. "DON'T OPEN THAT DOOR!" But Mary had children. Her husband was unemployed. Most dangerous for her, she was Armenian: a minority who, like the Jews, had been protected under the Shah and now feared for their safety. Good and loyal as she was, it was too much to ask her to jeopardize everything. By the time I had raced back into the outer room, its door was open.

The exultant victors squeezed in too fast to separate them as individuals. My first impression was of unkemptness. I noticed several girls with clubs among the first dozen. They were in chadors or kerchiefs wrapped heavily around their heads.

"GET OUT!" I shouted in Farsi.

"Either you move out of this room or we're going to drag you out," several voices answered simultaneously.

"This is United States property. Get out of this building immediately!"

This was more than bravado. The presence of that mob in my office made me very angry. To sympathize with the revolution's original aim was one thing, but to believe that revolutionaries had a right to violate diplomatic immunity and custom—to commit this barefaced offense against America—was quite another.

But this was probably too abstract and too patriotic to explain my stubbornness. Most of all I was acting on a childish insistence that I, which in this case meant my country, be treated with dignity. And although I was quaking, something in me was confident that I wasn't courting death. Perhaps it was naïve, but I reckoned the revolution, despite its anti-foreign passion, had killed very few foreigners.

Half a dozen intruders began ransacking the office, tearing through my press files and news-agency teletape rolls. Mary hunched in a corner, trembling. (She would be released that evening.) But most of the attention was devoted to me. My resistance seemed both to infuriate and, by enhancing their image of themselves as valiant fighters, to please the intruders.

"Leave this room immediately or you will be hurt," barked one of the leaders while his closest assistants waved clubs in the direction of my head. "This is no joke. You are flouting the will of the Iranian people."

"*You* leave immediately. You have no right to set foot in here, any of you. It is totally illegal."

I was also aware of the element of gamesmanship in my defense of principle. Iranians love to bargain and play brinksmanship, pitting one side against the other. Although the outcome was inevitable, I wanted to see how far I could go with *this* game. They respected a show of strength, which I was determined to carry through.

I gave up when the closest clubs swished inches from my nose. A squad led me to join the others in the Commercial Library. If I had dreamed that this was going to be the first of a dozen substitute cells, I would have been appalled and depressed instead of cocky.

*

I was never able to fully explain what prompted so much indignation in me. It was surely some combination of personal and national affront. But it seemed odd even to me that someone of so little flag-waving patriotism became, before the end of the day, so deeply insulted for his country and its flag. My "those half-baked kids can't do this to *me*" was mixed up with everything I believed I was, and deserved to be, as a free citizen. When the pinch came, I raged that they "couldn't" do this to me largely because I presumed I had the inalienable rights of an American.

The exhilaration of watching the action developed into a kind of euphoria. This was probably the end of an era. It seemed likely that Washington would break diplomatic relations with Iran within hours, and sorry as that would make me when the incident was over, I was high on excitement while it was taking place. If anything was clear, it was that we would be on our way to a new life that evening or the following day. After all, even Bazargan's government could not permit students, if they were what they seemed to me, to roam around their capital capturing diplomats. During the past weeks, they had seized hotels to convert into free dormitories for themselves. This was different.

The ebullience began petering out in late afternoon. By then I wondered whether this interesting adventure would be as short-lived as I had first assumed. I had to admit I liked the thrill of danger, even though it made my heart pump like a machine run wild and my mouth so dry I could hardly open it. I had to say too that in the crucial moments I behaved with a certain bravery—which was no virtue but a reflection of my capacity for taking offense over insults. But what was much worse than I imagined, even after a few hours, was being captive. Powerlessness and impotence were the ultimate insult, and how could I respond?

"It's going to be a trade: the Shah for you," said one of the group guarding us in the Commercial Library. That was the first hint that we might be in for something longer than the brief encounter of the Embassy's seizure and its personnel's expulsion. Surely Washington wouldn't, and shouldn't, succumb to terrorism by surrendering the Shah. I felt bitter about the staff meeting of October 22, when we were told about the decision to admit him for medical treatment. But once there, he could not be given up on a plate by a humbled American Government. And if he was not, would we in fact be flying home to a nice holiday with our families the next day?

I was in a group of about fifty captives in the Commercial Library. A handful were Americans. Many of our Iranian staff became panicky and pleaded to call home. Something had snapped in Mary's back; she lay on the floor with my jacket to ease the pain. My attempt to soothe and calm lost out to the wailing of our ordinarily cheerful cleaning woman: "You don't know how brutal they can be. I have children; let me out."

I thought the first seizure did give me an idea of how brutal they could be. But if I had even suspected that I'd have a chance to sample that for more than a few hours, I hope I would have had the sense to hold my Brooklyn tongue. As it was, the wise guy in me kept popping up while I waited. A lanky youth with a safety pin securing Khomeini's rain-soaked picture to his chest pointed his automatic pistol toward *my* chest and demanded where the *gav-sanduq* was. *Gav-sanduq* is a large safe in Farsi, but its literal meaning is "ox box." "We keep no oxen in the Embassy," I informed him. The Iranians in the room laughed despite themselves, while the overwrought kid shouted, *"Khafe-sho"*—the most insulting form of "shut up"—to me. Its literal meaning is "Choke yourself."

My jokes stopped with that, and the minutes turned sweaty. Peering out the window, I saw young men and women spray-painting "Nest of Spies" on the chancery walls, while others denounced the Shah through bullhorns. If the Chancery's steel doors held, as I was certain they would, at least some of our staff were calling for help from the government. However, there were no signs of anyone arriving to restore order. After two heavy hours, the Americans in the library were selected to leave, but not to pack our things or for a ride directly to the airport, as I'd half assumed.

As the other Americans were being blindfolded, I kissed Mary good-bye and shook as many Iranian hands as I could. My own blind-fold, a piece of khaki that might have been ripped from the uniform of one of our marines, was an outrage—yet I wanted it, in a way. When one guard asked another, "Is he an American too?" I almost shouted, "Yes I am, and take me with the others!" The blindfold was tight, but I could tell I was being led—alone—to the back end of the compound, toward the Ambassador's residence. The guards debated in whispers. I was pulled one way and then another. Apparently only the break-in itself had been organized.

When the blindfold came off, I was in a bedroom of one of the Embassy's Pakistani kitchen staff. From across the hall I heard one of the military attachés answering his captors in single syllables. My own guards, who would answer no question about who they were and whom they represented, took up the argument about the United States handing over the Shah.

"Whatever *you* say, your government will give in. You're more important to them than the Shah, that blood-sucking dictator, that animal!"

"I might agree with some things you say about the Shah, but our policy is not to surrender to terrorism—which is what you're engaged in."

"Do any of you Americans, even now, have any idea of what the Shah committed?"

"I can't answer for his mistakes or supposed mistakes. Have *you* made any? Are you going to answer for the one you're committing today?"

After our little debate, my guards posted themselves outside the door, and I strained to hear a radio playing in a nearby room. A local news broadcast announced with near glee that our captors called themselves Students Following the Line of the Imam and that support for their brave and righteous action was pouring in from all over the country. The implication that the seizure might be more, or become more, than an impulse of a band of irate zealots was a glum new hint that our confinement might not end in time for dinner. As if in development of a captive's habits, I took the opportunity of not being watched to look through the room's chest of drawers and half-consciously calculate what little thing I might make use of in the future.

On the surface, the interrogator who strode angrily into the room was typical of the girls who participated in the seizure. She wore baggy trousers, a long, shapeless coat to hide her figure, and a carefully knotted kerchief to hide everything but a few inches of her face. Her speech revealed that she was middle-class, possibly a university student. Her eyes were unusually attractive. Her behavior symbolized everything unpleasant and potentially tragic that was overtaking Iran.

My admiration for Iranian women, even tough ones, remained as great as ever. But this person was hostile and contemptuous, rather than tough: a personification of the threat to everything I loved in the country. She spit out her questions in a hiss as if to an animal, trying to find out who I was, what work I did, where I fit into the embassy hierarchy. Her questions revealed how little her band knew and how much they had taken upon themselves. What was the true function of a press attaché? What Iranian journalists did I "work with"?

"I understand how you feel about certain political things," I said, trying to establish a bit of self-respect and to reach her as a human being. "But this isn't the time or the place to talk about them. This is the territory of the United States—which you've invaded."

"No invasion; this is *our* country. This spy den—it is not an embassy—belongs to *us*. We are doing nothing that is not our absolute right and duty. *You* committed the invasion with your criminal conspiracies and corruption."

Suddenly I was exhausted by the day's activities. I'd had enough shoving from room to corridor to room—and I could not bear her tone. Perhaps it would have been easier if she were not a woman violating my notion of Iranian womanhood. No matter how much I cared for Iranians, I wasn't going to be lowered by her attempt to treat me like a viper.

But what I found myself doing was as unplanned as unthinkable. I got up for a bottle of scotch I had seen in one of the bureau drawers. It was as if I was trying not only to short-circuit this interrogator whose arrogance was making me twitch but also negate all I knew about Iran and Islam. To offer alcohol to a Muslim woman of those convictions in these circumstances was a kind of madness—which I proceeded to demonstrate. I held the bottle between our faces.

"Would you please accept a calming drink?" I asked in my most polished Farsi.

If she were combustible, she would have exploded. Her beautiful brown eyes turned murderous. Snorting through her nostrils, she threw up her arms, swung her long coat as she pivoted, and slammed the door behind her. The three male students who rushed in minutes later shoved me against the wall. "You beast!" one of them roared. "You have dishonored Iranian womanhood."

Again quaking inwardly, I nevertheless felt slightly relieved—for several minutes.

＊

That night I shared the room with Colonel Thomas Schaefer, the Air Attaché. We had been ordered not to talk. We whispered about the coincidence that he and I were two of but three "veterans" of the first seizure, in February. Although I had arrived in Tehran only a year before, the great reduction and turnover of staff since then made me one of the longest-serving officers there.

I also thought about the discussions early that morning of whether to fly the embassy flag at half-mast in memory of the students killed in riots a year before. Today's invaders might have come from the university demonstration to commemorate that anniversary. But a half-masted flag probably would have added no protection. Maybe nothing would have helped; maybe all our work since the revolution was the fumbling of illusion. Surely Washington's last illusion had been the weekend television flashing across Iran images of Bazargan in Algiers shaking Brzezinski's hand.

I was exhausted and freezing. The window in the little room had been smashed by a club or a boot. "Down with The Carter" was scrawled all over the walls with marker pens snatched from desk drawers. Our bedding was curtains ripped from the rods. We slept face-to-face, our hands and feet bound with nylon rope—except I hardly slept. The rope dug into my wrists and ankles. I kept seeing myself going off with Barbara and the children for a Sunday walk. It seemed possible now that I would not see them in the flesh for some time. The next morning, I shifted between surprise and anger when we were not released. Some of the students sported little badges with their names.

They were still unsure about who was who among embassy personnel, and still totally disorganized as to which brother or sister was responsible for which duties with respect to us. But they settled on a simple answer to their chaos. After breakfast I was moved again, this time to the large reception room of the Ambassador's residence, which was on the same floor. Blindfolded again, I could not count the Americans there, but coughing, shuffling, and occasional words suggested we numbered fifteen to twenty. I wondered whether the ghosts and goblins from last week's Halloween party were enriching the Iranians' imagination about our sinister activities. That day and the next, we were tied to chairs, our blindfolds remaining on. I got a masterpiece of modern design with a strip of leather for the seat and another supposedly to support the back. It was fairly torturous after the first few hours, but less than my thoughts of what this frenzied treatment might lead to.

A prohibition against talk accompanied the physical bondage. With shouts and threats we were ordered to say nothing except in answer to guards' questions. During the day I was fed a handful of dates while my blindfold remained on. Totally powerless, with ropes cutting into my hands and feet, I did not seriously consider disobeying. Still, it was demoralizing and shaming that we did obey. The only sentence in English I heard throughout the day was, "I'd like to go to the bathroom." I ate supper with the blindfold off in the already filthy kitchen. Contempt for myself was growing together with growing hatred for *them*.

They examined our watches for two-way radios. They checked our heels for hidden . . . what? Their nervousness was not totally misplaced: From their tone and from everything I knew about them, they were, despite their triumphant bluster, amazed by their success and frightened that American retribution for it was already on the way. But from what I knew about them too, they were operating on a knowledge of America that came chiefly from fantasies stimulated by spy thrillers.

My interrogator of yesterday was among the natural leaders. Most of the others were still too confused to know our names, but she could hardly have forgotten the beast who mocked her with whiskey. She directed her hiss to me. "What is your name?"

I did not answer.

Her voice filled with fury. "I am speaking to *you*. Give me your *name*."

"I don't have to give you anything."

Grabbing my beard, she spun my face around, giving me another moment of the relief of defiance. But despite this little show for her personally, I felt my moral strength declining, together with my energy. When our blindfolds were removed again and some bread and tea were thrown at us for the second day's supper, someone asked for a spoon. "Shut up!" screamed a guard. "Speak only when you are spoken to." Apparently incensed by the days of outrages, a marine tied up next to me protested with an assumption in his voice that seemed to come from my past. "You can't treat people like that." He was a handsome black in a dress uniform he had managed to keep immaculate: one of the new arrivals who had been posted in the Chancery. A squad of guards slammed him against the wall and waved fists in his face. "Forget about it," I whispered to the proud man when he was back in his place. "Don't try anything; it's not worth it."

Returning from the bathroom on the third day, I asked a young escort if I might see something from the press. Apparently he hadn't heard or understood the leaders' directive against this, for he gave me a copy of *Kayhan,* which bulged with copy about the seizure. The burning of the American flag and the "liberation" of our Iranian secretaries and drivers were featured among the saga of the Iranian people's glorious victory. Most depressing was the total absence of mention— and apparently of perception—that the take-over was a stunning violation of diplomatic immunity. As with the students themselves, the editorialists I read might never have heard of international law. It meant nothing whatever to them. It was a Western, not an Iranian concept, a concept invented to aid the rape of Third World countries. And Iranians were *finished* with everything Western; the seizure itself was proof of that.

What the newspaper did declare, and what the average Iranians surely felt, was that America had for too long used its laws—and not only laws—to oppress Iran. When I understood that the Embassy's seizure was regarded as no wrong, certainly not a crime, I felt a sharp stab of longing to leave the country forever.

The second floor of "The House" reminded me of a circus car packed with too many bodies. My parents had one bedroom. I had shared the second with my younger sister—who was sleeping there again, with her husband and baby. They had just moved back from Pennsylvania and would stay almost three years while looking for a place of their own. The cramped third bedroom, with a slanted, attic-like ceiling and just enough space for a high-rise bed and crib, used to be my brother's. In August, a month before Ariana was due, Alexander and I moved in there, while Barry remained in Washington completing his training for Iran. The single bathroom, which adjoined my bedroom, was as busy as one in a rooming house. In the morning, family members joined visitors and their children in the line at the door. "Hurry up, I've gotta get to *work!*"

Sundays were slower, especially for those not going to church. Everyone wandered down to the kitchen to fix his own breakfast. Someone went out for bagels, cream cheese, and lox. My mother would return from church with the Sunday papers, shortly before my uncles and aunts would start arriving.

November 4 would have been that kind of lazy morning if the telephone hadn't rung at seven-thirty. My mother answered downstairs, her voice quickly turning anxious. "Calm down, stop crying," I heard her say. "What are you so excited about?"

Barry's mother was often excited even at normal hours. Having guessed it was she, I went back to playing with the children. When Ariana had awakened in her crib, at seven, I had changed her and taken her into my bed. Then Alexander had crawled in to join us. I was sure my mother would calm Sarah until later—but she couldn't, and called me down.

"Your mother-in-law is on the phone, Barbara. The Embassy's been taken."

"Not again," I said to myself matter-of-factly. "Haven't we had enough of those shenanigans?" I went down to help compose Sarah. Before we hung up I convinced her to go to the dance she had planned to attend that evening.

I stayed reasonably calm, because the last time we spoke, during the previous week, Barry had told me he was planning to visit the town of Isfahan that weekend. There was a fair chance he wasn't in the Embassy when trouble began again. Besides, he could look after himself. And he had told me Iranians are essentially peaceful: people who argue in the street over something like a car accident, scream, wave their fists in each other's faces—but almost never punch. When they had demonstrated to the bystanders how fierce they were, they backed off before they could get hurt.

They'd make their point with storming the Embassy, then back away—probably by evening—before anything serious developed. After all, that's what happened the previous February, when the Embassy was seized. That was my best reason for telling myself and others that everything would end safely after a miserable day. It would be frightening, no doubt, but if Barry was there rather than in Isfahan, he would handle himself well. In a way, he was made for danger; he needed movement and action. If things were as serious as they seemed—two invasions of American territory within the year—Washington might well decide to close the Embassy. Barry could be home early in the week and we'd have the vacation we were promising ourselves. If he *was* captive, he wouldn't be for long. Not even governments as weak as Iran's would let citizens make prisoners of accredited diplomats.

So I stayed calm and agreed with the reassuring call from the State Department when it finally came. It was from the wife of an official on the Iran Desk who was helping to notify the families. "Don't worry about it," I told her. "It's happened before. I'm sure everything will be okay." The fact that Barry didn't answer the telephone in "our" Tehran house might just as easily mean he was in Isfahan as in the Embassy. The State Department didn't know which embassy staff members were being held.

I stayed near the telephone during the next few days, feeling my confidence wobble. Barry didn't call; no one knew anything about him. If he was in the Embassy, he might be in real trouble, because the militants weren't playing the scare-the-Americans game I had first imagined. This wasn't a one-day take-over with bluster but something new—which was getting worse instead of better. Americans remained captive, and nothing seemed to be getting done to lead to their release, while the fury against them appeared to be massing toward some terrible climax. I had no idea then that the crowds outside the Embassy were in fact tightly controlled, maybe even rehearsed. Watching them on television, especially the first few nights, was terrifying. The demonstrators seemed rabid with hate and revenge. My father and mother held my hands. I held my breath. I feared the crowd would march right in from their demonstration outside the gates to tear apart the hostages (that's what they were already being called) with bare hands.

The television screen was a nightly horror film. "Death to America, death to Carter," the crowd kept shrieking. I believe I had no prejudice against bearded men and women in chadors. It was the violence on their faces that sent waves of panic through me: insane hatred laced with ritual chanting that appeared to be building and building to inevitable blood. Yes, Barry had assured me Iranians almost always made a show of force rather than using it. But suddenly I remembered him describing a Russian envoy who was killed together with his entire mission in the first important antiforeign outbreak. That Russian had boorishly insulted Islam, but a century later, in the 1920s, an American vice-consul who had committed an accidental cultural affront was killed on the operating table by an impassioned crowd.

The first floor of our house was like one large room with the kitchen open to the living room and the dinette. The television set was in the far corner of the living room, visible from almost everywhere. Ordinarily the open space resembled a rumpus room—more messy than usual now, because my mother had postponed delivery of new furniture while the children were living there. Renovations had been interrupted midway.

Ordinarily too, everyone's behavior fit in with the "relaxed" surroundings. Toys were strewn about and Alexander and Ariana, together with my year-old nephew, had the run of the place. As she made goulash or macaroni at her kitchen "station," my mother would carry on simultaneous conversations with several relatives in various parts of the house. Barry and I had given her Star-of-David earrings the previous Christmas. She was putting them on for church the Sunday morning of my mother-in-law's fateful call and still had them on, having sworn not to remove them until Barry was home.

My father, just home from work, would be at his "station," a chair near the television set, like a tranquil Walter Matthau looking for a grandchild to wrap his loose arms around. The only other person who dared take that chair was Alexander, who sat like a squirrel on my father's shoulder, both of them almost sighing with contentment. My mushrooming sprawl of newspaper and magazine articles about the situation spilled over the table and onto the floor, advancing toward my father's chair. It was the house at its best: not idyllic and not without conflict, but with the warmth of an old-fashioned hearth.

The mood changed perceptibly as the hour for the evening news approached. Everyone tried not to mention the time, or the situation, at least during the afternoon "break" from it. But even our carefree mutt, Lucky, who also had the run of the house, felt the mounting tension. Ariana would became uncharacteristically quiet. Alexander made his "Khomeini face," with more furrowed brow, more sullen eyes, and more brooding mouth than three-year-olds should know about. My aunt Jeanette, who spent evenings with us, would be chatting with my mother. Minutes before news time, Aunt Jean, who lived a few doors away and spent the day in our house looking after my grandmother, would come in from my grandmother's room saying, "Quick, put it on!" My ninety-year-old grandmother would settle herself on a hard chair and glower at the set. Never had I heard an angry word from her about anyone. Now she trembled with fury at "those *animali"* who were "killing my Barry." She was especially fond of him, because he had spent hours talking with her about her youth.

Most evenings, Iran was the "tease" and the lead item, which meant it was on for five to ten full minutes. During commercials we flipped to another channel. Everyone watched in silence. My mother stopped cooking and for once focused her entire attention on one thing. The house was stony as never before. The bluish light radiating from the set kept us rigid, like paralyzing rays.

The eyes of some chanters were almost hypnotic. I wondered whether the ones who pushed right up to the camera were fully human. They kept calling us demons, and I was hearing an inner voice calling *them* demonic. One crazed man with blazing eyes yelled, "America will lose, Islam will win. The American hostages will be destroyed!" Alexander sensed the meaning and clutched my father's neck. My grandmother shook. I could think of nothing except when the rape would end.

But there was still a chance Barry wasn't in the Embassy. If he hadn't been there when it was seized, he would surely get away unharmed. His Farsi would enable him to get around, and he even looked Iranian, with his beard and high cheekbones. I studied the screen even more intently: Could he be in the screaming crowd? It would be like him to pause on his escape route for some excitement—and a comprehensive report to the State Department.

Barry and I had the same reaction to stress when we couldn't deal with it by taking action. We slept a lot. The news was becoming more bloodcurdling, and I went to bed.

It was a great relief to be at home. My parents sometimes talked about selling the house. I hadn't wanted them to, because I loved it. The wall that kept me in was now keeping the worst of the outside world out. The house was my family and my childhood. I understood Scarlett O'Hara's father explaining why land is more important than any one person: It is more enduring. I would have been miserable on my own.

Wherever Barry was, his children were getting the same stability and support as I was. However much we had disagreed about my wish to spend time with my family, he had the solace of knowing we were taken care of. Although I could have done this myself, here I was spared the details of food, laundry, cleaning—and of seeking deeply understanding confidants. My mother, father, aunts, and uncles generously met those needs, giving me a chance to escape.

I would go to sleep at three o'clock in the afternoon and awaken at six. Although I was losing weight rapidly, I could only pick at my supper before hurrying back to bed by eight o'clock, exhausted. That was the escape.

Barry's mother slept with a radio on all night. "Just turn it off, Sarah," I suggested when she complained that she couldn't sleep. "I can't, I can't," she answered. "I must know what is happening to Barry." I tried to reassure her but at that point was as uncertain as she. Only sleep made it tolerable for me—now up to fifteen hours of twenty-four.

I didn't dream. I didn't think, even about Barry. When my head touched the pillow at eight o'clock, I fell asleep evening after evening, and woke up still fatigued thirteen hours later. It was the sleep of the emotionally dead.

Still in bed in the morning, I reached for the radio. It stayed on all day, tuned to an all-news station endlessly repeating the same stories. The news from Iran never changed. The hostages remained hostages; the crowds kept screaming for their death. I dragged myself to the kitchen.

I was able to look after the children a bit during the day, read the newspaper, and answer constant telephone calls from the State Department, friends, ICA, or other concerned people. Otherwise I wasn't much use.

The overwhelming sleepiness was merciful, for it drugged me against the possibility that Barry was in desperate danger. I clutched at good omens. My younger brother visited a Puerto Rican fortune-teller, paid his two dollars, and the woman dealt him the cards.

"Richard, you are not here for yourself, you are here for your sister. Her husband is very far away. I see them separated by water. Yes, he's in some kind of prison."

Richard almost fell off his chair. His name was Bogutski, and he had been careful not to mention "Rosen" or anything to do with our preoccupation. "What's all those books?" the woman continued. "Her husband's so smart, but he's just sitting there; what's the matter with him?" When he recovered, Richard told her about Barry. The woman said *I* must be careful because I would be in a car accident, but Barry would return safely. He would be very nervous when he did, but there was no doubt that he would come home.

I started using seat belts on the children. When the front of the car was hit with my father at the wheel, they didn't get a scratch, thanks to the woman's warning. Stupid as I felt, her prediction calmed me. Somewhere I *knew* nothing disastrous would happen to Barry, but couldn't think more clearly than that.

Exposure of the genitals is sinful in Islamic culture. The same soldiers who linked pinkies on patrol became self-conscious when undressing. Otherwise the guards would surely have watched us in the toilet.

As it was, they followed us to the stall door, and the most persistent, who was also one of the meanest, stamped off when I asked him if he wanted to sit down beside me. Hungry for a moment's privacy, I would ask if I could be left alone to wash my hands. "Search me. I can't do anything dangerous, can I? Would you mind if I closed the bathroom door?" But they would plant themselves at the sink, fold their arms, and keep an eye on the lather while I washed. Their underlying fear of Americans mixed with their overactive imaginations led them to silliness as well as considerable cruelty.

The cruelty was no easier to take for being random and spontaneous. After two days tied up in the Ambassador's residence, I was moved to a large warehouse and barracks near the rear of the compound. The gloomy building was known as the Mushroom Inn in recognition of what might have grown there. Its black basement was used for showing films, with no darkening needed.

I was awakened in the middle of the night, and a towel was placed over my head, on top of the blindfold, for the two-minute drive to the Mushroom Inn in what felt like an embassy car. My new place was in its huge basement—a room that long before had housed monitoring equipment supposedly directed toward the Soviet Union. The ventilation was hopelessly inadequate. It remained an unusually cold November, but the thirty or so Americans held with me in the vaultlike enclosure roasted in stifling heat. A guard generously allowed me to roll up my sleeves and pants, but sweat kept pouring. We slept on the bare floor, trying in vain to soak up some coolness. No corner was less oppressive than any other. I got to try them all, because I tried to answer whispers of "What's going on? "Is there any news?" and I was moved every time I talked, even though it was only to say I knew nothing.

I first saw the full perimeters of the substitute cell in the morning, lit by feeble fluorescent light. It could have been an abandoned machinery room; apart from our bindings and separation from one another, we could have been bums squatting there. The huge ventilating units made a deafening noise but added to the heat rather than providing a fresh breath. I pushed my face against one exhaust to get at least its metallic breeze. The room was so crowded that the Americans placed against the posts seemed to be supporting them. The guards eyed a contingent of five or six marines with special attention. They were worried about what these young fighters might do, or they coveted their khakis, or both. Within days I began to see U.S. camouflage jackets and pants on the most style-conscious of our keepers.

Late that first morning, a television crew appeared with cameras, sound equipment, and interior lights. After panning around the room for an establishment shot, they took a pair of marine boots, placed them in the center of the floor, and let the camera linger over them. This was no doubt to symbolize the emptiness of U.S. power—a variation of a sign I saw on seizure day, just before the break-in: KHOMEINI STRUGGLES, CARTER TREMBLES.

The old-fashioned lights were horrendously hot and the crew turned them full on the humbled prisoners as they moved around the room, meticulously photographing faces and bound wrists. I turned my face from the lens as much as I thought wise. Did I want to say anything to my relatives at home? I was asked. Would I "care to comment about giving up the Shah for our own lives"? "Barbara, I'm okay," I answered tersely. "Don't worry."

Physically, I *was* okay. But my hatred of the guards was the strongest emotion I remembered feeling; I felt like pawing the earth to get at them. What was happening in that scorching basement was an outrage. When the crew moved to the next prisoner, I regretted having said anything at all.

❖

After lunch, a young guard who seemed the only English-speaker among them came in to announce that Ramsey Clark was on his way to Tehran on a special mission from "your Carter" to negotiate our release. This seemed to make sense. We had seen a television tape on the video equipment in the room, a summary of the 1977 World Series that happened to be lying about. The guards probably planned to release us momentarily; why would they entertain us otherwise? Ramsey Clark seemed a logical choice to see to any final arrangements between Washington and Tehran. The former Attorney General had become a human-rights activist, well regarded in Iranian revolutionary circles. He had met Khomeini personally and visited Iran several times. If any American had the Ayatollah's respect, it was Clark—and even prisoners who knew nothing of the background sighed with relief. I was surprised how quickly smiles formed and my own anger softened.

The guard cleared his throat. "But the Imam has said no. There will be no negotiations. We will not let your dirty Clark land in revolutionary Iran; let his plane stay in Turkey."

The room turned painfully silent. But though the smiles disappeared and resentment closed my throat, my calculating side detected something good in the guard's spiteful announcement. Once dickering had begun, it would surely go forward. What were Iranians if not bargainers? Clark would return in a day or two, as soon as a bit of last-minute negotiating had been seen to, no doubt prompted by the Iranians' desire to squeeze the political equivalent of a few extra rials from Washington. The only weak point in my optimism was Khomeini's disdain for compromise. If he had really said no to Clark, it might be decisive. Perhaps that would be best in a way: no negotiations, no pawns. On the other hand, Khomeini hated to change his mind about anything, not only because his was a black-and-white perception that stamped the rejected thing as evil. He rarely took political initiatives. If he *had* made up his mind about the taking of the Embassy, it was probably because he knew which decision would be popular. Anyway, dare he order troops to free us?

The guard nearest me studied my face while I was contemplating the possibilities. "There won't be any Entebbe here," he said defiantly. A raid was exactly what I had been thinking about. If negotiations did fail, I wondered what ways there were to escape. I couldn't imagine any from the Mushroom Inn.

*

Had I been less absorbed by hopes and anger, I might have been trying to figure out who our captors were and what they represented in the Iranian political scene. As it was, my interest in political analysis was amazingly feeble. I could hardly care less what the guards' claims were while they were "presenting" them this way.

I could only suppose they were a new group of some kind. The Embassy's first seizure was probably by a band of hard-core leftist guerrillas. The present invaders appeared ideologically different. They had come over the walls with women and continued to treat them as equals—whereas the first invaders were all male, seemingly not by accident. The present captors seemed more educated; in fact, well educated. One actually revealed to me that he was a student at a highly reputed polytechnic college.

Beyond this, it was impossible to find out anything about them. They called each other "brother" and "sister," indicating a distinctly un-Iranian dedication to purpose rather than to individual gain or glory. Otherwise they remained faceless, as if they had trained themselves to give nothing away.

I guessed their average age to be twenty-two or twenty-three, with not much variance either way. Had I seen them on the street before, I might have taken them for komiteh members. But the komitehs I had encountered were not nearly so cohesive. What struck me, despite my instinct to see nothing good in them, was their rare cooperation among themselves. They never argued, even when trying to accomplish something such as a move, which embroiled them in typical

Iranian disorder. They were as disorganized as a typical group their age, but only in seeing to arrangements and details. The unusual quality was their allegiance to some deeper internal organization and unity of purpose. I pictured them having deeply serious meetings before coming out on their assignments pertaining to us.

Naturally, some were less vicious and more personable by nature, which was difficult to hide. The English-speaking one quickly seemed a "good guy" relative to the others, despite the pleasure he took in announcing Khomeini's refusal to negotiate with Ramsey Clark—which they took as vindication of the seizure. Most of our shirts were reeking by this time. In a small but welcome mercy, English-Speaker invited us to remove them for washing. Never mind that I never got mine back and began wearing someone else's, with my only possessions now trousers, shoes, and one set of underwear. English-Speaker couldn't manage sorting the laundry, but he meant well. On the other hand, Handcuff Man was a loathsome bully who loved his work. He carried around several pairs over his forearm, like a self-important waiter with napkins. If someone said two words—such as "Ye gods!" —he slapped on a pair without a blink. If other guards heard something, or thought they did, they would walk out, and we knew who would appear within minutes. Much of the generalized hate I was feeling channeled itself to Handcuff Man's ugliness.

Shower Man hadn't revealed himself as such because we hadn't had a shower, despite the pressing need. I would develop a toleration for him, if only through the relief he brought. But I'd have bet my last dollar that no symptoms of the Stockholm Syndrome would appear among us for these slightly sanctimonious boys and girls. I saw too much of the old insecurity in them, which expressed itself too often in the familiar machismo. In their stunning ignorance of the wrong they were committing, they were very proud of themselves. Too many thought they were cool by pushing us around, almost always with two or three brothers to back them up even though they had the guns.

I sensed that at bottom they were surprised they still held us captive and that neither Iranian nor American authorities had forced them to give us up. This fed their morale; day by day they became more cocky. I doubted any of them would have proclaimed "no Entebbe here" the first day. Smashing the spy den and holding the wolves under their boots did wonders for their self-importance.

Curiously, some national characteristics I hadn't much noticed before, or had even found quaint, now sent me up the wall. The most jarring pertained to language. Since a vowel always precedes a consonant cluster in Farsi, almost all Iranians adapt English by prefixing an "e" to many words. "E-smell this," "E-brush your teeth," "E-stop the car," they would say, and, in the phrase that now filled me with disgust, "Don't e-speak." Many said nothing more than "Don't e-speak" much of the time. I hated their accent.

But their predominant quality was conviction of America's evil thoughts and evil deeds. Even the quieter, softer ones were totally certain their cause was the most just on earth. "Do you know how much I felt for this country?" I asked a skinny, seemingly nonhostile boy taking me to the bathroom after the usual wait. "I was here with the Peace Corps. I spent a good part of my life thinking about Iran."

"Hah, you mean War Corps," he answered. "The United States never sent anyone here or did anything here unless to exploit and corrupt Iran for its own purposes. It will learn that fact when we put the Shah on trial."

※

If I had my wits about me the first day, or suspected there would be a second, I would have concealed my knowledge of Farsi. It might have been discovered in time. But if not, perhaps I would have overheard valuable scraps from the guards.

As it was, they were careful about talking in my presence, except to use me to give orders to others. "Tell him not to signal," they would say to me as intermediary for whomever they wanted to warn. "Tell him he must wait his turn for the toilet." "Tell him no talking." One or two guards seemed to feel I was responsible for whatever troubled them, just because I was the one to whom they spoke.

On the other hand, Farsi helped with things we were permitted to discuss with the guards, such as reading material. Among other things, the Mushroom Inn was a repository for thousands of books, almost all left by the Tehran American School, a well-equipped high school that disbanded almost immediately after the revolution. The stacks reached to the ceiling in one corner of our "machinery room."

Permission to read came in the form of a guard's unexpected "Want some books?" I made a selection and read on the floor, under the feeble fluorescent light. Time passed a little less slowly, but not much. I had read in libraries all day; why was it so much more difficult to spend eight hours that way here?

Almost immediately, I found myself immersed in "prison literature." It included Solzhenitsyn's *The Gulag Archipelago*, about Stalin's concentration camps; *Andersonville*, about a group of Yankee soldiers in Confederate prison camps; *Midnight Express*, about a young American in a Turkish prison; and *Papillon*, about a Frenchman on notorious Devil's Island. These books related horrors so much worse than our conditions that I had no right to make the comparison. Many of those prisoners, all of whom were subject to starvation and/or bestiality, were totally innocent.

So I was not unique in having been imprisoned "for nothing." I might not even have been an exception to the rule; millions of people all over the world endured this. In the closest example, American servicemen as Japanese prisoners of war, suffering was a thousand times greater. I tried to learn from this, and to reconcile myself to the books' implied warning that once "in," you're usually in for a long time. I tried to see my plight in the perspective of those infinitely worse ones, to master the lesson that people who survive with the least damage are those who keep their internal defenses strong. Perhaps it helped.

But it was hard to feel better about our situation because others had known worse. The perception of others' misfortunes and my own clearly came from two different sources in the brain—or the nerves. And the interesting thing was that I felt less sympathy for the innocent victims of the Shah's regime, although logically they deserved no less.

Another videotape of some sort was shown to entertain us. I noticed Americans being removed, seemingly one by one, from the darkened room. "What's going on?" I whispered to a neighbor. "Guess we're being questioned," the reply came back. "Kind of interrogation."

When my turn came, I was blindfolded and walked to what felt like one of the storage rooms in the same basement. The pushes of one of my escorts were hard enough to qualify as punches. The other escort, English-Speaker, seemed to want to protect me. There was no time to figure out their roles.

When my blindfold came off, I saw that the storeroom held the Embassy's generous supply of liquor. Pointing a revolver at my jaw, the pushing guard showed me a list of combinations to ICA safes. "Where are they?" he demanded. "What building are they in?" I said I knew nothing about them; the people who did had left the Embassy ten days before the seizure.

"You are lying. You will not like the punishment for lying."

"Believe it or not, I'm telling you the truth."

He produced another list, this one for the building we had evacuated months before, after it was ransacked. About this one, I did tell the truth, giving him the address and adding, "Go check it yourself."

He did not want to believe that the safes were not on the compound. Furious, he grabbed my shirt. "You tell lies and nothing but lies. This will be very bad for you."

I thought I had been rather clever to think of stressing the old building, which no longer mattered. Now I was stupid with bravado. "Even if I knew the combinations, I wouldn't tell you," I said defiantly and totally superfluously.

Before he could hit me, the other guard intervened. "Look at this list," he said, studying the second one. "They seem to be old dates from another building; nothing to do with the Embassy. Let's check it first."

Gun Waver pushed me out the door. My heart was beating furiously but I felt wonderful. Back in the vault with the others, I gave a thumbs-up sign to the Embassy's security officer. "They got nothing from me," I mouthed. When he had read my lips, he indicated that his concern now was that the embassy staff not be hurt. He was right. Menace had entered the air. If I had been sloppy enough to leave the names of some of my Iranian contacts in my desk, or if the guards found any unburned cables mentioning names, I felt certain those people were going to suffer with us. For just a moment, my thoughts went beyond our own tests to my Iranian friends and millions of others who might soon be confronted with worse. How ironic if the editors I talked to, even those who disagreed with me flatly, would be punished for this.

My return to the Ambassador's residence after three days in the Mushroom Inn was as unexpected and unexplained as my midnight transfer from there. This time I was brought to the Ambassador's sitting room and tied to an ornate chair facing the fireplace, just loosely enough so I could hold up a book. I was reading President Truman's memoirs, which went into detail about how the United States restored Iranian sovereignty after World War II by "nudging" Soviet troops out of the country. The sign I saw when I looked up from the book was "Down with Carter," painted crudely with a spray can, directly over the Ambassador's handsome mantelpiece.

The formerly homey sitting room with a chintz-covered sofa was shabby from days of people camping out in it. The three others who shared it with me were Colonel Charles Scott, the second-highest-ranking army officer at the time of the seizure, and two civilian embassy officials. Our chairs faced outward so we could not see each other; a particularly vigilant guard leaped on the first word of any attempted whisper. This quasi-solitary confinement made an extremely long day.

Our untying for the night, at nine o'clock, might have been the guards' way of tucking us in. For a few minutes I weighed the advantage of exchanging the tedium of sitting in one place all day for the tedium of trying to fall asleep on the floor. Then the electricity went off. In case we might stage a breakout with our freed bare hands, a pair of guards hurried into the darkened room with something raised over their heads. When the lights came on, I noticed that the weapons were the ripped-off legs of the chair to which I'd been tied on the second day in the Ambassador's guest room.

On the second evening there, our sixth of captivity, the door leading to the Ambassador's bedroom opened. Several guards ushered in a tall, distinguished-looking gentleman in a dark suit, followed by four or five other well-dressed men in their forties. Before I had time to wonder whether this was going to be a show or the beginning of something positive, the lead man introduced himself as the Swedish Ambassador and the others as members of the diplomatic corps from France, Algeria, and Syria. The Swedish Ambassador did not try to hide the pain in his eyes at the sight of his captive diplomatic colleagues. I felt more and more certain that our captors—and whoever was supporting them among the Iranian authorities—did not understand that the image of bound, disheveled diplomats would not make good propaganda for them. They had been photographing us repeatedly in our humiliation, and photographed us again in the presence of the delegation. But our condition clearly shocked the visitors. Passing quickly through our room, apparently on their way to see the other Americans, they shook their heads in welcomed sympathy.

When the same door opened the next day, the photographers entered first to take our pictures with a Polaroid camera, probably appropriated in the Embassy. I turned around and tried to block my face with my bound hands until a team of guards grabbed me by the neck, almost strangling me to get their photograph. A few minutes later, a priest came in with other guards: the picture of a benign, devoted soul, exactly the kind who paid "house calls" on Barbara's grandmother when she was too weak to go to church. Quickly, yet with great warmth, he introduced himself as Monsignor Annibale Bugnini, the Papal Nuncio to Iran. Putting his hand on my shoulder instead of shaking my tied hand, he gripped me in a substitute embrace while looking into my eyes with deep compassion. "I know, I know," he said in English with a thick Italian accent. I recognized his final word to me, "patience," from hearing it at Barbara's house: "Pazienza." He said it as if the strength of the Church, and of all the outside world, were being passed to me.

Although he too left after only a minute, his visit stayed with me permanently. To give his advice great effect, I tried to remember his accent and gentle tone. *Pazienza.*

The lingering glow of his presence seemed to stimulate my analytical powers. Surely the Pope's representative did not come to see us, I reasoned, without instructions from the Vatican. Maybe the Pope himself was interceding with Khomeini on our behalf; and everyone knew how morally forceful he could be. I lived on this speculation until evening, when a team of guards handed us each a piece of paper with English printing. Evidently the Pope *was* working for our release, for the paper reproduced an answering speech by Khomeini that berated the Vatican repeatedly for not having protested "fifty years of massacres and imprisonment under the most inhuman conditions" during Pahlavi rule, and praised the Embassy's invaders as "our youth, who had been under suppression for years [and] who went out and got a few people from the spy nest who are responsible for conspiracy against our nation."

How come the thirty-five million people of Iran for the fifty years the father and son reigned over this country and oppressed our people, while we were under the suppression of the United States as well, and recently under the suppression of Mr. Carter as well, the millions of oppressed people expected some fatherly sympathy from the great Pope to lessen our miseries at least slightly.

But our ears have never heard such a sound. . . . Those who are pretending to be Christians in the big countries should stop using the name of Christ to cover their treacheries.

So Khomeini *was* supporting our captivity; it was not just these students acting in his name. And I knew the Ayatollah's self-righteous intransigence all too well. When he felt he was dealing with evil, which we had obviously come to represent, nothing would move him. The prospect of dying for a cause, rather than compromising, even appealed to him, for this was part of his vision.

"We are a nation of thirty-five million, and many of these people are looking forward to martyrdom," he said. "We will move with the thirty-five million. After they have all been martyred, then they can do what they want with Iran."

I suppose it should have been clear that the students couldn't have continued to hold us without the Imam's approval. But it took this confirmation to make us accept that we were at a dead end. Khomeini's speech was crushing because it indicated that he had made us the new focus of his righteous moral wrath. Surely the guards gave it to us with the intention of breaking our spirit so that we would "see reason" and beg our own government to let them have their way.

❂

The next day, guards brought in a copy of something from our side to further deepen everyone's pessimism. It was a copy of an August cable from Washington to the Embassy marked "Secret/Sensitive" and entitled "Planning for the Shah to Come to the United States": one of the documents that obviously hadn't been destroyed during the storming of the Embassy. The guards flourished it in triumph. To them it was proof—especially since the cable had been sent almost four months before the Shah actually arrived in New York—that his medical condition was a subterfuge; Washington had been scheming all along to receive him, the better to plot the counterrevolution.

They were wrong in this, either because they could not or did not want to understand the cable's slightly bureaucratic language. The two major sections dealt with the Shah's possible admission to America pretty much in keeping with the administration's policy from the time he left Iran. Hoping to stall him, the drafters recommended that the Shah be urged to renounce the Pahlavi claim to the throne. In my reading, it supported the view that the Shah's illness brought an end to stalling and to the State Department's attempts to resolve a tricky issue with the least possible offense to everyone.

But it was the cable's third section that mattered to us now. This was entitled "Security," and it read like a tasteless joke.

> We have the impression that the threat to U.S. Embassy personnel is less now than it was in the Spring; presumably the threat will diminish somewhat further by the end of this year. Nevertheless, the danger of hostages being taken in Iran will persist.

We should make no move towards admitting the Shah until we have obtained and tested a new and substantially more effective guard force for the Embassy. Secondly, when the decision is made to admit the Shah, we should quietly assign additional American security guards to the Embassy to provide protection for key personnel until the danger period is considered over. . . .

My wrists still tied to the arms of the chair, I held the cable as best I could with my fingertips, remarking to myself that the "threat to U.S. Embassy personnel" hadn't quite diminished. And the "additional American security guards" were a trifle too late. No embassy, whatever measures it took, could be made secure without the host country's protection, so our security and policy failures weren't the deciding factors. But it was difficult to keep my thoughts at this analytical level.

*

Another dreary note handed us was signed "Abolhassan Bani-Sadr, Foreign Minister." So there had been changes in the government! Ibrahim Yazdi, the previous Foreign Minister, was the man we'd been dealing with during most of the year before the seizure. He maneuvered deftly, switched from hot to cold with us, and always demonstrated what a good revolutionary he was, even when he had to take a caricaturishly uncompromising stance to do it. But at least he worked through diplomatic channels, according to diplomatic norms—and during the first invasion of the Embassy, he clearly did his best to end the violation, after which he came to the compound to apologize. If Yazdi was out, maybe Prime Minister Bazargan had been forced out with him. Maybe the radicalization or "mullahization" that began with rejection of the moderate Bakhtiar was still going on, taking the country still closer to Khomeini's vision of a clerical state. In this case, who was now running the show under the Imam's guidance? There was little hope that Bazargan's replacement, if he was actually gone, would have his degree of tolerance and respect for international codes of conduct.

The political speculation I used to spend so much time with now interested me only insofar as it might affect *us,* all the more because our whole Iranian policy of the past decade seemed a mess. My own fumblings to improve relations struck me as pathetic. Maybe Bani-Sadr, the new Foreign Minister, was just what Iran needed; but I already considered him an enemy. The newspaper he controlled when I was Press Attaché and he was an "Islamic economist" high in the radical Revolutionary Council consistently attacked America and smeared those who were willing to talk to us. Bani-Sadr personally refused to see me. From what I sifted from informants who made the most sense, his personal vendettas against the previous Foreign Minister were vile.

And here was his note, which fell into place with everything I knew about him. Apparently he had just taken over as Foreign Minister, and his first act was to declare support for our captors. The ones who handed me the paper pointed to a Bani-Sadr line about the Embassy not being really that "but a vital spy center." Another line identified the Shah as "the greatest criminal history has seen."

A guard told me that he and his brothers had placed a new banner over the Embassy's main gate: NO NEGOTIATIONS—JUST DELIVERING SHAH. Bani-Sadr's appointment and support appeared to have given the skinny twenty-year-old the confidence of an outsider whose formerly far-out proposals had been adopted into law.

✦

Guards took Colonel Scott from our room on the evening of November 14. Perhaps this was for interrogation. Perhaps, as a leading army officer, he faced something worse. The shots we had been hearing somewhere in or just outside the compound for several evenings involuntarily brought to mind photographs of bloodied corpses that had used to greet me in the morning newspapers. With the gesture of a finger to the temple, someone put about a rumor that we were being taken from our various rooms one by one for shooting. I tried to be cheery when I wished the Colonel good luck. A wave wasn't enough. At the difficult moment when someone was selected for individual removal from a room, one had an obligation to bolster him by saying at least a quick phrase in good old English.

My whisper was overheard; Handcuff Man rushed in. "You e-spoke," he certified. "We told you not to e-speak! Put out your hands."

"It's a pleasure," I said in Farsi. It was, for the moment, but the pinching handcuffs stayed on when I went to bed. With the difficulty of sleeping that way, I stared at my watch much of the night. At two o'clock in the morning a different guard entered the room, bent down, and told me to gather my things—a toothbrush and spare underwear I'd been given—and follow him.

I was blindfolded in the corridor, and the handcuffs were replaced with strips of cloth. Was this, I wondered, because it was easier to save the handcuffs now than to remove them from my body? But I had to swallow the terror of being led alone to the dreaded wall or stake for only five minutes or so. The others in the room—and other rooms too—must have been treated to the same "good morning," for after the usual delays for guards to whisper and fumble, I was led past a screen door that I knew to be at the rear entrance to the Ambassador's residence, then pushed into what felt like a small van parked a few steps outside the building. Just as they say, blocked vision heightens other senses. To my great relief I heard coughs and arms slapping chests there, and also "felt" they were American. The slapping was an attempt to keep warm. It was a bitterly cold night. I had at last been able to wash my socks that evening, and they were still wet. Soon my teeth were chattering louder than anyone's, but I picked up some body heat from the crush. When everything was finally organized, the van was so packed that not another rib could have fit.

"I heard you there, in the back," warned one of the guards. "Don't e-speak!"

But mouths were too close to ears to keep us from whispering. "What's going on?" we asked each other. "Where are we headed?" A few former roommates who had been worried about people taken from their rooms made contact with each other, but no one I heard had an answer to what this group move might mean.

To slow traffic, the Embassy had poured three concrete mounds in the roadway leading to the main gate. I felt a twinge of panic when we crossed them. Not only I; our makeshift paddy wagon went silent for a moment as our breath was collectively held. Whatever happened in the Embassy, it offered a measure of protection, if only in our minds. I realized that captivity had turned me slightly Iranian: The outside world—outside the compound—was full of frightening uncertainty and danger.

The van strained under its load. It pulled slowly uphill, which meant we were being taken north. Why? "Resettlement" was the end of hope. This was no way to release us; and we wouldn't have been sneaked out of the Embassy for that. Or was it a devious route to the airport? The outside chance was that the guards were *so* caught in the nest-of-spies fantasy that they were resorting to this secrecy and camouflage to smuggle us onto a plane. But this fantasy of our own evaporated as we continued driving north. I guessed we went to or just beyond the city limits, for we traveled—like market cattle, I kept thinking—for almost half an hour. Then we stopped, were unloaded, and herded for a few minutes in the cold drizzle. Our destination was a large house. Once inside, I dislodged my blindfold enough to see french doors and a chandelier that seemed to drip oil money. I assumed it was the mansion of a fled *taghuti:* a term Khomeini and his followers coined—from *taghut,* one of the idols smashed by the Prophet Mohammed—for the former regime's evil, idle rich.

It was even colder inside the massive stone walls. Sleeping arrangements hadn't been organized. We spent the night on the floor of a large reception room: eight or ten of us, I reckoned from the sounds of tossing. Our hands remained tied and blindfolds remained on. My teeth chattered on like a riveting machine.

The next morning, several of us were led up what felt like a magnificent staircase. When the blindfold came off, I almost smiled at the sight of my new quarters. I was in a comically luxurious bedroom with a purple brocade spread on an oversized bed. I couldn't have drawn a better caricature of the taste of the Iranian nouveaux riches.

A vanity in someone's vulgar conception of Louis XIV style stood in one corner. Within a few hours I was so bored that I risked a little investigating, despite the menacing warning to touch nothing. The vanity's top drawer held an assortment of mascara from the best Western makers and a stock of little jeweled stars for decorating monied Persian eyelids. The mirror over the vanity was soon covered with a sheet to keep us from signaling one another—which, in our guards' still fertile imagination, we were waiting to do in order to plan our escape. The curtains, so thick that it was impossible to tell the time of day or night, were not parted for a second. Three of us slept in this room, on the carpeted floor around the bed. It must have had more chairs in the decadent days. We shared the one that remained.

*

Perhaps the former mistress was fond of chocolates. My place on the floor teemed with little red ants. They liked hostage meat, for their several columns headed toward the meal between the musty blanket that served as my mattress and the dirty one that gave marginally more warmth. (The room remained so cold that I slept in my clothes.) For diversion I watched army groups make for me from the walls, from behind a bed post, and from under the door—each crack force under its own commander, who, however, appeared to coordinate his advance with the others'. My shoes and books blocked them only long enough for them to regroup and attack with hundreds of reinforcements. Soon I used shoes, then my palms, for lethal counterattacks. Maybe I took the battle analogy too seriously. Maybe I identified the attackers with those who had breached the embassy gate. In any case, my blows to the floor made a considerable bang, though I doubt a fully rational man would have detected a pattern in them.

If "Adolf" had been rational before the seizure, his work with us was steadily leading him from that state. My nickname for this guard had nothing to do with his outward appearance. A bulky young man with an abnormally short forehead and outsized feet, he had sported a new pair of shoes during the first days of our capture. They became my weather report: dust indicated clear skies, and drops of moisture —which probably remained on the leather because it was already so dirty—meant rain. He was constantly angry with us, and suspicious of everything—even why I didn't "e-smoke." What was I trying to disguise by pretending not to?

Evidently to display the poverty the Shah's policies had engendered, the guards had decorated the Ambassador's once-luxurious bedroom with a photograph of Tehran's "tin town," where former villagers lived in wretchedness. That was back in the embassy compound, directly over a mattress on which I would eventually sleep. One day Adolf nodded to the photograph to make a point to a captive he was trying to intimidate. "What's the big deal?" answered the American. "After all, it's just a slum."

"Islam?" shouted Adolf, with blood in his voice. "*This* is *Islam?*" He moved his bulk threateningly to the hostage, who didn't know whether to giggle or weep.

In this house, wherever it was, Adolf was posted to our room for eight hours at a stretch. He became proportionately more irritable as he grew more tired; but he stuck doggedly to his reading of Islamic treatises, looking up at us every thirty seconds or so, then down to search for his place. During one of my blitzes on the ants, I saw him growing darker and darker with each squint in my direction. Finally he leaped up, putting iron in his voice.

"Do not e-signal. I know what you are doing. Your code does not fool me." In the two seconds it took to reach me, he had worked himself into a tirade of orders and threats. I looked up at him, shaking my head to suggest he was mad. "You're unbelievable," I said in Farsi.

"Shut your face. Do not e-speak!"

The ants won the day, until I began squeezing them quietly, under the blanket.

∗

My roommates were Donald Cooke, a young vice-consul, and Jerry Miele, a communications officer in his early forties. Don wore his hair almost to his shoulders. Guards constantly told him to do something about this "unmanliness." Don's gifts included an admirable ability to sleep and an imperviousness to everything nasty when he was awake. Jerry and I would grimace to each other at the suppers of cold beans garnished with okra from commissary cans. Don ate his with a cheerful smile. *Sangak* bread saved Jerry and me on those occasions. A bit artificially, we winked to each other—carefully, in order to avoid charges of signaling—for companionship.

We all instinctively looked to each other for support when an English-speaking guard came in one morning after our weekly shower. Unexpected entries now caused more anxiety than hope. The guard handed each of us a sheet of paper. It was a short questionnaire asking name, home address in Iran or a map to the house if street address wasn't known, location of other Americans in the neighborhood, and name of the caretaker if any.

Jerry told the guard he had just moved to a new address and did not remember the name of the street. "Then draw a map," said the guard. Jerry stopped drawing when he saw me cautiously shaking my head and wincing "no." Seeing this too, the guard turned his attention to me. "Excuse me," I said before he could begin working me over. "Why do you want this private information?"

"We need to know everything about you. Where you live, what you have in your house. All your secret messages are. . . ."

"Excuse me, I'm a diplomat," I interrupted. "Maybe you don't know the provisions of the Vienna Convention, but you have no right to enter my house."

"Yeah, right on," chortled Don. The sound of Jerry's pen dropping to the floor was the final declaration of our modest revolt.

The guard's pause for thought lasted several disagreeable minutes. "All right," he said at last, not making clear whether this was a threat or an expression of agreement. "All right, you can do this action if that is what you want."

When he withdrew, I sat with my back against the wall, trying to guess how speedy his return would be. Although I myself knew almost nothing about the Vienna Convention governing diplomatic immunity, I did know he wasn't looking it up. He was consulting with his brothers, the most influential of whom seemed invariably to be the most forceful. In fact, he did not return for several hours, and I almost began to believe that resistance was the answer. Then the door opened and he pointed to me. "You, come with me."

I was blindfolded and led downstairs, deeply regretting my impulsive mouth. The blindfold was removed when I stood in the middle of a vast hall with even larger and gaudier furniture than in the upstairs bedroom. The chandeliers looked as heavy as the massive, overstuffed divans. Spotlights played on metallic curtains and a glittering gold carpet.

But my thoughts could not linger for long on the trappings. Adolf and another guard were waiting in the room. Both marched two paces forward so they were standing directly in front of me, G-3 automatic rifles at the ready. After a moment for me to become fully aware of their significance, I was led past them to a corner of the room. A desk there, seemingly plated in gold leaf, was even more ludicrously ornate than the rest of the furniture. The chubby young man seated behind it was so short that his feet barely touched the floor. I had never seen him before. "My" guard pushed me into a chair beside him. He could not have been more than eighteen years old.

He deserved a role in a Woody Allen satire. Opening a dossier, he extracted the questionnaire I hadn't filled out and pointed to it as though it were the key evidence in the crime of the century. His demands for my instant, unqualified "obedience" were marked by bad grammar—in Farsi.

"I'm sorry, I'd like to give you my address," I answered. "But the fact is, I can't."

He waved Adolf and the other armed guard nearer. "I will now count from ten to one," he said. "If you do not tell me your address, these men will blow your head off. We have no time for people who oppose the will of the Iranian people."

Adolf's companion stuck the cold barrel of his rifle against my temple. The count was as slow as might be expected from someone of his age who enjoyed playing this particular game. "Ten . . . nine . . . eight. . . ." Somehow, I was certain it *was* a game, and this boy was not authorized to kill me. Of course, there was an outside chance, but I wasn't going to give in to this squirt. My residence really was supposed to be protected by diplomatic immunity, and just because it had been trampled on at the Embassy didn't mean I should help repeat the process at my house. Duty to my government overrode the very slim possibility that this was more than a performance.

Then I thought of a solution.

"Three . . . two. . . ."

"*Sabr kon,*" I said. "Wait a moment; I know I have no choice."

The boy could hardly suppress his grin as he handed me the questionnaire. I wrote down the address of my *old* house, the looted one in which I had hardly slept since then.

I was led back upstairs. After the excitement of the confrontation, I grew panicky that they might really hurt me when they discovered my trick. During the next few days, I jumped at every creak of the stairway. But no one came for me. And I never had the chance to ask Don or Jerry whether they went through the same performance when it was their turn to be taken downstairs.

*

"What's going on in Washington?" I asked myself. "Where are the Marines?"

"Do you really want America to use force?" another inner voice asked. In low moods I couldn't answer that honestly, because I didn't know what I wanted—beyond GETTING OUT.

Thanksgiving Day, my favorite holiday, left me feeling forsaken and resentful. We had been prisoners *two and a half weeks*. What did the bastards want from us?

One of them noticed the ring I'd had made in the Tehran bazaar in 1968. We were reduced to so few possessions, and were so carefully scrutinized, that I might have been surprised that it hadn't been noticed earlier. It had hardly rubbed down at all in eleven years of constant wearing, and of course the inscription in Farsi, a line from a great thirteenth-century Iranian poet, remained the same: "The People of Adam Belong to Each Other, and Their Creation Is of One Essence." This particular guard didn't waste words. "I want that," he said.

"It's mine," I answered stupidly. "I want to keep it."

"I said to give it to me. I want to . . . show it to my brothers."

The ring represented something precious to me. Without it I would be stripped of much of what remained of my identity and individuality. I almost pleaded with the guard, but wasn't up to defying him. When he closed the door behind him, I was certain I would never see it again. For half an hour I felt more miserable than since the beginning of our confinement. Then he reappeared with the ring, which he said he and his brothers found "very interesting." But I felt only slightly better with it back on my finger. I had been violated again; it had been tarnished.

The television remained on almost constantly, waiting for the announcement I kept hearing in my inner ear: The hostages were released and are flying home. About a week after the seizure, a news report showed one of them being paraded before an angry Tehran crowd. The thick blindfold covering his face from mouth to forehead had the grisliness of terrorist handiwork. The announcer identified this helpless being as Barry Rosen.

I felt a stab in my stomach, but something stopped me from crying out. The hostage on the screen was balding and bearded like Barry, but clearly not he. I called ABC News and asked to speak with the producer, who assured me that one of their correspondents who had worked in Iran had made a positive identification.

"But I know my own husband. And that's not him," I said, trying to control myself.

"It is, according to *our* information," he answered as though correcting a pupil's mistake. That was my introduction to the backstage of American television journalism. The producer led me to believe the reporter who identified the hostage as Barry knew him well. Actually he had met him once. But soon I'd consider myself lucky to encounter nothing worse than this kind of sloppiness.

Until that evening, I had had a mindless confidence in the American press. I was almost a patriotic caricature: a schoolteacher genuinely convinced the great American public was being served in the best possible way by honest and accurate American news services. I was so inexperienced I didn't know network and local news come from separate organizations. I also didn't know the mere mention that I was a hostage's wife would get me connected to almost anyone in the network hierarchies. That realization, and the reason for it, would dawn later.

In the coming fifteen months the blindfolded man would be solemnly identified as Harry, Gary, and Barry Rosen hundreds of times throughout the country. The clip of him being humiliated and paraded was shown at every tense moment, and became a symbol of the hostages. I immediately started telephoning other stations that picked it up, then newspapers that splashed the photograph over their front pages. I explained that his closest relatives, including me, were certain he wasn't Barry. "That's not my husband. After the first minute, it doesn't even *look* like him."

After a month, the sister of the pictured man told me who he was. Although I of course would not reveal his identity, I stressed that I knew it. Nothing I said, however, stopped journalists from calling the blindfolded man Barry—even the same ABC News with whom I had had a long, detailed conversation that first evening. It was as though reporters, editors, and producers were determined to prove themselves right not by checking with people who would know but by backing each other up with endless repetition of the same mistake. "We got it from television news," said newspaper editors. "We got it from the newspapers," said television producers. One paper printed a retraction, adding the wonderfully helpful information that Barry Rosen was definitely one of the hostages! That finally taught me it was better to let some things go than to protest.

The inaccuracy was baffling, but wasn't what maddened me. As I tried to explain, wrong identity could be disastrous. No one, including the State Department, still knew for certain whether Barry had been in the Embassy when it was taken or on his weekend trip to Isfahan. The militants themselves were least likely to know, unless they were far better organized than during the first seizure. What if Barry was indeed a hostage but using an assumed name on his own initiative or on orders of security people? Did the press have the right to take these defenses from him?

If Barry *was* away, he could probably blend in with the natives, perhaps even get by bus to the Turkish or Pakistani border—*unless he was being searched for*. But constant repetition of his name was a sure guarantee he *would* be searched for. It was a straight tip-off to the very militants our media so angrily condemned. Whose side were they on? Obviously, I thought then, their first concern was the well-being of the hostages. How could they make such a dangerous mistake—and keep making it, as though they didn't care about the truth *or* the people involved?

Nothing could be worse for Barry.

"Yes, my husband is in Iran," I would say to one media person after another. "But we don't know whether he's a hostage. The State Department hasn't released his name—unless to you privately. Where did you check your identification? . . . How can you identify him publicly when you don't really know who the man is and could be putting the real Barry Rosen in terrible danger?"

The unfailingly reassuring voice on the other end of the line was edged with surprise, sometimes amusement, at my venture into matters best left to professionals. Patronizingly or not, it almost always promised to check before using the picture of the blindfolded man again. But in a day or two Barry's name and the photograph would be linked yet again. Slowly it dawned on me that the journalists I had assumed so responsible were lying, in a sense, for they had failed to check with the best source: Barry's family. Even if the film clip had been of Barry, didn't anyone care that they might be putting a life at stake for the sake of . . . what? And Barry was one of many. As the State Department kept repeating the danger of revealing names, journalists kept trying to uncover and make public those names. That was "the story"; but should it take precedence over everything? Even the New York *Times* contributed to damaging revelations by noting that Barry is Jewish—and when I called to complain, asked, "Well, isn't he?" "That's not your business now," I answered. What was it all about, this fantastic push of the most powerful networks and most reputable newspapers to do things *their* way, even when it was so obviously wrong?

*

The journalist, or entertainer, who next moved to center stage was less powerful but equally dangerous. Half a dozen friends and relatives called me to say they had heard Barry Farber, host of a radio show on a local New York station, talking about the situation in a very enterprising way. Since the names of the hostages still hadn't been released, he presumably knew as little as anyone who they were. But he shrewdly guessed that some of their relatives lived in WMCA's listening area of New York, New Jersey, and Connecticut.

My friends said his program mixed national outrage with supposed personal sympathy. Every American was deeply concerned, he pronounced, about the dreadful Iranian abuse of the United States in general and intolerable treatment of American diplomats in particular. Relatives of the hostages were of course especially concerned, but since these were *Americans* being mistreated, the whole country was with them. Surely a relative was listening in right now and would want to give his or her personal opinion about the scandal by telephoning in and speaking to Barry Farber on the air. We all feel so bad, he said. So helpless. Tell us about your hostage and let us at least sympathize with you.

Who accepted this awful invitation? My mother-in-law, a regular listener to the show, heard it as a chance to help Barry. At that anxious time she didn't realize the potential harm of what she was doing, and gave her favorite radio personality a big slice of the melodrama he reveled in. After all, Barry Farber said maybe he could help—without, of course, specifying how.

My mother-in-law's tendency to see herself as jinxed had grown stronger since her husband died, and enough rotten luck plagued her those nine years to confirm her conviction. She was mugged twice; a wheel fell off her car while she was on a highway; when she and I were driving to meet Barry at the airport, her gas tank sprung a leak. While we were being towed away, she recited the litany of her misfortune and kept asking *why*. Her car broke down so often that she took a train to suburban New Jersey to visit Barry's brother; someone threw a stone at the train and a splinter from the cracked window lodged in Sarah's eye.

Naturally, she was gravely distressed and depressed by Barry's still unclear situation. She needed to talk; like a mother in mourning alone, she needed a sympathetic listener. She answered Farber's self-serving overture immediately and opened up to him over the telephone and onto the airwaves. In great detail she told how difficult her life had become even before the hostage burden. She also told him—and Iranians in New York could quickly pass on the particulars to Tehran—about Barry's command of Farsi, his yeshiva education, and much else that filled her with pride. It would have been hard to invent more-damaging information. If a captive wants his captors to know he speaks their language, *he* must decide; that could be crucial. If he is zany enough to want zealous Muslim militants to know they have a Jewish prisoner—no less a yeshiva graduate—that, too, must be his decision.

I had never contradicted Sarah, much less raised my voice with her. This time I began losing control as I dialed her number. My lack of respect was completely out of character. "How dare you broadcast that information?" I challenged. "If you want comfort, why don't you talk to somebody in the family, not to an outsider who wants only to use you? Don't you realize why the State Department is silent about who the hostages are?"

"Barry is my son. Don't tell me what to do about him. I'll talk to whomever I want."

"I'll tell you what to do when you're endangering my husband's life," I said in a voice I hated.

"You think you care about Barry more than I do? I brought him up. Suffered for him. *I'll* do what needs to be done for him—like always."

Our shouts launched a long conflict about who should "represent" Barry to the press. It wasn't prestige or "exposure" that was at issue, but the vital question of who would decide what to stress; who had the right to make public what information. At that point I was furious with Sarah and didn't speak to her for days after slamming down the telephone. Then I waged a long, mostly futile war to get her to discuss matters before revealing them, or at least consider the possible consequences of her emotional releases. But I couldn't really blame her. Understandably, Barry's safety obsessed her, and I felt partly responsible for her anguish after having reassured her so blithely the first day that everything would be settled quickly and happily. Having the ear of my extended family made it easier for me to control my comments to others.

On the other hand, I blamed Farber with all my vengeance. Publicizing Barry's Jewishness made him a possible target for charges of Zionist espionage, or whatever else the "Death to America" chanters might concoct. And Farber outdid himself on his next program, the following afternoon. WMCA advertised the upcoming sensation all day, and Farber was as good as the promises. Over the air, he telephoned the American Embassy in Tehran. This time I was listening, to my horror.

When one of the militants answered, he began yelling. How terrible their behavior was! What were they doing? he demanded to know. Who the hell did they think they were to mistreat American diplomats? I hardly believed what I was hearing. It was so mindless, the potential harm to the hostages was so great, that I blocked the reality. Then I succumbed to visions of the more macho of the militants answering Farber's antics with their own brand: physical pain for the hostages to show who was in charge.

The longer he screamed, the more I heard self-satisfaction in his voice, and without doubt, the more the audience relished the program. Don't you realize what the United States can do to you? he thundered. We can level your oil fields. We can wipe you off the face of the earth!

It was fine third-rate stuff, appealing to the most basic—and base—patriotic instincts. America was not really impotent, you see: Here was brave Barry Farber putting things straight with the militants. Finally he demanded to speak to . . . Barry Rosen, whom he named in another informational giveaway as Press Attaché. I know his mother, he announced, as if threatening the naughty boys. "I demand to speak to Barry Rosen right now."

Never in my thirty-one years had I been so frustrated and angry. Or so helpless. My mother genuinely feared I would have a stroke. What right did Farber have to shout Barry's name to the very people threatening the captives with death? Yet, if something in our broadcasting industry was unhealthy, I was powerless to do anything about it. While my husband's life was at stake, Farber made perfectly clear I was defenseless against journalists who *used* our desperation. *Our* side was shooting away whatever protection anonymity could give. Few names had been divulged at that point. Barry's was by far the most publicized. I was terrified for his safety.

Our telephone had a very long cord. On good days I took it out the front door to the steps, where I would sit with one eye on the children. While Alexander and Ariana played in the yard, often under the maple tree where Barry and I were married, I would talk seemingly to every friend I'd ever had and to an equal flock of new acquaintances. November was unusually warm, although, as luck had it, the month was unusually cold in Tehran. I kept watch of temperature charts in the newspapers. I spent most mornings on the steps in the sunshine of a late Indian summer I didn't think to enjoy. The leaves of the maple, in which Alexander buried himself, were their reddest. Ariana, approaching her sweetest age, made mud pies, leaving the icing on her face. I made an effort to give them their emotional due, but my family had to help. My attention kept going elsewhere.

The telephone rang from nine o'clock in the morning or earlier. Everyone's question was the same: "Any news from Barry?" After I happened to mention to someone in Washington that I had a touch of the flu, five people from five State Department and ICA branches called in the course of an afternoon to ask how I was. There were too many people to talk to for me to need a psychiatrist. I probably wouldn't have had time to fit one in anyway.

A number of Muslims I'd met expressed something near mortification at what was happening in the name of Islam. The Ambassador from Bangladesh, for example, whom I met at a party for the hostages given by the U. S. Mission to the United Nations, apologized profusely for what he called "the terrible, regretful holding of your people, which is a violation, not an expression, of true Islamic law and feeling."

Barry's Iranian friends were among the most concerned of my sympathizers. One, a warm man named David who looked a lot like Barry and acted like my brother, would call in the evening. Barry was close to him during his Peace Corps days and the friendship resumed when David moved to the States in 1970.

He was an Iranian Jew, with shame and guilt that seemed identical to that of the Muslims. The only difference was he apologized for Iran, not Islam. David had nothing whatever to do with the new regime; "the crazy mullahs," as he called them, were "ruining the country and tearing apart family after family—and now yours." He felt so ashamed of what was being done that I often ended by comforting *him.*

He talked about the irony of Barry's treatment in view of his deep feeling for Iran and the wonderful country it used to be—with David no doubt romanticizing life under the Shah. "It's the lunatic fringe who are in control, Barbara, not the Iranian people Barry loved. It's been destroyed now; there's nothing to go back to."

Although I tried not to make it worse for David, one evening he called just after I watched the daily performance on television news. "Did you see the crowds? Day after day! What are they chanting, David? It sounds like 'Bye Bye Carter.'"

"No, Barbara. I'm afraid it's '*Marg bar Karter:* Death to Carter.' But try not to worry. The crowds are making a show. The captives may be held for a while, but Iranians aren't killers."

I didn't ask David why Iranians, who weren't killers, were destroying so many of their own, as he himself had just bitterly regretted. I wanted to believe the hostages would only be held.

I tried not to count days or attach importance to anniversaries, but could not ignore December 4. Passage of a month was sufficient to convince even original optimists like me that something was seriously wrong. Most of the hostage families had been more anxious—or less casual—from the beginning. I was in telephone touch with a number of them through the State Department's Iran Working Group, an outgrowth of the volunteers who had come in to inform the families on the day of the seizure. The approaching holiday season underlined the lack of progress—and the nervousness.

The Iranian situation appeared chaotic, and not only in their government, which was split into jockeying, competing centers of power. Independence movements in Azerbaijan, Kurdestan, and other regions were in armed rebellion and threatening greater disunity, and the economy was disrupted. The captives became the best agent for whipping up nationalistic fervor with which to hold things together. They were being used to blackmail America, but also more and more as a weapon in the struggle to win control of Iran. The more radical politicians, mostly mullahs, accused anyone who favored release, as some in the Foreign Ministry apparently did, of "being soft on American imperialism." Discrediting moderate voices was a way of keeping the revolutionary momentum going, which was ideal for ambitious politicians exploiting issues for personal advantage—and terrible for the hostages.

In my first conversation with the wife of Barry's ICA boss in the Embassy, she predicted the hostages, who included her husband, would be held a long time, maybe even until Christmas. "You must be joking," I said in my näiveté. Although no one had told me officially, it was clear now that Barry was in the Embassy. A newsmagazine ran a photograph of him in mid-November. He and other officers seemed to be eating—standing up—in a messy kitchen, under the eyes of young guards in khaki. Barry's beard had lost its usual neatness and he was standing listlessly, but otherwise he appeared himself. Other hostage families, however, had seen nothing, heard nothing, and knew nothing about their people. Anger was soaring. Bumper stickers and buttons were seen everywhere with warnings to Iran that expressed the outrage of more and more people as their patience ran out.

In their telephone calls to reassure me, I sensed the State Department was becoming nervous lest some families break off and start criticizing the Administration's handling of the situation. It seemed important to them that we remain unified—under their guidance—so as to show no disunity to the outside world and open up no opportunity for ambitious American politicians to exploit the frustration. In any case, the Administration clearly felt the time had come to soothe the growing "hysteria," as a State Department official put it, and answer some of the families' questions. A briefing was arranged and one round-trip ticket to Washington sent to each family.

The briefing was to be held in the State Department Building, which was enough to make me nervous. It didn't help that this was to be my first meeting with a dozen important officials, or that we were directed to the impressive entrance for visiting dignitaries with an array of flags hanging over marble floors. I was always able to express my opinion to Barry easily enough. The problem never presented itself when I was with my family. But meeting new people could make me ill, especially when a gathering involved something official.

A year and a half before, when Barry was working for Voice of America and we were living in a Washington suburb, I would have been happier to receive a court summons than an invitation to an ICA reception. Barry wasn't fond of the diplomatic social scene either; he preferred spending time with family or close friends, very informally. But once inside the most elegant or intellectual door, he was off discussing, analyzing, and joking with the best of them. I never knew what to say and would beg Barry to find an excuse for going without me. "What can I possibly discuss with those people?" I would appeal. "My torture doesn't even produce interesting conversation for them, so why do you have to take me along?"

I had a master's degree in teaching and a respectable record in the classroom. I was a thirty-year-old mother of two whose husband had been away a full year. Yet I remained dependent in many ways. I wouldn't dream of staying in a hotel alone, or even dining by myself in a restaurant. Unless I could gobble something at a counter, I would rather not eat when I had no company.

But events in Tehran modified that. Who else could deal with the press and the State Department? I had to, and having a concrete issue made it easier. I had firm ideas about the subject; there was no need to search for something to say. I was surprised at how easy "socializing" was when the purpose was essential business.

The morning I flew to Washington I still didn't quite know what to make of the Iranian revolution. But the rights and wrongs of the hostage situation were clear. There was no reason to pretend the revolutionaries didn't have sound grievances—which gave them no right to commit their own wrongs. Whatever America did have to answer for in its relationship with the Shah, the CIA didn't teach SAVAK to beat on soles of feet; torture was a long tradition there. It was Iranians practicing it on other Iranians, and now it was Iranians acting out their revenge on innocents, including some who cared deeply for their country. My willingness to make allowances for an oppressed people was used up.

And it seemed to me our approaches to Tehran were flabby. My initial expectation of quick release was probably shared by the Administration. Holding diplomats hostage was so outlandish and outrageous that it might not have been taken seriously as a long-term possibility at first. Reassuring calls from the State Department made sense to me then. But wasn't it time to recognize we were going nowhere?

After the first few weeks of seizure, the "tone" of the situation was clear and my reaction had begun to take shape. We were faced with completely abnormal diplomatic practice. Therefore I believed President Carter should order an end to every interaction with Iran under his control. Whether he did that quietly or dramatically probably wouldn't matter much. The main consideration was that the United States be seen turning away from criminals, not trying to deal with them. *All* contact with Iran, without exception, should have been ended until the hostages were returned. It had to be made absolutely clear there would be no negotiation and no compromise on that one issue.

If the President had no right to direct American journalists to leave Tehran, he should have exerted moral pressure on them to do so. I felt he could have done that relatively easily by pointing to the moral wrong of giving publicity to terrorists committing a repugnant act. The press couldn't be expected to leave Iran of its own accord, but surely would have heeded the appeal of genuine leadership. War and other emergencies provided precedents of sacrificing some of "the story" for larger national interest—and we were in one of those emergencies.

I was convinced that if the President had done this on the first day, the captives would have been home quickly. From what Barry had told me, Iranians are bargainers almost by nature. What good would their "prizes" do if we refused to bid for them? The other comparison that occurred to me after watching the screaming crowds in Tehran was that of children rebelling against their parents and taking satisfaction from the act itself, irrespective of whatever demands went with it. Had we walked away, leaving the student militants howling on the kitchen floor, they might have soon given up. The pleasure is almost all in observing the effect achieved.

The earlier the intended audience makes apparent it will *not* watch, the better. The strategy, it seemed to me, was for the President to pull everything American out of Iran, enforce a total embargo on words and goods, and wait, as a strong parent waits. His one warning should have been about the hostages' safety. "This much I caution you," the President should have said. "Do not let harm come to any of our people. We can do nothing about your holding them short of military action, which we are not planning now. But we will not deal with you or with any intermediary in any manner until those men and women are free."

Of course I understood such a stance involved risk. I'd have willingly taken it for Barry, since I felt certain the risk of our present policy—playing into the militants' hands by showing how much their tantrum pained us—was greater. It encouraged them to push their price higher, increasing the possibility of accident and ensuring a longer hold on their human goods. At the same time, something told me they wouldn't physically harm the hostages. People who are going to punch *do* it, rather than wave fists into the camera every day.

We needed to play their game, behind a captain with good nerves and will as strong as theirs. The President's intentions seemed fine and he made some good points, such as insisting he was not interested in debates about the Shah or Iranian history but only "in the day when we will see the hostages come home." That wasn't enough.

I had paid too little attention to the presidency until that Sunday-morning telephone call about the Embassy. But the criticism of Mr. Carter's indecisiveness in general was beginning to seem justified, judging by his handling of the Iran crisis. He acted on a bit of this and threatened a bit of that, and appeared unable to take a decisive step and stick to it—while the militants jeered "Carter cannot do anything." But only he could provide the genuine leadership needed in a troubled period.

Because he lacked the strength to take painful but probably peace-ensuring decisions, I feared he might give in to pressure to take the "easier" course of military action, for which some editorialists had begun to call. If war did erupt, surely the hostages would be among the first casualties. Aside from that, what would war accomplish besides more death and more trouble? Yet, the President would be facing reelection soon. Dispatching the troops in a patriotic cause almost always got even unpopular leaders reelected. . . .

＊

The briefing for family members was a kind of preventive medicine against anger, which was "not what we need," an undersecretary of state told us. We were asked to support the policy of negotiations with the "coolness of determination." The opening session was devoted to summaries of what had happened since November 4 and countermeasures under consideration.

Secretary of State Cyrus Vance visited the afternoon session with President Carter, who came to hearten us. They walked in together from behind a curtain in the auditorium as if to a news conference. Too folksy to appear presidential, Jimmy Carter said nothing that reassured me about the necessary strong leadership.

But he reassured us on another point: Visibly moved and perhaps even slightly nervous by the sight of us all together, he stressed how sorry he felt for the hostages and for us, and how committed he was to using only diplomatic means to free our people. He would not endanger a single life, he pledged; his goals were protecting the lives of the hostages and preserving the national honor—in that order. "I am not going to take any military action that would cause bloodshed or arouse the unstable captors of our hostages to attack them or punish them."

Then it was time for photographs, during which individuals and groups went up to speak with the President. In my moment with him I mentioned how relieved I was by his promise. I wanted to say more about how dangerous military force would be but felt that would be out of place. Handing Mr. Carter snapshots of Alexander and Ariana I carried in my wallet, I asked him to remember that their father was trapped in Iran. "If you consider using guns, I hope you'll think of the chance Barry will have," I said.

The President put the photos in his pocket and shook my hand before moving to the next person. I hoped I hadn't been presumptuous with the world's most powerful man.

Barry Farber's telephone "confrontation" with the Tehran militants was only act one, scene one, of the treatment of the crisis by the press. During the first weeks, I continued to believe there might be some strength in anonymity and in numbers: in trying to get the militants to see their captives as a group, not as individuals they would like more or less, therefore punish more or less. The less attention focused on an individual hostage the better, I felt. Journalists worked at the opposite, searching furiously for names and personal data. The hunt was on. Anyone who might know something about a hostage was steadily hounded, especially relatives.

Despite my efforts to restrain Barry's mother, she remained vulnerable to most inquiries. Once she revealed herself to Farber, seemingly every local reporter on the hostage story called her. They also bombarded a Barbara Rosen of Brooklyn with day and night calls. Later they told me that in trying to track me down they had run through the thousands of Rosens in the telephone directories of the five boroughs. But I was living with my parents, the Bogutskis. Two years later, that other Mrs. Rosen is still receiving calls intended for me.

I managed to "hide" for months. A reporter at my first news conference asked where I lived. "In the greater metropolitan area," some instinct told me to answer. "Can you narrow that down for us?" she pressed. I stuck to my vagueness. By then people recognized me on the street, for I had become a kind of standby on programs about the hostages. But my press "career" began accidentally.

I had no direct contact with reporters until the Iran Working Group asked if I was willing to be interviewed. If there was any likelihood the program would be seen in Iran, I thought, the chance of reaching Iranian wives and mothers seemed worth the effort. It was more productive than sitting home and bottling up my worry. And now that Barry was known to be held, there was no point to remaining silent to shield him. On the contrary, publicity might offer some protection—provided, of course, I said nothing inciting. It might even protect against our own government. "Hostage" was an abstraction with no real identification to the public. If hostages became individuals, it might be less easy to sacrifice them in pursuit of a larger national objective.

I also felt I had something to say by that time. Much of it was in reaction to false and misleading impressions the press itself was spreading. It seemed to me most journalists were failing by far to provide a balanced, useful picture of Iran. Apart from a few exceptions, they were dealing more in stereotyped images of the bearded bad guys with the religious fanaticism than in sober—therefore useful—information. Almost no background of Iran's people, history, or culture was given. I was far from an expert, but no one could know Barry for eight years without picking up at least some rudimentary knowledge.

Apart from worry about him, I had originally felt some sympathy with the revolution. That came from his explanations of the shortcomings of the Shah's regime. Iranians who wanted genuine, deep reform probably had to do something fairly drastic to put across their point of view, especially to most Americans, whose impressions of the country were so colored by the Shah's perspective. Releasing the hostages after a week would have made their point, and perhaps even won prestige, especially among Third World countries. Now they were losing almost everyone's respect and soiling their own cause.

The cowardice of the Tehran government, demonstrated by its rush to jump on the bandwagon of the embassy invaders rather than halting their flagrant misconduct, had rapidly thinned my sympathy for the revolution. But one didn't have to support one side or the other to object to the nonsense in so much American reporting. It was one thing to present Khomeini as a diabolical genius hypnotizing a great mass of Iranian fanatics, which could be someone's honest opinion. But maintaining that the American prisoners were being starved because they got only soup and crackers for dinner showed little more than ignorance of Iran, where the main meal is usually in the afternoon and supper often consists of soup. Cultural differences were at least part of the problem. Apparently some of the hostages had trouble adjusting to Iranian food, because this was their first contact with it, having lived in the patch of American suburbia known as the diplomatic enclave. In any case, it seemed to me that no good was being accomplished by leaping on departure from American habit as automatically sinister.

I was astonished at the abysmally low level of knowledge about Iran and that so few introduced balanced information into the emoting and guessing. The most serious failure, it seemed, was inability, or unwillingness, to convey the depth of anti-Americanism and its sources. How could we find a solution to the problem when we were fooling ourselves with caricatures? Most of the press was offering comic-book pictures of the militants as religious kooks, together with "human interest" stories, a kind of gossip about the personal lives of the hostages. I decided to try to give some of the in-between factual information I had, about Iran's background as well as Barry.

The first interview was with a European news service, which is why I hoped it might be shown in Iran. The children were to appear too, and I prayed they would draw the camera away from Barry's "darling introvert."

Shortly after the first session with the foreign crew, the State Department asked me to a second, for the American public. Together with a sister of Kathryn Koob, one of the two remaining women hostages, I was to be interviewed by Tom Snyder, of NBC's "Tomorrow" show. We were very nervous as we waited in the studio, watching the taping of earlier segments of the program. With lives at stake, every word seemed crucial, but no one gave us any suggestion of the questions we would be asked so we could think about intelligent responses. At the last moment, during the commercial preceding our segment, we were ushered in to Mr. Snyder.

Nothing was said about reimbursement for travel expenses to the studio, and I was too green to ask. But when the interview ended, I did ask if I might have a copy of the tape for Barry to view when he came home. "It will cost you one hundred and fifty dollars," the producer said without embarrassment. I also asked whether something I said could be changed. For the first time, I had referred to the militants as "terrorists" and panicked the moment it left my mouth: What if my slip hurt Barry?

"Can't you *please* do something about that one word?" I pleaded. "It's not a silly whim."

"I'm sorry, the tape's completed. And you signed a release." Indeed I had signed a release—and still didn't know that completed tapes were spliced at will to make interviewers and masters of ceremonies appear as impressive as possible. I backed off apologetically, to days of fretting over my mistake.

A third interview followed shortly, on CBS. This time I appeared with Louisa Kennedy, wife of Moorhead Kennedy and probably the most active member of a hostage family. But the star of that show was so impressed with himself, he barely noticed Louisa, let alone me. We were in the makeup room when Stanley Siegel entered. I was less nervous about the camera by then but submerged in pessimism about the lack of progress in freeing our people. The militants seemed to be gaining rather than losing support, and the Iranian Government was apparently too weak or simply unwilling to take control of the Embassy. I wanted to talk about the whole, grim situation, with its growing complexity and hazards, but the show had other priorities. After a brief hello, a long speech about his girl friend, and a longer monologue about his dog, Mr. Siegel approached a mirror to perform a set of facial exercises. While he stretched his mouth open like a fish against the glass, my own mouth dropped open. Finally the star turned back to us and in a tone that suggested we would now move on to the business at hand, he began talking about . . . a Central Park walk he'd just enjoyed. It was as though he had made up his mind to avoid all thought of the tiresome Iranian problem by sticking to chatter about himself.

Self-absorption was the rule; few interviewers raised serious questions. Few seemed able to, because most had done little homework on Iran. Questions ranged from the irrelevant to the silly, and repetition of the obvious appeared more sought after than complexity or ambiguity. *Everyone* asked how long the hostages had been held. Instead of dealing with what motivated Iranians and how this derived from their social and political realities, it was always vitally important to establish the precise number of days—as if that weren't in the newspapers every day anyway; as if that were the key concept.

No matter how empty their questions, almost all interviewers preened for them. The primary goal seemed appearance, not substance: making as striking an impression as possible on the screen. Shallowness almost crossed the line to phoniness.

It took time to comprehend that not Barry, not all the hostages together, and certainly not Iran was what mattered; *looking good* was top priority. There were exceptions among individual reporters, of course, but each studio I visited was pervaded by a striving for the *image* that would deliver success. Celebrity—not the news, not the truth—paid off in the local news scramble.

Having to look good meant sometimes reshooting sequences several times when the effect, not the content, was judged wanting. It was also why producers told hosts and others what expressions to assume during cutaway shots. "No, no—furrow your brow a bit more . . . now look straight ahead, and a little more serious." The serious look was often requested of interviewers who had asked ridiculous questions, stumbling over themselves when something slightly serious arose. That kind of direction, more suitable to movie-making than news-reporting, startled me.

I participated in several documentaries that did *not* sensationalize or trivialize the issues. Some, such as *The Hostages: One Year,* were simply a summing up, in this case on the anniversary of the Embassy's seizure. But even these conveyed something false. They were made into little dramas, slick *shows.* I understood that there would be insufficient audience without a comprehensible narrative. What bothered me was the extent to which selling techniques were introduced, such as hammy lead-ups to commercial breaks and neat endings, maybe to compete with cute audience-grabbers elsewhere on television. Even those better documentaries were packaged as a commercial product that wasn't straightforward. If they weren't selling advertising time, they were selling the network itself, which promoted its own stars and crowed praise for its own work in the same-pitched tones as ordinary advertising. Promoting of news people as stars, incidentally, transformed the profession partly into show business. And the "look-at-me" attitude hardly helped viewers grapple with the issues.

The format itself of most shows was distracting. With one segment devoted to a publicity-puff chat with a Hollywood personality and the next to a demonstration by a snake charmer or fashion designer, how could the audience take seriously the third segment's conversation about Iran? Jumps from one to the other brought the hostage issue to the level of the others: entertainment.

Was all broadcast journalism so superficial? I wondered. Apparently not. A day in advance of a scheduled interview for the BBC, the producer discussed possible relevant questions with me. Reporters were well informed and allowed me to express my thoughts without interjecting quips to take the spotlight on themselves. This was professionalism: The objective was information, not drama. Notes were even taken, to make follow-up questions more meaningful.

Public television, especially "Bill Moyers' Journal" and "The Mac-Neil-Lehrer Report," were outstanding. Among newspapers, the shining exception was *The Christian Science Monitor,* which, like the BBC, is run on noncommercial principles. Their interview too was free of the Hollywood slant—or any slant—and another example that confirmed my impression that most of what I, a fairly average reader and listener, had been accepting as intelligent, valid reporting, was not.

It was—in contrast especially to the BBC—a collection of snippets of Iranian excesses, with almost no social and political background. It was Iranian fists being waved in the faces of blindfolded Americans, without explanation of what caused the outrage. It was vivid, dramatic crisis journalism, perfect for the camera and for stimulating emotion without thought. To me, the proof of this came when a media expert named William Adams discovered that in the entire year of 1973, when American military aid to and involvement in Iran were enormous, ABC, NBC, and CBS devoted an average of four and a half minutes of airtime to coverage of the country. When Americans were physically threatened, this coverage was multiplied by *over a hundred and fifty times,* to seven hundred minutes. For two solid months after the second Embassy seizure, over half of every weeknight newscast went to the crisis, night after night. And very little more was explained, or learned, about essential facts and underlying causes.

Was personal involvement making me too harsh a critic? Pains in my neck and lower back developed after the first week, when my nonchalant confidence in Barry's quick return faded. A day of bad news laid me low, and I wondered whether I was relieving some anxiety by being overcritical of television people, who were naturally less involved.

Television helped in certain ways—which is why I kept appearing. It was the best medium for expressing an opinion to a large audience. It also brought Barry from a faceless hostage to an individual people felt they knew, therefore were more concerned about. That was accomplished by the very personal approach that was so cheapening when carried too far.

My complaint was the tendency to concentrate almost entirely on

July 1972.

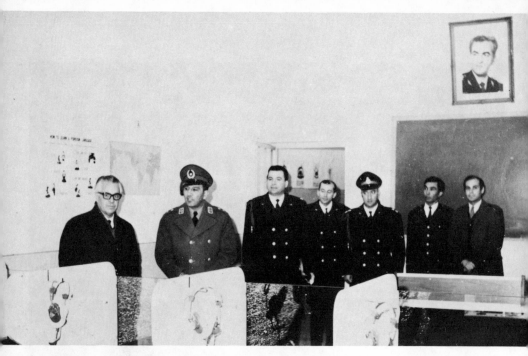

Barry (r.) and his class in language lab. (Note Shah's picture.)

Last family photo before Barry left for Iran.

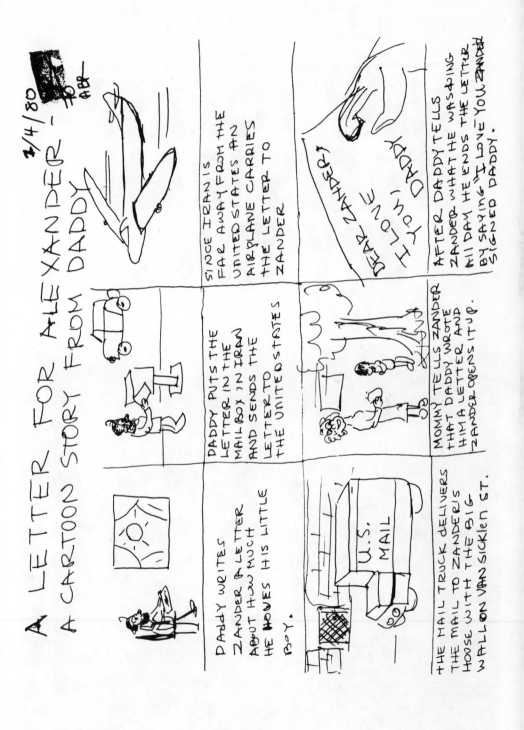

Carey to dump Ted unless he sweeps N.H.: Page 4

NEW YORK POST

TODAY
Cloudy, windy, 30s

TONIGHT
Mostly clear, teens

TOMORROW
Partly sunny, high 20s
Details, Page 2

FINAL
TODAY'S PRICES

TV listings: P. 27   WEDNESDAY, JANUARY 23, 1980   25 CENTS

© 1980 News Group Publications Inc. Vol. 179, No. 56

LARGEST-SELLING AFTERNOON NEWSPAPER IN AMERICA

DAILY
SALES
EXCEED 640,000

NEW YORKER FACES IRAN SPY TRIAL

President Carter is holding pictures of Rosen children.

*Picture sent to Barbara to reassure her
during his confinement.*

Grandma kisses Congressman Biaggi after receiving her citizenship.
COURTESY, THE NEWS

SPORTS FINAL

★★★★

DAILY ◎ NEWS

Showers.
Afternoon clearing.
High in low 60s.
Details on page 79.

Vol. 61. No. 262   New York, Friday, April 25, 1980   Price 25 cents

IRAN RESCUE TRY FAILS

8 Yanks die as planes collide

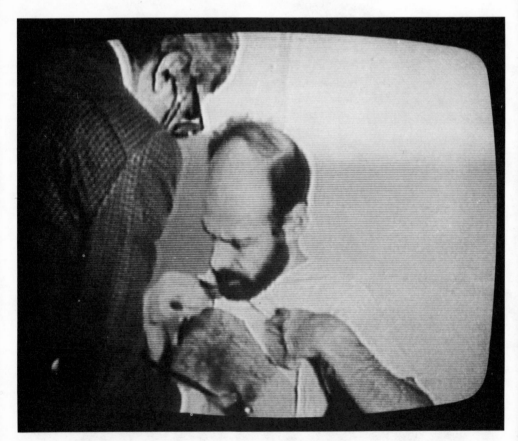

An Iranian Red Cross doctor examines Barry during the worst of his illness. This was shown on American television.
COURTESY, WIDE WORLD PHOTOS

Barry carried this with him always.

Left to right: Giscard d'Estaing, Barbara Rosen, Pearl Golacinski, Louise Kennedy, Jeanne Queen.

With Chancellor Helmut Schmidt.

BJB006(0524)(1-000038I019045)PD 01/19/81 0512
TWX WHITEHOUSE WSH DLY PD
045 DLY GOVT WHITE HOUSE DC JAN 18
PMS MRS. BARBARA ROSEN
C/O JOHN BOGUTSKI, DLR DONT DWR
354 VAN SICKLEN ST.
BROOKLYN NY 11223

    I HAVE JUST LEARNED THAT AN AGREEMENT FOR THE HOSTAGES'
RELEASE HAS BEEN REACHED. THE STATE DEPARTMENT WILL KEEP
YOU INFORMED OF FURTHER DETAILS AS WE LEARN THEM. WITH THE
HOSTAGES' RELEASE THE PRAYERS OF MILLIONS OF AMERICANS AND
PEOPLE AROUND THE WORLD WILL BE ANSWERED. THE DIGNITY AND
COURAGE THAT YOU HAVE SHOWN DURING THE MONTHS YOU HAVE WAITED
FOR THE HOSTAGES' SAFE RETURN WILL BE REMEMBERED.

    JIMMY CARTER AND ROSALYNN CARTER

SF-1001 (R5-69)

Boarding Algerian airplane to leave Iran.

"All the News That's Fit to Print"

The New York Times

CITY EDITION

Metropolitan area weather: Partly sunny today; cloudy tonight, tomorrow. Temperature range: today 28-38; yesterday 36-43. Details on page D21.

VOL.CXXX .... No. 44,835   Copyright © 1981 The New York Times   —NEW YORK, WEDNESDAY, JANUARY 21, 1981—   30 cents beyond 50-mile zone from New York City. Higher at air delivery cities.   25 CENTS

REAGAN TAKES OATH AS 40TH PRESIDENT; PROMISES AN 'ERA OF NATIONAL RENEWAL'

MINUTES LATER, 52 U.S. HOSTAGES IN IRAN FLY TO FREEDOM AFTER 444-DAY ORDEAL

The children with Barbara's parents.

Haggard but free, Wiesbaden, January 21, 1981.

Barry's first night home.

Brooklyn neighbors greeting Barry.

Barbara and Barry in ticker-tape parade, New York City.
COURTESY, PAUL MONASTER, THE NEWS

President Reagan presenting Barry with a box containing a miniature United States flag.

Barry, his mother, and family, with Robert Hess (r.), President of Brooklyn College. (COURTESY, GEORGE BING / BROOKLYN COLLEGE)

emotion: "We wonder what you are really feeling now that Barry has been captive for _____ days." Didn't the issues lie in Tehran and Washington? Wasn't how I felt largely irrelevant? In any case, didn't those feelings belong to *me?* I soon sensed *they* regarded events and policy as decidedly secondary.

What was accomplished by the public observing Barry's mother weeping? They milked her for tears, which made dramatic viewing. And I realized they didn't care whom they hurt for a "heart-stirring" clip on the evening news—instead of facts and opinions to provoke thought.

Watching our own set with my new insights, I realized that all the hostage families, and even the hostages themselves, were being used in competition for audience rating. Slotted among panty-hose and peanut-butter commercials, cartoons and product-pushing quiz shows, news people tried to maintain they were serious islands in the sea of makebelieve. Their pretense was all the shakier because the news, too, used movie techniques and the star system in quest of the same end: rating.

I came to view the key influence on the treatment of public affairs as soap opera. That genre was becoming the most successful seller, making inroads into evening prime time too. I couldn't help likening "Tune in to Dallas to learn what happens to J.R." to "Don't miss the evening news to learn what is happening with Bani-Sadr and our captives." It was the "soap" of 1980: Every effort was made to sell it as a continuing story.

＊

On a personal level, almost without exception reporters were gracious. Who would risk rudeness to the wife of a hostage, for whom the country now spilled over with sympathy? Only a rare aggressive type and the few who announced pure invention, such as my alleged diction lessons, as a news item. My grievance wasn't with the reporters.

On the contrary, I began to feel a bond with many. It was turning out that while they were exploiting the Iran situation, they in turn were being exploited. When I walked off-camera with some journalists, I didn't hide my sometimes extremely critical feelings. Most of them agreed with me.

Included were big names of network news, some of whom had reported from Iran themselves before American journalists were expelled. They said that even then the impression of the country given by the American press, especially television, was shallow and misleading. Khomeini, for example, was portrayed as an evil fanatic without explanation of *why* the majority of Iranians almost worshiped him.

"But you people were reporting from the field," I would reply. "Are you saying your own coverage was bad?"

It almost had to be bad, I was told, because producers of news shows demanded good footage, meaning *action*. Reporters explaining a complex story lacked punch; they wanted the crowds frothing at the mouth outside the Embassy. "I sent all the serious background stuff I dared to New York," one respected reporter told me. "But it never made the evening news. I kept getting orders for more of the chanting crowds." I ended by feeling sympathy for many reporters in their frustration.

The producers, some of whom agreed with the criticism, blamed the executives. The executives blamed their bosses in corporate headquarters—who, in turn, were under pressure from ratings figures and their effect on advertisers.

I had been taught that competition is good for quality and essential to full freedom of the press. But the BBC was better by far without scrambling for advertising dollars. The effects I saw of competition in the electronic media were largely degrading. Everyone could excuse his failure—departure from his professional and moral standards—as inherently necessary to stay in business. Competition often seemed more a rat race to disseminate rumor and innuendo than a spur to better reporting. Many fine reporters, apologetic or defensive, knew what was wrong but couldn't even begin to change the system.

I was beginning to grasp that a press both reflects and molds a country. The news is crucial in forming our view of the world—but who decides what news we see and read, and according to what criteria? The damage from the race for ratings goes farther than the studio and even than the television screen. I was also beginning to see the connection between that and other ills—the commercial frenzy, sinking standards in education and taste—and the same race for ratings. I had read about the effects of television violence and advertising, but what about hyped news? That seemed another poison in the national bloodstream. While these thoughts were forming, I happened to see a clip of a father who had just been told his wife had burned their son to death in their oven. The camera zoomed in on the father in his disbelieving grief, cut to the oven, then back to the father's pitiful face. Was that "news" edifying? Did the man have a right to private grief? Why was that item used when the program skipped legislation pending in City Hall and Albany, not to mention developments in Asia and Africa? We hear almost nothing about South American countries until an American businessman is kidnaped in one.

Within months I was solidly—but privately—skeptical about the press. I kept my smile intact because I had a job to do. A boycott for my new principles would be no use to Barry, so I clenched my teeth, let them use me for their purposes, and used them for mine. I thought of the paradox of Barry's yearning to return to America, which never looked better to him, while my eyes were being opened for the first time by involvement in governmental and journalistic realities.

*

Even in the hostage affair, there was no bad without good. One of the positive effects of my press involvement was the civic maturing of my grandmother.

It wasn't *necessarily* true that she was ninety years old. Various papers testified to various dates of birth. When her worried Italian father said she was too young to go to America, she got the required documents without his permission by using an elder sister's birth certificate. That accounted for at least one discrepancy.

Although she emigrated in the early 1900s she hardly learned to speak English, let alone write it, and therefore could not become a citizen. Gabe Pressman, a well-known New York newsman, arrived at the house one day despite my having said I couldn't squeeze in an interview. Waiting to catch me between errands, he got into conversation with my grandmother, who told him her life story. He passed it on to Mario Biaggi, a Bronx congressman. Within a month, Congress passed a law enabling her to apply for citizenship. "Who was the first President of the United States?" was the sum and substance of her test.

She answered with great pride, and the entire family celebrated royally what my grandmother kept calling the happiest day of her life. "The only thing that could make me more happy is Barry's return," she announced. Too feeble to leave the house to pray for him in church, she did it in her rocking chair at her picture window, fingering a worn rosary. She is extremely religious, but I had never seen her pray more intensely. It was as if her devotion to family had shifted almost entirely to "her" Barry. Sometimes she growled that he was being "tortured" because that man Carter was doing nothing to get him home. The President's image on television occasionally provoked a loud "Pooh!"

My own doubts about President Carter were growing, but to blame him alone was like cursing him for the oil squeeze. The more I thought about it, the more responsibility I attributed to the media.

When Secretary of Defense Brown and others appeared on talk shows, interviewers badgered them about what military action was planned. Would Iranian ships be sunk in the Persian Gulf? Would cities be bombed? Which cities? What facilities would our planes use to get there? I wanted to shout into the screen that television is not the place for discussing military plans.

It was no accident that the crowds outside the Embassy came to life, like so many of our own demonstrators, when television crews arrived. After the first weeks, chanting of hate-America slogans began only when the cameras were ready for what a British journalist called "the greatest show in Tehran." "The big crowds were like professional extras," he observed, "as they chanted and raised their fists for the cameras." No other cue was needed. Those people knew how to use our media.

Did the media mind being used? Weren't they actually working *with* the captors, to mutual advantage? It was hard to believe Iranian diplomats in New York telling our television audiences that the militants had every right to seize the Embassy, that holding the hostages was a humanitarian act! It was less believable when American reporters in Tehran asked the militants, for benefit of the camera, how they would respond to a military attack from Washington. During World War II, would the country have tolerated American reporters asking Japanese officers how they would react to specified actions by President Roosevelt?

Maybe in a free country it is necessary to give airtime to people who have committed aggression against its territory and citizens. But I couldn't believe it was necessary to subsidize the aggressors. When American networks *bought films from them,* I felt they had touched bottom in their morality. Surely they had lost all sense of right and wrong, abandoned all concern for anything except selfish interest. Never mind that on one occasion they handed over $36,000 to the kidnapers. The principle would be as despicable if they had paid less.

For the networks' blood money, hostage families were given the privilege of seeing their loved ones on film for a minute or two. But seeing Barry on the screen as a prisoner had to be measured in terms of the crucial matter of getting him home, which was almost certainly delayed by the networks' willingness to do business with the kidnapers. A few principled people refused the temptation. John Kifner, of the New York *Times,* wrote with great honesty about the militants and the American journalists tending to "serve each others' needs"— which were far from the needs of the hostages or the country. Ford Rowan, NBC's Pentagon reporter, resigned in protest over network manipulation by the militants. But these courageous acts only underscored the general willingness to sell out.

The networks explained their action in terms of "public interest" and concern for the families. But of course it wasn't for the families that these tainted clips were bought and broadcast. If it were, the networks would first have shown them privately to family members, which was never done.

The closest approximation in my case was a call from NBC two minutes before they were going to run a film shot inside the embassy compound. That gave just time enough to alert Barry's mother and brother. Then the clip was aired, and I had to fight against blacking out. The shock came in waves. Barry looked as though he was being eaten alive by some desperate illness.

Regret for having called his mother mixed with despair. With no warning, alone in her apartment, she was confronted with that ghastly portrait of her son. But the network had said nothing to prepare me, and minutes after the showing, the representative phoned again to invite me to the studio. He suggested a film of me watching and reacting to the devastating sight of Barry—which, he said, would be very effective.

Even without this particular callousness, television's dealings with the militants were abhorrent. Had they hyped so many products, shows, and stars that they didn't recognize what hyping the militants meant? Many Americans were warning that terrorism would be the prime security problem of the 1980s. Few went on to note that the media were part of the problem. Most terrorist groups were small and would wither without publicity. American television was supplying that now, together with dollars—and the militants were thriving.

The problem of how to report as accurately and fully as possible *without* nourishing terrorist groups was real, and sharpened in this case by expulsion of American correspondents from Iran. I was as far as anyone from a solution. To enact any form of censorship would also be a victory for extremists, who placed a free press high on their list of dislikes. A sense of responsibility seemed the only answer, as it had always been. The critical issue was how to apply that responsibility in the new age of network competition with its "Dramatic New Hostage Film! Stay Tuned to This Channel!"

When I recovered from the futile rage over this dishonorable deal for "good footage," I thought about freedom of the press and the national interest. I agreed that journalists were right in trying to establish their own code of conduct and guarding against others seeking to impose standards on them. If that right were given to Washington officials, I realized, they would soon be using it for *their* interests. Yet I couldn't reconcile journalists fighting against outside control only to succumb to advertising pressure.

"It's what they want. If we don't show it, the other channels will." "Who's going to pay if we don't get the ratings?" These were comments by respected correspondents with reputations for exposing other people's failures. They didn't need me to tell them some of their "best" stories weakened and cheapened our country. Maybe it was only natural that so few were willing to sacrifice salary and celebrity, even when their own films pricked their conscience. But not having protested their networks doing business with terrorists, where would they draw the line?

The Personnel Department of ICA had promised to bring me back from Iran just about now, in early December. A year without family was considered enough. And what a year this one had been! I realized I had been living under "revolutionary stress" since the evening of my arrival. Again I remembered that the entire embassy staff of November 1978 was now home or reassigned except for two political officers, two military attachés, and me.

In fact, I had agreed to extend two more months while my replacement was being crash-trained in Farsi. Washington had requested this, although I had made no secret of my wish to go home. My new target date was February 14, 1980, the anniversary of the Embassy's first seizure. So I might have considered this little confinement as part of my service. Living conditions were still slightly uncomfortable, especially the prohibition against talking. But what was so terrible about a month of silence? Ordinarily we all chattered too much, myself as much as anyone. Instead of chewing over this new experience, I might have used the silence to think more deeply about it. There was certainly much to think about, from the way most revolutions disappoint and degenerate, to what I wanted to do with my career now that Iran was a dead end. If I'd been offered such a spell—of thinking and reading my fill—I might have thought seriously about taking it.

However, I thought of little beyond the fact of captivity. The reality was worse than what I'd have imagined. It seemed that this, on top of the previous year's tension, was pushing me toward some kind of limit. The recognition was sinking in that we were *prisoners,* with no real hope of ending the condition. It wasn't an adventure but a seemingly permanent pushing of our noses in dirt.

Although I sensed that I had to stay busy to keep from reaching that limit, preoccupation with indignity drained my concentration on anything else. The long hours to do what I wanted was in fact the opposite of free time. Maybe the opportunity to analyze and joke with my "cell mates" could have relieved the oppressiveness, but I doubted that. I could not adjust to loss of control over my life.

I brooded over the reasons for this because a peculiar bug had begun to work on me. The symptoms were physical, but what was the cause? I tried to ignore them, with almost no success. Ordinary sounds began to affect me strangely. The opening and closing of our door cut through me like a rusty blade; the slight creak—which the others whispered was all it was—made me jump. At the same time, I was growing restless, so much so that sitting still had become a minor agony. It was as if some relentless internal growth were putting pressure on my skin from the inside. The problem sounded silly, even to me, but not being able to move from our tiny confines gave no way to relieve it. Whatever was building inside me seemed harder than my nerves, stronger than my will.

I was also having trouble sleeping. I wasn't really afraid, yet couldn't shut off a motor that generated a growing current of anxiety. Anxiety about nothing specific; anxiety, it seemed, for the sake of anxiety. My ritual was to picture Barbara and the children in the Brooklyn yard. The children would wave and I'd wave back. "Go inside, kids; it's cold," I would tell them. "I'll see you soon." I replayed the scene hundreds of times after the lights went out, at 10 P.M. Sleep never came until early morning and rarely lasted more than an hour at a time.

During the day, I ran in place as much as I could. But this didn't satisfy my craving to get up, get out, and *move*. It was as though my need to walk had been compressed into a black hole that sucked the rest of me into its vortex. I cut the days up: If I made it without trouble until lunch; if I could make it to supper. . . . "Keep going, Barry. Don't dwell on it. Read your book!"

But a clutch of bright omens appeared. During the first week of December, heavy gunfire broke out somewhere in Tehran and lasted a full fifteen minutes. I sensed it was south of us. Was the Embassy being stormed? It was maddening to think we would be missed; surely no one on our side knew where we were. But the appearance alone of something *different* lifted my spirits and put new color into my daily daydreams of slipping out the window, if the guard fell asleep, then out of the country via Tehran's alleys. For a few days I felt almost good. Things might be turning.

On December 6 or 7, the whispering and rustling of a move sounded through the night. The next night, we three were blindfolded, packed into what felt like the same van, and driven . . . somewhere downhill, in the general direction of central Tehran. Things *were* turning! Downhill was toward the American Embassy. Sure enough, a gate was opened and our van crossed three mounds in the road. The only ones I knew in Tehran were the Embassy's. The bump-bump-bump made the springs creak and my heart soar. "My God, we're back! It must mean we're going to be released. Maybe tomorrow!"

I couldn't sleep that evening, either, but because anticipation kept leapfrogging my happiness. All night I kept feeling the bump-bump-bump, which inflated me more and more into a marvelous high. Besides, not sleeping was almost a pleasure there.

I was assigned to the Green Room, in the guest quarters of the Ambassador's residence. For the first time since we were captured, we spent the night in a heated room and on a genuine mattress. It felt like a royal bed.

The following days brought more hopeful signs. I was shifted twice to other rooms on the same floor of the Ambassador's private residence. The bindings were removed from our hands. We were permitted to use the toilet and shower adjoining our room by asking and without escort. We were served steak (from commissary supplies), and I remembered from my prison reading the better food that often precedes release, when captors want captives to look healthy and remember them well. We even got a daily Geritol and joked in gestures that we sure *did* have tired blood.

To crown the improvement, we were taken outside, one at a time, for exercise. *Outside!* Never mind that it was a courtyard of about twenty by thirty feet facing the cook's quarters, with air-conditioning motors and a metal pole for drying the Ambassador's laundry. Every tired and trite phrase about the preciousness of being free raced through my thoughts. I realized I had known nothing about freedom —and couldn't have known anything until I was deprived of it, then given back this tiny portion in the courtyard, with promise of the rest of it very soon.

When my turn came, I jogged as much as I could during the allotted twenty minutes. When I was called back in, I carefully removed a leaf from an ivy vine and put it in my pocket. The guard who was watching my every move charged toward me, but I was too "up" to care. I had once read about an obstetrician who never ceased to marvel at the miracle of birth: He entered the delivery room when one person was on the table, and left when there were two. The leaf seemed miraculous in the same way, like my own Alexander and Ariana. Back inside my new room, which I shared now with four people, including John Graves, my ICA boss, I flattened it between pages of a book to preserve the symbol of the day and of my children. When we left for home, which would surely be any day now, I planned to take it with me. I couldn't think of anything else I wanted from Iran.

When we were given paper to write home a few days later—the first genuine letter after one brief note previously permitted through the Red Cross—I described the prohibition against talking as "the most unbearable restriction, given the need for human contact." But I said also that the treatment since we had been returned to the Embassy had been "inordinately nice."

For a week or so, my hopes hovered in the sky. They had a long way to fall, but not that—or anything else—could explain the revolt of my nerves.

Above all, the "Holiday Season" was confirmation that we would not be freed—not now; not any time in the foreseeable future. If it was going to happen, Christmas or New Year's would have been the time. I swallowed the bitter probability that we had been returned to the Embassy only because the militants no longer feared an American raid to free us. The realization that we were prisoners *indefinitely* was worse than the initial adjustment to capture.

Our hands were bound again after December 16 or so, maybe after a rumored—by gesture—escape attempt. They used strips of sheet, tying us so loosely that I could stretch my arms to almost their full reach. When I went to the bathroom I untied one hand, washed, and retied myself. The bindings were symbolic, and perhaps intended to humiliate us—which they did. They stayed on twenty-four hours a day. I took the dried leaf from my book and looked at it to rekindle my hope of just ten days before—and to remind me of my children, whom it represented even more to me.

*

It was closer to a vision than a dream. I could conjure it up almost whenever I needed it, and I needed it often.

It was Barbara, almost exactly as I had seen her the last time we were together, when I was called back to Washington from Tehran for consultations after the February 14 raid. I went up to Brooklyn and we left the children with her mother while spending a weekend alone in Manhattan, indulging our whims. We stayed in a good hotel. We went to the theater, to exotic restaurants, and on long walks, as in our courting days. Her cool hand in mine was proof that I had survived.

On Sunday morning we got up late for brunch, which was the setting of the vision. It was blurry around the edges, but so distinct in the center that I wanted to reach out and touch the silk of Barbara's blouse. She was radiant: a princess without the trappings, as when I first met her. As when she secretly uplifted me almost every time we went out.

This time we went to an elegant restaurant for the brunch. A rose was on our table. A string quartet played Mendelssohn, but I couldn't hear it; the room was wonderfully hushed. We had bloody marys and omelets with truffles. The curious thing was we didn't converse at all, although in real life we hardly stopped talking. I just looked at her deliciousness and felt my heart respond.

"Do you think Barbara is in love with you?" I asked myself.

"Yes!"

"Do you think she *likes* you?"

"I think she likes me very much."

*

A few days before Christmas the guards gave each of us a little clipping from the English-language Tehran *Times*. It announced that the Imam had invited "suitable" priests and ministers to conduct Christmas services for the hostages. This was official confirmation that we were not going home.

By the time we went to bed Christmas Eve, no visitors had materialized. This was not unusual in a country and a situation where normal procedures had disappeared, where everything changed from one hour to the next. I tried to sleep by remembering my first Christmas with Barbara's family, when dozens of her relations crowded into her parents' living room and some of the uncles tried to put me at ease by telling innocent Jewish jokes. In those days, Barbara's family and I were feeling each other out, and I thought I was being adventurous eating squid and scungilli for Christmas Eve dinner. What wonderful troubles the world had for me then!

I dozed off. At three o'clock in the morning a guard tapped me on the shoulder. "Wake up, Rosen. Merry Christmas."

The guards woke the others and rushed us all to dress. Five minutes later, we five were blindfolded and led downstairs to the reception room where I had spent my first few days after the seizure, tied up as well as mute. Our blindfolds were removed. The door was opened and we were pushed through into a fantasy world. Television lights illuminated a large table heavy with fruits, nuts, and cakes: props for the little play about to be staged.

A small forest of microphones attached to Coke bottles stood among the goodies. While the Reverend William Sloane Coffin conducted a short ecumenical Christmas service, Iranian television cameras panned from food to our hymn-singing American faces, no doubt to broadcast to the world the good news of our well-being. In case the dozens of our captors present for the service weren't enough to intimidate us, some of them pointedly seated themselves between each two of us hostages so that we couldn't talk to one another.

We five roommates saw no other Americans, including no other American clergymen. Where were the other prisoners? I knew nothing more about anything important except that the anti-American posters sharing the walls with traditional Christmas decorations should have alerted the clergyman to *something*. Maybe it was the Reverend Coffin's religious duty to conduct the service, but did he know how he was being used?

He passed on messages from some Columbia University friends, then did something beautiful in a beautiful way. "I just saw Barbara and your son, Alexander, in New York," he said. "He's a lovely, remarkable boy. He gave me this for you, . . ." and he placed a kiss on my cheek.

That moved me so much that I had to fight tears. The Reverend Coffin was a *good* man. Yet I wondered whether he should have come under these conditions, wondered too what compromises he and the others had accepted to see us. He kept referring to someone on *their* side, evidently a man who was escorting him or who had taken part in negotiations, as "my good friend Mohammed here." Could a jailer be such a good friend?

Although guards pushed their faces between us during our brief conversation, I whispered quickly to him, "What's happening on the outside? Are there negotiations for getting us out?"

"We must straighten out the mess from our end," he answered—which I took to mean that he considered the American Government the cause of our imprisonment. The Reverend Coffin had been a prominent protester against the Vietnam War. I was with him then, but he struck me now, for all his goodness, as one of the apologetic, uninformed, myth-making people who assume the United States is at fault in every conflict. God save us from that naïveté.

I stuffed myself with oranges and nuts. When my group was led from the room, we were blindfolded again the instant the door closed. I could tell that some of the hostages had been relieved by the service and the opportunity to meet the kindly clergyman, while others were enraged by their exploitation for Iranian propaganda. I was somewhere in between. The brief contact, even that kind of contact, was reassuring. But where did it leave us?

✳

The guards' Christmas card contained a handsomely printed message from Khomeini entitled "Ring Bells for God." The greeting informed us in English that "Carter, as the ringleader of the oppressors of the world, has demanded that the bells throughout the U.S. be chimed for the sake of spies against the oppressed people of Iran." But it gave "comfort"—actually a dry laugh—since "our youth treat the spies in a Godly way because Islam orders us to have mercy on captives, even if they are oppressors or spies." He neglected to mention that Shi'ite Islam specifically rejected taking us hostage. Scholar that he was, Khomeini surely knew that Shi'ite law was especially protective of non-Muslim diplomats, and that since the time of the Prophet Mohammed, it insisted on a guarantee of diplomatic safe-conduct, even in time of war and always if the foreigners entered Iran reasonably assuming that they had that guarantee.

Luckily there was more mail. A few hours after our meeting with Dr. Coffin, we were handed some Christmas letters from American well-wishers, including schoolchildren. The guards told us that a vast amount of mail had arrived for us, of which they distributed the contents of one bag only. The messages of love and solidarity from strangers in the letters given to me were a great joy. In our snatches of conversation we'd been saying to one another that the state of the economy, not eighty prisoners* five thousand miles away, was on people's minds. "A few diplomats held hostage, yeah, and what's for dinner tonight?" was what we imagined the country was thinking; maybe

* We did not know that thirteen hostages had been released on November 19 and 20, nor that six diplomats had avoided capture and were secluded in the Canadian Embassy on leave outside Iran on November 4.

I'd have felt the same if I had been there instead of here. These letters showed that some Americans did care, and I was deeply grateful.

The guards ordered that all be returned; we were not permitted to keep anything so dangerous. I kept one, hiding it in the little plastic garbage bag we'd been given for our belongings. It was from a young boy in Minneapolis—a typical representative, as I pictured him, of the goodness of American children. The envelope contained an ounce or so of what he identified as "Good old U.S. soil." I decided I would try to take it with me too when I left Iran. It would go well with my leaf.

I never had Barry's need for privacy; now I was even happy that my mother's house had so little of it. There was no place to go off and feel sorry for myself, no secluded corner for a private cry. The children slept in my room and I tried not to disturb them. The bathroom was the only possible place. When tension got the better of me, as it did some nights after watching the news or reading newspaper predictions of war, I cried in the shower. Water bounced off my face until the tears were gone, and when someone noticed my bloodshot eyes, I could say soap had gotten into them.

Why was my life spoiled this way? It had been a good life. I was happy with Barry. We had a solid relationship and two beautiful children. We knew we were lucky and were thankful. What would happen now?

By early December I felt unsure enough to call Washington for some practical information. I had often reassured Barry that I could always support myself, but what about the children if Barry was away permanently, disabled permanently, or worse? He hadn't told me about financial matters or insurance. Maybe he didn't know himself. He read his office documents with amazing care but signed personal papers after barely a glance.

"What will happen to my family if the hostages remain hostages?" I asked a State Department personnel official. "Are there any steps I should be taking?"

"Don't worry about it, Barbara. We'll let you know exactly what you're entitled to if anything happens."

"I think it's time I did some planning."

"You've got enough on your mind right now. Don't worry about these other things; we'll take care of them."

His words were pleasant enough, but his tone said, "Don't bother your poor little head about matters you can't understand." The briefing in Washington had covered a good deal of ground but in fact explained little. It didn't bother me yet that the State Department hadn't shared its basic strategy with the hostage families, for I still assumed they knew better and would make the right decisions in our interest. But not being treated as an adult in matters that directly concerned my dependents was something else. I could have done without that unintentional slap in the face. The fact that I made the call at all worried me as much as how it was received. I was thinking of what I would be entitled to if Barry didn't get out of Tehran! The shock had passed, and so had my optimism. Resignation was better than fear for my husband's life—but not much. And I didn't exactly admire myself for it.

We were expecting him home for Christmas. We had been apart on several Thanksgivings because of his assignments, but Christmas was something else: The entire family was together every year. We had arranged it before the seizure. Barry was to have a good, long leave, from the beginning of Hanukkah through New Year's. Wasn't this the time for the militants to make a gesture, to show they weren't heartless?

*

I had never seen so much coverage devoted to one story. America in Captivity had become a national preoccupation, and I watched, listened to, and read everything available. Most stories were repetitive and empty, implying that nothing was being done because nothing could be.

I had not received one letter from Barry, nor had the other families had mail. Some wondered whether all the hostages were still alive and speculated that the demonstrators were keeping everyone out of the Embassy to conceal the truth.

Christmas Day would be Tuesday. It was difficult to force myself into stores festooned with holiday gaiety, and I shopped only for gifts for the children. I was less anguished now; the intensity of emotion had to fade somewhat over time. But inner emptiness was the antithesis of Christmas spirit. The most difficult task that holiday week was to make myself fully comprehend that Barry wouldn't be with us, after all. A concession from the militants, allowing four American clergymen to go to Tehran to conduct Christmas services, helped me face reality. If they were planning to release the hostages as a dramatic gesture of good will, they wouldn't have agreed to let the clergymen in. I kept myself from questioning, "If not Christmas, when?"

The clergymen planned to leave on Sunday, December 23. I heard their names on the radio the evening before. One was the Reverend William Sloane Coffin, Senior Minister of Riverside Church, in Manhattan. I called the church immediately and asked to see him in the morning.

Waiting with Alexander for him to appear from his office, I was startled to see the State Department's Iran Desk Officer, one of the people who had been keeping in touch with me. His briefcase was stuffed with photographs and other material obviously for briefing the Reverend Coffin. I could think of no reason why I shouldn't speak to the minister, but something in the Desk Officer's attitude told me I was wrong to have come without informing the State Department. Although I was only seeking a link to my husband, I had the unmistakable sense that they didn't like my independent action.

The Reverend Coffin, though, whom I was soon calling "Bill," was extremely hospitable. He asked about the family so he would have specifics to tell Barry if he saw him. He also asked for a message from me—and just before we left, from Alexander, too.

"Do you have anything you want me to give Daddy?" he asked gently.

I suggested to Alexander that he give him a big kiss which could be passed on to Daddy. Bill Coffin departed for Tehran later that day, and I drifted deeper into depression. Barry was thirty-one when Alexander was born. The longer he waited for fatherhood, the stronger his paternal instincts grew, and he was a superb father. He adored his son and spent a great deal of time exclusively with him; this came from his heart. Now Ariana was becoming aware of her surroundings, which included no father. What deprivation for them all!

Monday, the day before Christmas, I felt guilty for having no gifts for my grandmother, sister, and aunts, all of whom were helping so much, and even more for my mother and father, whose love and encouragement were truly boundless. It would be self-indulgent to spoil *their* Christmas with my gloom.

Off I went to smart mid-Manhattan, where I felt even worse. Twinkling lights were little stabs of recollections of happy strolls with Barry to see Fifth Avenue's decorations. I lugged two shopping bags as though they were buckets of cement.

Christmas morning radio news reported that the American clergymen had seen some, though not all, of the hostages and the names of those seen weren't yet known. The children coaxed me downstairs to see what Santa Claus had brought and were playing with their new toys when the State Department called to say Barry was one of those seen. Later Bill Coffin appeared on television reporting on what had happened in the Embassy. Among many moving moments, he said, the one that would remain most in his mind came when Barry Rosen appeared among a group of hostages brought to see him. Barry was downcast until he was told he was going to receive a kiss from Alexander.

"Suddenly it was as if a Christmas tree had turned on inside Barry's head. I've never seen such instant illumination. That was the most beautiful moment of my whole time in Iran."

I had my Christmas lift after all, a fine one.

*

My New Year's present was almost as "thoughtful." Some hostages had been filmed during the clergymen's Christmas visit. The State Department called to say they had seen all the clips, but Barry didn't appear in any. We kept the television on nonetheless to see what we could of the other hostages.

Two of my aunts were "celebrating" with my parents while I dozed on a couch in the living room. When the hostage clips came on, just after midnight, Barry *was* there, with the Reverend Coffin! He had gathered a handful of oranges from a holiday table and was working on adding cookies to his prize. I guessed his slightly awkward smile came from embarrassment at appearing greedy. But I *saw* him, and he looked well, considering the six weeks of strain he was surely living with. I called my mother-in-law to share the good news and went to bed almost content. The threat of death had surely passed, and his health seemed sound. They had to release him soon, didn't they?

From the Green Room I was shifted to another of the Ambassador's guest rooms across the corridor, then to the Ambassador's own bedroom, in the same wing. A guard still believed I was signaling my roommates, not with any instrument now but by looking at the others with supposedly significant expressions. First I'd be assigned another mattress in the same room. Then all of us were made to sit so we would not see each other. The room shift followed, a few days later.

In general, the moving of many of us from room to room was obviously a security measure to prevent communication and keep us off balance. The guards betrayed signs of still worrying about a raid or a rescue attempt by an American strike force. Perhaps they also feared our forming an internal "resistance movement" and made certain we did not get settled in any one group. For our part, we still worried about accidental shooting. We had heard shots outside our room in the mansion in northern Tehran. This was followed by much scurrying about in the corridor and a large, fresh bandage on one of the guards' hands. I had to acknowledge a certain disappointment that his accident hadn't been more serious.

Bad news cut short our gloating. Since the seizure, I had comforted myself with the probability that Kate Koob and Bill Royer, my two ICA colleagues, had not been taken. As the Director of the Iran-America Society and the chief language co-ordinator, they had offices outside the compound. But on a visit to the toilet shortly after Christmas, I caught sight of Bill Royer in a neighboring room—which meant Kate might have been taken too. This defeat of my personal hope was another blow.

On December 30 I was moved again, this time to a former budget-and-fiscal office in the chancery basement. It was four o'clock in the morning. Three others were sleeping in the room, watched by a yawning guard stationed at a desk.

As I entered, I heard someone bellow at the guard in a nasal American twang. "Does he smoke? If this one smokes, get him another room!"

The extender of that welcome, just when we all needed each other so badly, was a middle-aged commercial officer who had developed paranoia about tobacco smoke invading the room. He feared all air currents from the corridor and other rooms as potential bearers of smoke. The guards called him "E-shut the Door," which is all he would say to them. If not for his concern about air quality, he'd have said nothing.

The small basement room had two little windows high on one of the walls. I would have been happy with less-crowded quarters, but

my escort marched off with only a warning about talking. I lay down
on the leather couch assigned to me and tried to get my bearings. It
was still dark. The guards had locked the door that led between our
room and the adjoining one. At first light, "E-shut the Door" began
stuffing the cracks with toilet paper, in a way that suggested resumption of a vital project. His yards of compacted toilet paper failed to
satisfy him and he asked for masking tape. When he had taped and
retaped every crevice, he placed a little flag on the bottom of the door
as a draft detector. When it fluttered, he would ask for more tape and
set to work again. I wondered whether this was the remote man's
usual behavior or whether the confinement was getting to him.

It was certainly getting to me. My physical symptoms were worsening so fast that I feared I might lose control of myself. I was becoming enormously restless, many times more so than before. I *had* to
move the next second or scream—or explode. Confinement had become a tremendous hardship, like a cosmic itch I couldn't scratch.
Every second lasted an hour.

Screaming was out of the question because noises had begun to
affect me just as bizarrely. A guard's whisper or sneeze ripped at my
insides. This complaint sounded so farfetched that if we had been allowed to talk, I might not have rushed to tell the others. And the
growth of my insomnia was keeping step. The sleepless hours were
accompanied by an unusually strong, very worrying heartbeat.

*

"E-shut the Door" hopped like a lame buzzard to avoid dirtying his
soles on the floor. Apparently he had been known as a great pain in
Embassy work, and our living conditions failed to sweeten his nature.
Wrapped in a blanket to fight the nonexistent drafts, he began complaining about cigarette smoke in other rooms as well as ours. "They're
always having smoking parties outside," he twanged to the guards
like the archetypal tattletale. The marines quartered in the next room
were evidently permitted to talk, since we often heard them using
normal speaking voices. "E-shut the Door" complained about this too
to the guards, when the others were asleep and I couldn't reach that
blessed state. "Tell them to shut up. Tell them to stop bouncing that
tennis ball against the wall!" He protested against anyone exercising
in our room because of the dust it raised. When I tried to jog, he
donned a handkerchief mask. Every few minutes throughout the day,
he cleared his nose with a grand snort. The others in the room disliked
him thoroughly, not for such unfortunate habits but for his lofty
opinion of himself and his arrogant dismissal of others' political opinions.

The elder of those two others—and oldest of all the hostages—was
Robert Ode, a sixty-four-year-old retired Foreign Service officer who
has returned for temporary duty in Iran. Although he had a congenital

heart problem that was very worrying in our circumstances, he stayed tough, unfailingly supportive, and generous with his rich sense of humor. Some of the guards would allow us a sentence or two during the day. One quite young student even seemed sympathetic. When he was on duty and we felt we could risk a few moments of talk, we loved to hear Bob Ode's one-line stories about his work as a consul in postwar Poland, and his repertoire of punch lines. "Under a new trade agreement with Russia, the Poles began sending their wheat to Moscow," he deadpanned, "in exchange for . . . the Polish sugar the Soviets were taking." Bob received an amazing number of letters, even including some with swatches of wallpaper on which his wife wanted his opinion for their new house, in Sun City, Arizona. By sheer force of personality he compelled the guards to mail, registered, a ten-page letter he had written about legal matters concerning the house.

Bruce German, the fourth man in the room, was a budget officer in his early forties, a Greek Orthodox who read from the Bible every morning. I envied him for his religious commitment, which clearly helped sustain him and gave him composure. On top of this, he was a thoroughly decent person.

Some of the conflict in the room was political. A guard named Hamid, who was in charge of mail and seemed to be in command generally, tried to entice us to write to Washington saying how terrible the Shah had been and how wrong America was to shelter him. The prizes for this were promises of more letters from the family and a telephone call home for the winner of a kind of most-cooperative-hostage-in-the-room competition organized by Hamid and joined by no one. From Bruce German's conversations with the guards, it became apparent that he did write something about American foreign-policy mistakes. From everything I knew about him, it was even clearer that Bruce wrote nothing he did not sincerely believe, certainly nothing to play into Hamid's oily hands. But E-shut the Door, who was an arch-conservative, called Bruce a collaborator. This held as much water as his suspicion that I was talking about him every time I said something in Farsi to a guard.

I had to ignore as much as I could of the political controversy because dealing with my symptoms was becoming a full-time job. Our room was in front of the Chancery, which faced almost due south. I lay in my underwear on the floor next to my bed, trying to absorb the feeble winter sun that penetrated to the basement. I had become too jumpy to read. I wanted only to relax in warmth, to soften my pulsations.

A taxi's honk on Takht-e Jamshid Avenue, outside the Embassy drove into my chest. E-shut the Door's nose snorts were like a chain saw ripping at my ribs. But they frightened me less than the question of their origin. Was internalizing of outside noises a symptom of madness?

The five o'clock prayer call provided a test of my condition. When preoccupation with images of disintegration was strongest, I didn't even hear it. When I was feeling slightly better, I had to hold my chest to keep the reverberations from bursting it. "God is great. I am a witness that Mohammed is the Prophet of God and I am a witness that Ali is the Friend of God." Ali, the martyred first Imam, was the son-in-law of Mohammed, who carried the Shi'ite line. I used to enjoy this drawn-out call with its direct insight into what distinguished Iranian Islam from the larger tradition it departed from, with its reminder that Shi'ite Islam is the religion of the injured and insulted. Now I detested it.

But although noises laced me with pain, a heart specialist who happened to give us a desultory check one morning pronounced, "There's nothing wrong with you; just nerves." He gave the guards a supply of Valium tablets from the Embassy's clinic, with careful instructions for handing them out to me. They provided a few hours of drowsing each night but seemed to intensify the restlessness during the day. I wouldn't have believed such agony was possible in the absence of a wound. It was impossible to sit, impossible to stand, impossible to lie down. I felt like laundry squeezed between two great rollers, one commanding me to *move*, the other forbidding it.

I had always disliked drugs and stopped using the Valium out of worry about dependence. But sleepless nights and the current of undefined anxiety were too much. I twitched for a few days; then, in the dead of night on January 4 or 5, popped another pill. In seconds, blue and white stars exploded behind my eyes. Cold sweat ran all over my body.

I'd had depressions during my life, including the one following the breakup with my Iranian girl friend. Whatever was attacking me now was so much worse that I yearned for the sweet days when I merely felt too blue to get out of bed. My pulse raced too fast to get a count. My heart had become a crazed pump, sending excruciating pulsations throughout my body. My limbs jerked like a puppet's, and I had no control over the terrifying throbbing in my diaphragm.

Had I guessed that an hour-by-hour battle with the demon would continue throughout almost four hundred days of captivity ahead, I would have wept for mercy. Not knowing what was attacking me, not believing I could possibly endure it, was as bad as the physical symptoms. This doubled the anxiety, even from its previous unbearable level. The worst of the hell would last two months: an exhausting trial physically as well as mentally. During much of that time I doubted I would survive. During some of it, I didn't want to.

✳

After the first night, I gestured to the others, one at a time, that I had had an attack of something overpowering and wondered whether I could continue. Bob Ode guessed something had happened before I could turn to him. The bathroom mirror reflected someone whose eyes could have been sunken with horror-movie makeup.

In addition to a weak heart, Bob had a bad back, which I had been given permission to massage. I didn't know how much I helped him, but making the motions allowed me to be close enough for whispers. Bob worked on me with the patience of a father, sometimes scolding under his breath, sometimes joking, mostly assuring me directly that I wasn't going crazy and would not die a miserable death here.

"Feel my legs, Bob. What do those terrible pulsations *mean?*"

"Barry, you're going to be fine. Once you get out of here, all that will disappear."

"You can't imagine what 'all that' feels like. Can't you see my face?"

"It's not exactly bright lights under your eyes, but we're all in the dumps."

"I can't sleep. I don't think I'll make it."

"Cut that out and get hold of yourself. I know you're down with something, but I also know there's nothing wrong with you except reaction to this."

I was lucky to have someone of Bob's experience and good nature for a roommate. Both qualities were needed to put up with me. One of the guards, a pharmacology student who occasionally came by to ask about our health, was much less patient. I tried to explain what was happening. He said I must control myself; everything was in my head.

The specialist who had examined Bob Ode's heart and given me the Valium appeared. I was desperate to see him again—to see *any* doctor—and several guards helped by whispering to him in Farsi that I had cracked up. To the best of my knowledge, I hadn't. I think I remained rational even when I was paralyzed with fear. But I was willing to be called a cockroach if that would convince the doctor to look at me. I needed explanations, a father confessor, *an answer,* and all my hope and yearning went to him.

He sported an excellent English suit with foulard haberdashery. It didn't matter that his very natty appearance on top of his recently discovered nationalism put him among the least likable Iranians: the opportunist who took what he could from the West—this one had been well educated in America—the better to denounce his former hosts when it paid. All that counted was his medical knowledge, which might *explain what was happening to me,* even if I was beyond help. For this reason his professional arrogance even appealed to me. He had introduced himself to Bob as "the most renowned heart specialist in Iran." Although my heart was only part of my problem, surely he could interpret the symptoms.

I was led to another room in the same basement, probably one from which the militants had yanked the window bars with a truck when storming the Embassy. I had wanted to be strong enough to endure whatever captivity brought. Now I was ashamed of my condition, mortified that I appeared to be collapsing, and grateful that my request to be alone with the specialist was granted.

Although down from its nocturnal rage, my pulse still raced and my blood pressure approached twice its normal reading. "You're very nervous," chuckled the smooth-faced doctor. "But there's nothing wrong with your heart."

I tried to describe what I was going through. Even as I talked, pulsations convulsed my stomach. I said my system seemed to be running out of control.

"It's your government that's out of control. I can tell you your problems would disappear if your country would hand back the Shah to where he belongs." He wasn't joking. On the contrary, he clearly wanted triumph over me in a political debate. "Do you know that President Carter is Satan?" he said. "And this is how he treats you."

"Doctor, Satan or no Satan, I'm *here,* and I need your help." I didn't have the physical resources to answer his charges even if I had wanted to. He settled for a monologue about the virtue of the revolution and evils of American imperialism, which was responsible for Iran's troubles.

"Dr. Arefi, I'm not in Washington and I can't concentrate on the Shah right now. Please help me." If he had prescribed a long leap as the only way to stop the inexplicable surges, I'd have begged the guards to take me to a roof. In my desperation I attributed magical powers to him and his medical training. But he preferred diagnosing the CIA. I could tell him nothing more about my heart. He had pronounced it sound, and he knew all the answers.

I tried to prevent him from leaving. "Doctor, I have this opportunity to be with you now; I want you to understand my symptoms." I was trying to get myself to a hospital for a complete examination. He said he had no authorization for that and had to leave. The guards who took me to my room must have thought me the most wretched of human beings. "You shouldn't be having such difficulties here," said one we nicknamed "Spectacles." "Why aren't you tougher?"

I couldn't lie down because the furies became even stronger when my head was level with my heart. I sat on my bed and tried to answer Spectacles' question. The high basement windows had been barred in iron during the campaign to improve embassy security after the first takeover. How ironic that we had helped jail ourselves! A cushion between my back and the wall behind the mattress slightly softened the reverberations inside me. I stared at the windows until they became floating rectangles of light. There was no answer for me.

The richest gift in the world belonged to my roommates, who seemed to be able to doze almost at will. If my sleep came at all, it sneaked in at five or six o'clock in the morning. I was still a prisoner of insomnia as much as of the militants.

"At least you have the knack of losing yourself in sleep when something bothers you badly," wrote Barbara in a letter. "Thank goodness we're both lucky that way." I used to tuck my problems under the covers and wake up refreshed. Now I'd have given almost anything to lose myself in sleep, but my luck had run out.

Breakfast was nourishing Iranian bread with butter and jam or cheese. The drink was tea, of which I'd had my fill for a lifetime. It usually came around eight o'clock, without the precision of a proper prison.

Unlike prison too, no one forced us to get up. For others, staying in bed was a sane way to pass a few boring morning hours. For me, it would have been surrender. There was nothing to get up for, but I forced my dead weight off the mattress to show myself I wasn't giving in.

I forced myself to eat for the same reason. I didn't want the guards to have the satisfaction of my sinking deeper into depression, even though I felt I had lost much of my battle to bear imprisonment well.

After breakfast we were permitted to go to a small room at the end of the basement corridor. Printing equipment that used to operate there had been pushed against a wall, leaving space the size of an average bathroom for jogging. There was also some muscle-building equipment, probably taken from the marines' apartments.

Bob Ode was permitted to exercise there three times a day because of his heart condition. I used the room every day, no matter what, and was grateful for my compulsion.

The rest of the morning was spent reading, if I was up to it, or writing one of the two letters permitted a week, neither of which could exceed two hundred words. On a few occasions this rule was relaxed, apparently when someone going directly to America would serve as courier. But in general the limit was enforced, for no purpose I could think of other than to cut down the work of the guards who censored letters.

"Shorter letters or they'll be thrown out," admonished Hamid, known as Number One because he was now more obviously in charge of our living arrangements. Ours was a "bad" room, he informed us— in contrast to that of the non-political marines, who were permitted to talk.

"When will this end?" I asked him.

"It can't end now," Hamid replied. "We haven't yet determined which of you are spies. Those who aren't have nothing to worry about."

Spies? More intimidation, or something real to worry about on top of everything else? My roommates had just arrived in Iran or had noncontroversial duties. I was the logical candidate, and Hamid had also told me he didn't like my letters. I tried not to think about it.

❖

Lunch was at one-thirty or two o'clock. The Embassy's Pakistani cook, who was also prevented from leaving although he was a Muslim, usually prepared the meal, which ranged from spaghetti with meat sauce to frozen chicken to an occasional hunk of "mystery meat," probably beef. Brussels sprouts garnished every other meal. Once or twice, I got a few down.

The next highlight was tea, without which few Iranians can make it through the day. The guards came around at four o'clock or so, and even those of us who had never liked tea began to demand it when it was late or forgotten. Every little privilege was precious. Usually we were asked whether we preferred light or dark tea—which I supposed was a form of *ta'arof* even here.

Plastic plates and embassy silverware were stored on the table in the center of the room. We ate there or on our mattresses—still not talking, which seemed most unnatural at mealtime.

The climate usually reminded me of a slightly warmer, much drier Washington, D.C., but this winter was unusually cold and snowy. There was little sun to try to absorb during the day as I put my face up to the feeble rays. As it got colder, standing around the gas stove, which was not far from the table, became the central activity. Then it was back to my book, thoughts of our weekly shower in the Ambassador's residence, or rereading Barbara's letters. "Zander really does miss you a lot. I think he is taking it out on me because he will not let me leave him even for a moment. The baby recognizes you in the picture we took in Ocean City and says 'Dada' when she sees it. I think she is looking more and more like you."

Would we ever get out of here? Of course we would. But I did not believe I could endure many more months. I kept thinking I would try to get myself shot if I had to spend the rest of my life in this condition. In whispers, Bob Ode assured me that American public opinion wouldn't stand for our continued imprisonment. He became almost incensed when I said, in gestures and three-word phrases, that American public opinion had no effect whatever on Khomeini—who was, I assumed, ultimately responsible for this situation.

Anyway, how could American public opinion change our policy? Emotionally I didn't care if Air Force One delivered the Shah to

Tehran in a black box. All I cared about was ending my hour-by-hour struggle against my symptoms by getting out. Logically I knew the United States could not and should not accept the guards' demand for a trade. Whether or not the students or their backers understood it, the United States could not hand over the Shah or anyone else without proper proceedings—and we had no extradition treaty with Iran. It could not do so under threat, nor in exchange for its own citizens. I had told that to some of the guards, and to the self-righteous heart specialist. If he didn't understand, surely some of the highest officials of the revolutionary government did, for they had spent years in America, protected against the Shah's repressive instruments. We didn't hand *them* over, after all.

This didn't count with them. They distributed cards for our signature saying America was wrong and ought to return the Shah. With no second thoughts, I handed mine back unsigned. Whatever our past mistakes, that was not the way to right them.

I told Bob Ode that unless the guards and their supporters dropped their demands, we were in for a drawn-out experience. It might last a year, I said, despite my emotional unwillingness to contemplate that. The American elections *in November* might be the first chance to break the deadlock. Then I stopped talking about it, because Bob, in his straightforward patriotism and optimism, became angry again: a foolish thing for me to provoke in this friend of constant good cheer and fellowship. Bob thought me pessimistic and cynical, and probably attributed it to my condition.

A photograph from the Washington *Post* got through in one of his letters. It showed President Carter bent in prayer for the hostages at the National Cathedral, in Washington. With his humble stance and pained face, I saw him as unknowingly vulnerable to the Iranian authorities. Personally, it reassured me to learn he was taking our plight so seriously. Professionally I sensed he was taking a wrong approach. It was a great shame to show him pained. It would make our captors stronger, not make them relent.

Whatever the President was or wasn't doing to get us out, he had to play it cool. I wondered whether he knew that the worst he could do was let the Iranians feel he badly wanted what they were selling. They were bargaining people. The ways of the bazaar were among their earliest formative experiences. Anything that might prompt them to increase their own assessment of the value of their goods had to be avoided—but not, I hoped, by forgetting us; perhaps by pretending we were not important, the customer wasn't interested. Nothing lowers price so quickly as walking away from an Iranian's stall.

It was either that or making a full commitment to use force—which could be disastrous because of the Iranian martyr complex. Millions would *like* to die in the fight against American "evil." I hoped the President was being advised by people who knew the Iranian mentality well. I hoped even more he was playing his cards close to his chest and the press was cooperating by not making this a big story in which they told their readers—and Khomeini's lieutenants—every little thought.

❋

E-shut the Door returned from the bathroom with startling news he passed on when he felt he could risk one- or two-word phrases. He had found a message inside a toilet-paper roll saying that about a dozen hostages had been freed two or three weeks after the seizure, including most of the blacks and women. His tone of voice made clear that he resented the blacks for getting away with something or shirking their duty. I gave an inward cheer. It was good that at least some of us escaped the increasing misery. On the second day, I had seen one of the secretaries waiting at the door of the bathroom in the Ambassador's residence, looking exhausted and destroyed. I hoped she was one of those who was home now, enjoying all she had no doubt previously taken for granted.

I wished I were black or a woman myself. Being Jewish didn't help, although it hadn't hurt so far either. A few guards had suggested my "Zionist wife" should be in Tel-Aviv, not New York. I was relieved that it had been nothing more serious.

❋

I had received Barbara's first letters two or three days after my attack. About twenty were handed to me in one bunch, the earliest dated in November, just after the seizure. Had they come earlier, they might have prevented what happened. I wanted them very badly, *needed* Barbara's holding. Now I could read them in my better hours, but lacked the stuff to reply. I couldn't tell Barbara the truth—that I had little desire to live—and faking good spirits was too much for me then.

Somewhere deep in my psyche Barbara and the children remained my hope and mainstay, but not even they could help now. I was alone with my affliction. It could have come from an alien planet, for it was beyond my comprehension. I did not fear death but the relentlessness of the agony and inexplicability of its source.

❋

During the day I read a biography of Montgomery Clift, whose degeneration in mind and body was a form of self-destruction. My anxiety was overwhelming. I had believed that if I lived through the Embassy's first capture, with guns at my head, I was hardened. But this constant helpless waiting was far worse. I had lost my leverage with the guards by revealing I was no longer a person who could cope with everything.

The goal was to make it from one hour to the next. I looked for-

ward to eating because it sometimes provided twenty minutes of partial relief: Symptoms receded to the extent that I could concentrate
on chewing. But the rest of the day was interminable and the night
was a nonstop nightmare. I sat up in bed and tried to control myself.
What could cause such furious pulsations? I seemed to be undergoing
a heart attack that went on for hours. My system had obviously been
unable to adjust and was self-destructing, but why was it happening
to *me?*

My roommates were asleep. I didn't want to wake them, or had too
little command of myself to do it. Anyway, the guard who slept in the
room would have punished me for talking. I huddled in a corner, my
body thundering unbearably. "Calm!" I whispered to myself. "For
God's sake, calm, nobody's killing you." My arms trembled and nausea
rose to my throat.

January 19 was a date to remember: Two weeks of terror had convinced me I was dying. Relieved by the certainty, I composed a last
will and testament in the form of a note to Barbara saying I loved her
and the children dearly, that something mystifying had happened,
and I would probably never be the same even if we were together
again. I said I hoped they would have fond memories of me, not
spoiled by disappointment in this end. I wanted to stress what a pity
it was that this had happened, considering the life we could have had.
I put the scrap of paper in a Bible I'd been reading and asked Bob
Ode to give it to Barbara if he got out and I didn't.

In moments when I was able to put things in perspective, I thought
I understood at least the cause of the trouble. I had always over-
reacted to being *wronged*—which, as I grew older, included restrictions on my freedom. My cheek just wouldn't turn when my dignity
was slighted. I struck back in some way, even against people I liked.
A few years before I met Barbara, I'd had a rousing argument with a
woman in Berne. Typically I slammed the door and walked off my
tension—which took hours, despite a chilling rain. I came back dripping wet, and feeling good enough for drinks and laughs.

I had always taken things seriously but was able to discharge
"heavy" emotions quickly. In one way or another, what was happening here must have been caused by inability to release my anger in
words or walking. I yearned to scream but knew that would land me
in handcuffs. My whole self was being squashed, together with my
supposedly inalienable rights, and my outrage could find outlet only
in my own body. And having no power of initiative, no power over
myself, produced deep anxiety.

What my captors were doing to me was bad enough. What I was
doing to myself was worse. It was no consolation that I hadn't dis-
graced myself earlier in the term, when there were opportunities for
action. When it came to endurance rather than a quick shot, here I
was with limbs twitching like a spastic's.

❖

I kept my letters to Barbara as circumspect as I could about my condition. I mentioned depression and nervousness but spelled out nothing about my symptoms. Maybe they would go away; maybe I'd overcome them. There was no need to burden her with a problem she could do nothing to relieve and which I didn't really understand myself.

We had been told what we could and couldn't write. Descriptions of food and frequency of showers were permitted, but not where and how we were being confined; not the real story or conditions. Sometimes I wrote the truth anyway, knowing the letters would be intercepted. Getting something down on paper served as a small safety valve.

Letters to the children required more thought. I wanted them to know how much their father loved them, yet not to wonder or worry why he wasn't with them. What were they making of my absence—especially Alexander, my little cohort? Good-cheer messages were the answer; yet I didn't want them to suspect I was *happy* to be separated from them. The hardest part was not telling them fully how much I missed them, for this would surely have made them feel something was very wrong.

I hoped they would know one day; I hoped I was writing nothing to distress them. I detested the students for putting me in this difficult situation.

❖

It was bad luck that this was a leap year. One extra day was twenty-four hours too many. The day before that, February 28, was my birthday. That brought good luck, although not as a birthday present.

For weeks the guards had been calming me with promises about "an important specialist," evidently a neurologist, who would see me when he returned from meetings in Austria. They described him as a very well known consultant or official of the Ministry of Health. On February 28 "Shower Man" told me to get ready immediately; I was going to see the famous doctor. Despite my experience with the slogan-spouting heart specialist, my hopes soared. Again I had visions of a Wise Man who would explain all, even if he couldn't cure all.

Blindfolded, I was driven in the back seat of a car several minutes from the Chancery. It was easy to guess that this was the embassy clinic. Waiting in one of the clinic rooms the guards had taken over for a dormitory, I learned the specialist's name was Dr. Fakhr.

A small man in his fifties, he was less natty than the heart expert—and also more professional with me; in this sense, more compassionate. After routine checks of pulse, blood pressure, and reflexes, he examined my eyes. Unhurried questions about my background and what was bothering me followed, after which Dr. Fakhr said I was suffering from a form of depression that was straining my system. "You must be more positive," he said in Farsi. "If the Shah is returned, you will become more positive very quickly. Meanwhile, I think I can help with some medicines."

He wrote several prescriptions and gave them to a guard I knew was a medical student. I tried to prolong the time with him by asking what exactly had gone wrong; whether it could be called medical. Now eager to finish with me, he said my reaction was not unusual. "I'm surprised more people are not afflicted."

"But why is my body so out of control? Will it ever be normal again?"

"Just take the medicines that will be given to you. It won't be so bad."

The pills came to my room the following day, again with detailed instructions to the guards to give me just enough each morning for that day. They were made by a Danish company. From the circular in English I learned that Amitriptyline, the major one, was an antidepressant with strong sedative effects.

It solved none of the problems but made them less frightening by easing their grip. The first night, I slept deeply for five straight hours: incredible relief. Five hours away from the world of the guards seemed almost to make my escape plan come true.

At last a letter from Barry! *Seven* letters, brought directly from Tehran by what Barry would have called "unlikely" messengers. They were members of an organization called the American Indian Treaty Council who had met some embassy militants while attending a Third World Conference in the Iranian capital and offered to hand-deliver letters to hostage families all over the United States.

This stroke of good news came literally out of the blue. I learned about it when a man named John Thomas called soon after his plane landed in New York. I invited him to come to Brooklyn immediately, even before I understood just who gave him the letters and why.

A full-blooded Delaware, John was accompanied by five other Indians in long braids and covered with turquoise and silver. One, a tall man with rawhide strips wound around his warrior braid, had been a leader of the 1975 takeover of Alcatraz Island in the name of America's Indians. Lucky went to the door to challenge them, then ran back. The old house had many visitors, but none quite as exotic.

John handed me Barry's letters. I controlled myself from opening them because I wanted to be alone when I did. Especially considering the visitors' sensitivity to slights, it would have been impolite to do what I yearned to: run upstairs to my bedroom and read them. The pile lay on the dinette table like yesterday's newspaper while we had cake and coffee—and discussed the problems of the American Indian.

The group didn't hide their pride that Indians served to bring out the first hostage mail—and more than that: to make the first contact with the militants. They were equally puzzled and angry that in a national crisis more smothered by publicity than any previous one, hardly any mention had been made of their role as messengers and possible intermediaries. They were certain the government was responsible. As members of an oppressed minority, they had offered to take custody of the hostages for transfer home. They saw that as a way of saving face for the Iranians and simultaneously a means of winning international prestige for themselves in their campaign for recognition as a sovereign nation.

We kept talking. The letters almost burned a hole in the table next to my cup, but I could not cut my guests off in mid-telling about the cause of their lives, though they were no longer intimidating. They stayed several hours.

I had to fetch Alexander before I could finish reading the letters and took the last one with me in the car. It described a winter day in

Brooklyn—which could have been that very day; the letter was uncannily real, as though Barry had spent the morning with me. He picked out each detail of my putting on the children's coats and hats before taking them out to the yard. I sobbed. This isn't me, I thought, with my great self-control. But Barry had captured the scene—said so much about our lives with such loving clarity—that I broke down.

Drivers honked from behind me at the light. The letter fell from my hands where I was holding it against the steering wheel. I had to pull over and wait to regain control.

New Year's Day, 1980

I know this may sound crazy, but I'd love to have a third when this is all over. He or she will be our "Love Child," conceived with all the love and devotion we can muster, and a sign of our hope in the future.

Letter to children, same day

I bet Ari is becoming a big girl, aren't you? And I know her big brother is helping his sister to learn all the good and beautiful things about trees and birds and flowers in Nanna's yard. And of course both of you help Mommy, and laugh and sing with her whenever you can. . . . Oh yes, Alexander, thank you for the kiss you sent me with that nice man, Mr. Coffin. He said you were so big and handsome and smart. I still have that kiss in my pocket, and I always love to look at it. So good-bye for now, you two.
Love and kisses,
Daddy

January 4th

Although it is 62 days now, I think I've finally gotten a handle on things. There was a long and dreadful period of self-pity, bitterness and almost self-defeating emotions. I've had trouble sleeping —but that, I hope, is also slowly dissipating. . . .

Mail is now coming through, although haphazardly, along with the many hundreds of Xmas cards from all over the U.S. You really can't understand what those cards meant—please communicate that feeling, baby.

Of course I wish you once again a Happy Birthday. That makes two of your birthdays I've missed. What can I say other than I'll wrap myself in a ribbon when I see you and I'll present you with me? . . . Nothing can ever be important again—that is, materially so—compared to what this bad television melodrama has done to *us*. I love you more and more each day.

January 6th

I'm in the midst of reading Turgenev's *The Home of the Gentry,*
but I'm having difficulty reading more than a few pages at a
time. I look up and see . . . you!

One of the few news organizations to cover the arrival of the Indians in New York with the hostages' letters was the local CBS News
bureau. Apparently they listened in when John Thomas called, and
with the directions I gave him, arrived at my parents' house even before he and his friends did. That ended the secret of my address,
which I had kept from the press for ten weeks.

A well-known correspondent knocked on my door while two cam-
eramen waited behind her. She asked for permission to film me as I
read Barry's first letters.

"What?" shouted my mother in quick fury. "Can't you tell the
difference between public and private?" She ordered them to leave
her property at once, threatening to call the police if they didn't. I
was calmer, but just as adamant.

The crew pulled back behind the wall and set about filming the
house through the front gate. Waiting for the arrival of Barry's letters
any minute, I was becoming increasingly disturbed at this intrusion
on my privacy. An American flag hanging in a window was going to
be used as the backdrop for their I-Found-a-Hostage-Family report. I
was so upset at their insensitivity—or maybe so tense waiting for messages from Barry—that I pulled the flag from the window and closed
the drapes. I didn't want them there, didn't want to be observed,
didn't want our relationship to the flag used for *their* purposes.

Inability to sleep still ate at my morale, as if it stood for larger failures. Why couldn't I at least doze off when most of the others seemed to be coping with more difficult problems? I lay awake throughout the night with my laments, my chest magnifying each wheeze and whisper like a giant echo chamber.

The night of February 5 was as miserable as the preceding ones. Suddenly I shot up from my mattress. In a nearby storage room, plates and glasses were being thrown to the floor, the crash of glass sending shock waves through me. But before I could fully react to the pain, my nerves switched to something more threatening: A howling group of guards raced up the corridor toward my room. Each of their thumps set off an internal explosion.

Something was terribly wrong. My watch read just after 3 A.M. My heart pounded like a battleship's salvos, totally out of my control and unreleated to anything in a normal body.

My bed was just inside the threshold. When the door burst open, I had no doubt whatever that we were going to be shot within minutes. Not even the usual "this can't happen to me" illusion protected me from acceptance of imminent death. I saw the scarves and masks covering the guards' faces as executioners' wear. My eyes wouldn't move from their automatic weapons, which they waved toward us like every picture of terrorists preparing to kill.

The suddenness of lights in our eyes made us blink; otherwise we were too numbed to move. The guards' shouts were not merely vicious but edged with murderous fanaticism. "Everybody up and out! Up and out NOW! Everybody. MOVE!"

I couldn't. I was like a cobra's victim. I wondered how other men forced themselves to walk to their place of execution. While I tried to push my legs down to the floor, one of three guards nodded in my direction and hoarsely whispered, "Don't speak Farsi here," to the others. Their emphasis on my not knowing what was going to happen seemed the ultimate proof of their intention: the ultimate deprivation of prisoners about to be shot.

The guards yanked me out of bed and shoved me toward the door, together with my three cell mates. I yearned for the comforting voice to assure me this wasn't real, wasn't happening to me. Instead I was filled with limitless dread and with vast sorrow for myself.

The killers herded us into the corridor. No doubt to bolster their own courage, they grew more and more frenzied. "Arms against the wall," they screamed. "Spread your legs. Do not drop your arms. Do not lower them a centimeter, or you die *right now*."

The others were near me in the corridor, but I lost track of them. As on every trip into the corridor, I was blindfolded—but even if I could have seen, I had lost the power to think about many things. My mind was utterly blank in large areas, including Barbara and the family, where I wanted to concentrate my final thoughts but couldn't. I could barely follow the movements of the guards, who had started ransacking our room with a violence that numbed me again. For a moment I thought it might be a search, but for what? No, it was a rage to destroy: the sounds were of ripping and breaking. But the questions that tormented me—What does this mean? Why are they killing us now?—were too much to cope with.

At last the imminence of death cleaved me in two. Part of me now detached itself from the rest, and this part—which had always been closest to me, which knew my secrets—was observing my final moments. This almost convinced me that Barry Rosen would somehow survive.

At the same time, I wanted the part that others were seeing to die like a man. The desire not to make a fool of myself grew in proportion to my fear—and filled me with yet more dismay, for I *was* making a fool of myself. My arms trembled like a pathetic weakling's. The right one had grown so treacherously heavy that I could not hold it against the wall any longer.

"I said up with those arms. Do not lower them *at all*."

But the arm continued to shake and slip. It had grown heavier than anything I had ever lifted. "Stop this," said a new voice within me—the voice of the secret self when I was a baby. "Somebody take me away from here."

A guard ordered me to drop my trousers for a search. My arms couldn't cope with pulling them up again. I thought maybe the pulsations that were buckling my knees would burst my heart before someone pulled a trigger.

It struck me that enraged captors shoot their captives against a basement wall in cheap television films. But I was also aware that the "heroes" of such drama don't struggle with puny worries about image. I wondered if I would make it to the shooting without breaking down, and how much longer that might take. I wondered why my arm couldn't support the weight of my hand against the wall. Caring only about saving my "honor" now, I cheated a few inches to lower its heaviness.

"*Dastet bala!*" screamed the guard. "Hands up!"

"Take me away from this misery," answered my baby's voice. "I don't *want* any more of it."

At the same time, I yearned to turn around and punch the guard who had shouted last. Punch, kick, smash. My whole being rebelled against standing there in passive acceptance of this humiliation. My cells craved some final dignity.

As if he had heard my hunger to punch him, the guard jerked his gun hard against my back. A cartridge clattered to the floor. Had I been shot? It no longer mattered much; I was glad the episode was finally ended. My mind went blank and my body turned to jelly.

Perhaps I passed out for a second, just to relieve the inconceivably powerful pounding of my heart. When I became aware of myself again, I was trying to dislodge the blindfold with my eyelids, if only to get a glimpse of the floor. The "What's going on here? What are you trying to do?" of other Americans gave me strength. When I realized I hadn't been shot, I wanted to strangle a guard for the humiliation. I made up my mind to start kicking if I heard shooting now. Even if I didn't land on anything, the attempt would give satisfaction.

I was again ordered to pick up my pants. Finally I managed to pull them on. After endless time—which probably lasted fifteen minutes—the guards told us to return to our room. I inched the few feet to the door like a baby taking its first steps.

Everything is relative. After the exposure to what I took for certain death, I longed to return to the comparative luxury and happiness of my "cell." I craved the security of not being threatened with extinction.

When we had been pushed through the door, our blindfolds were removed. The room was a shambles. Everything had been violently overturned or pulled apart, as if the guards had been searching frantically for something very small and very threatening—and decided to take revenge for failure to find it.

My mattress lay twisted on the floor. I clambered over it to look for my photographs of Barbara and the children: photographs that had carried me through hundreds of wretched hours by keeping me in touch with the most precious in life. Several of the most valuable, including our wedding photograph, were missing. My leaf was also gone from its place in a book, and I begged—in vain—for its return, together with the photographs.

I could understand the taking of my money, which amounted to a few rials. My "last will" note to Barbara was also gone. But what did they want with pictures of my family? Perhaps one of the sadistic guards took pleasure in ripping up pictures of Barbara and the children.

In time, I thought I also understood the taking of my belt and tie. Rumors circulated that an attempted suicide by one of us, or, as another rumor had it, an attempted escape—had prompted the raid; the guards were searching for any possible devices others might use to lay hands on themselves. This would be confirmed later by a man with whom I would room.

The first thing I noticed on entering my new quarters was his badly slashed wrists. Although I never mentioned the scars, he soon volunteered to tell me his story. He explained that he had appeared on

Iranian television to condemn American policy toward Iran, especially CIA support of the old regime. He had thought, he said, that his "confession" would be a way to earn our collective release—which is what the militants had promised him. When he realized he had been tricked, he felt that killing himself was the only way to escape his guilt, or at least to escape the solitary confinement he had been placed in.

No doubt he had been naïve. He seemed very oppressed by his confinement, which is partly what drew us together. My problems had given me a new perspective on weakness, and when I told him that I did not and could not condemn him—on the contrary, I could only sympathize with him—he knew this was more than the usual comforting noises. We became close friends.

❖

The other hostage who tried to commit suicide had had more than his share of punishment. The militants had seized him as he was bravely destroying secret material, and they roughed him up physically and psychologically. Yet it was less his treatment than the problem that troubled all of us to a greater or lesser degree—the indefiniteness of our term, not knowing what to count on—that caused him, according to the story that circulated, to bang his head against a wall and try to end his depression by ending his life.

When my symptoms eased enough so that I could think about something else, the attempted suicides made me aware that some of the other hostages were suffering more than I. No matter how painful my physical complaints, I rarely fell into the kind of despair that sees suicide as the solution. Even when I hoped I would die, I had no fantasies about doing it myself.

My other thought was that our kind of imprisonment created unusually difficult psychological pressures. The prison literature I read reminded me that we were incomparably better off than, for example, tens of thousands of American prisoners taken in the Second World War. Their ordeal of starvation and physical punishment beyond the limit of human endurance made the conditions of our confinement seem luxurious. Yet, as soldiers, they were better prepared. The chain of command, with all its support for individual prisoners, continued to function in most prison camps. They also had the purpose and unity of war to sustain them. The entire country was with them and behind them—in the case of World War II, behind them in a cause everyone knew to be necessary and just.

By contrast, we felt isolated and often purposeless. What were we fighting for? Where was the nobility, even the sense, in our suffering? Especially in my case, there was no pride to stiffen me. I had loved the country of my captivity. The Axis weren't holding me, but people whose intentions I had wanted to make clear to my own countrymen. How I had wanted to see the Shah's regime go!

The talking prohibition much reduced the moral support and sense of solidarity we could draw from ourselves. I remembered *King Rat*, a novel about life in a Japanese prisoner-of-war camp. Despite the extreme conditions of imprisonment, despite the scurvy and beatings, I wished I had the purpose of men who felt they were continuing their fight for a just cause from behind barbed wire—and who could organize their lives enough to maintain respect for themselves and each other. This is why I came to look back at the February 5 raid as a dramatic highlight in our demoralized existence. The succession of purposeless days was a much harder test than one life-or-death hour in the middle of a single night, and it seemed to me that Foreign Service personnel would have to be prepared in some way for these new pressures of "peacetime" imprisonment.

Two weeks after Barry's letters arrived, the telephone rang late in the evening. It was Ted Curran, head of ICA's Near East division in Washington: Barry's direct supervisor. "We've had bad news, Barbara," he said evenly. "Barry is accused of spying."

"Only Barry?" I heard myself sputtering. "What does that mean?" Spy charges were not entirely new. The invaders of the Embassy had let it be known that they considered the officers spies; during the first month, they threatened to put all the hostages on trial. The so-called "Hanging Judge," an ayatollah who had sentenced hundreds of Iranians to death, volunteered to preside at the hearings, amid reminders that espionage, too, was punishable by death.

That menace died away in December, after the militants apparently found no evidence for a mass trial. But here was Barry, specially selected for individual prosecution. Ted read to me what seemed to be pages of charges: a hodgepodge of fantasy and paranoia that could have come from a Soviet dissident trial. They were going to lay bare and put on public trial "the most famous spy and plotter in the United States" and his "evil conspiracies. . . . His ugly face and the conspiracies hatched by America in Iran will be exposed clearly and better than ever to the nation," ran the text.

The specifics confused me totally. Apparently on the basis of undestroyed documents found in the Embassy, Barry was accused of establishing contacts with editors of Tehran newspapers to discuss press affairs and persuade them not to publish anti-American material. The other charge was that he had tried to improve Iranian-American relations.

"But that's a press attaché's *job*," I said stupidly. If that was the sum and substance of the accusation, it was less worrying than I first thought.

"Of course that's his job, Barbara. I assure you, whatever anyone else was involved in, Barry never did anything illegal. Try not to take this too seriously."

I did try, and the Iranians made it easier. They had issued so many threats that one more couldn't have the impact they surely sought. This one produced a resurgence of my back pain from confirmation that attempts to negotiate with their government were futile.

I had visions of captors and captives growing old together, all with gray beards that made them indistinguishable. "They *won't* kill the hostages," I kept telling myself. They know America wouldn't tolerate that. They know also the hostages are their trump card, and corpses are less valuable for blackmail.

But I didn't try hard enough with Barry's mother. She couldn't be expected to minimize the seriousness of threats to try Barry as a spy. Newspapers reinforced her conviction that he was a prisoner of "Arab" fanatics intent on taking out their revenge on him, and her deep distress was understandable.

Our relations remained strained, but only because the situation was putting unusual pressure on us. In December she had gone to the office of Starrett City, the large Brooklyn housing complex where she lived, to arrange for a room for the party we planned for Barry on his return. The editor of the Starrett City newspaper happened to be in the office too, and Sarah couldn't refrain from talking about Barry's yeshiva education, which again appeared in print. "Are you trying to get him killed?" I exploded when I saw the article.

That was overreaction: The militants' New York contacts wouldn't be checking the Starrett City newspaper. Maybe vestiges of the old religious conflict made me overly critical; if I'd been Jewish, I might have had more compassion. When I took Alexander and Ariana for their next regular afternoon with Sarah, my heart went out to her. She was a loving grandmother and a kind person. If passion overrode the self-control necessary for coping with Barry's plight, she hid her grief and sparkled when she was with her grandchildren. I wished I were outgoing enough to put my arms around her and say I understood the pain and that Barry would return.

I couldn't make that therapeutic gesture, but I could provide protection against shocks that would dismay her. The spy charge was one. It was almost eleven o'clock when Ted Curran and I ended our conversation. I surmised what the morning newspapers would make of the story if they got it—which they would, since the espionage accusation was originally made over Iranian radio and television, which were monitored by the BBC and Reuters. The news should be broken to Sarah first by someone who could convince her that the threat was not as grave as it appeared. I called Barry's brother, who seemed the best person to soften the blow.

The press indulged itself indeed. One New York newspaper devoted its entire first and second pages to NEW YORKER FACES IRAN SPY TRIAL and connected articles (which once again identified Barry as the blindfolded hostage paraded days after the Embassy seizure). By then, I was able to handle the usual silly questions about what I felt about the accusation. Actually, I felt relief that Sarah would not be at the mercy of reporters hyping the news to get maximum reaction.

I was mistaken. Jeffrey's call came after she was besieged by reporters. The first team arrived at her apartment just after dawn. Sarah was wary: "I shouldn't be talking to you—my daughter-in-law will be angry," an afternoon paper quoted her. She refused to open the door, but enterprising reporters shouted questions through it and she couldn't keep herself from answering.

How did she feel about her son being tried as a spy? How *could* she feel, for goodness' sake! "If I don't have a heart attack now," she was quoted again, "I'll never get one." The door remained closed, but to make her point she shouted to a second set of reporters that Barry was no more a spy than Hodding Carter, the State Department's press secretary.

I had never known Sarah's love of conversation to flag, and when I telephoned her, she apologized for not being able to talk. "I just can't. I'm exhausted."

She sounded so weak that I drove to her apartment as soon as she hung up, thinking about how much more difficult it was for her to do our job of waiting. She even had learned that in the interim she couldn't share with the world her pride in her son.

As for the spy trial, it wasn't held, surely because there was no evidence. My guess was that embassy guards were responsible for the charges. When they found papers indicating that Barry was meeting with Iranian editors, they leaped to the attack: That was the jailers' intellectual level.

On my birthday, but again with no connection, the guards permitted us to play a game of chess with a board and pieces that were in the room. Bob Ode taught me the game in silence. Although we sneaked in "I'm an idiot" and "Can I take that move back?" here and there, the prohibition against talking remained in force and a guard was still permanently stationed at a desk in the room.

Bruce German had been moved soon after the raid in early February. Bob Ode and E-shut the Door were removed on February 29, the day following the chess game. After two months with them, I had come to feel something even for E-shut the Door. Although his views remained alien, I saw the humanness underneath, especially when we were alone, while others were in the bathroom, and he hinted at his loneliness and exhaustion. His voice seemed to change in these private exchanges of a word or phrase. As for Bob Ode, I liked him more than ever and had asked the guards if I could go with him. The answer was predictable.

To make up for the good-byes we weren't allowed to say, we waved for half an hour. Alone in the room, I missed the others badly and wondered how any Americans who had the terrible luck to be kept in solitary bore up. Notes left in the toilet suggested there were a few.

The next day, after nearly four months, talking was permitted. I assumed this from the guard leaving his desk and merely coming in to check every few hours. I also heard American voices from nearby rooms. The urge to tell someone what I had been experiencing and to ask what it might mean almost jumped out of my throat. But who was there to talk to?

In came an Iranian man in his forties who might have been a representative of a Western firm before the revolution. His suit was well cut, his cheeks were clean-shaven, his smile was like a car salesman's welcome to a customer. He told me he was a member of an Iranian human-rights organization of which I hadn't heard. The ten or so guards who had come in with him nodded "yes." By now they were all outfitted in khaki and boots—gifts, they told me proudly, of bazaar merchants—so they looked much alike. Their hair was cut not much longer than their scraggly beards. Maybe they were setting the style in Tehran at the moment.

The human-rights representative looked approvingly around the room. "Are you fed three times a day?" he asked in Farsi. "Allowed to go to the toilet when you need to? . . . And you look fine to me. I take it there are no complaints about your treatment."

When my patience snapped, resentment emerged as a challenge to the smug man's methods. "What kind of human-rights representative would expect me to tell him anything with those people in the room? Tell them to get out and maybe you'll get the truth instead of a show. Anyway, what does permission to go to the toilet mean when we're being held illegally—don't you understand *that* little violation of human rights?"

I turned away from his stutters of "Calm down, don't get excited." He quickly accepted my invitation to leave. I spent the rest of a very long day "in solitary," angry at first, then relieved by transporting myself home.

*

With all my supposed interest in other things, a woman's looks made the first impression on me, almost to the exclusion of everything else. It was pure biology, perhaps reinforced by heredity or conditioning: My mother also has a drive for the handsome and the neat. Barbara looked exceptional when I first saw her at the far end of a parked jumbo jet. She was beautiful, statuesque, and so immaculate that she seemed to radiate something exciting—which was refined by her reserve. I liked the control she kept over herself and her use of language. She didn't want to go out with me at first, which also didn't hurt my image of her.

On our first meeting, we had something to eat, walked a good deal, and talked nonstop. I never saw the point of impressing a new date by splurging on a play or fashionable movie and learning almost nothing about her. Besides, I had no money for that mistake. I knew Barbara was enjoying herself, and I liked her company as much as I'd imagined. Her lack of pretension and ceremony surprised me.

Most of our summer dates were like the first one. During the early days, I just wanted a good time. I had recently stopped seeing a beautiful Iranian woman I had met in Tehran and become very close to when she came to study in America. She represented all I loved about Iran, plus European sophistication and culture. She was an intriguing blend of East and West, and our parting devastated me; I promised myself not to get involved again.

But Barbara wasn't the type for casual amusement. She couldn't open to anything physical without deep involvement and commitment. She didn't have to tell me that—or many of her most important feelings. She was usually very quiet, but communicated more with her eyes alone than most women I had known who talked long and earnestly about every aspect of their feelings.

I even liked her original coolness to me, which was connected to respect for herself. Barbara had more than physical stature. Her eyes and lips were especially attractive, but less than her sensitivity and poise, which showed even in our small talk.

During the first months, after my total failure to impress her in the airplane, our relationship was idyllic. Barbara looked pretty, romantic, and sexy all at once. She always wore something striking, yet graceful. We'd do something interesting, then come back to my apartment. Her mother had warned her not to see me there, but Barbara disobeyed and kept quiet about it. Despite our passion for each other, however, we remained almost platonic until Barbara decided otherwise. I left this initiative to her because I knew I'd never be able to leave her once I took that step.

For some time I had the wrong impression about her mother. She is an unusually good person in all the traditional senses, a treasure of a woman in many ways. The trouble was that her moral concepts were difficult to apply in our less rigid age. And she kept her children in the grip of her love and demands, so they never quite grew to full independence. In the hierarchy of authority, she was third only to the President and the Chief Justice.

Barbara's father, a retired construction worker, was more easygoing. Not only Barbara's beauty and intelligence kept her the apple of his eye; she was the eldest of four children and the most devoted. When I met her, she was twenty-two and still kissed her parents goodnight. All the children grew up behind the walls of the family "fortress," almost untouched by the outside world except for the school across the street—where their mother went to work as an aide when Barbara was twelve. They were ideal children in certain senses, except for the rigid scheduling and discipline, which kept them "straight" but subdued.

Barbara's disposition prevented her from challenging her mother's authority. When I got angry, I shouted, "Get off my back," and pounded a table. When I felt I was being taken advantage of, or my independence or dignity was under pressure, I'd reach a limit of tolerance, then blow off steam. Barbara, by contrast, never lashed back, even when under pressure.

She was least able to defend herself against her mother's demands, reasonable or unreasonable. In the 1960s and their aftermath her mother, with her intense commitment to Catholic upbringing, felt threatened by rapidly changing morals, despite her political liberalism. When she treated Barbara like a pariah for miserable weeks after finding out that we were lovers, Barbara said nothing. She wasted away from not being able to eat and from being eaten alive by her mother's scorching silence. Finally I confronted her mother with her heartlessness to her own daughter. "You're killing her," I accused in my fever. "I love her."

"My daughter is my daughter," she snapped. "I know what's good for my family. And I know what your kind is looking for."

"What do you mean by my kind?" I asked, anger taking full control of me. "Get it out. Is what you really mean Jews?"

"I mean you're different. So educated, so willing to take advantage of others' innocence."

This drove me toward rage. "I don't want to spend another minute in this hypocritical house," I shouted. "You're so nice to me when my father dies, but this is what you really think, this rotten prejudice."

Actually, I spent a great deal more time in the house. Bringing the conflict into the open cleared the air. From that time on, Lillian and I developed a solid relationship; I understood why Barbara so loved and respected her. Although I could never accept many of her attitudes, they softened in time. On my side, I came to admire her as much more than a bright woman. For all her strictness with Barbara, she helped develop the distinctive qualities that made her different. Whatever lay ahead now, I was ahead because of my time with her.

I couldn't keep memories flowing indefinitely and was thrilled when an embassy administrative officer was moved in as my roommate the following day. One of the first things he did was pour himself some water from a jug on the table. His hands shook so badly that he could barely bring the glass to his mouth. Despite a serious nervous breakdown in the past, the State Department had decided to give him a tour of temporary duty in tranquil Iran.

The guard was still gone. "Do you want to talk?" I asked.

"Not particularly."

"You're sure?" I almost pleaded.

"I'd rather read."

Apart from determination to keep entirely to himself, he seemed a decent, pleasant person. I was desperate to find out where he'd been and what he knew, and to exchange any scrap of information and describe the rampage in my system. He propped up a book so it wouldn't dance about in his hands and buried himself in it, leaving me to go nuts.

Three nights later, while I was enjoying a spell of liberation in deep sleep under medication, he was moved out and replaced by Lieutenant Colonel David Roeder, Assistant Air Force Attaché. "Are you all right?" he asked in the morning.

"Why are you asking?"

"They made a wild racket bringing my stuff into the room and you stayed conked out. I thought maybe you had some kind of fever."

Everything about what *was* wrong poured out: the start to one of the deepest, most trusting friendships I'd ever shared with a man, thanks in the first place to Dave's profound concern. The paradox is that under ordinary circumstances, I'd probably never have guessed what a splendid person he is.

✳

I was raised an Orthodox Jew. My parents sent my brother and me to a yeshiva in Brooklyn's East Flatbush, partly because they believed we would be better educated there than in public schools, partly because they wanted us to be very good Jewish boys. Under the yeshiva's influence we became more religious than our parents. A man gave me a lollipop when I was nine years old, and while I was licking it, my father gently told me it was not kosher for Passover. I ran with all my might to a water fountain to wash out my mouth, hoping it wasn't too late to be saved from doom and begging God to forgive me. Although I later lost almost all my belief, my decision not to wear a yarmulke every day—part of a larger decision to attend a secular Brooklyn high school instead of advanced yeshiva—was difficult.

*

Dave Roeder was a deeply dedicated Presbyterian. The deacon of a small church near Washington, D.C., he lived his religion and his belief in God. I had always taken for granted it was the kind of religion that by nature had something—or a great deal—against Jews. I couldn't have been more wrong.

The rest of my bias was equally groundless. Dave had the smooth good looks and rah-rah optimism of a football coach, a type I assumed dismissed most social and intellectual interests. He was also, of course, a military man: a highly skilled pilot who had flown more than a hundred missions into North Vietnam while I was taking part in demonstrations against our participation in that war and recovering from tear gas, convinced we protesters embodied higher virtue and fighter-bomber pilots embodied evil. I had an almost instinctive antagonism to military men and military attitudes.

In short, Dave would have seemed to me—and *had* seemed in our one embassy meeting before the takeover—a man of unthinking patriotism, to avoid or to counter: a natural adversary to my beliefs. My underlying mistake was perceiving him as a type in the first place, which closed me to as keen a sensitivity and deep an understanding as *my* "type." Dave was bright, articulate, and thoughtful. More important to me was his great compassion. I hoped I'd never forget what he, with his sharply contrasting background, taught me about my own prejudice.

Although we never agreed about Vietnam, I quickly came to admire his courage and dedication to duty there. Perhaps partly because his military work required it, he had great inner strength. He had trouble sleeping too, but took no pills.

"Dave, maybe you'll have to compromise a little on that."

"I'm not against compromise, Barry. But I can't submit to something that would control me."

After listening with deep empathy to monologues and meditations about my symptoms, he urged me not to give in to them. "Barry, you don't even have to tell me you're hurting; I can see something is on the blink. But you're stronger than it; I know that, too. Whatever other faith you have or don't have, you must have it in yourself—justified faith, because you're the only one who's going to see this through."

He never gave in to his own problems, of which he had his share. His elder son, an unusually intelligent boy, had been stricken with a muscular disease that severely disturbed his movements. Dave's suffering over this didn't shake his faith; he believed the affliction was

God's will. Although I could not accept this kind of reasoning, it was reassuring coming from someone so solid who believed it with all his being.

Shortly after Dave moved in, his son underwent crucial CAT-scan tests that would reveal much more about his condition than had been known before. The guards assured him he would be permitted to telephone home to find out about the tests and discuss options for treatment with his wife. They repeated the assurances in front of representatives of the Iranian Red Cross. When Dave discovered they were lies, he held to his self-control. "Hate," he would say, "achieves nothing. It isn't God's way and shouldn't be man's."

But he was far from a prude or a self-righteous condemner of others' weaknesses. He felt he had enough of his own to sympathize. He told me of his failures and doubts in such detail and with such honesty that the trust we developed became almost bigger—and better—than either of us. We kept back nothing. From time to time, I remembered my instinctive suspicion when Dave moved in. If he was the stereotyped American Christian in my eyes and I the stereotyped American Jew in his, we learned from living together that our country need never be troubled again by that particular problem.

He had deep respect for Judaism. When I told him about my grounding in it, he was astounded that I had come from there to my vague agnosticism.

"Dave, I believe in my family, but I don't know whether I believe in God any longer. My faith is shaky at best."

"But you're losing so much, Barry. A Jew who doesn't believe, especially with your knowledge, is a kind of tragedy."

"That's a big issue, Rev. Let's work on something else while that sun's peeking through the bars. Let's do a crossword puzzle."

We had been given seventy-five "blockbuster" crossword puzzles from the Washington *Star,* apparently sent to us by the newspaper. Later, other snippets of newspapers would come, including sports and classified advertising sections: clippings that had no mention of news on the other side. Growing up in White Fish Bay, Wisconsin, Dave had spent half his childhood on the water, including much time wreaking havoc and almost killing himself in speedboats before he attained Bar Mitzvah age (when my great adventure was getting on the Church Avenue trolley alone to get to my yeshiva). The classified advertisements for boats still fascinated him, and the magic began to work on me.

"Read them out loud, Dave. I want to go on a holiday."

"Where to?"

"Chesapeake Bay. That was weekend fun for Barbara and me when we first moved to Washington."

When we returned from our imaginary holiday, we played a "pick-up" game of baseball-basketball with a wastepaper basket and old coasters we'd sneaked out of the Mushroom Inn shower room (where we showered because the hot-water system in the Ambassador's residence no longer worked). Coasters navigated through the air like flying saucers, and a good hour passed in something like enjoyment. Dave won consistently, thanks to his skill as a pilot and athlete—or just because he was a winner.

*

The other games were played by proxy with the guards. They had used the chancery printing equipment to design leaflets for—among other things, we supposed—pinning to our walls. One favorite was entitled "Down withthe deciiwing Carter. [sic!]"One of its photographs showed the President embracing a healthy, well-dressed Mexican girl —whom the guards insisted, despite anything we said, was his daughter, Amy. The other photograph was of a starving Biafran child. The leaflet was supposed to expose, once again, American exploitation of the Third World. But the "rich" girl wasn't even his Amy; they had mixed up so much! Every other day, we removed one of these propaganda jumbles from our wall and disposed of it in a hole in the ceiling tile.

The guards were even more upset by *our* "deciiwing" in the bathroom. Near the toilet, American hands had scratched "Sit" in front of the "Down with Carter!" slogan. Below the *Marg bar Amrika* (Death to America) invocation, someone added *Marg bar Iran*. The guards obliterated "Iran"; it kept reappearing. Ahmad, who was no slouch in deceit himself, rushed into our room one day as Hamid's lieutenant.

"*You* did it!"

We had been waiting in pleasant anticipation. "Did what?"

"You'll pay, Rosen. You're the only one who speaks Farsi here. . . ."

When his tirade ended, I put on my slippers and knocked on the door to use the bathroom. They were Iranian rubber slippers, the kind most people wear everywhere there. Our shoes had been removed after the February raid, presumably as an added precaution. At that same time locks were installed on the outside of our doors—which incensed Dave. "When a fire breaks out here," he'd say, "what chance will there be of *them* figuring out how to open the locks?"

*

Although Dave was only two years my senior, his marriage and parenthood at an earlier age made him seem older. It seemed natural that our fond and trusting hours prompted memories of my father. When he died, eight years before, I deeply regretted the long talks with *him* I should have had. A heart attack killed him immediately.

My mother was often distressed: by bills to meet and by our apartment, which was kept scrupulously clean, by life's burdens in general and by her health in particular. We never went hungry, partly because she was skilled at producing wholesome meals, but also never had enough for her not to worry about paying next month's rent. My father never seemed anxious, perhaps because he shunted the financial worries to my mother. He was a loving man to whom Isaac Bashevis Singer would do justice. People would stop me on the street to tell me how much they liked him. He had an impish twinkle in his eye and a little joke for everyone.

He was a young boy when he came to America from Poland, which was considered slightly down the social scale from my mother's Russia. His place on the floor in the ship's cheapest hold was next to barrels of herring and butter, neither of which he ate for the rest of his life.

Despite his intelligence and reputation, he also never got his electrician's license. He was an imaginative designer of electrical systems as well as a skillful craftsman—but the examination stymied him. Although he could read well enough, he was afraid to express himself in written English. He coped by working for other electricians, who exploited him, or, on the quiet, for contractors who exploited him even more shamelessly. He struggled and suffered under a misplaced, permanent pall of inadequacy. He never complained to me or my brother.

He also behaved very bravely in the face of death, which happened twice when I was with him. The most terrifying time came when I was nine years old and he was running a line through an old dumbwaiter shaft. He was standing in the dumbwaiter on the seventh floor when the floorboards collapsed and he prevented himself from taking the sheer drop by a last-second jump to the inch or so of framework remaining at the dumbwaiter's walls. "Barry," he said calmly, "open up the little door and hold on to my legs as tightly as you can." While doing this, I cried and screamed, "Dad, don't die. Dad, you can't die!" Even then, when he was trying to think how to pull himself out, he was able to soothe me.

"*Calm*, Barry, *calm*. . . ." When he was finally out, we sat together until he had me laughing as usual.

Caught in a group, my father sat in a corner and talked very little. I sensed how much this difficulty in verbalizing his knowledge and feelings thwarted him. But he loved to talk to my brother and me, especially in his storage room in the dark basement of our apartment house in Brooklyn's now notorious Brownsville section. He encouraged me to putter with anything and everything in the room's enticing mess.

He took me to work with him in his old station wagon with permanent vapor lock as often as he could when I wasn't in school. "Schnappsala," he'd grin—his Yiddish coinage for "little jigger of whiskey"—"c'mon with me." I would drop everything to run gleefully ahead of him to the jalopy. It was clear that in addition to loving me as a father, he liked my company almost as a best friend. And his heart attack killed him before I got to his bedside.

My brother could not make himself go into the bedroom. I took him by the hand so we could say good-bye. We hugged my father and tried to control our tears.

"I want you to know that I love you," I said, still holding him. Surely he did know. Without talking about the important things, he knew a great deal about them. But I wish I had said it before he died.

Why had I put off so much that was essential before this situation? The inclination to assume there would always be time, that nothing disastrous would happen, was wrong. I resolved that when I was freed, if I was freed, I would stop giving so much time to empty errands. I'd stop chasing around in pursuit of—what?

I closed my eyes and conjured up a picture of my smiling father.

*

Our room faced the former Takht-e Jamshid Avenue, at the front of the Embassy. Although there was no explanation of our move one day to another room, just across the corridor, Dave and I assumed the guards suspected I could hear the words of almost constant demonstrations outside the main gate. Actually I could decipher nothing apart from old slogans whose rhythms I knew: "Death to America!" "America, the enemy of the people of Iran!" "America, the Great Satan!" The daily crescendo might have unnerved the calmest, most impervious prisoner. It was a pleasure to get away from it, but I wondered how to escape the guards' steady boasts that revolutionary Iran had destroyed America's power: "America can do nothing to us any more."

I returned from a visit to the toilet to find Dave's blood pressure being taken in the new room by a doctor who said he was from the Red Lion and Sun, the Iranian Red Cross. A camera crew photographed Dave's brief examination, while I tried to calculate the advantages of speaking English or Farsi to the camera when my turn came. The doctor spoke almost no English, but maybe if I did, I could publicize my condition to an international audience if the film would be shown abroad.

I did speak English. As the doctor was using his stethoscope, I told him about my convulsion in January and the heart beats and pulsations since then. He appeared to understand nothing. Furious because they felt I was complaining about the medical care, the guards in the room said I would never see a doctor again.

Afterward I regretted my appeal. If the film was shown in America, I knew I would look unwell and maybe humbled. I might even seem weird enough to embarrass Barbara. Dave assured me I had said nothing to hurt the country or my self-respect and that I must stop putting myself through the wringer. I tried to believe him.

Having arrived in Tehran only eight days before the takeover, Dave was almost totally dependent on my knowledge of Iran, as I was increasingly dependent on his personal support. I hated using drugs, but when I tried to skip a day, the pulsations and fear of physical disintegration were stronger than ever. Dave would not let me dwell on it.

"But why *me?*" I would ask. "What does it *mean?*"

"It's not only you. Everybody's affected in different ways. Yours just happens to take a physical form."

When I succumbed to deeper pessimism, he would resort to stronger verbal medicine.

"I don't know if I can make it, Dave," I said, huddling on my mattress against the wall. "It may be too much for me."

"You have to make it," he snapped. "There's no other way. You *will* make it; that's final."

I grew panicky when the guards ran out of my pills one day. While my limbs twitched, Dave got me through the night by relaxing me. Sometimes he let me talk on and on; other times he would "order" me to change the subject. I thought about my luck in meeting him, and did change it.

*

I wouldn't have believed how important it was to find out what was happening "outside," especially negotiations for our release—if they were going on—and other matters affecting our fate. Craving for information derived from craving for freedom. I'd learned in perhaps the only way that these were no clichés but essentials of life without which Westerners, at least, cannot easily exist. We were starving for the kind of news I used to take totally for granted.

Our mail continued to be censored—rarely by removing sentences, for the guards apparently had no time for that; "offensive" letters were simply thrown out. (Garbage pails brought later to a room for peeling potatoes yielded one or two sopping nondelivered letters at the bottom.) Only occasional words were blacked out. "Now that this has happened," someone wrote—but I couldn't read beneath the censored words that came before, no matter how long and hard I tried. Still, some people were delightfully clever in getting scraps of information to us. In late March I received a letter my twelve-year-old nephew had mailed in January. The censor had obviously seen it, since it bore the usual little "okay" in Farsi. "We all love you and miss you and hope you'll be back for my Bar Mitzvah," my nephew wrote in unusually tight handwriting. "The latest news is the Steelers beat the Rams in the Super Bowl. They think you're a spy and Russia is invading Afghanistan and Carter boycotted the Olympics." Then on he went again about domestic matters. Whatever he meant about being considered a spy didn't worry me much since months had passed since he wrote it; the main thing was getting *any* news.

Inside, there were also occasional opportunities. Guards sometimes used Iranian newspapers as mats for the bathroom floor, maybe assuming no one could read Farsi easily enough for it to make a difference. Almost all the pages had nothing whatever to do with anything political, but I scurried around quietly, reading what I could while a keeper waited outside the door.

One day, I spied an article that appeared to summarize developments in the Iranian political situation with reference to the hostage problem, which was evidently causing conflict. I jammed it into my underpants, but apparently with too much noise. Shower Man searched me when I walked out. Finding the contraband, he threw me against the wall and growled.

"You'll be in real trouble if you try that again. Believe me, deep trouble."

Deep trouble might mean deprivation of mail, which would close another channel of information as well as contact with Barbara. I worried about that. The smaller our privileges the more I cherished them.

*

Whatever was happening on the outside, I sensed the guards were no longer quite so certain the Shah would be exchanged for us. In fact they seemed less certain what to do with us in general, and I guessed there was no unified policy among the clerical and political leaders who counted. They were probably improvising—and, unless Iranian politics had experienced a transformation, trying to use us for their personal advantage in infighting.

A questionnaire handed out by the guards seemed to support this view. It asked for name, address, religion; then inquired, "What ideas do you have for solving this crisis?" I had to laugh at *their* asking *us* how to get *them* out of the mess. I handed back the piece of paper with the space for religion blank, saying I didn't want to talk about my faith. In answer to the laughable question, I wrote: "I have no idea other than what you are doing is totally illegal and morally wrong. If you are smart enough to release us, you will look much better. The world now knows how you feel about the Shah. Each day you keep us makes *you* look more and more like a bunch of terrorists."

When another camera crew moved its equipment into the room soon after distribution of the questionnaire, Dave and I took it as confirmation that something important, maybe even positive, was in the offing. We had been told to clean up the room. This crew, apparently for a full-sized film, was half a dozen strong, seemingly professional, and clearly deferential to a young woman who followed them in.

She was about twenty years old, younger than the woman I had insulted the first day by offering her whiskey. She wore a tight black scarf around her chubby face. Her manner was direct and cold, as though she had come to receive a surrender document from us.

She came to my bed first, while Dave waited on his. "I am going to ask you questions about yourself and your job," she said. "You will answer them truthfully—in Farsi, if you want." I held my breath while she got quickly to work.

"And what were your duties in the Embassy?"

My old anger flared. I hated submitting to her matter-of-fact imperiousness. "I was Press Attaché," I said, "at the time you illegally climbed the walls and invaded our territory."

"CUT!" shouted Hamid, who was still Number One. Without another word I was out of the room and into a toilet off the corridor. There Hamid told me I would not be interviewed again or retain a single one of my "privileges."

Dave was next. Although this was perfectly obvious, Hamid announced it to me in a menacing tone, as if he didn't really care about me anyway; Dave was the real target. During the first week of capture he had been interrogated long and hard as a "war criminal." Their intention was to collect evidence that he had just come from his job as a "baby killer" in Vietnam and to include this in a general picture of the United States playing the same role in Iran. Dissatisfied with his answers, they put him in a Mushroom Inn elevator, closed the door, and let him freeze in pitch-black solitary.

Now I strained to hear *his* "interview," and wasn't surprised when it immediately turned into an accusation for the camera. The dour young woman hardly asked his name before holding up a sheet of paper to the camera, Dave told me later. It contained biographical material: his seven years in the Pentagon, his Vietnam "war mongering," his medals, bombing missions, and "plotting against Iran. . . ."

I was returned to the room a few minutes later, just as Dave was throwing an empty film can at the departing crew. "And take your garbage with you," he said with admirable moderation and great precision in what we felt about the woman and her work.

We sat in silence for a few minutes, perhaps a little amazed at the anger that had flashed out of us so quickly. Were we the only ones filmed? Were they actually preparing a trial, as they had hinted? For a moment it didn't matter; we felt very close and very good.

✳

We looked forward to every holiday like children. Easter was next, and wouldn't releasing us then make fine propaganda for the students? That's what *we* would do, we assured ourselves during our makeshift religious observances. A Brooklyn family had sent me a box of matzohs for Passover. Dave and I shared it while he read Jim Bishop's *The Day Christ Died*, timing it to Christ's agony and explaining the significance of Easter.

Easter Sunday we were told that several ministers, not further identified, would see us that evening. I tried to make myself as presentable as possible in case there would be a television film that Barbara might see. This would show that I was coping much better now.

When our blindfolds came off, on the top floor of the Chancery, we found ourselves being greeted by three clergymen in the office of the Deputy Chief of Mission. The Papal Nuncio, my old friend "Pazienza," gripped my shoulders with great warmth. The Reverend Jack Bremer, a Methodist minister, was more reserved but seemingly no less genuine in his concern for us. The third man's immaculate beard was in keeping with his neat cassock and gold ring. An archbishop of the Melchite (Eastern Catholic) Church, he did not identify himself at first but said we would get the opportunity immediately to answer notes from our families.

He handed me one from Barbara. "I was very concerned about your health," she wrote, obviously referring to the interview with the Red Cross doctor. "I think you should try as hard as you can to think positively. I know how difficult captivity is for you, but I have faith that your inner strength will see you through. Most of all, I send you all my love and hope. Please know that I am waiting for the day you will be home with me and the children."

With the camera focused on me, I answered that I was "making it" with Dave's help, adding, "Please don't worry," for my mother. After Dave's turn, the third clergyman took it upon himself to add that things were going very well with us. He ran down a list of our "amenities," including access to books, use of the new exercise room, chances to watch videotapes. . . . It was the old story of the sleek prison visitor telling prisoners how lucky they are. Oranges, Easter cakes, and other props were of course neatly in place.

Instead of giving in to anger, I tried to make sense of the feeling that I knew the Archbishop from somewhere. Under my breath I asked the Reverend Bremer to repeat his name. So *that* was it! I exclaimed to myself. Hilarion Capucci was the very same man the Israelis had jailed for running guns to PLO guerrillas in Jerusalem. Caught red-handed, he was later freed after intercession by the Pope. I tried to shake off the bear hug he had given me when I first entered the room. What would Americans make of me embracing *that* character on television!

But the Reverend Bremer's sympathy more than compensated. He was clearly pained when I told him this half hour was a show. "I know, I know," he said before we were taken away. "But meanwhile, take what comfort you can from it." Stuffing oranges and Hershey bars into a little bag I had, I said I felt like a scavenger. "Don't worry about that, Barry," he replied. "We're all scavengers."

Barry's letters never said he was sick. His mention of depression and nervousness seemed normal. Anyone who loved free physical movement as much as he would of course become depressed and nervous under guard. His type worries a little, even in normal circumstances—which spurs them to accomplish a lot. This came and went, like his concern with symptoms when he came down with a cold. He let you know how he felt rather than pretending everything was fine. But in anything major, he was a fighter. If anyone in the Embassy could deal with captivity, it was surely Barry, who would be in there observing, analyzing, and probing for loopholes. The situation was worrying, but not his condition.

Then I saw the television clip of him filmed in March, when international concern for the hostages' condition and very existence—seven families had received no mail whatever—was becoming acute. A New York station called minutes before to alert me that it was to be aired. I turned on the set with a surge of girlish anticipation that made me flush. My mother and aunt were thrilled for me but ran to bring me water before we could say a word. Barry's appearance shocked them, too. His face was gaunt and haggard, like a concentration-camp prisoner's. Only real suffering could have hollowed out the dark circles under his eyes. His arms were sticks. I felt like a fool for not taking the hints in his letters more seriously.

Of the dozen or so hostages in the footage, only Barry was talking. He appeared to be sitting on the floor, looking up at an Iranian Red Cross doctor and describing pulsations he was experiencing. He seemed to be almost pleading with the doctor, in phrases that suggested he was seeing one for the first time. The Iranians had obviously released the film to answer worldwide concern with this evidence that the hostages were well and receiving medical care. "Are they crazy?" I said to myself more than to my mother and aunt. "To convince us they're fine, they show Barry looking like death?"

The clip of him entreating the doctor was a television favorite for months. Station after station played and replayed it. The second and third times, I concentrated on Barry's barely audible words. It seemed odd that he, who always spoke Farsi to Iranians, was using English. He was telling the doctor that he had had an attack that started his heart beating furiously, but the way he said it frightened us more than what he said. His voice was hesitant. He was reduced to the choppy speech of people who lack the breath or strength to get out more than a few words at a time.

When I turned off the sound for the next few viewings, some of the other hostages looked as bad as Barry. All had gaunt faces with dark circles under their eyes. One man hunched in fetal position on a couch, holding a blanket over his head; others walked listlessly or stared at nothing. I reassured myself that what made Barry appear so much worse was his being the focus as the only one who talked. Then it struck me that his speaking English wasn't odd at all: He was trying to get a message to me: *He needed a proper doctor.* After that viewing, I went to bed knowing I must do something for him in the morning. My first idea was to appeal to the militants, either directly or through a press campaign. Neither route offered much hope. Then I thought of something that was less likely to provoke the militants' automatic rejection. The Iranian Embassy in Washington was closed, but the Iranian Mission to the United Nations remained a diplomatic channel. I decided it would be best to approach them privately, on humanitarian grounds.

Within an hour after release of the startling footage of Barry, reporters began camping outside our front gate. The collection of network and local vans, with their instant-replay equipment, spread down the street in both directions. I didn't want to comment on Barry's condition until I had thought about what might be best for him. I decided not even to express the shock and worry we *had* to be feeling. When reporters kept shouting my name, one of my brothers-in-law went out to tell them I had nothing to say for the moment. His Alaskan malamute accompanied him to the gate. The item was so "hot" that even my brother-in-law's "Barbara has no comment now," together with the dog's howl at the moon, featured on the evening news.

The next morning, I was even more certain my only chance for a doctor would be through strictly private intercession. If my appeal became public, it would be transformed into a political issue, pushing the militants to demonstrate their ideological purity and revolutionary "toughness" by rejecting it. But I had learned not to count on journalists to see it that way. Too many lessons had taught that their job was getting the story, whatever the implications for Barry.

I had to get past the encampment without their suspecting my destination or their following me. I got into the car casually, as though for local shopping, then drove around, watching my rearview mirror until I felt "safe"—before heading for Manhattan.

*

One reason I was intent on avoiding publicity was the disastrous failure of a United Nations commission to Iran just a few weeks before. In February, five distinguished public figures from Algeria, Venezuela, Syria, Sri Lanka, and France had flown to Tehran under the auspices of UN Secretary-General Kurt Waldheim. All five were highly acceptable to the revolutionary authorities; the Frenchman, for example, had investigated torture practices under the Shah. Together, they exuded optimism about breaking the long deadlock. Two days before they flew from Geneva to Tehran, President Bani-Sadr said that Khomeini had accepted their plan for a solution to the crisis. The day before they left, the commission chairman announced, "We have a gentleman's agreement for the hostages' release."

But their visit was a fiasco, and I felt certain that Kurt Waldheim and President Carter's premature announcement of triumph was at least partly responsible. Hard-line Iranian politicians opposed freeing the hostages, largely because it would diminish their own power in political infighting for control of the revolution. They used the hasty public congratulations to win Khomeini to their side; a few words from the leader torpedoed the supposed settlement. For two weeks, the commission was subjected to treatment similar to what Dr. Waldheim himself had endured on a January visit to Tehran. Demonstrators screamed at them and pounded on their cars. Despite solemn promises and "guarantees," they weren't even allowed to *see* the hostages!

Finally they felt jostled, twisted, and humiliated enough and decided to leave Tehran, as empty-handed as previous intermediaries. The trip to the airport ended in a ludicrous car chase, with militants trying to force them to accept photocopied documents from the Embassy as proof of American evil and the justice of their cause. The commission's failure left the situation even worse than before.

It also left me with nothing but disgust for the revolutionaries. Remembering Barry's descriptions of suffering under the Shah, I had tried to understand their motives. But those who won't allow even friendly observers to check the health of wrongly taken, wrongly held prisoners sacrifice the right to sympathetic understanding. My interest now was singular and straightforward: how to influence the new regime to provide medical attention for Barry. From everything I knew, the only way was through the friend-of-a-friend route: the opposite of confrontation, which would threaten the bullies. . . .

*

I parked the car in a garage near the United Nations and walked the few blocks to the Iranian Mission, which was on an upper floor of a new Third Avenue office complex. Although the building's lobby guards recognized me and sympathized with Barry, they would allow no one to enter the elevator without permission from above. A sharp argument followed when I called upstairs to ask for that permission. The voice on the other end of the telephone obviously belonged to a secretary. He said I could not come up.

"You are holding my husband illegally," I answered, sensing my approach would come to nothing unless I hurdled this first obstacle quickly. "I saw him on television yesterday and he looked awful. I've come to talk to you about that privately, and if you don't give me the courtesy, I'll round up the press—which I've been avoiding. Let them take some good strong film of you people refusing to see me."

An armed guard came down to escort me upstairs. The officer who met me there was obviously a career diplomat, the antithesis of the student militants in dress and manner. He cordially led me to a large meeting room with a mahogany table and Persian art on the walls. Both the room and the diplomat could have "belonged" to a large European corporation.

While the fastidious man poured tea, I took out some of my "teaching aids" and displayed them on the table. I had brought a medallion with a saying from the Koran and little necklaces with "Ariana" and the Farsi for "Alexander" wrought in gold. Arranging these around a revolutionary painting Barry had sent home. I launched into my speech. Since my host was very polite, I kept it friendly—but didn't pare it.

"My husband has always respected your people and your country," I said, looking him straight in the eye. "He went to Tehran fully aware of the revolutionary situation and determined to do everything he could to advance mutual understanding. Now he looks ghastly, he's so sick that he can't even stand. What kind of people treat someone like that who loves your country?"

The First Secretary waited courteously until I finished: a good sign, I thought. "I am truly sorry for the way the hostages are being treated," he answered after a pause. "As a diplomat myself, I know the importance of diplomatic immunity and I am personally convinced that holding your people is wrong."

It wasn't the fault of the Iranian people and certainly not of Ayatollah Khomeini, he said. It was all the doing of "those wild militants," whom no one could control. "But I give you my word that I will do what I can to obtain a medical examination for Mr. Rosen. I will be in touch with the highest authorities."

"Does that mean President Bani-Sadr?"

"The highest authorities. I cannot tell you more, but I promise your request will receive the most serious attention."

I did not believe a word about Khomeini not being able to control the students. He even claimed the Ayatollah had to play along with them to guarantee the hostages' safety and ensure that they would come out alive. Yet he changed tone—became intense and seemingly earnest—when talking about his distaste for what was happening and when promising to intervene. There was nothing more I could do for the moment.

*

During the next weeks, the clip of Barry talking to the doctor seemed to show almost every time I turned on the television. When I didn't turn on the set, the footage played in my mind. Barry clasped his heart, then held his hands up to the doctor. I still made no public comment, because I didn't want to give the militants the satisfaction of knowing how I felt, or the encouragement to keep up their game and keep raising the stakes. If I had spoken out then, I might have revealed hatred.

I knew Barry wasn't afraid to die. An engine once fell off a plane he was on, in the middle of the Atlantic. He comforted everyone, including the hysterical English psychiatrist sitting next to him shouting that he couldn't lose his life this senseless way. ("Pull yourself together, man," said Barry, who was returning from a visit to England. "If it's going to happen, we can't change much.") During the first seizure of the Embassy, Barry calmly said good-bye to his photos of the children and me. Maybe his willingness to face death was another outcome of religious training that persisted after he lost conventional belief.

But I also knew he couldn't stand much inactivity, and should have realized earlier how badly the hostage situation must be affecting him for that reason. In difficult situations, Barry has to *act,* if only by jumping up for a brisk walk. One of the experts interviewed by NBC News said Barry exhibited "the classic symptoms of profound depression" associated with hostage victims. Five months of doing nothing had to be a great strain on him. When my father saw the film, he said he wished he could trade places. He was so relaxed he could doze through a bombing; in this sense, he was Barry's opposite.

Each time I saw him pleading to the doctor, I felt a twinge of my nausea of the first afternoon. It was no exaggeration to say that death would be less hard on Barry than imprisonment for much longer. This was not because he was heroic, which he could be at times, but because nothing could damage him more than the constant humiliation —which is how he would interpret it—of being submissive.

I sensed he was truly sick, and hoped fervently that my visit to the Iranian mission would achieve something. After leaving there, I went to see Donald McHenry, American Ambassador to the United Nations, whom I had talked to previously. He wasn't in, but his second-in-command had seen the clip of Barry and promised to speak to Kurt Waldheim at a meeting later that day. He called that evening to say it was done and that Dr. Waldheim too promised to intercede with "the highest Iranian authorities." I tried not to think of the consequences if neither approach worked. The hostage crisis had become much more acute for those who loved Barry. We were in a new dimension.

*

We were also in a new time of pain-sharing. In the old days, prisoners of war languished in camps for years, but families and loved ones were spared the sight and sound of them. With the occasional letters that got out taking weeks or months to reach home, imprisonment was a *distant* ache.

The electronic age, with instant satellite transmission of armed captors and the perfect international medium of videotape, changed that. Most of my friends assumed that seeing the hostages was a comfort—except for Barry's debilitation. In one way it *was* a relief. In a more dominating sense, it made waiting harder.

Barry was an arm's reach away, but he might as well have been in space, because his cathode image conjured up only what I couldn't say to him or do for him when he needed my help more than ever. The screen tortured with a contemporary twist. I was glued to it—and hated it.

What was gained by seeing him except feelings of powerlessness and hopelessness? Barry remained unreachable and maybe would never be reached. After all the fictitious kidnap and prisoner episodes on that never-blinking television eye, this real one was perverted and repelling.

The effect on Alexander was very disturbing. When his father's image appeared, he ran out of the room, buried his head in my lap, or asked me to shut off the set, because he "had a headache." I was afraid it meant he had developed negative feelings toward Barry. Then I realized the child was avoiding the pain of seeing his father a prisoner—or of seeing him when he couldn't "have" him in a normal way. I often wished I could do that too. Maybe one day families of crime victims will take in stride seeing and hearing them as they undergo their ordeal. Meanwhile, I had yet to adjust to this bit of progress.

One of the lessons taught again and again was that there were no simple answers to difficult diplomatic questions—or to large issues at home. The more I observed the media, the more I resented their sacrifice of so many values to commercialism and the surer I felt that their greed was poisoning our country. The most disappointing realization was that so few people recognized what they were being fed. They turned on their television sets and passively swallowed the poison—just as I had, before a pressing need forced me to think for myself.

Yet much remained resistant both to greed and the newer kind of poison. Americans had amazingly strong constitutions. So many spent most of their free hours watching a screen whose basic message was *sell*, yet many kept it from perverting their senses.

Some were remarkably generous. My pediatrician saw the children a dozen times and wouldn't accept a penny. The owner of a toy company—a graduate of Lincoln High School, which I also had attended —sent a box of toys to each hostage family with no publicity whatever; his reward was in the giving. Total strangers sent stacks of letters and invitations—for example, to attend a festival in the town of Salamanca, New York, near Niagara Falls. The wife of a prominent furniture manufacturer took me, my mother, and the children on a week's vacation in Florida. I hadn't known her before she telephoned.

On a personal level, many people overflowed with spontaneous kindness. If I added them up, the expressions of concern and eagerness to help probably would have made me as optimistic about human nature as media attitudes made me gloomy. There was no simple answer to that, either.

The letters I received with advice for maintaining my equilibrium and for freeing Barry were almost all motivated by good will. That didn't keep some from deserving the label of crank. A few were followed up by telephone calls—to Barry's mother, since I still managed to keep my number confidential.

One of the most persistent callers identified himself as "Mr. Graham from New Jersey." He rang so often that Sarah gave him my number, having checked with me. He called promptly, announcing that he had a nearly foolproof plan to free Barry within weeks. He would reveal nothing about it on the telephone but sounded so intriguing that I gave in to his power of persuasion and agreed to meet him.

But something told me to keep him away from the children; meeting at Sarah's seemed safer. He drove to her apartment in Starrett City almost as soon as I put down the phone. Mr. Graham was even more conspiratorially "intimate" than his voice. A thrusting man in his fifties, he sported gold rings on his fingers and a gold eagle dangling from a gold chain around his neck. He introduced himself by means of some rather personal stories about his several wives. Coming to the point, he asked whether we would mind his spending some time in the bathroom. He wanted Sarah and me, he explained, to listen in private to a cassette he had brought. He put it into a little recorder he also had brought, then absented himself to wait among the stockings drying on Sarah's shower rod.

Sarah and I blinked. Our surprise grew even greater when the tape began with Mr. Graham's voice announcing that wasn't really his name. He could not reveal the true one now because he was . . . one of America's best-known second-story men. Although he used no gun and had harmed no one, he was, he allowed, "very, very famous" nevertheless. If we wanted to check, he would supply articles about his exploits.

But in our case he wanted no publicity for himself. His only interest was helping the hostages, to whom he felt a duty deep in his heart. The government, he said indignantly, had done far too little for them. "I can't stand it any more," he growled, "that Americans are over there being treated like, excuse me, you-know-what, and nobody doing a damn' thing for them." His own plan was a bit complicated, he went on, but was *certain to work.*

It would start with the State Department leaking to the press that there had been a recent series of burglaries of homes of important Washington officials. Sometime later, he would reveal to the Iranian Embassy in Canada that during one of *his* burglaries in Washington—he would make the connection for them in case they didn't do it themselves—he had found a set of papers in a safe. The papers would indicate that American agents had planted bombs in major Iranian cities and that the bombs would be exploded if the hostages weren't released by a certain date. To save the Iranian cities and the Iranian face, he, the burglar, would suggest that the hostages be freed before the State Department presented them with the ultimatum.

The tape laid this out in a straightforward manner, as though one conspirator were talking to another. To strengthen "Mr. Graham's" credibility with the Iranians, he would offer to *sell* them the plans for just enough to make the caper look believable. The U. S. Government would be spared all embarrassment, for if it wanted, it could deny knowledge of everything, stressing that a thief could have no knowledge of its plans.

If "Mr. Graham" wasn't actually a criminal, he had watched some realistic crime films. His idea sounded just plausible enough for me to put him in touch with someone in the State Department, and he drove down to Washington without wasting a minute. He used all his persuasive power to get me to come along, but despite his charm I preferred not to embark on a six-hour ride with him. When I insisted I couldn't leave the children, he set off alone, at his own expense.

He spoke to my State Department contact, but apparently the government didn't appreciate his ingenuity. I regretted not taking his telephone number, for when I didn't hear from him again, I wanted to make sure he was well and not in the clink.

*

Most of the other "solutions" were simpler, but often as farfetched. One couple was connected with a Kansas group called The Committee for Free Americans and the Resolution of the Iran Crisis. Their idea was to draft a letter—which they assured me they could smuggle to Barry—that Barry would copy in his own hand and present to the militants. It would expose American "crimes" in Iran in detail, making clear that the high-minded students had every right to seize the Embassy and hold the hostages. It would be written in a way that the militants could easily exploit in the American press, simultaneously winning Barry his freedom and doing a great service to Israel, because it would show the world a Jew could defend Muslim activists!

They were utterly serious. Their own family had suffered grievously when they were forcibly repatriated to Romania after World War II, and they hoped with all their hearts to spare us a similar tragedy, although I was hard pressed to find the connection to our situation.

The neatest suggestion—even though it took him many pages to describe it—came from a Santa Monica man. As confirmation that *his* plan was certain to work, the instructions included selected quotations from the Bible and Shakespeare. "All things be ready if the mind be so." To accomplish Barry's release, all we had to do was make the mind ready by writing down two sentences and repeating them upon awakening, at noon, and just before retiring:

All the hostages in Iran have been released and they are now home and safe. They are all healthy, happy, and well adjusted, and I give thanks that this has happened.

The letter was beautifully typed on luxurious stationery. The advice was the only indication the writer wasn't a pillar of society. His P.S. was a crowning touch:

Visualize in your mind your loved one's first night back. You are having a big celebration, a very festive homecoming dinner. Everyone is happy. . . . Make this very real to you. IT HAS ALREADY HAPPENED.

On evenings when things looked dismal, I sometimes reread this advice. It brought laughs through my tears.

Barry's letters kept coming, irregularly and in batches. I picked up some at the offices of the American Indian Treaty Council in Manhattan. Others came with the ministers who visited in April or through the Red Cross. When my local post office received some, almost always three or four at a time, they called me at 7 A.M., just after sorting, so I could fetch them even before the official opening, an hour later.

Letters brought momentary happiness because they were tangible evidence that things could be worse: As long as Barry could write, he couldn't be *impossibly* unwell. But they were misery to read.

January 8th

I'm holding up as best I can given the circumstances. But truthfully, I'm no hero, and this experience will never leave me the same. I try hard to take it in stride, but my condition makes this difficult.

January 10th

I'm doing my best to stay as calm as possible. But it's a tough battle. . . . If only I weren't the nervous type! How I wish I had your father's ability to stay cool. This is the 68th day, enough is enough.

January 15th

I try to cheer myself up, but I have to be honest with you, it's not easy. I think about you and the children all the time, and hope and pray to see you soon. . . . If I sound depressed, take it for what it is, a release to the only person who can really understand me. I know you are undergoing similar pressures, but I'm now too realistic to keep up the proverbial stiff upper lip and make believe that all is fine and dandy.

January 25th

I am trying to keep up the game, but it's very difficult and painful. I need your prayers.

January 26th

Today is the 84th day, that makes it 12 weeks. I can hardly believe it. It seems there is very little hope left. . . . There's no need to hide the truth from you. I'm depressed, but trying to hold my own for all our sakes. . . . I know the only way for me to really get back to myself will be with good loving care at home and freedom from this nightmare. Try not to worry, but I had to tell you. . . . Although I used to exercise as often as possible, either in our room or a makeshift exercise room, I've lost interest. I've also cut down on reading due to a lack of concentration.

January 29th

I want to concentrate on *you* and *the children*. I want to devote my time to you because I worry about how all this has affected you, and made your life, once very joyful, into less than you deserve. I admire you and respect your intelligence and honest courage while undergoing such an experience. It must be terrible for you to spend the entire day under the expectation that something good might occur. . . . I look forward to holding you in my arms and telling you how much I love you.

February 6th

We, you and I, go back a bit, and your love is all that is keeping me going. I'm selfish enough to say that I can't think of anything any more but *you*, and that thought is all I have.

February 20th

Don't smirk, but I've been reading the Old and New Testaments for solace. . . . My favorite selection is from the Song of Solomon, sensuous poetry describing a love relationship. Although many can interpret it in a religious sense—God and His people— I choose to accept it at face value and think of us. This quote is how I feel about you.
"My beloved is a bouquet of flowers in the gardens of Engedi. How beautiful you are, my love, how beautiful! Your eyes are soft as doves'. What a lovely, pleasant thing you are, lying here upon the grass, shaded by cedar trees and firs."

I never reread the letters. It took self-control, but what was the sense of hurting myself? I could do nothing to ease his pain.
And that pain hurt less than his terrible guilt about the children. When we lived together, we did everything together, even shopped for food—and especially for clothes, since he liked supervising what I wore. Many weeks we were side by side twenty-four hours a day except for work. Yet Barry had been a bachelor long enough to look after himself in the practical sense. He took our long separations in stride.
Not seeing his children is what ate at him. He was tortured by in-

ability to hold Alexander and talk to him as he had used to for hours whenever he could. His letters to the children were harder to read than my own. I was overwhelmingly sorry for them all.

"I can't express the guilt I have concerning the children," he wrote to me. "Sometimes I believe I don't deserve to be their father. I've spent so much time away from them—and now, given the present circumstances. . . . My guilt is especially directed to Alexander, whom I miss more than words can tell. I dream of taking him for a walk; just talking to him—for that alone is a joy. I'm losing his childhood, which I dearly want to be part of."

That was no exaggeration. Although he hardly knew Ariana, he had been an extraordinary father to Alexander. When we lived in Washington, he was chief of Voice of America's Uzbek service. Broadcasts went out at 9 A.M. Washington time. To supervise their preparation, he went to work at 5 A.M. and returned at two o'clock in the afternoon. The rest of the day was his and Alexander's, until they bathed together every evening and Barry put his boy to bed. They were unusually close.

Alexander had a seat on the back of Barry's bicycle. They chatted as Barry pedaled around the grounds of our apartment complex every afternoon. I watched from the balcony, refraining from interfering with their closeness, which was as beautiful as the best of Barry and me.

Letters that reached me made clear that other letters never did, including some to the children. Those that got through made me cry. Why was this happening to *us*? I wondered. There were so many empty marriages, and we, who were so much part of each other, were being pulled apart. But masochistic thoughts would accomplish nothing, and I blanked them out. Crying couldn't help, only being as active as possible in whatever real work might be done to end the hurt.

I wanted Barry, not television clips or even letters. I was beginning to prefer the long periods without news, when my feelings would go numb and I could concentrate on the children. Letters ripped at the wound.

For that reason, I learned to ignore Barry's advice about keeping his relationship with the children active. "Please keep talking to the kids about me," he had written in his very first letter. "Don't let them forget me." Later, obviously desperate, he went so far as to suggest I find a friend with a voice like his to call on the telephone to speak to the children as "Daddy." Alexander's reaction to film clips—and common sense—told me not to keep mentioning him.

Ariana was too young to understand, but Alexander became upset when I tried to talk to him about Barry. He put up a very determined resistance for a three-year-old and grew visibly depressed when I persisted—which I soon stopped doing.

"Try to keep the children aware that they have a father, don't let them forget me," Barry would write—but Alexander was *trying* to forget. He had a surprising amount of information about what was happening in Iran from television, radio, the family reading newspapers aloud, telephone conversations, and visitors talking about our preoccupation. He knew the names of Khomeini, Bani-Sadr, Ghotbzadeh, and half a dozen others, and could locate Iran on a map. Even one-year-old Ariana absorbed something from our immersion in Iran. Sitting in her high chair, she would bang her cup on the little tray and pronounce one of her first words: "Kho-mei-ni, Kho-mei-ni."

Alexander was able to discuss the crisis at the level of a child twice his age, yet wouldn't discuss his father, as if the two things weren't related. I thought I understood. Death is a final, irrevocable separation to which people must adjust if they are to remain normal. But the periodic appearance of film clips interrupted the healing process for Alexander, and he was trying to protect himself in an appropriate way for a child his age. Having been so close to his father, separation was especially cruel. He was avoiding having his unavailable daddy dangled before him, then having to begin the painful "forgetting" process yet again. And I stopped reminding him. After all, who knew how long the crisis would last? And if the worst happened, it would be better for healing to have begun.

Then, entirely of his own accord one summer day, he asked with a twinge of impatience, "Where's Daddy? Whatever happened to Daddy?" Nine long months had passed. I told him what of course he already knew. If I perceived correctly, it had taken Alexander all that time to come to terms with his problem sufficiently to verbalize it. He didn't accept it fully, for he "blanked it out" again after the summer. But when he sensed Sarah was distressed after this, he would reassure her: "Don't worry, Grandma Sarah, Daddy will come soon. Everything will be okay."

I hugged him hard, wishing I could wipe away his hurt—but I couldn't. Pretending everything was fine would only confuse him more or hatch new resentments.

The weeks with Dave seemed shorter than the first period of captivity. He often did one thing and I quite another, but we managed never to get in each other's way. He widened the margin of his wins in our coaster game.

We reckoned it was the morning of April 25 when Hamid ran into the room in a lather. I was taking my after-breakfast jog and Dave was resting in bed. "Pack up!" barked Number One as if someone above him had ordered an evacuation. "Everything in one bag and be ready in an hour!"

This was the start of our removal from Tehran, a more frenzied operation than any previous one. Guards jigged about as if the Embassy had put ants in their pants and they were suddenly itching to leave the compound. Naturally, we were even more anxious. Where were we going? What did their goddamn jumpiness mean?

What did it mean that they had masked the windows of our van with fresh spray paint to prevent even Iranians from seeing the move, yet kept photographing us as if they wanted hourly proof that we were still alive? Despite their running about, it took them all day to get organized and pack a van with about a dozen of us. We supposed there were other vehicles for most or all of the other hostages. Conversation was forbidden, and blindfolds kept us literally in the dark, but we risked whispers when the motor strained.

"Is that you, Dave?"

"Yes, Barry, it's me."

His voice provided enough security to fend off the worst of the anxiety. After nearly eight weeks together, our little room had become almost comfortable, and the International Red Cross had visited just ten days before, with a promise of returning every two weeks. The Red Cross promised genuine medical checkups and regular mail from Barbara. Above all, it was a token of the Iranians' giving in on something, which must have been at least a small step toward release. Maybe this move had been ordered precisely because a group opposing release had triumphed in an internal political struggle and was sending us out of Tehran so no more concessions to us would be granted. The future seemed so bleak that I needed something solid to steady me. Dave—and our trust in each other—would make it easier.

We seemed to drive south between two and three hours. Shortly before we stopped, we passed a large collection of railroad noises, reinforcing my guess that we'd come to Qom, the closest major center to the south with a railroad yard. The holy city of Qom was the site of one of Iran's two most sacred places and Khomeini's present residence. Dave Roeder, a naval officer named Robert Englemann, and I were unloaded there. Our residence, a tiny room just big enough for two bunk beds, was tiled in white. "The White Hole," as we called it, provided clinical surroundings for going mad, in case that was in the cards.

Bob Englemann, a Lieutenant Commander, had been working before the seizure with Iranian counterparts, trying to settle claims and counterclaims about the supply of spare parts for American military equipment. He was suffering so badly from dysentery that he could barely eat. An Iranian doctor taken in to examine him seemed almost as anxious as we about his condition, which he bore without complaint. Again I saw a military officer who was bright, well educated, and behaving with admirable inner strength.

A week or so later, he was removed from the room, to our intense concern. Hours later, Dave Roeder and I were driven to another town, seemingly farther south. During our month there we were given a bottle of milk. The label revealed it had been produced in Isfahan. Since almost all Iranian milk is distributed locally, my supposition that we were in or near a town in Isfahan Province was strengthened. This was "The Tan Hole": a larger room with a little opening in the ceiling that provided a thin shaft of light. The windows were boarded up. Iron bars had been welded over the ceiling opening too, as if to symbolize our status as crudely as possible. Oddly, however, the guards here seemed less aggressive than in Tehran. Some even knocked on the door and asked permission before entering our room. A certain relaxed, provincial feeling penetrated even into our "hole," starting with the morning crow of roosters.

Mr. Nice, our favorite guard, seemed embarrassed even to step inside, lest he disturb us. But he ran in one day, flushed with excitement.

"It's come. I *told* you. The black revolution in America!"

What he had told me, politely but often, was, "You'll get yours"—which was inevitable when the blacks revolted, as the Iranians had.

"In Florida," he continued. "Streets being burned in a big city; it's the end of your imperialism."

He went on about how events—I still knew nothing about the Miami riots—had vindicated his conviction that, among other crimes, America had calculatedly ruined Iranian agriculture to make her dependent. At that point I grew tired of Mr. Nice—who, I remembered, had tied Dave's hands so tightly with plastic fasteners for garbage bags that his hands stayed numb for four days after the ride to The Tan Hole.

From a balcony of whatever building we were in, Mr. Nice and others ranted to vast-sounding crowds below. Clearly eager to be whipped into hysteria, the crowds screamed back. This was not the usual "Death to America, death to Carter" generalizations, but specific charges that the American Sixth Fleet had steamed into the Persian Gulf to bomb Iran and land an invasion force. "Could *this* be why we had been rushed out of Tehran?" Dave and I tried to fathom. Obviously the Iranians had information we did not, and feared an imminent attack. The implications took us to new levels of pessimism. If an attack came, we surely would never be found. If we were the only two still away from the Embassy, we'd probably be the Iranians' ace in the hole in any bargaining. Dave held his breath while I strained for every word from the balcony.

We were moved again on the night of May 30–31—back to what I reckoned was Qom. Whatever had stimulated the passion for shifting us about was clearly still operating, and this time it devastated me: Dave Roeder and I were separated, which left me more depressed in the classical sense than anytime since the seizure, seven months before. Dave and I had remained extraordinarily close. Without him, I felt hopelessly deprived. He had been taken somewhere in the same building, and I felt like risking a bullet to try to track him down.

What eased me back toward my "normal" state of incomprehensible physical symptoms was the discovery that I could help someone else. One of the three others into whose room I was moved was severely depressed. "Could you imagine *you* encouraging someone else?" I asked myself. For my own encouragement, I extracted a set of compressed, self-evident homilies from a book in the room and placed it on the wall directly over my mattress, with my own underlining.

THE WELL ADJUSTED

1. WHEN YOU FEEL GOOD, BE HAPPY
2. LOOK ON THE BRIGHT SIDE
3. PROBLEMS USUALLY WORK OUT
4. EVERYONE IS IN THE SAME BOAT
5. LOWER YOUR DAILY GOALS
6. STOP GUILT FEELINGS—NO SELF-PITY
7. REPLACE HURTFUL EMOTIONS WITH HEALTHFUL ONES: PRACTICE REPLACING HARMFUL EMOTIONS LIKE WORRY, FEAR, ANXIETY, APPREHENSION AND DISCOURAGEMENT WITH CHEERFUL ONES LIKE HOPE, SERENITY AND SATISFACTION.

It also helped to be spending the time there in as highly organized and productive ways as possible. Colonel Thomas Schaefer, Air Force Attaché and Dave Roeder's superior officer, measured the dimensions of the room with his belt and calculated that our several daily walks, which he led somewhat like Alec Guinness before the sun got him in *The Bridge over the River Kwai,* covered eight to ten miles. Our healthily distracting daily agenda also included half an hour of yoga and thorough, analytical talk about where we had all been and whom we had seen before coming to this room.

In addition to Tom, my new roommates were Steven Lauterbach and Robert Englemann. Steve was a young administrative officer on his first assignment abroad; Bob, with whom I had spent the week in Qom, had fully recovered from his dysentery. I would come to know them very well in eight months together. We spent the early days going over our captive pasts in minute detail for the benefit of each other and any common deductions we might reach. But at first I was much distracted by the room in which they had already been held for several weeks.

Known as The Pink Palace in tribute to the gaudy color of its paint and the bathroom's marble floor and shower, it was possibly the guest quarters of a museum or large government institution. The pink became as dreary as lavatory green, because we could see nothing whatever through the windows. They were entirely blocked by steel window boxes filled with sand: exact copies of those that had been installed in the Embassy to protect against gunfire, except these leaked sand over everything. The ventilation was from a small fan that pushed air through four or five metal slats that opened over a vent. This also supplied the only daylight.

The fan often stopped, because electricity came on and off erratically, suggesting that the country's economic difficulties might be worsening. But although the room became suffocating and slightly foul in the June heat without ventilation, I didn't mind when the electricity went off. Lying on my bed, I could see a view of the outside, upside down on the ceiling. It was reflected off the motionless fan blades. I recognized a pair of doves on a branch. Smudges of people and orange taxis passed on what I imagined was the pleasant provincial street. I dozed and daydreamed.

It worried me that visions of Barbara were no longer sexual. Perhaps energy shifts from the libido to something even more basic at times like those. But I missed her even more than before: She had given me strengths no one else could. When things were difficult, I could blurt out anything without worrying that she would think less of me. Her quiet hug helped me say what I wanted and be what I was.

From the other hostages' talk about their families, I realized more than ever that we had a rare understanding. We made up in a minute after an argument. When we discussed what we had done at the end of the day, it was never perfunctory or mechanical. She was a genuine listener and partner.

I wished I had been as good a husband. Early in our marriage I was sometimes stupidly aggressive. I wanted to see if she would convert to Judaism, which was too much for her. She wasn't a practicing Catholic by then; why should she respond to another religion?

It was narrow, unnecessary, and unfair. It could only have hurt her. If I had another chance to live with her, I'd undo my mistakes.

Maybe it was another form of feeling sorry for myself: I was in trouble and often thought of the unthinking, unnecessary troubles I had caused others. Why had I been untrue to myself?

My other main regret was for time frittered away. I wished I were a happier person: less bothered by petty, self-set tasks. If I had learned anything from months of reading and thinking since the seizure, it was that each day we lived—except in prison—passed very quickly. I now saw the search itself for happiness as an intrinsic destroyer of it. "Someday we'll have . . ." "Someday we'll get to . . ." was self-deception, whether or not encouraged by pressures to "score."

Maybe Iranians' unusual emphasis on family used to appeal so much because it answered a lack in me. I had spent a fair amount of time with my wife and children—but never as much as I wanted—free of striving and "business" thoughts. Barbara and I were separated too much of the time. We spent too many hours worrying about externals instead of dropping them simply to be together as a family, with no other purpose.

I had wanted to "get ahead." I didn't get very far, and paid too high a price anyway. "Finding yourself" sounded like mush when I heard it from an earnest young person in a Manhattan bar; now I felt I had found just that. When I got home, I was going to remember that my deepest instincts are most important, and these instincts are to stop rushing around. I would spend more time with Barbara and the children. I would stop sacrificing one day urgently arranging something that promised greater happiness for the next—when some new telephone call would set me running again.

Each day had to be used as though there might be no more, not wasted in the scramble for tomorrow's paradise. If I could put that into practice when I got out, maybe the hostage experience would be worth something.

＊

Missing Barbara wasn't the hardest burden. Our relationship was strong enough to withstand almost any length of separation. But depriving children of a father in their formative years was irreparable damage. They were too young to understand where Daddy was or why he had "abandoned" them. I felt guilt and self-pity, rage and outrage, all at once. Most of all, I felt each passing day was not only lost, but a further opening of the children's wounds. Sometimes frustration built up in my throat so that I could hardly swallow.

Other times, I partially released it on those guards who revealed themselves as human beings—who even expressed sorrow at the personal pain they were causing.

"What you are doing is killing a family," I would say. "Destroying a wife and two little children who have *nothing whatever to do with Iran;* do you understand?"

"Maybe I do," answered "Spectacles." "Do *you* understand how many Iranian families were destroyed under the Shah?"

"I sympathize with the mothers and children of families ruined under the Shah, during the revolution, or any time. But what you are doing to my children is no better. They *need* me."

"You will go home, maybe in a few months. Stop thinking about *your* problems."

"I'm not your property. What right do *you* have to decide how long my family and I will be apart?"

"The Iranian people suffered and died in the tens of thousands. Nothing has happened to you but a temporary separation."

"You think death is the only form of suffering. What you're putting us through is living death."

On it would go, with no conclusion and certainly no satisfaction. Never getting the guards to see the hypocrisy of causing human misery for the sake of supposed human happiness burned me with resentment like a log in a fire. As with our attitudes toward international law, we lived in two separate systems of logic.

*

I never kept it a secret from Barbara that I felt she had an almost suffocating relationship with her family, especially her mother. When we lived in Washington, Barbara could not go more than a few weeks without seeing her, so up we drove to Brooklyn, weekend after weekend. Now, however, I was relieved that she was living in the walled-in house. Many practical worries were eliminated for her there, and it was enriching for the children to be surrounded by relatives, as they always were in the old house, probably even more while I was "away."

Barbara's letters made clear that her family were looking after Alexander and Ariana as though they were their own children. I was deeply grateful for that; I owed many thanks for what *everyone* was doing. But they were *my* children. I wanted to expose them to *my* values and longed to bathe them and take them for walks. I had to blame myself too for whatever my absence was doing to them. I had been away too long even before the seizure. I had volunteered to come to Tehran without my family and volunteered to extend my stay, which was wrong for them.

It was the usual mistake of not following one's instincts. Somewhere, I knew the children were more important than anything else. But off I went without them, and here was the reward.

The State Department's December briefing of the hostage families had been followed by one in February. Many family members arrived full of demands—at least for information—and even anger over lack of progress. The Washington weekends began with cocktails and a pleasant dinner on Friday. A full day of briefings on Saturday was capped by a handsome Sunday brunch.

Although we learned almost nothing new, the opportunity to talk with high officials—and with each other, which was equally important —vented our frustration, as the organizers of the briefings knew it would. The applause of what seemed the entire State Department as we filed out of the auditorium put a collective lump of pride and patriotism in our throats. Most people remained reassured for a month or two, when questions about policy arose again and rage over our impotence built. The military families in particular grew heated. Some demanded action, even if it meant risking their husbands and sons.

Apart from that, there was general resentment that holding our hands and patting our shoulders were substitutes for facts about negotiations and attempted negotiations. The conflict between our right to know and the government's need for secrecy was real. Some people rushed out of the briefings to hand notes to journalists massed outside, or walked in with their hometown reporters at their sides. Others recorded the full first briefing and made the tapes available to the press. Without solving the question of how much information we deserved and how much could be dangerous for us to have, everyone wanted the families' interests and views to be better represented in Washington.

An association called the Family Liaison Action Group—FLAG— had been formed there in March. The prime movers were Penne Laingen, wife of Bruce Laingen, the Chargé d'Affaires, and Louisa Kennedy, wife of Moorhead Kennedy, an economics officer at the Embassy, and Katherine Keough, wife of William Keough, head of the Tehran American School. We saw the new organization not as an extension of the State Department, like the Iran Working Group, but as a cooperative of the families to which we all could turn for information, advice, and a channel of influence on the various branches of government. To what extent it remained free of State Department influence was difficult to measure, just as it was difficult to maintain complete independence of the government. For months, until funds for its own premises could be raised, the FLAG office remained in the State Department Building, where free use was made of a WATS line, without which we could not possibly have afforded calls around the country. But despite our big brothers in government with their vast resources, FLAG acquired a personality of its own, with which I felt more comfortable than with the Iran Working Group.

Tireless Louisa Kennedy was elected spokesperson. She called me in early April to ask if I wanted to join a few wives and mothers whom FLAG was planning to send to Europe. The purpose was to obtain support for the hostages by personalizing their situation to the European people. Most Europeans perceived the fifty-three Americans as merely a news item—which was natural. A hostage without a name or face is an abstract. Perhaps seeing close relatives would help them view the problem in terms of real lives.

My first question to myself was whether appearances by me in Europe would harm Barry. I decided they probably wouldn't, and possibly might even help. The second question was whether I had something to say, rather than going along for the ride. I indeed wanted to "push" an idea if I could, and joined the group.

My attitude was opposite, in a way, to that of most military families. At a press conference before departing, I said I was increasingly worried that military action was being contemplated. With continuing failure to make diplomatic progress, I sensed that increasing frustration was bringing an increasing inclination to resort to force, and risking tens of thousands of lives to save fifty-three wasn't my idea of a sensible solution. I was still convinced that war would bring more suffering, but patience, if we had enough, would eventually lead to release. As friendly bystanders, Europeans might exercise a moderating influence or serve as intermediaries. The more involved they became, especially in the American economic boycott, the better I saw the chance for avoiding tragedy.

The danger of military conflict seemed great. More and more patriots were calling for *action*, such as mining Iranian ports and blockading the Persian Gulf by American aircraft carriers already there. Since we had met President Carter, in December, he had kept repeating that his goals were safe return of the hostages and preserving the national honor, but when he reversed the order in his most recent speech, my ears pricked up at this apparent signal. Given the country's mood, it didn't seem accidental.

Some in Washington assumed the Iranians would crumble at the first show of force. But what if it fed the Iranian martyr complex, sparking them to take immediate revenge on the hostages? So far, our allies had been less than gallant in coming to our aid and, it seemed, less than far-sighted in recognizing the threat to *all* diplomats in the outrage against our own. The more vocal their support the less the chance that the situation would lead to tragedy through calculation or miscalculation. But I also wanted to go to Europe to listen and learn.

Not being directly involved, Europeans might suggest new approaches to Tehran or offer dispassionate advice.

Our group of four was led informally by Louisa Kennedy, who still did most of the organizing and talking for FLAG. The others were Jeanne Queen, mother of Richard Queen, the young vice-consul who would develop multiple sclerosis and be released in June; and Pearl Golacinski, mother of Alan Golacinski, a security officer. On April 22, we left on an evening flight from Washington as representatives of FLAG, without the State Department's direct involvement but with their approval and support, especially with cooperation after we had made our arrangements abroad.

We arrived in Paris the next morning, a few hours before our first appointment, with Giscard d'Estaing, President of France. There was time to ponder secondary questions—whether to wear gloves, how to address the French President—but not enough for our excitement to become nervousness. Traffic delayed the government cars sent to fetch us. They arrived just as we were about to take a taxi, then got free of our hotel by driving a block on the sidewalk. While I absorbed my first view of Paris, we crawled to the Élysée Palace, which seemed to cross a magnificent mansion with a lavish museum.

A red carpet led up the grand stairway to the door, with soldiers on guard who could have been in costume. Inside, the Palace was unrelieved luxury. Its immense rooms featured huge Persian carpets, sumptuously ornate furniture, and more gold leaf on more elaborate moldings than I could have fantasied. I practiced my "Bonjour, Monsieur le Président" until it was nearly intelligible, but when M. le Président appeared, I found myself murmuring, "Hello," in English.

Giscard d'Estaing was polite, concerned, and well informed about the crisis. He said he did not understand why all Iranian students had not been expelled immediately from the United States—and also assured us that he would never have permitted Khomeini to settle in France had he known he would have been "so political." This sounded a bit unlikely to me, perhaps offered in the expectation that we would like to hear it.

After personal details about "our" hostages, we talked about the need for unity and the importance of economic sanctions—which, however, he felt France should not fully support. Presumably to signal Tehran that he took our visit—therefore the holding of the hostages—seriously, he kept us almost an hour longer than scheduled. Still, the visit was a slight disappointment. The French President was impressive, but not totally persuasive. He did not think economic boycott of Iran a good idea, and I wondered how much that had to do with French trading interests. I must have been expecting something more.

The rest of the afternoon went to press conferences and interviews, with pushing and shoving even more aggressive than in America. The

following morning, Louisa Kennedy went to England to meet Prime
Minister Margaret Thatcher and the Archbishop of Canterbury;
Jeanne Queen traveled to Rome to talk to President Pertini and Prime
Minister Cossiga of Italy, and Pearl Golacinski remained in Paris for
radio and television interviews.

I traveled to Bonn for press appearances and a meeting with the
German Chancellor. When I arrived, the American Embassy's Press
Officer, Barry's counterpart, settled me in a charming inn just outside
the city limits. This was my first long trip without Barry, who had always selected the itinerary and plotted our sight-seeing. The "what
am I doing here?" feeling was submerged in irritation at myself for
knowing so little about European history and politics. After a drive
around the countryside, the Press Officer brought me to the Chan-
cellery of the Federal Republic, an ultramodern building. The Chancellor's offices were on a high floor. He came out to greet me and led
me inside.

Of the men in power I had met, none radiated it like Helmut
Schmidt. The ceremoniousness of the aristocratic and faintly aloof
Giscard d'Estaing seemed to some extent a substitute for states-
manship. Schmidt, by contrast, carried an aura of natural, powerful
leadership. His every word and gesture exuded ability to command.

He was also so warm that my nervousness quickly disappeared. It
was like having a good talk with a favorite uncle. We talked, in fact,
for more than an hour: just the two of us in his businesslike office,
with his secretary taking notes.

Schmidt never resorted to clichés, small talk, or a pat on the wifely
head. Without condescension he expressed the kind of sympathy for
relatives of the hostages that could come only from genuine concern.
He also described with great precision the dilemma of whether to
resort to force against those who take captives—as he had done in
1977 to liberate a Lufthansa jet from terrorist hijackers. He told me
that when a Baader-Meinhof band held the plane in Mogadishu,
Somalia, he sought advice from families of the passengers and crew.
One son in particular was very helpful, he said, offering cool, logical
suggestions, even though his father faced death at any moment. I
couldn't help comparing that to the American administration, which
from the beginning took an almost opposite approach. Their public
concern and attention to our comfort were no substitutes for sharing
ideas. Like a man hurrying to light a woman's cigarette but not really
talking to her, they kept us from all substantive discussion of the alternatives, as though anyone personally involved *ipso facto* could
have nothing sensible to contribute. It was always "Everything possible is being done"; "We are exploring every avenue"; and "Negotiations are being pursued with all our ability. . . ."

At that point Chancellor Schmidt felt American force against Iran
would probably be counterproductive and perhaps disastrous for

many more innocent victims than the hostages. I agreed, of course, but would have felt at ease in objecting if I didn't. In previous meetings, with top American officials, I sensed an artificiality veneered with a false camaraderie. The families and the leaders had been cast into roles, and performed them by telling each other what they were "supposed" to. Schmidt's directness and concentration on the issues cut through that awkwardness.

His vision ranged from details of politicians' personalities to a total international picture. He was deeply concerned about Barry's physical condition, but also about pushing Iran toward the Soviet camp and feeding the growth of radicalism throughout the Middle East. And he felt the student militants were feeding too richly on their publicity in the American press. There had been too much of it for too long, he said—and President Carter opened the way by admitting his obsession with the crisis. "Tell my friend Jimmy to get it off the front pages," Schmidt suggested. "Let him concentrate on Afghanistan or even the old Russian threat—anything to stop giving the militants exactly what they need."

To say he expressed my thoughts precisely would have been conceited *and* wrong; his were much more developed and refined. But essentially he said what I believed, especially about the need for patience and for Europeans to be more active as intermediaries. The Chancellor too wanted more concerted action, but backed by the patience of maturity.

When I asked whether I should speak out against President Carter if he resorted to force, he responded very forcefully. "It is *most* important not to embarrass your own country," he replied. "Do everything you can to influence, but do not oppose. It's your government; you'll gain nothing from it."

Naturally it was flattering that he talked to me with this openness, unlike most of Washington. But beyond that, the Chancellor's remarks about specific actions, such as sanctions against Iran, seemed more acute and knowledgeable than the observations of American politicians. Above all, his manner inspired confidence. Just because he used no hyperbole, Schmidt radiated strength. When I added listening and learning to my initial goal of publicizing the "family angle" in Europe, I didn't imagine it would be so rewarding.

*

The rest of the day was filled by interviews with German and American journalists. Barbara Timm, mother of a twenty-year-old marine hostage, had just flown to Iran, in defiance of President Carter's ban on visits there. Her first stop too had been Paris, and reporters asked me repeatedly whether Tehran would be our next stop, while I tried to discuss substance instead of that kind of speculation.

It was an exhilarating day, and when I returned to the immaculate inn just outside Bonn, I ate and went straight to bed. Sleep was still the most reliable escape from worry; I never awakened at night. But in a comfortable bed in the charming inn the night following my talk with the Chancellor, I did wake up—and felt too strange to get back to sleep. Closing my eyes, I saw bodies wrapped in white lying in a flat, distant place I couldn't recognize.

Unable to shake the vision, I got up before dawn and dressed slowly for a breakfast interview. The telephone rang at about seven-thirty. It was a television producer in New York asking whether I had heard the news. "What news?" I asked, trying to stay calm as my mind leaped to *the* news I'd been hoping for since November. I had a quick, rich vision of meeting Barry in Europe on his way home and spending a peaceful day together in an inn like mine. Then I accidentally dropped the telephone, and while I was telling the hotel operator I'd been disconnected, someone pounded at my door. It was a reporter who was traveling with us. "Barbara," he began, "I don't know how to tell you this so I'd better make it quick. Last night. . . ." That is how I learned of the American rescue mission which had failed at a cost of eight lives.

For the first time since the crisis began, I felt my emotions winning over my control. The eight lives were a tragic waste. I was miserable with guilt and sorrow. If someone had to die in Iran, hostages would be bad enough. These were disassociated strangers, whose families were now shattered. I remembered thinking, shortly before Barry left for Tehran, that our family had been spared serious sacrifice to war. My father, uncles, brother-in-law, and half a dozen cousins served in World War II, Korea, and Vietnam. All of them returned unharmed. "We've been too lucky," I said to myself. "Something is bound to happen." Now the sacrifice had come, not by, but *for* our family—and it seemed like blood money of innocents who were paying for us.

I went into the bathroom to hide my tears from the reporter. They came from frustration as well as grief: recognition that ordinary people have so little control over their destiny. President Carter had *promised* to refrain from military action. Despite the concern that convinced me to participate in this trip, I didn't really believe he would use force. He had, and eight men lay dead in the Iranian desert.

It was 2 A.M. in Brooklyn, but as soon as I could steady my voice, I called my mother to tell her not to take Alexander to school that day. I wanted him protected from the press and *everyone* in case my dread materialized: that the militants would shoot the hostages in reprisal. I felt fairly certain they wouldn't do it out of calculation. But there was a good chance ideology or anger would get the better of them when they learned American troops had landed on their soil. From the beginning, their motivation was laced with revenge. They took the hostages in revenge not only for admission of the Shah to the United States but also for the long association that evoked deep resentment. This new American "invasion," as they would view it, could prod their self-pitying image as perpetually invaded underdogs and lead to retaliatory murder.

I had tried since the takeover to keep myself from contemplating life without Barry. I thought it healthier to cope only with what each day brought. Now I had to force myself from picturing a husbandless future. The trick was to get through the next few hours. If there was to be a massacre, it would probably take place before the morning was over in Europe. If sufficient time passed for discussion with Khomeini or his advisers, the hostages might be "punished," but I felt certain they wouldn't be killed. Surely even the most radical of the new authorities understood that would provoke strong American retaliation.

At my wit's end, I called my mother-in-law to try to comfort her from four thousand miles away. Then I waited. Halfway between home and Barry, I held my breath. Once the Iranians start thinking about consequences, I told myself, they won't shoot an American. I almost believed it. Pacing the hotel room, I thought I had a glimpse of Barry's days in whatever room he was in.

"They can't shoot him."

"They can't shoot them."

"Stop that talk!"

❊

When I called the American Embassy and asked to speak to the Press Officer, he answered with cheery hope that I'd had a good night's rest in preparation for my morning appointments.

"Don't you know what happened?"

"I've just walked into my office, Barbara. *What* happened?"

He sent a car for me immediately. It brought me through a crowd of reporters—asking *how I felt* about the failed rescue attempt—and into the Embassy. There had been no further word from Tehran. If no news ever really meant good news, it was now. The extreme edge of my anxiety retreated enough to think about my own position in Germany.

The first question was what to do the rest of that day. A full schedule of interviews and press conferences was supposed to follow the breakfast meeting. What I planned to say would be nearly useless in the clamor for my reaction to the rescue mission. What could I answer? To condemn it would be to speak against my own government in a foreign country—which I wouldn't do, especially if the militants were about to kill the hostages. I kept hearing Chancellor Schmidt's "never embarrass your country." Yet I couldn't pretend I approved, having spoken again and again against the use of force. I was afraid if

I did meet the press, my feeling would emerge about Carter's ignoring his guarantee not to endanger the lives of the hostages.

I canceled the individual interviews and waited for news until late afternoon, just before I was scheduled to leave Bonn. Still nothing had been reported from Tehran. At a large press conference, I tried to pick my way through questions without endangering or embarrassing anyone. "What is your opinion of United States military preparedness in light of all the mechanical failures in the helicopters?" one reporter asked. I said that even the most pampered car sometimes won't start in the morning; that was known as bad luck. What I really thought was the mechanical failures were appalling. Who on earth was in charge of those things? Having undertaken the mission, how did they let something like *that* happen?

❋

From Bonn I returned to Paris, where Louisa, Pearl, and Jeanne were waiting, as shocked as I. Back in the same hotel, we gathered in one room to recount similar experiences and share what comfort we could contribute. We were still listening to news broadcasts and buying newspapers hourly. Reports about the charred remains of the dead servicemen diluted joy that the hostages apparently remained unharmed. The militants had warned repeatedly that military action would bring about immediate execution, but the fifty-three were clearly too important, if only as a trump card, to be disposed of.

Early the next morning, we took a train to Luxembourg, site of the Council of the European Economic Community. Jeanne Queen is Russian Orthodox; Pearl Golacinski, Unitarian; and Louisa Kennedy, Episcopalian; but we all attended a mass for the hostages in a magnificent Catholic cathedral.

Barry's mother had been lighting candles in her menorah every day since he was taken. My mother attended church every morning, and my grandmother prayed throughout the day. But I had stopped going to church after our marriage and couldn't resume when Barry was under threat. I had no right to ask favors after ignoring my religion during good days.

Now the best of the Church enveloped me with comfort and more. The mass was glorious. Maybe because it was celebrated in French, which had the same effect on me as Latin; it was so inspiring that I was moved to receive communion for the first time in a dozen years. With tears in their eyes, many of the congregation reached out to hold our hands. I wondered whether it would always take a crisis to instill me with spirituality. In this case the mass made us feel that ours was a genuine mission of peace—not limited to Iran, but linked to something older and more universal.

We had seen gruesome photographs of the dead servicemen. There was nothing noble there, nor in the danger still facing the hostages; yet we were uplifted. How logical—or fair—was that?

＊

When she was in Rome, Jeanne had requested an audience with the Pope. Back in Paris, we postponed our return home, waiting for the answer.

Jeanne's initiative came after discussions among us four. We had been seeing various leaders; why not try the Pope, whose influence might be at least as strong? After the rescue mission, it seemed even more important to put our "case" to him.

The answer came early that evening: The Pope would indeed give us an audience. The next morning, we drove to the airport in taxis, glancing through rear windows for reporters and feeling like conspirators. Publicity was the original purpose of our trip, of course, but we felt that if the Vatican wanted to reveal our papal audience, they should be the ones to make the announcement.

＊

Jeanne was originally Bulgarian but had lived in Italy. We put it about that she had a house there, to which we were going for rest. At the airport, Alitalia put us in a secluded back office. We spent most of the morning waiting for a delayed flight behind a stack of air-freight cases.

In Rome we spent the night in the apartment of a friend of Jeanne's, and had time the next day for a long walk before our audience. It was my first visit to Italy; I couldn't ignore the beauty, even in the circumstances. If anything, Saint Peter's Square was grander than photographs of it, with so much space that it seemed empty with hundreds of people standing about. We entered on the side of the square opposite the Vatican offices, where two cardinals greeted and escorted us.

After a twisting, confusing route through corridors, verandas, passageways and courtyards, we were delivered to a great, dark hall with magnificent paintings, immense red drapes, and no chairs. I assumed we would meet the Pope in his office, but apparently it would be here. We were asked to form a rank, spacing ourselves as in a receiving line. On our walk that morning, it occurred to one of us that women meeting the Pope were supposed to wear gloves and cover their heads. Jeanne's friend produced lacy black mantillas for our heads; my gloves were the white cotton kind used for gardening, found the last minute in a drugstore.

We waited and waited—uncomfortable in high heels on the marble floor. The pain in my arches made me think of penance. I thought also of Barry and his difficulties, compared to which my discomfort was laughable.

Looking about at the opulent room—the ceiling was a painting of angels, with God reaching down to touch their hands—it struck me that my girlish notion about an uncommon future was coming true. How odd that of all the Catholics I knew, many more religious than I, it was I who was meeting the Pope—because my husband, a Jew whom my family hadn't wanted me to marry, was in trouble. Although rooted to reality by aching feet, I felt exalted and slightly faint from touching my childhood fantasy.

The Pope emerged finally from a doorway about two stories high, accompanied by an entourage of half a dozen bishops and priests. His face was pink and sparkling, with eyes of intense blue that surpassed even the brilliance of his white robes. It was angelic.

The Vatican reputedly has the largest Foreign Service in the world, and we hoped the Pope would discuss the crisis in political or diplomatic terms. However, he simply shook our hands in turn, saying "we" were praying and working for the hostages. Giving each of us a set of beautiful rosary beads, he moved on.

But although the meeting was short and ceremonial, the fact that he received us demonstrated more important support outside America. News of our audience would be broadcast to Iran, indicating that they were becoming isolated, at least in Europe. This was an encouraging ending to our trip.

I thought about what had been accomplished to mitigate the plight of Barry and the others—and the by-product of a deeply rewarding personal experience for me, for which I felt guilty. I was vastly enriched by meeting Helmut Schmidt and by the Pope's glowing spirituality. Then it was time to fly home, away from that and from Barry.

Back in Brooklyn I used to enjoy a daydream in which I asked President Carter what had possessed him to order the rescue mission. I saw myself reminding him, politely but firmly, of his specific promise, when he dropped in on our State Department briefing the previous December, not to use force. It seemed to me the President was caught in an increasingly difficult, maybe otherwise unwinnable campaign for reelection. He felt he had to do *something* to end the crisis, even if some of the hostages were sacrificed. When the President invited us four to the White House, I felt lucky for the chance to tell him what I felt about his betrayal.

The White House surprised me with its lack of surprises. The Oval Office, which looked out on the Rose Garden, was really oval. The Élysée Palace had been the perfect expression of French aristocracy, and Bonn's modern offices seemed to say something about the new Germany. The Oval Office matched them in that respect, for its Early American furniture made it a handsome, unpretentious living room.

Sipping coffee, we waited, amid the sun and flowers, for the President. When he entered, he seemed as warmly relaxed as the room—so much so that it was hard to remember we were in a "national crisis," as he himself kept calling it.

"Hi," I said in a slightly falsetto voice. "I'm Barbara Rosen." As the words emerged, I wanted to bite my tongue for being disrespectful. Couldn't I at least have said, "Hello, Mr. President"? On the other hand, that was what Jimmy Carter prompted. During this second look at him, I was relaxed enough to observe. Although I couldn't say precisely why, I sensed that he lacked the presence, and leadership qualities, that radiated from the other statesmen I'd met, including the Pope. My tongue would never have tossed out a "Hi" to Giscard d'Estaing or Helmut Schmidt.

"Hi, nice to meet you," answered our President.

I remembered Mr. Schmidt referring to him as "my friend Jimmy," as if talking about a school chum. That was what he was: earnest, maybe well-intentioned, and certainly boyish. He wasn't "James," and again I feared he wasn't really presidential timber.

We sat on a chintz-covered couch, he in a chair directly opposite. We began with the unavoidable photographs, which wasted nearly half our time. When the photographers finally withdrew, Louisa Kennedy did most of the talking about our trip. As I listened, the President's amazingly blue eyes and pearly teeth half hypnotized me and I lost concentration. I also noticed how many years he had aged during the past few months. It showed mostly in his deeply wrinkled neck, which suggested an exhausted man hidden under a crisp suit.

Maybe if he and I had been alone, I would have asked what I wanted. As it was, our twenty minutes with him slipped by without my finding a place for the question. It seemed too late when he stood to say good-bye.

I blamed myself less for missing my chance than I would have thought. I still believed the President risked lives needlessly and in violation of his promise, but as he talked, a painful concern for the fate of the hostages pulled at his face. Although he didn't mention religion, I sensed his strong Christian commitment was putting him to a kind of torture. He *wanted* to do the right thing and seemed lost about how to proceed with an Iranian Government that promoted the wrong thing when it revealed its motives at all. How to fight evil with good in this case? Nothing was working for him.

We were considering a letter to the new Iranian Parliament and asked his advice. He said he would support us in any way he could, but privately; most Iranians hated him so much that public support would bring about automatic rejection of anything positive. That, too, seemed to show humility—and acceptance of a cross he had to bear.

I also sensed strong guilt feelings in him. It was his decision to admit the Shah, despite warnings about the possible consequences—and now he seemed to accept that as his personal responsibility. I still believed that had he been decisive at the beginning, Barry and the others might have been home months before. But I no longer wanted to point a finger at his inconsistencies or indecisiveness. What was the point, with a person haunted by worry and awareness of his own mistakes? Maybe he didn't have the leadership qualities of the other statesmen, but he lacked nothing for warmth, openness, and compassion.

When we four were returned to Tehran, it was not to the embassy compound but to a cavernous maximum-security prison. For weeks I believed it was one that adjoined the National Police Academy, past which Farhad and I had used to walk on our merry way to his apartment. This was partly because I never saw the building's exterior.

We were driven from Qom, if that was the location of The Pink Palace, in the middle of the night of June 16 to June 17. Tom Schaefer, Bob Englemann, Steve Lauterbach, and I quietly said good-bye to each other, not knowing we would be together again in the next place. Even the most spirited men were apprehensive: The uncertainty surrounding every transfer fragmented all support struts and self-confidence.

Preparation of the van apparently took hours. When it was time at last to be stuffed inside, a guard who had gone so far as to hint that the taking of hostages might have been wrong hissed that we would be shot if we failed to move fast enough. Although no one took such threats seriously any longer, goading for its own sake or to humiliate set our teeth on edge.

The van sped so fast that it teetered on the edge of losing control. We would learn later that one van turned over, badly injuring several hostages. For the moment, we guessed only that the driver was demonstrating more of the usual bluster and self-importance. He flew over a rock or curb and almost killed us before getting his wheels under him again. Suddenly he stopped, and we were transferred to another van. At this point I wondered whether the guards feared attack by government police, American Green Berets, or perhaps even rival groups who wanted us as prizes. Flashlights were constantly turned on our blindfolds and wrists to check the security of plastic bindings that pinched the circulation enough to make my hands numb.

"Don't e-speak!"

After an hour, one of the hostages said he had to relieve himself urgently. The guard inside with us reluctantly ordered a stop. "If you do not hurry," he said to the man being let out, "you will be keelled." A groan of disgust and derision went up inside the van. "Shot for a piss," someone risked saying.

After another hour, we arrived in what felt like the outskirts of a city. Despite the van's twisting and turning, presumably to fashion a circuitous route, I felt certain it was Tehran. When we stopped, we were led up a maze of staircases whose clang produced an echo from what could have been dungeon walls. Guards kept telling me to lift my legs over what seemed to be low metal walls. In fact, they were the bottom rims of bulkheads to cellblocks. When my blindfold came off, at 3 A.M., I was in a cell with three heavily barred windows, the glass broken in all of them. Guards came in with cans of soda. A fluorescent moon shone through the shattered windowpanes, putting shadows of the bars on the floor. A thin green carpet had just been laid, and the walls were freshly painted in gray over cracks that were already reappearing. A steel door with a judas-hole slammed shut. "When will it end?" I asked myself.

❖

Whatever the petty personality conflicts, we four were happy to be sharing the same cell. No one wanted the emotional drain of adjusting to new people once more. We even protested when guards wanted to settle another hostage with us, despite sacrifice of the information he would have brought with him. The guards almost insisted on additions, because, they said, our moderate-size cell had housed sixteen prisoners under the Shah. But little time went to commiseration for previous occupants.

Like a spoke of a wheel, our corridor led to a hub in the form of a central courtyard. During our six months in this prison, we would be taken to the courtyard for fresh air a total of three times: *one hour* in all. The inside air could not have belonged anywhere but in a prison. Nor could the sounds, especially of whipping. Since the screams and pleas in Farsi were often even louder when we couldn't hear strokes being laid on, we assumed other torture was also being applied to Iranian prisoners somewhere in the building. In a frivolous moment I remembered I was supposed to be a diplomat.

Loud playing of Bach and Brahms usually started within a few moments of the screams. The devotee of classical music was short, balding Ahmad. Slightly better-dressed than his brothers, he had a round face and a thick, dark mustache. Ahmad was our chief guard there. In the Embassy we had called him Number Two: He was subordinate, and deferential, to Hamid—until Hamid appeared to lose authority for being insufficiently ideological. Ahmad played a cozy role with us then, bringing around chewing gum and rancid chocolates from the embassy commissary. But when Bob Ode mentioned "those SOBs" in a letter to his wife, Ahmad turned furious. He was the distributor—and censor—of mail, and he knew much slang from his American education.

"What do you mean by SOB? What is that expression?"

"Sons of bitches," said sixty-four-year-old Bob, standing up to Ahmad's violent temper.

"You called us sons of bitches? *Us?*" Ahmad knew how much Bob's letters from his wife meant to him, and he took visible pleasure in his captive's distress. "You will never receive a letter again. From anybody. That's final!"

Here in prison Ahmad exercised leadership partly by tightening security precautions everywhere. As a supplement to his old job of censoring mail, which he performed with smirking zeal, he installed closed-circuit television cameras in the toilets and shower stalls. His purpose was to deprive us even more methodically of information, and he nearly succeeded.

The knothole in his elaborately constructed fence was a plastic bag of garbage that lay on the floor near the entrance to the bathroom. Steve Lauterbach and I made certain to take scraps of paper along to throw into the bag—and while we were doing it, to rummage inside like famished bums. We would count paper plates to guess who was in what cell, examine old medicine bottles, dig in any kind of dirt. The slightest scrap of information might prove valuable if properly analyzed with other scraps. Sometimes there were even pieces of newspapers, from which we learned, or guessed at, some extraordinary developments. A half-ripped fragment from an editorial page that accused Iraq of helping train anti-Iranian dissidents was a startling clue that the Iran-Iraq relationship, never happy in recent years, was deteriorating rapidly. Another grease-soaked fragment from a newspaper of the religious Islamic Republican Party accused the current President, Abolhassan Bani-Sadr, of anti-Islamic behavior and trying to undermine traditional elements of Iranian society. Putting two and two together, we guessed that one of Bani-Sadr's difficulties was his attempt to extricate the country from growing crises by negotiating our release, which was encountering impassioned resistance.

Meanwhile, Ahmad did his best to keep us from knowing anything. We had no way of knowing for certain whether his urge to hear concertos and symphonies just as the screaming began was prompted by desire to cover up torture, but this fit everything we knew about him. One irony among hundreds was that Ahmad developed his enthusiasm for classical music in America.

❖

Whipping was prescribed by custom and sanctioned by the new regime as punishment for certain crimes. The ghastly ripping of flesh by leather could be heard more distinctly in the bathroom than in our cell. Sounds of men crying and howling were no easier to endure, even though we were confident by now that we would not get the same treatment. I had to hold my hands over my ears.

Although most guards did not threaten us with physical punishment, some would have liked to if their instructions had permitted it. "Bedside Manner," named in a spurt of deep sarcasm, was one of the uglier ones: a tall, well-built thug with a bulldog face frozen into an expression of dumb hatred. He would answer a knock on the door with a snarl of "Waddya want?"

"I want to go to the toilet."

"Wait!" he would order scornfully. In the fullness of time, having prepared himself for the prison break he *knew* the evil Americans were planning, he would crack open the door. If his eyes had been gun muzzles, few of us would have survived.

To foil the plot we would be trying to hatch in the bathroom—or simply to give expression to his personality—he would pound on the door. "Hurry up in there. Get out. You go back right now!" To ensure that we were locked up again fast enough for his liking, he would shove from behind as we returned to the cell. "Faster. Keep *moving*, I said." His pushing and browbeating grew worse the longer they went unchallenged. "One day I'm going to hit him back," I said to myself, hoping the promise would "satisfy my honor." But the urge to get even welled up until it broke the dam one evening. "I'm a human being," I shouted in Farsi as I pushed his bulk against the corridor wall and dug my elbow in. "I'm not an animal!" Although he was twice my size and had thirty times my power, he raced away to report me to Ahmad, who arrived in a moment at my cell with his second-in-command, like a third-rate hit team. "That is not the way to behave here," they screamed. "One more episode and you will live in solitary."

"Joker," whose real name was Reza, teetered between maintaining control of himself and giving in to savage outbursts. These could be provoked even by a too vigorous shuffling of playing cards. "Someone's making too much noise," Reza would accuse, charging into our cell. "*Who is it?*"

Other guards by contrast, were decent and more. "Space Cadet" was so named because most of the Americans thought he was spaced out. In fact, his "nuttiness" was nothing more than ordinary Iranian concern for our comfort, as much as comfort was possible in the prison. He was a walking bundle of *ta'arof*, which is what most of the others couldn't correlate with his role as a captor.

Space Cadet usually sported pajama bottoms, a T-shirt, and the slippers almost all the guards wore indoors. In time I learned he was an engineer—who now helped out in the prison kitchen. I hardly saw him without a book, often by Ali Shariati, who was, even more than Khomeini, the theoretical godfather of the young revolutionaries. Shariati, a sociologist, was profoundly disillusioned with the West and Westernization, and tried to fuse Shi'ite Islam with modern developments and resistance to cultural and political oppression. Throughout the revolutionary period, his pamphlets were at least as popular among lower-middle-class students as Khomeini's cassettes.

Shariati appealed to dislocated youth by offering them a way to find their identity in Shi'ite Islam, which he presented as a religion of revolutionaries, not perpetual victims. Their culture, he insisted, was progressive, not inferior as the West insinuated. Had he not died in 1977, perhaps at the hands of SAVAK, the revolution might have taken a less doctrinaire if not a less anti-Western turn, for despite his devotion to Islam, he distrusted the mullahs and would have disapproved of a theocratic state.

Although Space Cadet supported the revolution as fervently as his brothers, he also believed in securing all possible extra food for us, like a good Iranian host. He served as our nutritionist and chief cook, but protested when we praised him for this. "I am not a cooker. I am an e-student."

"Give them extra, let these boys have more cheese," he would say after slipping us some hard-boiled eggs and carrots when we were peeling potatoes in the cell. The pull between devotion to revolutionary ideals and concern for us as human beings almost showed on his eager face.

But the guard who meant most to me was a law student whose dark circles under his eyes looked larger than the rest of him combined. He appeared shortly after my medical "episode," when I was at my lowest. Talking was still forbidden then, and many of his fellows shouted "Don't e-speak!" at the slightest whisper from us. Gentle Jamshid, by contrast, would almost apologize for asking us to obey the rule.

"Excuse me, that was interesting, but I believe you are required not to speak," he would say, having waited so as not to interrupt anyone, patiently fingering his worry beads.

"But we were only talking about our families," I would answer. "Just for a minute?"

"Well, for a minute. What harm is there in that?"

Little Jamshid would sit on my bed and ask help in translating terms in his English lawbook. "Why are you bothering to study law, Jamshid?" I would taunt him. "You know there's no law in Iran now; just look at us."

"But the whole world knows what harm you were doing here," he would answer almost apologetically.

Jamshid penned Alexander a note on the back of a picture I had drawn for him. "Your father is a very nice man," it began, "although the Shah is evil. . . ." He was consistently solicitous, even deferential. "Please don't be upset, Mr. Rosen. Things will soon be all right. Please don't worry so about your family. I know how terrible this may sound, but sometimes adversity brings out good things in people. I was in prison for rioting against the Shah. Maybe it will be a learning experience for you, too. Anyway, let's have a good talk."

The "good talks" always ended the same way. Jamshid did not want to hear that Iran, as well as America, may have overemphasized the Soviet threat, any more than he wanted to learn that not every American black was mercilessly downtrodden. He was as narrow in his political thought as most of the others but never failed to explain that he felt deeply sorry that I had fallen victim of *the American Government's* actions that had made me a hostage.

"I like you, Mr. Rosen. I respect your knowledge of Iran. I'd love for you to be home with your lovely family—but you are a symbol and you must remain until the Shah is returned and your government apologizes for what it has done to my country. Until it admits its very great guilt."

"Don't you know by now this will never happen? So you're going to be our waiter for a very long time, you terrorist."

"Me, a terrorist?"

"Yes, because you are holding me here against my will. What else could that make you?"

"Then, call me a terrorist, Mr. Imperialist."

Unless I was feeling too bitter or depressed, we would end with a good laugh—until I tired of it.

Jamshid began coming in to see me whenever he could. There was no official reason for him to pass hours on my bed; evidently he simply wanted company.

"How is the imperialist doing today? Have you heard from your wife and children?" It was the old Iranian urge to forge a deep personal contact, to *touch* as people—but in such ludicrous circumstances that I continued to shame Jamshid despite my affection for him.

"How dare you ask about my wife and children when you are doing this to them? You say the revolution is for the oppressed, but did you ever think about how you are oppressing *me*? I don't want this building a warm relationship. I don't want to like you. Just leave me alone."

Jamshid would drag himself away, only to return in several minutes, his little face still twisted with hurt. "I know you think we are causing you pain. Honestly, *we're* not keeping you here, it's your President; there's nothing I can do about that. What I *can* do is get you something nice to eat. Or here—please take some chewing gum. Excellent Iranian chewing gum; it will make you feel better. Things will be fine very, very soon."

Excellent Iranian chewing gum. An Iranian terrorist who was attentive and for hours seemed to want nothing more than to sit and talk. Once, Jamshid dashed out for a jar of peanut butter for a snack. Again, when we were reunited in the Embassy after a separation, he rushed up to embrace me: "How have you been? I was so worried about you!"

In our debates I would sometimes accuse him of destroying my life. It was more complicated than that.

*

There were Hamid the Red, Hossein the Tooth,* Sailor, Rookie, Dizzy, Spectacles, Shortshit (a walking Napoleonic complex), and a dozen others we recognized by name or sight. Enduring devotion to their mission held these widely differing personalities together. Some hostages were convinced that they were not primarily students but professional terrorists trained by the Palestine Liberation Organization or "the Communist conspiracy." The more I saw and heard them, the more I believed the opposite: that these young men and women were motivated by exactly what they professed: an extreme form of Iranian Islamic patriotism. Some seemed to lean left, many took Arabic lessons, but the main source of inspiration was not external; it was something connected to their conception of their own religious and national identity. Even during the early period, when they were very nervous about guarding us, they would spread newspapers on the floor as a prayer mat and pray every day, no matter what else was happening. Most of the students I knew had scientific or engineering backgrounds. They were as devout as the others, and perhaps even more nationalist in the sense of "anti-imperialist." "Neither East nor West," one of their favorite slogans for bathroom walls, seemed to express their groping for something of their own, which they felt had to be contained somewhere in Islam.

I came to believe that even they hadn't expected their stunning success when they attacked the Embassy; some believed they might be martyred. Nor did they expect the nation to support them, as it apparently did. They acted out of an urge to do something shining for Iran, even if it turned out to be futile or suicidal.

In this sense they were idealistically pure, no matter how misguided. Sometimes I hated them all, even Jamshid—and especially those who blended belief in simple solutions with personal insecurity, and strutted about blustering and threatening. But to call them dupes of some foreign power was to miss the point of the revolution, whose vanguard they might be now. It would be the old easy way out of not answering underlying questions by pretending they didn't exist: one of the "solutions" that had landed us in this mess.

*

On the few happy Iranian holidays, the guards brought cookies and candies. Including the monthly commemoration of our capture in their happy holidays, they gave us extra treats on the fourth of every month. On July Fourth, the eighth commemoration, Joker, now in his

---

* Hossein Sheikholislam stood out among those destined to rise high in the Khomeini regime. Early in 1982, he was reported to have been appointed to the number three position in the Iranian Foreign Ministry.

forced playful mood, bore gifts of greasy sausage and lumpy straw-
berry cake.

We had planned our own celebration. Tom Schaefer's American
flag, which he had made from paper in The Pink Palace, was high on
the wall above our table. We sat beneath it, choked down our holiday
meal, and began reading from the Declaration of Independence and
the Gettysburg Address, which were printed in a copy of an almanac
that had come to us with other books.

I had memorized the usual parts of both in school but had no idea
until now of their greatness and relevance. Our revolution had
stressed political rights and protection from tyranny. How different
that seemed from the Iranian one, with its willing surrender of leadership to a single imam. Lincoln's concepts and eloquence moved me as
much as Jefferson's. Both seemed majestic, because they defined and
limited rights and duties.

Tom and Steve read excerpts: ". . . deriving their just powers from
the consent of the governed," he said in a normal voice that rang full
in the hushed room. I wanted only to listen and absorb the dignity.
To an outsider we could have appeared stereotypes of American prisoners in a corny movie. Among ourselves we felt no embarrassment
reaching for our roots and strength. We wanted to know what made
us feel developed as political animals, therefore continued reading
sections of the Declaration I had always skimmed.

During my Peace Corps years I sometimes felt like a drop of water
thrown on a hot skillet. Iranians constantly tried to discover who I
was, culturally and nationally. When I spoke of my ancestry, people
insisted I was Russian. When I said I was Jewish, I was told I should
be in Israel, not the United States. I spent a good deal of time trying
to figure out for myself who Americans were. Now, in prison, we were
all taken several steps farther, partly just because we were together,
sensing what linked us. A wave of respect for each other built, along
with gratitude for the luck of the accident of our birth. We looked
into each other's face from across the scraps of the unappetizing meal
and absorbed the civic nourishment. I knew I would not spend another Fourth of July at a baseball game or watching fireworks without
deep gratitude and conscious thought of what is precious and essential in our national identity and remembering its antithesis.

*

It has to be said that the spectrum of American personalities was as
wide in its way as that of our guards. I was very lucky with my cell
mates. Here, as in my previous "cells," I came to know some of the
best Americans, in every sense, I had ever met. But only outsiders to
our experience could imagine that it brought out exclusively noble instincts, or that being American was a guarantee of admirable behavior.
There were good and bad among captives as well as captors, and I

would just as soon talk to certain of the oppressors as to a few of my fellow victims.

One hostage became a new Joe McCarthy when any of us spoke Farsi, as if this was a collaborationist gesture. "And don't laugh," he would add whenever we let go in a joke—as though anything but grimness and groaning was also a betrayal of the Stars and Stripes. The man to make difficult times more difficult in every little way, he was confirmation of the truism that imprisonment brings out the best in some—as in Dave Roeder—and the worst in others.

A few hostages seemed compelled to score one-upmanship points on their cell mates by trying to seem bigger and tougher. One or two dictators took it upon themselves to criticize everyone else and attempt to censor conversation by insisting this or that topic was not fit for discussion. And of course some had annoying personal habits whose effect was multiplied many times by our confines and claustrophobia. "E-shut the Door" had company in this.

Sometimes prison conduct might have been predicted from personality revealed in normal embassy routine. On the other hand, stress sometimes brought out unexpected qualities. Here in prison, I was showering with one of the highest-ranking military attachés, who bolstered others with his quiet fortitude. I described how much I missed my family. He said he had just received a beautiful letter from his daughter-in-law which thanked him for having given her such a wonderful husband. The water of the shower mingled with his tears as the brave man broke down and wept. He composed himself before leaving the bathroom, but I never forgot the side of him that had been revealed to me, for which I respected him more than ever.

We were a full range of types, from the generous to the nasty. But I was happy to see that the general standard of behavior was higher than I would have expected. Most people's first instinct was to support and help. With me, they had a lot of supporting and helping to do, and I couldn't put myself in the better half of any of the spectrums.

*

In prison we four continued our long daily walks, and also went "back to school." Steve Lauterbach and I studied French from a high school review book. Tom Schaefer worked on his German. For an hour or so in the afternoon I taught Steve and Bob Englemann Farsi from primary school readers, and we often followed this with a predinner hour of yoga under Bob's increasingly guru-like direction.

Waiting for our meal on the evening of September 22, we heard a series of distant thuds surely caused by bombs. Racing feet in slippers sounded next, followed by ladders urgently being pushed against walls, then automatic pistols and rifles being fired into the air as if in imitation of a Pancho Villa victory celebration.

Spurts of cannon or antiaircraft fire sounded from farther away. For a few wild moments we guessed *this was the American Air Force*—until it occurred to us that an American bombing run would surely be heavier.

Joker shouted into our cell: "Put out your light! No more lights!" Our light remained out each evening for the remainder of our stay in prison.

The lights went out during the day as well, because electricity began failing for hours at a time, while we tried to make sense of the new events. I interpreted the thuds and firing as air-raid drills, concocted to instill Iranians with a more martial spirit and sterner discipline. Long periods without electricity might also have served to prepare the public for a difficult future.

The chanting of political slogans at evening prayers in the prison courtyard finally provided another clue. The "Death to America, death to Carter" ran on as before, but something new was added: a refrain whose rhythm fit nothing we had heard before. Only the beats penetrated the walls from the courtyard. I pressed my ear to the steel door, worked on the puzzle for a few days, and finally came up with "Death to Sad-dam Hos-sein," the President of Iraq. Had Iran started a war with Iraq, its none-too-friendly neighbor? If so, the Iranian Government surely would want to patch things up with America more quickly, at least to obtain spare military parts—which would have to start with our release. On the other hand, war might mean that our case was set aside for the duration. Not taken to the courtyard for fresh air for almost two months, we had nothing to do except read and talk. By candlelight we tried to decipher the undecipherable: What was happening out there; whether anything good would ever happen to us. I wished fervently that Iraq would beat the hell out of Iran. Maybe that would somehow get us out of there.

✿

It wasn't quite true that we had nothing to do but read and talk. On shower days, I would toss my soap into the spray and see how many times I could catch it, or let it fall to the floor and see how long I could delay my kick before saving it from the drain. This was relief from boredom, even though I lost a lot of bars of soap. The guards generously supplied more from our still-bountiful commissary's supplies.

From the day of the first firing, a blackout had been imposed at six o'clock every evening, which led to the most exciting activity: Stealing candles from the bathroom became an achievement and a form of competition; making them out of old wax became a cottage industry and *another* form of competition. We kept "fulfilling our five-year plan" even when dozens of candles were stashed in caches around the room. Guards would ask us if we needed another one. "Yes!" we chorused, "we're all out; can't you see?" One day, the commissary supply would run out and we didn't want to live in darkness the rest of our lives.

For exercise, I ran around the cell an hour a day, then paced the same perimeter. For escape, Tom had managed to bring a Monopoly set from a previous "hotel." We played on Friday, our day off from everything else. Sometimes I got so involved that I preferred to sit one out. Arguments over the trading value of good old Baltic Avenue, Park Place, and the others became ever more heated. Eventually we hid money under our trousers and pleaded poverty—in order to pick up properties cheaply at auction—and gave the wrong change from the bank. When the bubble of competition broke, we laughed and laughed.

Screaming that he would confiscate the game unless we played in whispers, Reza never saw the irony of his "imperialist" captives playing the classic game of capitalism under his revolutionary nose. Nor did he penetrate our cover-up. The military men in our cell were working hard to decipher the code of tapping from the adjoining cell. Soon they were exchanging messages, a slow process through the thick cement walls, but done so well that we learned that a new Iranian Parliament, soon to be convened, would decide on what to do with us. A hot game of Monopoly disguised the tapping sounds and made things look normal. The messages kept coming, almost all dealing with our constant preoccupation: scraps of information from anywhere about our fate.

*

It was in search of visual information that a hostage in another cell tried to peer out the bathroom window one day. The window was high on the wall against which the toilet stood. The hostage stepped on top of the tank, whose cracking made an explosion like a small bomb. The guards raced in—and broke into belly laughter. For them, the rupture might have been another triumph over America. The ordinary Iranian toilet was a hole in the ground. This one, again from the Embassy, had been installed—complete with buckets of water for flushing, for it had not been plumbed in—for our comfort.

To go to the bathroom we had to knock on our cell door and toss "the flag," a white towel, through the grating on top of the door. The flag indicated from which cell the knock had come. If you threw it first and knocked afterward, you were certain to enjoy a lecture from Ahmad when news of the transgression reached him. "If you do not follow the rules," he would declare, "you will not be allowed to use the toilet again!"

One of us did not follow rules, and Ahmad dashed in again. "Yeah, I goofed," said the American. "But I gotta go badly. And the wait's probably too long with all that knocking I heard."

"You must follow the rules," came Ahmad's standard solution.

"Damn you, I've got to go. Do you want me to do it right here?"

Ahmad ran out of the cell and a moment later ran back in with a bucket. "Yes, do it right here," he screeched.

The toilets themselves were dismal, despite our own efforts to keep them clean. In the Embassy, before we were given responsibility for this, they became flooded and filthy almost overnight. The Ambassador's luxurious bathroom was transformed into little better than a slop bucket with revolutionary graffiti—such as "We Support the Struggling People Against the Karter Imperialists"—all over the walls. By nature I am fastidious about such things as toilets. That was one thing we all had to learn not to let disturb us, and they gave us a surfeit of practice.

We also washed our clothes in the bathrooms—in prison in a shower room with a belching, often exploding kerosene heater across from the toilets. It occurred to me that when the nightmare was over, if ever, I might make a fortune in endorsements. I had been wearing the same pair of Levi Strauss trousers, bought in Macy's Brooklyn branch, for what would soon be four hundred days. I could introduce myself to viewers, tell my story, and with great conviction, advertise the superior quality of Levi Strauss products: in my case, superior to the wearer. I washed them every two months or so, watched in amazement as the dirt flowed out, and when they were dry and the permanent crease back in place, put them on again for every occasion of day-and-evening prison wear.

As months passed, the support system of my extended family became even more essential. Practically and emotionally I was sustained better than anyone in my circumstances could have hoped for. Most important, the children appeared normal and essentially happy. The country was seething and sometimes I seethed too, but they lived in a haven from strain. In their father's absence their grandfather played with them long and lovingly; the houseful of relatives all parented.

Barry had been away for almost two years. Missing our anniversary, in July, and Alexander's birthday, in August, tore at him. "Surely Zand and Ari will resent my absence and always feel I've deserted them in some way," he wrote. "Please tell Zand that I love him with all my heart on his fourth birthday. I want to hug him so hard it hurts."

I knew how he felt by instinct and experience, not from the letter—which came only in the fall. From April to late August not one arrived, for me or the children. That was obviously one result of the failed rescue mission. It was almost certain the hostages were scattered from Tehran immediately afterward. With little doubt that Barry was alive but no idea where he was being held, a kind of vacuum set in.

In some ways, it made dealing with separation easier. The children were enveloped in protective warmth and I was too, to some extent. There was a lull in television appearances, since I could offer nothing "new." Except after reading newspaper speculation about a second rescue mission or the possibility of stronger military action, anxiety lay dormant. I occupied myself with daily trivia, blanking out painful prospects as much as I could.

I kept myself from checking the calendar to see on what day July 29 would fall. This was self-protection, evidenced by my response to my father's question about our anniversary. "I don't know and don't want to know," I disappointed him by answering.

In the same way, I put off planning a party for Alexander's birthday until I realized it was unfair to him; it was *his* day. We invited a few of his friends to see the play *Peter Pan*, which Barry would have enjoyed especially. It was the second consecutive birthday of Alexander's he missed. I tried to hide my depression, but it probably would have been better if my parents had hosted.

On our way to the play, we passed a little fountain in a shopping mall and Alexander asked, as always, for a penny to toss in with a wish. He made the same expression as just before blowing out his birthday candles, but this time announced his thought: "I wish my Daddy was home." He still wasn't speaking of where Barry was and why he wasn't with us. I wasn't certain what he felt, but thought it better not to probe while I myself was depressed.

I tried to adhere to my dictum of one day at a time, no longer even keeping the radio on all day. In fact, I avoided broadcast journalism except for the evening news on the channel my father had watched before the crisis. The inevitable questioning by reporters who called about speculation as to when it would all be over was nonsense that helped no one. What did help was filling the day with routine, caring for the children. By the time I got them to bed, I was ready for it too.

The State Department even worked out a routine for contacting Barry's mother. The rescue mission frightened her badly—and drew us together. When they called her, she was rife with accusations. "You almost got my son killed, didn't you? Now, what ideas do you have for getting him *out?*" With no answers, they started calling me with messages to be passed on to her. Often I would have liked to ask similar questions but learned that the person calling was blameless and kept my feelings to myself.

We could have been taken for a happy family with a sad secret. My grandmother prayed for Barry with the rosary the Pope gave me, then put it away, saying she wanted to be buried with it. Photographs of the Pope shaking hands with me gave her deep satisfaction. She held them inches from her failing eyes and joy appeared on her face for her granddaughter's "anointment." She was fulfilled—and that paradox had some elements that were taking control of my life.

Without Barry, I lacked someone to talk to—not about the mundane, which was as easy as ever with my family, but about topics and feelings that Barry had opened up. Deprivation of our openness was usually harder to accept than his physical absence.

That couldn't be explained to my family; it could come out only in talk with *him*, with whom my own thoughts were refined. I couldn't even discuss Iran with anyone as I would have with Barry—although I sensed I was starting to grasp things on my own as he would. It was the intimacy of our kind of uninhibited exchange that I most missed. That was what had made me feel more a whole person than with anyone else. He helped me reach to the limits of my powers of observation and expression.

The paradox was that now I was having glimmers of feeling like a whole person on my own. Maybe nature abhors a vacuum in the psyche as well as in space. A striving for independence seemed to be moving into the vacuum. With Barry missing, I was developing *on my own* some of the qualities he had brought out—which was leading to a conflict I didn't suspect.

＊

When I returned from Europe, the First Secretary for Political Affairs of the German Embassy in Washington called regularly to discuss the situation. Like Helmut Schmidt, he was direct, politically astute, and knew about Iran. The First Secretary probably was instructed by the office of Helmut Schmidt to stay in touch, for the Chancellor sent a cable on November 4 expressing concern that the crisis was a year old with the hostages still held and asking me to pass on his feelings to the other families.

When the Chancellor was in New York, several days later, he asked me to attend a dinner for the Family of Man awards. It was an unusually elegant event, and I was glad I was wearing a new dress, my first since Barry left. The evening was a combination of beauty and engaging conversation. I was pleased too with my new competence in negotiating such affairs when I ventured out of the numbing limbo at home.

Other oddities struck me. There I was, surrounded by Germans in dinner suits—Germans of my father's age, which meant they might have been shooting at him thirty-five years before. Yet it was Germans who were being most helpful in this time of trouble for the wife of a former Orthodox Jew. When Barry's letters started arriving again, I instinctively called the German Embassy before the State Department with medical problems he raised.

The greatest oddity was my presence at the glittering table. While Barry was rotting in confinement—*because* he was there—I was enjoying this stimulating evening. It wasn't a happy irony. Out in the world, I was learning it was a less sensible and happy place than I had imagined from my perspective at the stove or behind the teacher's desk. But it was also more interesting than I had suspected. There were clever people to listen to and even exchange opinions with. I knew Barry would be pleased in a way—and perhaps worried in another. One of his letters betrayed a hint of hurt that while he was languishing I was finding so much excitement in related activities. I wrote only sketchily about them, but relatives filled in gaps. He more than anyone had encouraged me to develop my potential. But together with his applause I gleaned a twinge of resentment that it was happening this way.

It would have done no good, I told myself, not to have attended the Family of Man party. On the contrary, I talked there to Donald McHenry, American Ambassador to the United Nations, and Walter Stoessel, American Ambassador in Bonn when I visited, now Undersecretary of State. I knew those contacts were potentially helpful to Barry.

❋

In August a FLAG meeting was held in San Francisco so hostage families living in the West and the Midwest would not have to travel to Washington again. I, who had not even gone away to college, settled into my seat on the plane *liking* being alone. Often I had questioned Barry about his extensive travel. Wasn't he frightened? At least lonely? It was a question I would never again put to him or anyone. I even looked forward to the few hours of solitude in my hotel room. I would have loved exploring the city with Barry—but discovered I could enjoy it alone. I knew I was not independent in the sense of being completely responsible for myself and the children. Nor did I want to be; but I did like the taste of self-sufficiency.

The hostage who disapproved of our laughing fought a losing battle as time dragged on. Conditions grew no better. Lack of fresh air—a glimpse of outdoors—became increasingly cruel after months in prison. But courageous comics from neighboring cells began bolstering our morale.

One of them would occasionally sing "The Lord High Executioner," from Gilbert and Sullivan's *The Mikado,* at the top of his lungs. This sent the guards, with Reza in the lead, flying into our cells. Who's *making* that noise?" Later we learned it was John Limbert, one of the Farsi-speaking political officers. At the time, we were not covering up when we said we had no idea who our talented hero was.

The same voice proclaimed its dignity with a might cry of "Ahhhhh SHIT!" It would have been funny even if it hadn't sent the guards into a frenzy, like ants under a just-removed rock. Whatever they tried, they couldn't identify our daring spokesman, who seemed to use their fury to develop into yet stronger voice. The humorless Reza, driven to paranoia by far less than this, salivated at the first note of the liberty cry—while we gave in to glee, like boys in school. It rang out every few hours, never so nobly as in the middle of the night. It was the perfect expression of our innermost feelings.

"Ahhhhhhhhhhh *SHIT!*"

✿

Our other recreation was being moved to a nearby room to watch old videotapes. We could only guess at Ahmad's criteria for selecting them from the Embassy's collection. Anything involving a motorcycle appealed deeply. The guards licked their chops at the appearance of the California Highway Patrol, or whatever it was called, and revved up passionately—"hrrum hhrrrumm—at the sight of a Harley-Davidson. Most of the programs, with or without motorcycles, represented the worst of American police dramas, which appealed just as deeply. There was no end to the ironies. The guards inflicted this network junk on us because they loved it.

We were permitted to peruse a collection of books and comic books in the television room. One of the comic books published by the Born Again movement featured a smiling, superconfident Chuck Colson, former Watergate conspirator, leaping out of the pages to announce to the world that he had been born again: He was no longer a schemer and intriguer. Some concerned American had mailed it to the hostages as a group to remind us that good old Chuck had also endured a great trial but emerged from it an honest man, at peace with himself. This time the irony came from the American side—or was this *my* time for rebirth? Was I undergoing the labor pains of self-discovery, after which I would perceive the Nixon mouthpiece as my new buddy in truth and God?

Our television diet was liberally spiced with the new regime's driving images. Most of us had seen one of the most popular tapes when we were being held in the Embassy compound. It was a long documentary, much like some I had seen in slides at the University, of the beating, maiming, and shooting of Iranian citizens during the martial law of the Shah's last year, when blood flowed heavily from sometimes hideous brutality as the Army broke up demonstrations. To make the point that our countrymen, too, protested the Shah's tyranny, the room was festooned with posters of American demonstrations. But the photographs were clearly of 1960s protests against the Vietnam War and had nothing to do with Iran. The guards kept pointing to American "fascists"—the very motorcycle-and-helmet types they adored in the television pulp—brutalizing Americans who were trying to become their revolutionary brothers and sisters. Their little deception was so feeble that at another time I might have patted them.

But none of us saw anything remotely funny in the program featuring one Father Rupiper, a member of a group who had visited the Embassy in February and spoken to some of the hostages. We were subjected to a broadcast he made somewhere in the States in which he maintained that the militants were fine fellows, really, who were treating us well; the real problem behind our imprisonment was American foreign policy. I needed no one to tell me that American foreign policy toward Iran was indeed a problem, but the notion that it justified taking and keeping hostages turned our stomachs. How we wished for Father Rupiper to sample our fine treatment for himself!

Prisoners seemed fated to receive the attentions of outside investigators who bend over backward not to offend the captors and violators. We felt the self-satisfied clergyman was more interested in putting forth our guards' political viewpoint than in improving our welfare, for which he had presumably come. His totally misleading "oh-they're-fine" impression went to an outside world *we* could not reach. In the creeping passage of weeks in prison, most of us came to despise the duped or duping Father Rupiper.

❋

More news trickled in, each tidbit provoking hours of speculation. The adjoining cell tapped that someone had heard Richard Queen, a young vice-consul, had been released and was back in America. Why had this happened, *if* it had? We knew the students were determined to release no one and surmised the government was too weak to make them, even if it wanted to. Later someone else heard, and of course immediately passed along, that Richard was dangerously ill with multiple sclerosis.

By now, tapping was supplemented with a set of hand signals for communication with the cell across the corridor. Using the same code, we would stand on a chair far enough from the corridor to impede the guards' view from there, but where the two signalers could see each other's fingers. While guards passed in the corridor and we muffled our giggles of success, news was passed—including a report that several marines had been fed intravenously after the crash of a truck in which they were being transported. I remembered what interest I used to take in national habits such as the mad way of driving, how much affection I used to feel for even the foibles of a people I knew and loved.

Far more portentous news came in the bathroom in early September. Picking up the soap one day, I saw "Shah dead" traced into the bar, probably with a fingernail. At another time, I might have remembered that no death is a happy event. But the two words were eloquent then. I put down the soap without using it so others would see the message.

If the Shah *was* dead, they'd give up trying to trade us for him, wouldn't they? But maybe one of us had engraved his wishful thinking. Rumors ballooned during the following week; discussion and speculation were carried on by tapping and hand signals. Then came almost joyful confirmation in a carelessly censored sports magazine: An article about a golf match mentioned an interruption by a news report of the death of the Shah in Egypt. And I received a letter from a New Jersey woman which, among news of a heat wave, the pollen count, a gasoline shortage, and her neighborhood diner, announced that "the Shah is dead, the excuse is dead." We were full of expectation—and nothing happened. Why were we still here *now*? Then we realized the death had occurred more than a month before. Would President Carter or some other American "Satan" have to die before this ended?

The death of the Shah, on which we had pinned so much hope, changed nothing except to bring on the inevitable new deflation after puncture of that hope. However, it illustrated the Iranian hatred of him was still tinged with another kind of nationalism. A month later, Space Cadet was giving me a haircut. I sprang my question suddenly.

"Ali, who went to the Shah's funeral?" (Ali was his proper name.)

He tried to feign a blank expression. "What funeral?"

"Come on, don't give me the act."

The blankness changed slowly to pride. He was like a youth taking satisfaction in a parade that excited the senses and flattered the national vanity.

"The Shahbanu [the Empress of Iran] was there," he said loftily.

"President Nixon was there too, and a big gathering of important people. It was a very impressive funeral."

That the Shah was the reviled enemy hardly dented Ali's pride. He had been deeply impressed. It was thoroughly Iranian.

❁

Not all of our reading was what is usually called edifying. A novel entitled *Trading Up* featured a sexy girl in a black dress on the cover, thrusting her leg onto a border of gold. The book followed three young women from marriage to marriage, each a move up in society. The jealous second husband of one tries constantly to test her to prove his suspicion of disloyalty. In one episode he hires a man to lie on a beach near his wife, nude and with an erection. Overwhelmed by the sun, surf, and the other thing, the wife succumbs—and is beaten bloody when she returns to her husband.

Another man seduces women day and night, left and right, including one of the heroines. The amazing California cat can barely control himself, even on his marriage day—until the ceremony has been performed, which renders him impotent with his bride.

A third man, black and beautiful, sweats in a joyful orgy with several women on someone's makeshift stage as the third heroine watches. In the heat of the fun he drops dead of a heart attack.

The book earned unanimous protestations of "trash." When someone read aloud a passage he believed had redeeming quality, jeering resounded. But everyone in the room read it twice, turned to the wall. By my second turn the cover had fallen off. The girl in the black dress had evidently been fondled to death. Thank goodness for such books in such situations; I seemed to be making a comeback.

❁

The event that plunged our despair deeper than ever began with bestowal on us of a crossword puzzle ripped from an American newspaper. Steve Lauterbach flipped the little square over to examine the television listing printed there. "You won't believe it! Guys, listen to this." In one chance of a million, the program list included a documentary history of American military intelligence from the Bay of Pigs to *the aborted attempt to rescue the hostages on April 24!* A bomb seemed to have exploded in the cell. The conclusion hit us like searing shrapnel. *That's* why we'd been rushed out of Tehran in such panic the next morning.

Steve read the little item a second time, then passed the square around. Crushing disappointment followed our shock: We concluded that if not for the rescue attempt, we might have been home by now instead of in our miserable cell. Any attempt to negotiate for us *must* have been obliterated by the attempt. Since it had obviously failed, we had been stashed away in provincial hideaways and jail cells. Now when would we be freed?

In any case, I could not fathom how any rescue mission could have succeeded without heavy loss of life, including many of our own lives. Surely intelligence experts would not have planned a raid, if that's what it was, without cause to expect reasonable success. And reasonable success must have depended on meticulously devised plans that included "inside" help from Iranians. We knew nothing about such arrangements, and perhaps never would. From our vantage point on the ground, however, the notion seemed highly improbable. The Embassy, near the very center of a city of four million hostile inhabitants, had been protected and patrolled like a fortification. Even if a rescue force had managed to penetrate the compound, probably by helicopter, it still would have to deal with the armed guards and their sandbagged emplacements in the corridors. Thinking about the consequences in the cell, our mouths fell open. We felt certain that the attempt had brought us much closer to death than to rescue, that we had been saved by its failure—but also pushed much farther from real salvation.

✲

A few weeks later, Steve and I were escorted to a shower while Bob Englemann waited his turn. Tom Schaefer had been removed several nights before, on October 22. While Tom was packing, we agreed on a signal: If he was kept in the same cellblock, he would bend the corner of a photograph on the wall of the videotape room. The corner was not bent, indicating he had been taken farther. We never saw him again in the prison, which gave us many painful nights.

The shower room was at the far end of our corridor, with the treasure of the garbage bag just inside its door. "Stand in front of the water heater, Steve," I said so he would block Ahmad's television camera. Something told me the console wasn't being manned; it was worth the risk. I picked quickly at the slimy mess inside the bag and extracted part of an American newspaper that seemed to indicate that Ramsey Clark, who earlier had been refused entry to Iran, attended a Tehran conference about "American crimes" during the summer. A soggy letter to the editor called for Clark's prosecution for violating President Carter's travel ban to Iran. We dared not take more time at the garbage bag. In the shower, I stuck the scrap of newspaper against a corner of the wall—and felt the worst shock, the hardest blow, since the seizure of the Embassy. The final sentence of the letter stated that Ramsey Clark deserved prosecution all the more because *eight American servicemen had died in the attempt to rescue the hostages.* Only momentary incredulity—or disbelief—kept me from shouting out.

"What's wrong?" whispered Steve.

"Something insane. Let's get back to the cell."

The wet cutting was in my underpants when we left the shower room. Back in the cell we dried it over a lamp and tried to make sense of the dismaying, bewildering scrap of information, while Bob Englemann stood at the door. American servicemen had died trying to free us? How? We hadn't heard a single shot.

Months would pass before we learned that the doomed raiding party never even reached Tehran. Now, knowing only that eight people had somehow given their lives for us, we felt utterly miserable. This was the terrible, final reality that our absurd experience had wrought tragedy, and not even our own.

However bleak our future seemed, however disturbing our individual conditions, we were alive and had hope. Whoever they were and however they perished, the eight had no chance for anything, and their families were permanently maimed. This sacrifice was for us. We ate in silence. Hours of discussion and speculation would come later.

We tapped a signal to the neighboring cell but didn't share the information with everyone. Even a few evenings later, when a guard fell asleep on duty and we had the corridor's air space to ourselves, we kept quiet about the deaths for the sake of embassy marines imprisoned near us. For some reason we assumed the casualties were marines and the news would upset their comrades unduly in prison.

It was probably inevitable that the crisis became an issue in the presidential campaign, despite the best intentions, if that's what they were, to maintain a united front to the Iranians. Some Republicans accused President Carter of manipulating the situation to help him win reelection. At one point, Ronald Reagan almost sneered at Carter for the "humiliation and disgrace to the country" of allowing Americans to remain prisoners for almost a year. But beyond hinting that Iranians were barbarians and fuming at them, Reagan offered no concrete plan to compete with Carter's softer approach. I called the State Department for advice. Reporters were asking my opinion of Reagan's stance and I didn't want to say something that could damage the President's efforts.

"Are Carter and Reagan playing good-guy/bad-guy?" I asked.

"We don't know what they're doing. In this case we really can't give you advice."

"Maybe just guidelines," I persisted. "Something that would keep me clued in to your thinking so what I say will be in concert."

"Sorry, you're on your own."

Press interest in me came in cycles. This was an "up" period, as newspapers and television stations prepared reports for the first anniversary of the seizure. I still had friendly relations with almost all the journalists I knew, but if anything, my disappointment in the profession had grown.

Television remained the most likely to indulge in the superficial and the crass. One reporter finished interviewing me and turned to some closing chat. "Barbara," she said amiably, "what are you going to do when Barry comes home and all these cameras won't be on you any longer?"

After my year-long exposure to network machinations, her question shouldn't have surprised me as it did. Did she really believe I was there because I liked my screen image, not because it was a way to try to help Barry? Many in television so hungered to become celebrities that they projected this onto others.

Television's commingling of Hollywood and news reporting became even more apparent over the months. What remained to be said about "the domestic story"—that is, husbandless and fatherless life at home? But most reporters probed harder than ever. "Barbara, how do you *feel?*" they kept asking, as if the significance of the crisis lay in my yearning for Barry. If I would reveal my tears, they would have a fine story. I wanted talk about foreign policy; they wanted to peer into my "heart"—which was easier than preparing a program on the issues.

One of the strongest drives was to place the camera where it would broadcast directly over the air. Minutes after the film we saw of Barry in which his appalling appearance introduced us to his condition, a producer called to ask if I would come to the studio so he could record my reaction. Even in the shock of seeing Barry's state, his intrusion on that private moment amazed my parents and me.

It went on relentlessly. After five extremely anxious months, many families first heard of their hostages when International Red Cross doctors visited in April. When the doctors returned to Geneva, they called families with messages from their loved ones. The press plagued us all: Can we be there when you get your call from Geneva? Can we listen in? Will you give us the content of the message? If the messages had public interest, surely the familes would make them public. Striving to participate in—and thus degrade—private matters grew more persistent.

Most families tried to behave with dignity in the face of the assault on their privacy and senses, but producers persevered to obtain and air what they wanted. The worst moment for me—the most blatant violation of decency and taste—came during the broadcast of photographs of the charred remains of the rescue-mission servicemen. Ayatollah Khalkhali, the "Hanging Judge," had rushed to the Embassy, where the bodies had been brought, and was shown holding up limbs and gloating. It was revolting—but, to me, so was the decision to show the film. There were also pictures of the hideously burned face of one of the men: someone's husband, father, brother, or son, who had died in agony and was now an ashen skeleton with eyes burned out. Was the airing worth the pain inflicted? Was it necessary?

But part of my resentment stemmed from my own participation in the great television scandal. I still justified my appearance in terms of need to counter as much as I could that appeared damaging. Yet I was tainted by the prevailing ethics, just like everyone else.

I hadn't seen Barry since the Easter hostage film. ABC News offered to let me see him again by rerunning the Christmas tape for me. At the studio an executive producer insisted on a reporter joining me in the screening room. I protested that even my cousin, who had accompanied me to Manhattan, would wait outside because I wanted to view the tape alone. The producer said the machine was too complicated for me to operate.

The model featured clearly visible "on" and "off" buttons. After an exchange of words I said I wouldn't accept the studio's offer under those conditions. It was obvious why the reporter "had" to be with me. Someone decided a film of me watching the film of Barry would be an effective twist for a television piece. But it was known by then for certain that Iranians in New York were monitoring programs concerning Iran. I wouldn't give them the satisfaction of seeing my reaction. Furthermore, I wanted to see Barry in *privacy*.

I thanked the producer and left. She relented as I rang for the elevator and chatted with my cousin while I watched the film alone. "So Barbara is for real," she said. "Now I feel sorry for her, going through this ordeal." This is what it took, even for someone so intimately involved, to make the screen image represent a living person. But she hadn't met the hostages personally. Were *they* for real? Were all strangers fair game to develop for the network's advantage?

Sometimes I met reporters at the door of the house and led them to the yard for interviews. Experience taught that once a camera got inside, it focused on details of family life—and it was domestic scenes that featured that evening, no matter what I said about events in Iran. I regretted my slowness in learning that lesson, but when I did, I declined requests to film our Barry-less Christmas for television. Everyone knew how people like us celebrate Christmas, and it surely didn't bear on the resolution of the crisis.

Exploiting the children rankled more than anything. Film of Alexander and Ariana was prized—more touching than my comments, which were often cut anyway. Alexander had a half-memorized paragraph beginning, "I want my Daddy to come home," for reporters who asked him to say something. It was moving and true, but I sensed his deepest feelings were being used. Adults who believe they can gain from publicity must be free to play the game, of course. But no matter how much Alexander believed his little speech, I shuddered when I remembered him making it for the camera. I learned too late about the children's need to be shielded.

Letters from Barry began coming again with some regularity in the fall. Now he sketched some details of his sickness, and by implication, his battle with it. This brought back the heavy numbness I had managed to shake.

November 4th

To be frank, I felt rather bad that the media picked up on my health problems last March. Perhaps it's a feeling that I'd like to be portrayed as "able to take it." I know that's foolish. If one is sick, one shouldn't think of it as weakness or fault. However, in this case I'm personally at a loss about my ailment.

November 12th

I've lived with the symptoms so long that they've become part of me. I don't know why they continue. I've been told that my environment still produces anxiety. I have to leave the stimulus, so to speak, to change my response.

November 18th

You can understand why I'm always reluctant to talk about what's bothering me. But then I say to myself that it's ludicrous to stick to the macho image. I used to think of myself as tough and I thought that in the year previous to the takeover I'd exhibited the ability to hold tight. . . .

I'm apprehensive about the future and question my former strength. I know that with you at my side I'll have the courage to face whatever awaits us. . . .

Frequent mention of the time we would spend in deep understanding and total harmony—now that captivity had taught him what is truly important—troubled me too. I thought I gleaned flights of fancy in that.

It seemed natural enough. More romantic than I by nature, Barry was protecting himself from the unpleasantness of his enforced surroundings by spinning images of the exquisite marriage and perfect family life we would share when he returned. That was my interpretation of the lush passages in his short letters. One of his favorites was of us running barefoot on a tropical beach. I had no such visions —which was equally natural, since I wasn't languishing in jail. While he was sustaining himself with idyllic images, I was dealing with insurance policies and runny noses.

Were our experiences reinforcing contrary elements of our personalities? I wondered. I was afraid he anticipated a fairy tale after the nightmare. I feared the opposite: We might face more difficulty than before.

After months of seminormal routine, my sleepiness was returning. Limbo, I was discovering, is a surprisingly enervating state. Imagining life when Barry returned was becoming a preoccupation. For the first time ever, I became impatient with my parents—for no reason except that, for all my gratitude for their care of the children and me, I had lived too long in a crowded house. I had learned to like time alone. Barry was right about my relying too much on my family. I thought of getting an apartment for the children and me.

That too brought conflict, especially with my duty to Alexander. As I was leaving him at school one day in early fall, he wrapped his arms around my legs and declared, "You're *my* hostage now. You can't leave me any more." There was seriousness in his joking, as well as clear indication of how well he understood the central issue of the crisis. And although I knew he was "at home," in all senses, with my mother and father, I didn't *like* leaving the children, even for a day or two.

Yet I had to get away. It was closer to need than desire. Although I took no action about an apartment, I did look forward more to travel. I remembered my tension when I had first flown to Washington alone for the State Department briefings. That had been less than a year before, but a year of more change than ever before. Even when I became a mother, I was back at the house with *my* mother to help.

Soon after the seizure, I started jotting down some thoughts in a notebook but gave up because there was nowhere to write in the house without someone peering over my shoulder. Now I continued the project, "on the road." In a hotel room in Boston I tried to confront my feelings:

December 1, 1980

Surrounded by the family, I've just spent one of the loneliest weekends of my life. I am tense with myself and on edge with everyone. Maybe the answer is in a feeling I thought I had completely repressed; at least it hasn't been bothering me. Love desire coming to the surface after all this time. Why?

I so want to be loved and held again. It has been so long, but what can I do in such a situation? I have been growing irritable, which isn't like me. I don't have the patience to attend to the children properly or even hold a decent conversation with Mom and Dad. I need to do something for myself. I must regain control over the forces that are distorting my life.

I spoke with Marge German* today. Some of the families are more upset than ever with the State Department. They feel it hasn't been honest with us. There are many complaints about depression and despair as we are entering our second holiday season alone.

My own feelings are turning more and more hostile toward Iran. We should *refuse* to negotiate with them until the hostages are released or until they agree to talk to us face to face. I've lost all respect for them as a nation since they ignore even the basic human needs of mail and proper medical attention. How cruel they are after all! But I'll never let them know how much they are hurting me. They won't get that satisfaction from me and won't be privy to my hopelessness.

I wish I could run away and forget that all this has happened! Just be alone. I'm tired of worrying about how others are feeling. I need someone to take care of me and my needs—and no one is here. . . .

* Wife of hostage Bruce German.

An intern or a medical student occasionally checked blood pressure and handed out laxatives, but we knew of no doctor visiting the prison. I was still on antidepressant pills, and so were others by this time. My dosage had come down to four pills a day but added up to hundreds over the months, and this continued to worry me; I couldn't forget Montgomery Clift's deterioration.

The guards ignored my requests to see a specialist for months—until Ahmad came to the cell one day to tell me to pack for the evening. In the van my hands were bound and a sheet was laid over me, corpse-like. We drove for twenty minutes and stopped soon after riding over the bump-bump-bump in the Embassy's main driveway. We had been wondering what had happened to the Embassy since we left —specifically, whether it was damaged in retribution for the rescue attempt. Before being unloaded, I shifted my blindfold against a support inside the van enough to see that the façade of the Chancery appeared intact. "It's nice to be home," I tried to joke with the guard. "What do you mean? *Where* are you?" he challenged. Later he told me the compound would be made into a revolutionary museum.

Dr. Fakhr, who originally prescribed my medication, examined me briefly in a room of the Chancery. He said nothing new. I saw some familiar guards but no Americans, and although it was good to know the Embassy was standing and even better to get a glimpse of the compound's trees and grass after months of being cut off from everything green in the concrete cell, I was happy to return to the friends with whom I shared it.

That evening, a young marine named William Gallegos put on one of his shows in the corridor on his way to the bathroom. Gallegos had courage to match his sense of fun. When his boredom became too much, he fashioned his own entertainment. He could be an Indian warrior, a dog with a strident yelp, or, as in this performance, a galloping, neighing horse. The guards didn't know what to make of him even before he handed them a bridle for his own neck. Listening at the door and laughing made my "homecoming" to prison even happier.

A few evenings later, an interlude took place that will live long in hostage memory. Ever since the 6 P.M. blackouts following the outbreak of war with Iraq, we had been going to bed early. But sleep was fitful, and not only for me. Prison sounds echoed loudly in the dismal corridor.

In the early hours of September 30, someone knocked repeatedly on his cell door to ask to go to the toilet. Bedside Manner was on duty that night, sitting on his couch in the corridor. His disposition hadn't improved over the months. The beanstalk with black eyes was as nasty as ever. But he did answer toilet calls, however reluctantly. When he failed to answer this incessant one, the amazing reason dawned on us. He had fallen asleep!

Within minutes, everyone was awake and shouting to everyone else. The corridor was a babble of rapid-fire questions and intense discussions, as if not twenty but two hundred men who hadn't seen each other for months had been ungagged.

It was our finest moment by far for exchanging information. For the first time, we were able to talk to everyone in the cellblock; more messages wafted and crisscrossed in a quarter of an hour than in all previous months taken together. Even Bill Daugherty, a political officer who had been kept in solitary confinement for almost three hundred days because he was suspected of working for the CIA, joined in.

"How are you, Bill?" three people shouted at once.

"I'm okay. Keeping myself very busy. The only thing is the food: Is there still something in the world besides bread?"

Suddenly I recognized Dave Roeder's voice and shouted to him.

"And how's everything with *you*, Barry? I hope to *see* you one of these days."

Information flew back and forth like shuttlecocks. Everyone analyzed possible consequences of the Shah's death; everyone gave a résumé of his own experiences. The lovely time enjoyed by all was heightened by Bedside Manner's dilemma when the pandemonium finally woke him. Still dopey from sleep, he staggered from door to door, pounding weakly and demanding silence. But he had lost his power, at least temporarily. If he reported the incident to his brothers or superiors, Ahmad would deduce that he had fallen asleep and make a mess of him.

Toward dawn that morning, as I tried to force myself to get some sleep, I ran through what I remembered of what everyone had said. It occurred to me that even in our fifteen minutes of manic "freedom," the death of the eight Americans had not been mentioned. We had discussed what we knew and guessed about the rescue attempt, but no one could bring himself to mention the most important news.

I had learned to value life as never before. After so much concern about my own, the loss of eight others seared. However indirectly and partially, we were the cause of those deaths, and I promised myself that if we were released, I would fulfill my obligation to the families.

*

It seemed the new Iranian Parliament, which was supposed to decide our fate, hadn't convened, was stalling, or was being blocked. We knew no details, of course, and our speculation shifted to the American elections, about which guards had told us Ronald Reagan would be running against Jimmy Carter. The guards seemed to favor Reagan, if only because they hated Carter so. That and the continuation of war with Iraq were our new hopes. Maybe Reagan would do what Carter obviously hadn't been able to. Maybe the President, in his striving to finesse Reagan, would take some action or make some compromise to bring about our release. If Reagan won, maybe the Iranians, reluctant to begin new negotiations, would make a last-minute deal with Carter. The discussions in our cell resembled a "Washington Week in Review" television panel. We were as solemn and full of supposed wisdom as the best commentators—without, however, having the slightest knowledge on which to pin our predictions.

Election Day would mark the first anniversary of our capture. The October preceding it was a day-by-day drag, even in comparison to earlier months. Daily topics of conversation had come down to increasing cold in the cell and the old, futile discussion of possibilities and expectations. The sounds of whipping had stopped. From the shortened wait for the toilet and fewer plates of food set out on the corridor floor at meal times—each cell door was opened separately to get them—it was clear that our own numbers were decreasing; and apart from us, the large prison seemed empty. We guessed that heating was the cause. The autumn chill almost froze the air inside the thick stone walls, and guards wore khaki coats over sweaters with hoods indoors.

Early on the morning of November 5, I knocked on the door and flew the ragged toilet flag. Ahmad himself answered.

"What's the news?" I asked.

"Reagan by three to one," he said. "I just heard it on the Voice of America."

Whatever my political opinion would have been in ordinary circumstances, I shouted an inward hurrah. It was a *change*, which *had* to be for the better, after Carter's obvious failure. Besides, if Reagan had remained anything like the tough talker of his previous campaigns, there was a chance he might learn how to beat the Iranians at their game.

"What will that mean for us?" I continued with Ahmad.

"It's just a matter of time now," he said almost comfortingly. I sensed that he wanted the business to end after the dreary year.

*

It was not just a matter of time in the ordinary sense, but a matter of false hope in the hostage sense. The only change was Ahmad's greater willingness to talk, or lesser resolution to keep us in ignorance as well as isolation. Pumping him for information every time I saw him, I summarized his replies on a calendar I labeled "Quotes from Chairman Ahmad." Every day, he would yield another scrap or implication.

Putting one with another, we concluded the Iranian Government had set four conditions for our release, of which three had already been met. They were a Washington pledge of noninterference in Iranian affairs, a promise to return the Shah's wealth to Iran, and an apology for past American crimes in the country. I could hardly believe that President Carter had apologized, and had no way of knowing Ahmad was lying about this, probably to soothe or bolster himself. But things sounded promising. The fourth and final condition "all comes down to money," Ahmad said. If this was true, the differences were negotiable and would surely be sorted out. The Iranians want *dollars* now, we said to ourselves—which means they've lost; their great campaign to demonstrate American evil has been abandoned. We decided their economy must be in shambles or the war with Iraq was going badly and they needed international support. It couldn't go on much longer.

Six remarkably tedious weeks later, the prison was a refrigerator. Despite plastic tacked around windows and a new kerosene stove in the corridor, it was virtually unheated. Reza's hints that there was a possibility of moving us to a warmer, more comfortable place meant another Christmas with him.

*

By the time the move came, on the evening of December 17, there had been enough talk about it to leave a taste of anticlimax. After half an hour's drive as the usual blindfolded sardines in back of a van, I assumed we were going farther than the Embassy. After another half hour we stopped in a place that smelled of snow and the country.

Delicious warmth greeted us inside the building. We were led up several flights of stairs and down a carpeted corridor. So it *was* going to be an improvement on the prison! When my blindfold was removed, I was in one of the handsomest offices I had seen in Iran, without a trace of warping wood or makeshift carpentry. Grass-cloth wallpaper and fine contemporary furniture matched the fine construction, and the adjoining bathroom was clean, modern, and pleasantly heated. Five others were installed in the same large room: my two prison roommates, two other embassy officers, and William Keough, former superintendent of the Tehran-American School, who had returned to Iran on what he believed would be a short trip to tie up loose ends.

Almost the entire wall opposite the door was a sliding window leading to a balcony. We were ordered not to part the curtains until morning. When we did, we made out a country-like panorama broken by a road, tin roofs tipped with snow, and the usual walls enclosing our well-kept building.

We assumed this pastoral district was in northern Tehran, near the Niavaran Palace. The building itself might have been an office in the

Shah's Imperial Court, perhaps even on the palace grounds—which would account for the high quality. A letterhead I found in a desk drawer seemed to confirm this, but weeks later, hints and remarks by guards led us to believe it was now a kind of Foreign Ministry club: a place for dinner and relaxation, with administrative offices on our floor.

Although our oversized window was densely crisscrossed with iron bars, the view of the outdoors and the privilege of looking out without restriction until the 6 P.M. curfew put us in good spirits. The first day, we gazed for hours at snow falling on fir trees, which was less captivating only than stories of where the three other hostages had been and what they had seen.

But our sense of well-being evaporated quickly. The tin roof apparently belonged to a girls' school. We were awakened every morning by "Khomeini Is the Imam," the revolution's most popular song, which was followed by chants of the never-ending "Death to America, death to Carter!" Evidently this was a central part of the morning assembly. "My God, are they still whipping themselves up?" I thought.

Bedside Manner and other guards from prison had moved with us. I quickly became so fed up with the chants and his deliberate rudeness that when he growled at me one day, I kicked the door of the room in a way that showed my foot was really aimed at him. He returned a few minutes later with the usual crew of henchman to try to frighten me. Their bluster had lost everything but the ability to disgust.

"One more time and it's back where you came from," shouted Bedside Manner. He did not say "prison," because the guards had always pretended we weren't in one.

"Do you think it makes any real difference?" I answered.

"What makes a difference is our orders. You're nothing here. You have no rights, you'll do what we tell you."

✣

One of my new roommates was Charles Jones, a communications specialist and the only black on the embassy staff who had not been released shortly after the seizure. Charlie willingly explained why. When the students broke into the communications vault, he and others were frantically destroying classified cables and equipment.

"What are you doing?" the leader of the unit shouted at him.

"What does it look like I'm doing? Step aside, man, I've got a job to finish."

In trouble from the first, he stayed in trouble, for he gave the guards no satisfaction, obedience, or rest. He talked incessantly. His gravelly bass boomed through the prison, where he was in a cell distant from ours, but always identifiable. When he sang in the shower like a seal trumpeting, the walls vibrated. He *never* lowered his voice, even when a team of guards descended on him. *He* intimidated *them.*

Charlie's dangerously high blood pressure also never stopped him. His patriotism was as revved up as his energy. Although he has suffered discrimination and all manner of insults even as a Foreign Service officer on leave in his native Detroit, he loves America with a combination of good nature and discerning wisdom that his years abroad matured. He was a vitalizing tonic for us all.

William Keough, another of the new roommates, also intimidated the guards—by sheer size and knowledge of student psychology. He was six feet nine inches tall; a kindergarten pupil once asked him in total seriousness whether he was a giant. An educator with decades of experience, he knew very well what impression he made on youth. When a guard opened the door in response to his banging and Bill thrust a plate at him—usually "Shortshit"—demanding "More bread!" he could have been Rostam, legendary hero of the Iranian epic *The Book of Kings,* who defeated hordes single-handedly. "Shortshit" was just over five feet tall. He and his slightly larger brothers looked up at Keough with unmistakable apprehension. He got whatever he wanted —except, of course, what he really wanted.

✿

The debate about what had brought us there continued straight through until Christmas Eve. Might it be because they were going to free us at Christmas, after all? Or were they going to take more holiday films of us, in which case a jail cell would never do?

We debated among and within ourselves whether we should participate if it was going to be photographs. I didn't want to be displayed again. We had all had too much of what we called "dog and pony shows": our contribution to vaudeville, with each of us going on to do his number. On the other hand, wasn't it my responsibility to show Barbara I was alive and managing? She hadn't seen me since April.

Late on Christmas Eve, the guards said we would be going very shortly to a celebration during which we would be given a chance to say what we wanted to the camera. I put on a shirt Barbara had sent me in February, which arrived in July. I had been saving it for Getting Out Day, but maybe that was pointless. I decided to take the opportunity to say something to her.

The room we were taken to, a reception hall on our floor, was supposedly cheered by pathetic-looking Christmas decorations. Five of us filed in; Charlie Jones, principled as always, had decided not to come. The Papal Nuncio, Father Bugnini, greeted me with a warm "Shalom, shalom." He and an Iranian bishop, probably Armenian or Assyrian, handed out small crosses. "Pazienza" smiled and held my hand when I said I didn't need one. Again I saw what a sweet man he was.

I read my little message to Barbara, very much on guard so no one could misinterpret my mood and explain to a distant audience how well off we were. I added greetings to my mother and brother, especially for Rosh Hashanah and Hanukkah. After the others had their turn, we returned to our room with jogging suits a large American manufacturer had sent us as presents. Their bright colors seemed to symbolize real Christmas. The senders could not have known how gloomy their touching gesture made us feel.

A few days later, a guard delivered a small package to me. To my amazement, the customs slip indicated it contained a menorah, a box of candles, a prayer sheet, and a yarmulke. The yarmulke was missing. The other articles, all obviously for Hanukkah, were untouched. Once again, I had to admit that being Jewish had brought me no extra hardship. Prepared for retribution, I had taken a deep breath before mentioning the Jewish holidays on-camera. None was handed out.

Hanukkah had already ended two weeks before. I suggested lighting the candles anyway on the principle that Christmas hadn't yet worked and we should try anything and everything. Agreeing enthusiastically, the others stood still to listen every evening as I covered my head with my hand, lit another candle, and read the appropriate prayer from the sheet in the parcel. We were the most ecumenical of Americans.

*

Something worked. We had visitors on Christmas Day: the first nonclergy foreigners since the International Red Cross representatives before we were rushed out of the Embassy in April. These were two well-suited men with briefcases who introduced themselves as the Algerian Ambassador to Iran and a member of the Algerian Foreign Ministry. Checking our names against a list, they also checked our condition visually.

This alone seemed a great breakthrough, even before they explained that Algeria was "helping with negotiations concerning you" and confirmed that the chief point of issue now was money. At the moment, they said, there was a deadlock. They were leaving for Washington that very night with an Iranian counterproposal.

We were astonished and gleeful in alternating waves. Not just the extraordinary news made us so, but our captors' willingness to allow foreigners to break it to us instead of controlling everything, especially information. Algeria, I knew, was one of the staunchest supporters of the Iranian revolution. But these two men conducted themselves as humane diplomats, *independent of our guards*. No matter how radical Algeria was or wasn't, they were treating us as human beings.

They said they would return in twenty minutes to pick up letters for delivery to the States. We postponed discussion, even conversation, in order to write furiously. When the two came back to gather our letters, they put them directly into their briefcases. This time we were stunned by our own foolishness. Had we thought, we would have realized the guards wouldn't dare to censor or confiscate what Algerian diplomats carried. We could have sent home the truth for the first time. I would have written as much and as fast about our treatment as I could, instead of the usual "I miss you, I love you" letter.

But this was a disappointment of luxury; our treatment was no longer the important thing. Negotiations had acquired a momentum, and we could almost taste the result. We shook the hands of the Algerians again, not embarrassed by the fact that in wishing them luck, we were actually wishing it to ourselves.

Bill Keough had long been predicting we would be released on a Sunday, in time for a major newspaper story the next day, Sunday itself being a poor news day. That would leave us three more days, for he now guaranteed we'd be out on Sunday, December 28. We smiled: This was his way of building morale. We also believed it.

At a FLAG meeting in December, we debated whether to ask clergymen to make another Christmas visit to the hostages. I argued against the proposal. Recently I had looked at the film of the previous year's "celebration," with the hostages singing "Silent Night" like a dirge. There was something perverted in the pretense at "normalcy" in those outrageous circumstances. Cooperating with the militants even to this degree allowed them to use their film for propaganda purposes —but beyond this, how could the hostages enjoy Christmas—or anything—there? We had enough tidbits: Decorations, goodies, even priests and ministers weren't enough. Our people deserved to be home.

Although our side was outvoted, the Iranians did not permit American clergymen to enter the country, in any case. They "attended to" the prisoners' spiritual needs by selecting priests and ministers of their own.

Maybe I should have been less cynical. After all, there appeared to be some progress toward release. As long ago as mid-September, Iran had presented four demands that seemed negotiable; they no longer included an apology for past American actions in Iran, and there was no longer mention of trials of the hostages, the threat of which had been hanging over them on and off since the seizure.

Negotiations indeed followed. But there had been so many twists and turns, so many conflicting statements from Tehran, so many "breakthroughs" that came to nothing—so many fiascoes and failures —that I no longer believed optimistic predictions. To reporters who called I said I had no comment beyond being happy that the parties were talking. I didn't want to say anything that might conflict with the spirit of the negotiations. Besides, I was skeptical, and not only purposely to keep my hopes from soaring.

The crisis had become a roller coaster of optimism and gloom. Foreign Minister Sadeq Ghotbzadeh was a Western-trained diplomat who apparently wanted to end the captivity. When he was forced out of office by radical politicians and clergymen, in early November, it seemed a disastrous blow. But by Thanksgiving the Iranian Government was saying that Washington had met its four demands in principle. A week before Christmas, the new Prime Minister, a creature of the radical forces if ever there was one, said the hostages could be freed by Christmas if the United States met Iran's financial terms. Three days later, those terms were made public: Iran wanted *twenty-four billion dollars* as part of the settlement. Not one hostage family was in favor of giving this colossal ransom, which amounted to $460 million for each captive. Every family made clear their feeling that no ransom should be paid—one reason, I think, that eventually forced the price down. Meanwhile, I saw the ridiculous figure as confirmation that the crisis might still be far from resolved; I had better control my feelings.

This took effort. Every day's newspaper was full of analysis and speculation. The signs did appear much more positive than at any time since the beginning. It seemed clear that more and more Iranians wanted to end the affair so they could get on to other problems, such as the war with Iraq and their shaky economy. I even scolded myself mildly for shutting myself off too much from positive indications. Then, on December 23, Iranian authorities renewed their threat to try the hostages.

*

Sarah was in fine form at our Christmas dinner. When she was not depressed by the situation, her sense of humor sparkled—and her generosity. She had had her wedding band dismantled and the individual diamonds made into earrings for me and my sister-in-law. It was a very moving gift.

Barry's cousin, an actor, was the funniest Santa Claus we had ever had. With his own black beard under the white one, he looked like a lumberjack in drag. The children were taken in until the padding began to slip out of his trousers. "Hey, that looks like my blanket!" sang Alexander.

My father had hung fifty-two yellow ribbons on our "wedding" tree, and at ten o'clock we went outside to light candles for the hostages, as people were doing all over the country. I appreciated the ritual, because there seemed nothing more to say about the subject; *doing* something, even ceremonial, was an outlet.

A happy by-product of the crisis was the uniting of four families—both lines of Barry and me—in one holiday and one cause. I remembered the commotion involving Sarah when we were married in the same spot. Eight years and one international crisis later, she was very dear to me, and would remain so.

But when tapes of the hostages' Christmas were aired, a few days later, thoughts of side benefits were submerged by the main concern. About half the hostages spoke to the camera with messages for family and friends. Their words were eerily stilted and enunciated, as if under threat.

The men in particular looked utterly drained and profoundly sad. Their voices were constricted, and almost all seemed to be saying with their eyes and behavior that they were depressed. Perhaps guns were pointed at them, out of camera range. Barry sat with his arms and legs tightly folded. Was it to keep them from trembling? I had never seen him in that position.

He sent best wishes to his mother and brother for Rosh Hashanah and Hanukkah. That surely took courage in face of his captors' hatred of Zionism. It was vintage Barry and gave a shot of pride to Jewish communities around the country. But I wondered why he *read* a message to his own family—and what made it so lifeless.

Alexander was sitting on my mother's lap when we first saw the clip. "Look," she said, "there's Daddy—Daddy's talking to us!" This time, Alexander didn't run away. He studied Barry for a moment, then looked up at my mother, raising his finger to his temple like a gun.

"I thought they went"—he made a shooting noise—"pftuut to Daddy," he said calmly.

He had been shown his celluloid father too many times, and ended the separation's sorrow in his own way.

As many suspected all along, the Iranians—even those who were making the most rigid ideological and most passionate emotional demands on the United States—were negotiators. They dropped their price fast: down from their original demand of twenty-four billion dollars to a little more than a third of that, by the first week of January. Just as important, the government at least appeared to be taking physical control of the hostages from the reluctant student captors, possibly in preparation for releasing them. Jimmy Carter's presidency would end in two weeks. Ronald Reagan might be a harder bargainer or tougher opponent.

Algeria was serving as intermediary, carrying proposals and counterproposals back and forth between Washington and Tehran since mid-October. Now Warren Christopher, head of our negotiating team, flew to Algiers to begin what showed signs of being final talks. They went on intensely every day, undoubtedly in an effort to reach a settlement before January 16, a deadline President Carter had set for reaching an agreement under his administration. Again the news was saturated with reports and supposition about progress. Barry might soon be home at last, and this time I couldn't suppress my optimism. But unexpected apprehension mixed with happy anticipation. How sick was he? How changed? Was I capable of nurturing him if he returned drastically altered?

There were broader concerns too, which I put on paper in a few solitary minutes at home.

January 15, 1981

It looks as though this ordeal will finally be over. Every time there is talk of another "almost certain" settlement, I feel as though I'm going through false labor, with cramps, sweaty palms, and a menacing insecurity about the future. I can hardly believe how frightened I am at the possibility of release.

I know I am very different from when Barry was taken hostage. To begin with, I don't want more children. I also don't want to be tied to the house again—but what I do want eludes me. I've been asked by producers if I'd like to try television news, but do I want to become part of the media that seems so corrupt and whose pressures are so hard to resist? The feelers are tempting, but how could I pursue them and justify—even to myself—how they handled the crisis?

What I know is that I don't want to move back to Washington, which is what Barry talks about in his last letter. More important: what about my own freedom? Sounds funny, doesn't it? "My freedom"—when Barry's freedom has been our whole concern these fourteen months—a concern that absorbed the entire country!

Admittedly mine doesn't have the urgency of his. I think these are different types of freedom, both of which are important. Maybe my reaction is understandable if I remind myself that I was in a state of shock when Barry was taken and it took weeks to adjust to the situation mentally as well as emotionally. But did I adjust too well? Have I found too many substitutes, too many protective walls? Can I break them down? Should I?

Why do I feel this need to establish myself as an independent person, with *my own* life and home? Now that I've finally reached that point, I fear I'll lose the opportunity to learn about myself. But what a price for Barry to pay for this independence of mine!

Am I being selfish? I tell myself I shouldn't feel guilty about my feelings. They are an outgrowth of unusual circumstances over which I had no control. With all my heart I hope I will be able to work out these conflicts and re-establish our family, which was so special.

I long to hold Barry. But he is not the same. Nor am I. This isn't a novel. What will happen when the "real" new couple meet?

Hope had been raised and dashed so often that this itself contributed to a sense of futility. When the Algerians left, we returned to our routine—except it had become even more tedious. Nothing changed. At various times, most in the room talked of the Algerians' visit as one more illusion of freedom, even though we felt we must be close to it. The girls' "Death to America," chanted like a college cheer—with various groups coming in to form a fugue-like production—was our alarm clock, starting us on another day.

Another day? We asked, "Why aren't we out *now?*" so often that it became a litany. Conditions were not onerous here; what we had trouble coping with was the possibility that even this period had no definite end.

Ahmad stopped coming. Perhaps he stayed away to avoid being pumped for information. Our talk was on the same subject, but with more lassitude—and eventually we stopped speculating, because it did no good. We had asked the Algerians, then Ahmad, how *much* money was involved in the negotiations. Somewhere the impossibly high figure of twenty-five billion dollars was mentioned. The U. S. Government would and should not pay that, certainly not as ransom for us. We wondered whether all fifty-two of us—we knew the number from the International Red Cross—were in this building. No one had seen Bruce Laingen and two other embassy officers since they left for the Iranian Foreign Ministry early on the morning of the takeover. There was much reminiscing about Bruce's positive effort on morale in the Embassy, and much hoping his disappearance was not for sinister causes.

January 15 tediously came and went. President Carter's last day in office was four days away: another "milestone"—maybe. We started a countdown: three, two, one . . . something *had* to give.

*

On January 19 sounds of guards scurrying urgently went on all morning, as if they were preparing another move. I was neither depressed nor exhilarated—just interested, because something seemed to be happening at last. At ten-thirty we still hadn't had our bread and jam. Even a bit of hunger was a welcome break from routine.

An hour later we were informed we hadn't been fed because blood tests were to be administered. "If you'd only *told* us, we might have cooperated," said Charlie, who had made his own breakfast from leftover bread. But of course they hadn't told us; still everything remained secretive.

Iranian technicians duly administered the blood tests, raising expectations a degree higher. Whether the Algerians had requested the samples or the Iranian Government wanted to prove something to the world, this was at least activity—something different.

In the early afternoon, guards began coming for us, one by one. Despite all our hope for what this meant, the "selection" procedure produced anxiety. Bruce German, the first man taken, did not return. The rest of us wanted to go, yet were extremely nervous. We sat around the table nibbling at bread and shuffling playing cards. First there were six anxious captives. An hour later, there were two.

When my turn came, at last, I was led to a room in which we had been permitted to watch television one hour a week. The television set was gone; the room was almost empty. Ahmad, whom I hadn't seen in days, was seated in a folding chair against the wall. He motioned for me to sit down opposite him.

For all his mellowing since our transfer from prison, I never forgot his penchant for Brahms at full volume while prisoners were flogged. Now he flashed a newspaper in my direction without allowing me to read it. Presumably the paper told of successful completion of negotiations. "You and several others have been selected for possible release," he said in Farsi. "There's a good chance. I just want to remind you how humane our treatment has been—so if you do get out, you'll tell the truth."

Once again I lost control, despite everything I'd learned. Ahmad's tricks—or hypocrisy, or machinations, whatever it was—ignited my temper. "You can stop there," I said. "First of all, no more Farsi, I've had enough. I want to say it in my language so I can tell you precisely what I feel. After the years I spent caring for Iran, you treated me and the others like animals. You've managed to make those who loved your country hate what you represent—and hate *you*. You Iranians never stop talking about love for your families. I'll never forget what you've done to *my* family. I'll never forgive you personally."

He turned crimson and threw the newspaper into the air. "You *were* a candidate for early release," he screamed. "Get out of here. Off the list! Out!"

It was *my* way all over again: my pride, my insistence on—what? I wanted to leave Iran so badly that I honestly felt I couldn't endure another day there. Yet I wouldn't beg. Apparently the Iranians were planning to release us in a staggered procedure, maybe the least "political" first. Typically, I'd ruined my chances. How many more months would I live as a prisoner—and with the memory of my empty "feat"?

＊

Within the hour, I was led to the room where we were televised on Christmas Eve and again placed before a camera. My interviewer was the same woman in the black chador whom I had "failed" as a talk-show guest in March. I still didn't know she was "Mary," a spokes-woman who appeared frequently on American television.

"Tell everyone how you were fed, how you were treated," she prompted in a soothing voice in English.

"I was treated . . . like the others."

"You were fed amply?"

"I was fed three times a day."

Our duel resembled a dance. The tapes were obviously destined for American consumption. I tried to give just enough of the "right" an-swer to avoid retribution, without dishonoring myself or my country. I wanted desperately TO GET OUT—but couldn't do it by turning into a Quisling.

"You received medical care?"

"Yes."

"Good medical care?"

"I received medical care."

Ahmad entered the room toward the end of the interview. Was it to pass the word that I should not be considered for release? My nerves threatened to give. I had no idea that all the others in my room had been put through the same routine, many with the same pained ac-tion.

I should have said what I really felt before the camera. I should have made a speech of outrage, or refused to answer any questions at all. But I was afraid of months added to my "sentence," even of never getting out. That night I couldn't sleep at all.

The negotiators squabbled about money—but they were edging closer to one another. Denials followed misunderstandings that prompted retractions, but the hitches were more like last-minute than interminable ones. Bankers were tallying up Iran's frozen assets and moving gold for the transfer. By the morning of President Reagan's inauguration, on January 20, we were almost certain the hostages would be free very soon.

I had to use the shower again for tears of relief. An embarrassing, yet thrilling thought wouldn't go away: Over the past fourteen months I had encountered some of the world's most powerful, in-teresting men, and Barry had the makings of the best of them. I

wanted him to be proud of what I had done at home, much of it orig-
inated by guessing what his responses would have been.

But the thought that the "new me" was more worthy of Barry alternated with fear, even guilt, that my growth would almost certainly
not have taken place without his ordeal. Thanks to both, he was coming home to a wife who no longer wanted him to make the major
decisions. Did he have to be away for me to speak for myself? Was it
terrible that my husband's imprisonment was the catalyst? Men
plunge guiltlessly into *their* adventures, especially in wartime—and this
had been a kind of war. But that wasn't a full answer for me.

I was afraid to think how much of our marriage was predicated on
the old roles. I loved Barry as much as ever, admired him more than
ever, and knew how important I was going to be to him in the coming
months. My passionate wish was that the Barbara who had evolved
would fill his need. I feared his fantasy veered in the opposite direction: a heightened version of the woman he left. It was silly to imagine we could be *the same* again. The greatest irony would be if I
found I needed privacy from him, too.

*

In Algiers, Washington, London, and Tehran, teams of diplomats
and bankers worked almost around the clock to settle the details of
frozen assets and accumulated interest, and to solve seemingly insolv-
able problems that cropped up. The tone of news bulletins seemed to
change hourly. I listened with one ear. The other was tuned to my
private station, which carried a talk show about domestic possibilities.
No one had answers.

Television vans were encamped outside our gate again, some for
the third day, in bitter cold. We knew many of the reporters and felt
sorry that they had been ordered not to leave until "something happened." The assemblage, larger than ever, had worked out a modus
vivendi that included a deft poke of fun at me. They would elect one
of their number to approach the front door and ask, with exaggerated
meekness, when I might favor them with two words of comment. We
bowed at each other and laughed. One of them drove Alexander and
me to school so I wouldn't lose my parking place. When I returned, a
pizza was waiting for my "second breakfast."

Tension still lurked beneath the carnival atmosphere. I didn't want
to comment until I was notified officially of the release—but uncertainty dragged on. I felt like a hungry person lurching for a meal that
kept being pulled out of reach. From early morning, reporters passed
on the news. They said the wires had confirmed that an Algerian jet
was on the tarmac at Mehrabad Airport, in Tehran, awaiting the hostages. The Iranians were awaiting confirmation that eight billion dollars had been transferred to their account in the Bank of England.
Since the Iranians trusted no one, physical movement of the money

was a problem. No one took up my suggestion of bombing Tehran with eight billion dollars worth of pennies.

Finally the reporters announced that the transfer was accomplished. The State Department would confirm nothing, however, until they received official notification from the Algerians or the Swiss that the hostages were free. Now suspense built on the question of when the plane would take off. Minutes dragged into nearly an hour. Television lights went on every time I went to the door for information. Reporters passed on bits of information, and the State Department remained silent.

Half jokingly, I had predicted in December that if release came, it would be during inauguration, just to steal the show for the militants. The television screen was indeed split: Ronald Reagan being sworn on one half and reports from Mehrabad Airport on the other. Unofficial word came during the inaugural address that the plane had taken off for Algiers. Our houseful of relatives cheered and embraced.

That was enough. I carried both children outside. Neighbors were streaming toward the yard when the State Department called and cameras rolled.

"Barbara, how does it feel . . ."

"It feels *wonderful*," I said, not protesting at the question I had grown to abhor.

Breakfast came at the expected time on January 20. Lunch was delayed. The hours between were excruciating.

The guards had stopped scurrying. There seemed to be fewer than usual, and it was very quiet. Minutes passed like weeks, and nothing happened. It turned dark by four o'clock in the afternoon.

Two hours later, Ahmad burst into the room with thug-like Reza. "It's all over," said the leader, in English. "Everybody's going home." Every cell of my body wanted to believe him, but I couldn't forget how many times he had lied. Perhaps that was why there was no cheering. Any six Americans would have made more noise at a quiz contest. Or perhaps instincts for self-protection kept us from opening up in front of the chief guards.

"Pack one bag with your belongings," he continued. "Any letters or written material in your pockets will be confiscated when you are searched at the bus. Put them in your bags."

Jubilation and mistrust canceled each other out, leaving us excited almost to the panic point, yet empty. "I'm free!" I whispered to myself. "You *think* you're free," answered another inner voice. Around the room, the others, too, were biting their lips: holding themselves back from flying high, to soften the crash if it was to come.

Iranians usually used the plastic bags for garbage. Ahmad tersely specified to what degree we could fill them. What to take in the tiny volume allowed? Still shutting off our emotions, we worked on packing in an eerie hush. Should I take the book on sailing Barbara had sent to give Dave Roeder and me our minutes of escape? Her letters to me, which I had almost memorized? My watercolors of the children? I shifted the items back and forth as if this were the decision of my life, then sat down and looked at the others, who were also trying to steady themselves.

Ahmad returned with his surliness in place. "Your packing must be completed at seven o'clock," he ordered. "In forty-five minutes." Looking down at the bags of those nearest the door, he grew furious. "Too big, they're TOO BIG," he shouted. "None of this clothing; we'll send it to you later. Just your letters and things."

He picked up a bag and ripped it. "Smaller" he shouted, and punched it. "Get rid of all the *junk*," he shouted again—and ran out. We looked at each other for explanation or support, but each face showed only the wary doubt of seasoned prisoners.

Blindfolded, we groped downstairs from the third floor, carrying our bags. The motor of a bus—surely it was a bus, and a large one—ran and ran. Platoons of guards were scurrying again, and Ahmad directed the operation as if it were the embarkation for the Normandy Invasion. Under his orders we handed over our bags, which were tossed aside. Somehow I knew they wouldn't be going with us.* What no one knew for certain—even less now, with the bags gone—was where we were going. A guard shoved me into the bus, on top of other Americans, whom other guards were shoving. Another one took away Barbara's book on sailing, and my little envelope of soil from the Minneapolis boy was confiscated in a final search.

The bus seemed to seat about forty. I was one of the dozen or so pushed onto the aisle floor. John Graves's cough sounded from almost on top of me. I hadn't seen him since we were moved from the Ambassador's residence, over a year before.

"Is that you, John?"

"Barry! How *are* you, man?"

A surge of affection for him went through me as we hugged from behind our blindfolds. Apart from this, my calm surprised me. Surely this wasn't a charade to destroy us emotionally. And if the end was indeed coming, I wanted to bear the last pushing around, the final hours of humiliation, with dignity.

But Michael Metrinko, a political officer, went further by cursing Ahmad in Farsi. He had been pushed one time too many, and despite months in solitary, used "son of a whore," an insult he knew would infuriate. I could hear him being taken off the bus. Slaps and punches sounded over the grumble of the motor. Perhaps this would be their last roughing up.

We barely had room to breathe. It was probably 7:30 P.M., though I couldn't see my watch. When the bus finally moved off, we were ordered not to talk. The pain of elbows and knees jamming into me at each bump in the road was sweet: I was too caught up in *movement* to hear my pulse or have any awareness of my physical state.

As the bus rolled on and on, I tried to think of how to determine whether it was headed toward the airport. What if it *was* the airport and one of the guards put out his hand to say good-bye? No, I couldn't take it. They had caused too much pain to too many people. And they didn't care about that. Born in opposition to oppressors, they had become oppressors themselves.

"Don't e-speak," snapped one of them. "Keep your mouth e-shut." But the need to find out who was on the bus was almost as great as the need to ask each other where we were going. Traffic noises gave no clue. The bus seemed to be crawling. Hope was so strong I could almost feel it; yet we controlled ourselves. It occurred to me that we were hardened enough to take ten years, if necessary. The next sec-

---

* Six months later, most of the contents was sent to me in Brooklyn via the Red Cross and the State Department.

ond I thought I'd risk a breakout if we were just being moved again, if today *wasn't* the day.

"Don't e-speak. None of you."

The bus jerked to a stop. There was no indication that we had come to an airport, or anywhere else; just a halt seemingly in the middle of nowhere. We were told to unload ourselves. As the first of us were getting off, screams of "God is great!" "Khomeini is our Leader!" "Death to America!" filled the air. I had never heard them laced with more venom. This was no ritual, but an expression of fury. I wondered whether we had arrived at a place for public display of us, like the pit where I watched the camel kill.

Slowly we groped down the aisle. As I fumbled to find the step leading to the ground, Ahmad ripped off my blindfold. Two human walls of khaki formed a passageway from the bus, but before I could make out faces, a spray of flashbulbs blinded me. Then there was a hand—not extended for me to shake, but used as a stiff-arm to whirl me in the right direction for my last appearance on Iranian television. More lights were brought to bear, this time for the camera crew. While I blinked them off, the screaming climbed to a higher pitch and gobs of spittle landed on my face.

Focusing again, I saw a large jet thirty yards from the bus. Khaki walls flanked the path to the boarding stairs. Whatever awaited us at the end of the bus ride, I expected the usual delay and last-minute racing around by the guards. Now things were happening too fast to take in; I felt as if I were watching action in a dream.

The howling young Iranians formed a kind of gauntlet. I recognized a few guards from my various places. This was their last hurrah —and a true expression of their emotion. "Death to America, DEATH TO AMERICA, *DEATH TO AMERICA!*" Two guards from the bus held me under my arms, maybe to protect me, maybe because they still felt they had to protect themselves from attack by a prisoner. I did not feel my feet on the ground. It was as if I floated to the stairs.

I raced up. The plane's markings were Algerian. As I approached the cabin door, a cheer went up—which I would be joining for the hostages behind me. Someone said, "Welcome, hello," in English. The Swiss Ambassador seemed to be there, if I remembered his face, and a squad of Algerian security men. Automatic weapons never looked so good as those in their hands. I stepped inside and felt myself start to laugh.

Almost a year before, I had described my symptoms to a Swiss doctor from the International Red Cross who visited our Embassy room, the only doctor I could fully trust. "What do you think it is?" I had asked anxiously. "I'm not sure," he had said, "but I'm fairly certain things will improve very quickly once you are out of here."

He couldn't have known how prophetic that was. Walking down

the aisle of the plane past kissing, jubilant faces, I understood the expression "feeling like a new man."

Everyone was there. I hugged Bob Ode, whom I hadn't seen since February, and we both started talking at once. A much thinner Dave Roeder grabbed me as hard as I grabbed him. "We made it, Barry. We finally *made* it!" A sergeant who had served with the military advisory group and with whom I had hardly had any contact embraced me too. Everyone loved everyone else; everyone's joy was for all the others.

The plane could not take off, because only fifty-one of us had signed the list as we came in. Then it was discovered that two people had signed in one space. The plane still could not take off, because no one would pull away from the big bubble of congratulations to take his seat. The crew and the squad of Algerian security men gently pressed us to settle down.

At last the engines sent up their reassuring whine. I broke into an involuntary grin, as when my father's old station wagon came to life after an hour of trying to start it. The takeoff was not interfered with. We were on our way!

I sat with Kate Koob, my ICA colleague, but everyone's talk was all over the cabin. The pilot interrupted with a gloriously eloquent announcement in English: "We are now entering the air space of Turkey." The cheer was louder and freer than all that had preceded it. I realized I had not been alone in holding back while we were still over Iran. Someone told me that even the Algerian security guards hadn't left the plane during its three days on the ground in Tehran.

"Kate, it's over," I said. "I wondered whether I'd ever say just that. Thank God, it's all over." While we kissed, the stewards poured champagne. After half a glass I was as high as the plane. People were singing "Deep in the Heart of Texas." Someone proposed a toast "To Freedom."

The Algerian Ambassador to Iran had remained in Tehran, but high officials of the Algerian Foreign Ministry were flying with us. Bruce Laingen made a short, moving speech of gratitude for their great help. We cheered again and individually thanked every Algerian in sight. The pilot came into the cabin for a drink with us. Another cheer. It was a sublime flight.

❋

We came down in Athens just long enough to refuel. The next stop, Boumediene Airport, outside Algiers, was longer. The Iranians apparently had refused to allow us to return directly to the jurisdiction of our own, evil country. Never mind that this made nonsense of their having used us as symbols of precisely that "evil"; to save face, we had to be delivered only to Algeria, with the pretense that where we went next was none of their business. At the airport, Foreign Minister

Mohammed Seddiq Ben Yahia formally transferred custody of us to Deputy Secretary of State Warren Christopher, who we now knew had been very prominent in the negotiations. The brief ceremony began toward 3 A.M.

The next flight would last two hours and take us to Wiesbaden, Germany. We were as giddy from happiness as from exhaustion. "What's the first thing you're going to do when you get home?" a reporter shouted as we made our way toward two U. S. Air Force medical evacuation planes. I told him the answer would have to stay between Barbara and me.

The crush of newsmen and cameras in Algiers should have been a clue to the story we had become for the press and concern we had been for the American people. But we didn't suspect the full scope. Not in our most hopeful moments, not even after bundles of Christmas cards from strangers, had we come close to guessing the extent of American preoccupation with our safety. It was on our predawn landing at Rhein-Main Air Base, outside Wiesbaden, that we got the first glimmers. A "WELCOME BACK HOME!" sign covered the entire terminal. Crowds waved and cheered in movielike lights, and we heard a chant that could have been prescribed as an antidote to all the proclamations of hatred and death. "USA, USA, We didn't forget you." Dave Roeder and Tom Schaefer ran from the plane like teenaged athletes to embrace everyone in sight.

We drove to the U. S. Air Force Hospital, outside Wiesbaden, where a band from the American Community School struck up "Tie a Yellow Ribbon," and airmen and their families from the base sang "God Bless America" and "The Star-spangled Banner."

❋

Our reception at the hospital was nothing less than perfect. Never in civilian life had I encountered such excellence and thoroughness among doctors and nurses. Treatment was tactful and sensitive; the mood was more compassionate and nurturing than I could have hoped for. There was no condescension or hero worship, but steady gentleness reinforced by skill, concern, and the most sophisticated medical tests. Above all, they *explained,* at last, what I had experienced. My symptoms were not some form of madness, they promised, but an understandable reaction to severe stress which would respond well to treatment. "You yourself don't know what your system was subjected to," said the doctor to whom I was assigned. "But everything can be put straight, and without drugs."

The great relief this provided was a partial cure in itself. I had promised myself to take no more pills. I was going to get well without them—and, the first night, slept three full hours unmedicated. The pulsations were still there, but the next night was halfway to a normal one. Improvement kept me grinning like an idiot.

For the first time since leaving Iran, I thought about that country. Lying in a clean bed, I realized my bitterness was already draining away in the hospital's caring warmth. If the revolution turned out a failure, they would have brought it on themselves. For the moment, I had other priorities.

The hospital PX did not carry toys. Two German saleswomen there brought a doll for Ariana and a car for Alexander. I had no money. "We wouldn't take any," the two insisted. They *knew* me, not as one of fifty-two hostages, but as Barry Rosen, husband of Barbara, who had made a beautiful impression in Germany the previous April. I could detect nothing false in their generosity. They sincerely wanted to buy presents for my children, whom they also "knew."

That told me as much as newspapers and magazines, including back issues in packets specially prepared for us. Between rest periods, conferences with doctors, and talks with a sensitive air-force rabbi, we caught a glimpse of the cause célèbre the Four Hundred and Forty-four Days, as we quickly learned to call our experience, had been throughout the world. Apparently America had made more of us than of the prisoners of war in Korea, Vietnam, and World War II combined, and the concern had spread throughout Europe.

I suspected much attention had gone to me thanks to Barbara's campaign. It also seemed I was being cast as a hero, which I considered a hoax and a reversal of what I had learned about captivity. I told the doctor it had gotten the better of me in ways others had avoided without loss of their dignity. They accepted and adapted. I allowed it to eat at me, or I ate at myself, then tried my best to fight the battle with remains.

I wanted very much to behave well—for my family, for my image of myself, for my country. If I passed, it was with a mark of sixty-five.

That disappointed me. I'd have thought I was better hostage material, but one doesn't know until the test comes—and I hoped others would not have to take it. In any case, I didn't want transformation into a giant. What was the point, except to fool people into believing oppressive situations are as easy to handle in life as in television Westerns? Fables about being tough could only belittle my months of gasping, while giving others the worst possible preparation.

The plane landed at Algiers in early evening New York time. I was at the CBS studios, commenting on live coverage with Richard Queen and Dan Rather. Richard, the former vice-consul, had recovered remarkably since his release in June because of multiple sclerosis. He introduced most of his former fellow hostages as they stepped off the plane—but when Barry appeared, I interrupted. "And that is Barry Rosen," I stated—leaving the rest unsaid. Barry looked so much like *Barry*, his distinctive self. A surge of pride swelled.

He turned toward the camera as if searching for me. Dan Rather looked to see if I had something to add, but I didn't want to spoil the moment. Dan's eyes were wet. Complaints about the media notwithstanding, I felt very close to him and the studio crew—and, of course, to Richard.

I kept seeing Barry's gaunt but happy face as I drove home to Brooklyn. The house was packed with relatives, friends, and neighbors. It was eleven o'clock: past bedtime in our working-class area, but champagne corks popped as I entered.

I stayed up alone to watch the arrival at Wiesbaden. It was nearly two o'clock when the hostages emerged from two American planes, clearly very tired, very happy—and sufficiently recovered to wave to well-wishers, which they had hardly done in Algiers. I saw Barry again, appearing less stunned and more lively.

How much I wanted to say even a word to him! But the television commentators indicated there would be several hours of check-in processing before the *former* hostages might call.

It seemed only minutes after I went to sleep in the little bedroom from which I'd been called to learn the news fourteen months before that the telephone rang. It was the first night in a week that I hadn't left the receiver off its hook. I had slept just long enough to be disoriented at the sharp awakening and outraged at the reporter who dared call at that hour.

"Hello!" I snapped, my newly self-confident voice at its sharpest.

I assumed the hesitation indicated intimidation. Finally a tentative response: "Hello . . . hon?"

"Who *is* this?" I demanded. Weeks before, I had begun fending off reporters' questions about what my first words would be to Barry with "Barry who?" Here it was, almost as in my joke—and not very funny. I knew, of course, before I finished my challenge.

"Barbara, it's me." There was a short, strained pause. "It's Barry."

Our conversation took its cue from the false start. We talked of everything at once, but in headlines. While I was asking about his health, he wanted to know about the children. He began to talk about hating Iran, but I wanted to hear about *him* and tried to sound him out about what had been troubling him and how it was now. He said he began feeling better the moment the plane took off.

He sounded better than his letters. The other good sign was equally encouraging. We spoke for more than an hour, and it felt like minutes. Even in that disjointed way, it was good to *talk* to Barry.

A communications center fit for the Super Bowl had been set up on our floor of the hospital. From any one of about twenty-five booths we could call anywhere in the world without charge. Every booth remained busy, doing excellent "business." We called, talked our heads off, then called someone else. Saying whatever to whomever we wanted was a reversal of the isolation of our confinement, and we indulged our appetite to communicate. On my first call to Barbara we talked almost two hours.

When I called again, the next morning, her mother said she was shopping for clothes for my arrival. My mother-in-law's happiness couldn't have been greater had I been her own son.

During our chat I felt a tapping on my shoulder, which I shrugged off as a signal from an impatient ex-hostage. The tapping continued, and I turned around. Jimmy Carter was standing inches behind me.

"Mom, I'd like you to say a word to somebody here," I said. As I handed our ex-President the telephone, he asked me whom I was talking to.

"Hello, Lillian, this is Jimmy Carter," he began.

An hour before, the President had met us all, in our pajamas, in a ward turned reception room. Former Secretary of State Cyrus Vance, former Vice-President Walter Mondale, and aides Hamilton Jordan and Jody Powell were with him. Mr. Carter entered the room first. It was obvious he did not feel easy—probably with reason, since hard feelings about the long "delay" in our release lingered among many of us.

The President shook three or four hands. The exchange seemed stiff, like the polite applause when he first appeared. Then someone broke the ice by hugging him impulsively. As he worked his way around the room embracing each of us, the atmosphere became warmer and warmer. When my turn came, I felt nothing perfunctory or awkward in his gesture. His eyes were wet. His grip conveyed that he had truly suffered for us.

Then he gave a brief, moving speech, looking at us rather than at notes. He said we had done the country a great service by unifying it in support of us. Nothing, even the presidency, meant more to him than our release, he continued. His last words, about being over-whelmed with happiness and gratitude for our safety, almost choked him.

I choked too. I believed him utterly.

After a few days of catching up on news, I was convinced he had made serious mistakes. To have declared himself "obsessed" with our fate was flattering to us but an invitation for the Iranians to manipu-late him. I believe he should have been more forceful and less public in his thinking and moves: less willing to beat his breast and air his hurt when it provided comfort for him—and encouragement to our captors. A strong declaration of rightful demands followed by a cou-rageous period of silence might have freed us much sooner. Certainly it would have given the Iranians less pleasure, and probably less to bargain with.

Other hostages expressed other complaints in questions after the President's words. Why had the Administration's reaction to the sei-zure been—or seemed—so weak? Was it morally or politically wise to have paid a ransom for our release? Why had the rescue mission come so late? Yet even those who were more bitter than I clearly felt great respect for the office of the presidency. And on two points, he put us all at ease. He confirmed that no ransom had been paid: No more than $2.9 billion of $11 billion of Iranian assets were released when we were. He also assured us the relatives of the dead members of the rescue mission had no regrets for the attempt. This was an-swered by a moment of pained silence; then a release of emotion in powerful applause.

On top of that, I found myself liking Jimmy Carter personally. It seemed his false moves—making the conflict into a personal test, in-decisiveness in the face of possibly disastrous consequences of force-ful action—derived from the very personality that nourished his visi-bly deep concern for us as individuals. No doubt it is more important to judge a President by presidential than by personal qualities. But that could come later. It was as a person, not an official, that he ap-peared before us now. Seeing what the trouble and perhaps even guilt had done to his face, seeing his genuine relief that we were alive and generally well, I couldn't blame him. So much for my concern for foreign-policy issues at moments like these.

We stayed four days in the hospital's meticulously programmed yet unrestrictive routine of tests, consultation, and debriefing. Some were eager to get home after the first day; the majority, including me, were grateful for every recuperative hour. Barbara encouraged me on the telephone to stay as long as necessary. Apparently some wives wanted to fly to Germany as soon as possible. Barbara's interest was in my needs.

She sounded loving, yet careful and almost guarded. Catching up with newspapers, magazines, and news summaries on video tape gave me an indication that she had been more active working for our release than I'd suspected, and reporters I had known in Tehran called to tell me, among other things, about her effectiveness as a campaigner. I wondered how much she had changed. She told me about the children, but otherwise let me do most of the talking. She wanted to know what my doctors thought and kept reassuring me that everything was going to be fine at home; but it occurred to me that she really didn't know what to expect. Although our conversations dwelled on love, they were slightly artificial, faintly strained.

I missed his calls the following mornings. I was shopping to outfit the children in something that would please him. He deserved to be proud in every way when he saw them at last. Or perhaps I needed the shopping to get myself out of the house and into something other than waiting and thinking.

The rest of the following days were a whirlwind of brightening our little bedroom and answering the telephone calls of a hundred well-wishers. Reporters hovered, looking for the peek into the heart that would make their story. "What's the first thing you're going to say to Barry when he steps off the plane?" asked one as I left the house with the children on the evening of January 25. I was so happy that I felt neither nervous nor resentful as I looked at him—only an awareness of what I had learned. "Don't you think *he* should be the one to hear that?" I answered.

That evening, the children and I flew to Washington, where the families were given a final briefing. In the morning, we went on to Stewart Air Force Base, not far from West Point. The plane from Wiesbaden, with its fifty-two passengers, was to land there.

We arrived at the base at about 10 A.M.—too early, because we had to wait what seemed hours. Alexander, who understood that it *was* truly over and he would soon see the real Barry, entertained the crowd with his Khomeini face.

Most of the waiting relatives paced up and down, back and forth, inside the terminal. It was another freezing day, but that did not explain the frequent trips to the bathroom. Although many of the families knew each other well by then, we were too jumpy for sustained conversation. Obviously I was not the only wife worried about the future. As the wait went on, we deteriorated into a collection of nervous wrecks.

If someone had asked me to sum up the crisis, I would have called it a shared misfortune for America and Iran. Both countries suffered much more than loss of face, thanks to deep misunderstanding of each other and grave miscalculations in Washington and Tehran. I could think of no silver lining. Yet both sides were already celebrating this tragedy as a national victory. The outpouring of jubilation, patriotism, self-congratulation, and publicity seemed to have much in common with the very causes of the misunderstanding. Of course the country was in a mood of thanksgiving after the long humiliation. But why was it being whipped into this degree of triumph? If anything, the drive of many reporters to let nothing speak for itself, no matter how obvious, was even more blatant. This was a time for some reflection to dignify the rejoicing. With all that Barry and I had to resolve, I wondered whether the pressure of publicity, which I knew he, too, didn't want, would make it more difficult. Perhaps, on the contrary, it would help reunite us. The key questions were still his health and how much recuperation he would need, which was impossible to estimate from our telephone talks.

"Freedom One," a duplicate of Air Force One, flew us back to the States. The superb plane was labeled "United State of America," and the flight was full of a calmer happiness: that of going *home*. At a refueling stop at Shannon Airport, the Prime Minister of Ireland lauded us as a group sang "Tie a Yellow Ribbon" in Gaelic. We were getting a feel of what was going to be made of us, and back in the luxurious cabin we signed for each other fifty-two copies of a special edition of *Stars and Stripes* featuring our photographs. E-shut the Door complained about the smoking. Everyone else was smiling and laughing, yet touched with slight apprehension and even sadness that this uplifting camaraderie couldn't last.

The apprehensiveness was over seeing our families after the long separation. My own was at least equal to the others'. How much had Barbara changed?

As we approached the coast of Maine, the weather was perfectly clear, with the sun reflecting brilliantly off rivers and lakes, as if ordered. When the plane touched down at Stewart Air Force Base, the uniformed marines disembarked first, as we had agreed. I followed soon afterward.

Barbara, with her radiance, stood out instantly in the crowd below the ramp. All uncertainty disappeared. Alexander let go of her hand and ran into my arms as though I were returning from a week in Washington. Ariana blinked big eyes as if to ask who on earth I was. I gave the toys to the children to distract them for a moment so I could be alone—surrounded by hundreds of others on the tarmac—with Barbara. This wasn't the Barbara who maintained her reserve. She sobbed, her tears washing away my doubt. Our embrace was tender and natural. Many questions were answered in her arms.

"It's all over," I kept saying. "Everything's going to be all right." I was convinced it was.

ONE YEAR LATER

What does one say when it's over? I said thank God—above all, that Barry and the others weren't seriously harmed, although nothing, of course, will return the eight servicemen to their families.

The reception for the fifty-two was overwhelming. Living daily with the burgeoning interest did not keep the explosion of patriotism and affection from amazing me. Barry had far less preparation—and was stunned.

The first month was like one long "Welcome Home" testimonial that shuttled us from a television studio to a parade to a dinner to a thanksgiving service and back to a television studio. I kept asking myself what was being celebrated. I was celebrating Barry's return, of course, and to some extent, the country was too. There was generous emotion in the personal involvement. People were rooting for the hostages as though they were old friends. They felt genuine relief and happiness at their safe release, just as they had felt genuine anxiety about their treatment. Beneath the excesses of excitement I also sensed a great desire for unity within the country, and the fifty-two were the perfect symbols for release of that understandable feeling.

But the shouting and fireworks also fueled deception and self-deception. What had we accomplished or learned during the sad affair? Very little, it seemed to me. The supercharged celebrations were something of an evasion. Hard questions about policy and the real causes of the Iranian mess that were explored minimally for the public during the crisis were pushed aside once again in favor of a torrent of self-congratulation. The idea of a full congressional investigation of Iranian-American relations was abandoned. Not even the question of why the Embassy remained open after the first seizure was publicly explored.

Television played the happy ending as big as possible. It was a gala show; nothing changed in the motives and methods of the commercial networks. If new anti-American action takes place in, say, South America, we will be as badly prepared as for what happened in Iran —and there is no reason to hope coverage will be less superficial. Our "victory" in getting the hostages back safely gave no grounds for optimism that the same kinds of illusions would not lead to new captives'

Finally the plane appeared. The big white craft seemed to hover in the air, then taxi forever. It looked like a jumbo jet: another good omen, considering where Barry and I had met.

At last the landing steps were in place. The families surged onto the tarmac. The marines emerged first, looking as polished as if they had come from a year of routine duty. My chest constricted; I could barely breathe. Then I saw Barry. There was a spring in his step. He was wearing a jaunty tweed cap and typically immaculate white turtleneck sweater. He looked wonderful and healthy!

"Look, Zand, there's Daddy!"

Alexander dropped my hand and ran toward Barry with no hesitation. My knees trembled. Barry trotted toward us, his face a big smile. I had forgotten how blue his eyes were—and how sensitive.

He scooped up Alexander with one arm and wrapped the other around Ariana and me. The crowd disappeared from my vision, together with thoughts. There was no worry or strangeness, only relief and joy, one feeding the other.

Alexander was elated. Ariana was frightened and began to wail. I cried too, for the opposite reason. Then I drew back for a moment and saw the dark circles under Barry's eyes. They confirmed what he would need now, but I couldn't stop crying.

I did not know why. It was everything at once: relief at touching him, abandoning the self-control I had worked so hard to maintain, realization that this test was finished. I let him comfort *me*.

"Don't worry, hon. It's all over. Everything's going to be all right."

It was too good to be together to question anything.

being taken in the future, and to more sensationalizing, trivializing, and false moves while they languish.

Yet the overwhelming welcome seemed to have a healing effect on Barry, even though part of him wanted to escape it, even though he insisted that the cheers for him were based on false premises. That was what he believed intellectually. Emotionally he was nourished by the outpouring of respect and affection.

He had been through more than I had guessed from his letters and even from television clips from Tehran. Coiled like a spring, he had also been laced with medications for sleeping. Even now, New York noise gives him a start, especially at night. When Alexander or Ariana suddenly slam a door, I can almost see the surge of tension before he jumps. But the damage isn't permanent. Treatment for his high blood pressure and pulsations is by biofeedback rather than drugs; and it is gradually returning him to normal. It was clear within weeks that he would recover completely.

It took even less time for the children to adjust to his return: in fact, no time whatever for Alexander. Ariana's wariness lasted a day or two, after which she decided he would make a good horse and began climbing onto his back. She opened to him totally and joyfully. Barry grew fond of her as fast as she grew accustomed to him and is now as close to her as he was to Alexander at the age of two.

When Barry left for his first trip after his return, Alexander asked, "You sure Daddy's coming home?"—but he soon stopped worrying. A few days after Barry's return from Tehran, Alexander asked him why he had been "taken away." After Barry's simple, straightforward explanation, neither child questioned again. I doubted they understood much about hostage-taking or why anyone considered Barry an enemy. His calm affection was what they wanted—and received. They were reassured, and Barry's fears of how the deprivation of their father would affect them receded.

After a vacation in Puerto Rico and a few months in the Brooklyn house, we moved to an apartment near Columbia University, where Barry was appointed the first Presidential Fellow. When I spoke to him from Wiesbaden, he volunteered that he hated Iran and wanted nothing more to do with it. From time to time he repeats that sentiment in diluted form—saying he's had enough Iran and plans soon to finish with it forever. No one believes that, and I doubt he does himself. In any case, he is more submerged than ever in Iranian affairs, and when he complains about sinking into quicksand, I smile at his little cover-up, and he smiles back. At Columbia he is working toward his doctorate—in Iranian studies, of course. His dissertation will examine aspects of the Iranian press during the revolution.

He is also much in demand as a lecturer—about Iran in general and the hostage experience in particular. He travels widely, speaking to university and religious groups. With all that, he has little time to rest and sometimes feels frazzled, but I'm not certain the long escape he regrets missing would have been best for him. The general policy of State Department doctors, to return the former hostages to work as quickly as possible, seems effective. The most difficult cases of readjustment have been chiefly among those who have *not* kept busy: marines, for example, who left the service and have not found a new vocation.

Despite hints by some television reporters that my life was all but over because my time on the screen had ended, "fame" lingered for a time. I received two mother-of-the-year awards, one from the prestigious Mother's Day Council.

Actually I was a mediocre mother during the crisis. As a parent, I'd give myself the bare passing grade Barry gave himself as a hostage. A good mother focuses on her children, whereas I was pulled from mine by pressure and obligations, and perhaps by new interests as I developed a taste for stepping out in the world. If anyone in my family deserved the award, it was *my* mother, who substituted for me so often and so well. If any in the country at large deserved it, it was the wives of the dead servicemen, now raising their children alone. But I "won" because television had created a public me. The Mother's Day Council had a pleasant award ceremony. I tried to shape my address around the mothers left widowed by the rescue attempt and the Simons Fund, which would later receive a donation from the council; the truth was that I accepted the award meekly. I wish I were better about following my own advice and listening to my own criticism. In retrospect, I enjoyed television appearances and other publicity-centered activities, despite resenting their emptiness. I was more skilled at knowing what was wrong than at resisting the temptations.

As for Barry and me, the year has been full of adjustment. As I imagined, my thoughts about work no longer center on *his* plans and hopes. I also want more time for myself, sometimes simply to be alone.

Is it paradoxical that the crisis that drew us so closely together in some ways, pulled us apart in others? In the fairy-tale version of our "adventure," we'd have lived happily ever after. In real life, we are groping for new roles.

In connection with dates still being marked—the second anniversary of the seizure of the Embassy, the first anniversary of the hostages' release—reporters ask me about adjustments, hidden scars, and effects on our marriage. I answer that Barry seems stronger for his experience and I feel stronger too, but it doesn't necessarily follow that the marriage has been strengthened—because ours, like almost every other I knew, was not an equal partnership. What will happen to it is still unclear.

The problem lies not with Barry but squarely with me. If I had chosen to elaborate at interviews, I would have mentioned the curious fact that family members seem to be having greater trouble adjusting to the hostages' return than the hostages themselves. Four divorces and three separations among the fifty-two families (twenty-six of the hostages were married) are not necessarily evidence of this, since some had been contemplated before. But most of the difficulties of the reunited couples are being felt principally by the wives—who are faced with the prospect, and in some cases the reality, of becoming *dependents* again.

Reassuming their previous identities, the men went back to work, most with direction, purpose, and a "future." Although this, too, may sound paradoxical, the women who took an active interest in the crisis changed more profoundly than their imprisoned men. Most of us began as sheltered homemakers, not quite trusted—even by ourselves —to ponder the most important matters. My own four hundred and forty-four days was the opposite: an unprecedented time of learning and development. But few of the women have yet found ways to express their new interests, and feel puzzled or sad.

Barry is busier than ever, and although he regrets not being able to lead a more studious life, I sense that—apart from concern about me —he is happier than ever. He has less time for the children than he had had for Alexander when we were in Washington. He regrets that even more, having promised himself as a hostage that his primary attention would go to his family when he returned. Still, he is in his element now. He has cultivated ease in speaking to large audiences and meeting roomfuls of new people—to whom he takes the opportunity to tell home truths about Iran. Hurrying from a day in the library to the airport for an evening speech, he feels as fulfilled as most people can in our jumpy age.

I believe I'd feel the same if I could plunge into something. I haven't been able to, chiefly, but not exclusively, because the children need me near them. They go to nursery school part of the day, but Ariana is only three years old and Alexander five: Someone from the family should pick them up, take them home, and be with them, especially as we settle into a new neighborhood. Beyond that, I've allowed myself to be spoiled by my brief encounter with politics, diplomacy, and journalism. I want a career, not a job. Considering my scanty training for the matters that interest me now, that wish is presumptuous. So I drift about in a second limbo, feeling distinctly more capable—and more depressed—than when I took for granted that the important decisions about myself did not depend on me.

Throughout much of the crisis, I congratulated myself on how calmly I took bad news and how firmly I kept my emotions from interfering with my activities. I simply would not let the situation depress me or the children. But something sneaked up from behind to affect me, as it turns out, more than the hostage in the family. Unlike Barry, my interests and needs have not remained essentially the same.

This is new territory for our marriage. We haven't charted it yet, chiefly because I haven't staked out *my* "future." Barry is supportive and willing to work at anything that would make me happy. When he dresses to fly to a lecture and I remain at home with my uncertainty, I watch him and muse. The lasting effects of his captivity seem to have settled on the unexpected person.

Just before he left on his last trip, we listened to a broadcast about yet more assassinations and retaliatory executions in Iran. "It is as though it never happened to me," he said of his captivity—and rushed for his taxi. Every day, his memories recede further, mercifully. Every day, my dilemma of what to make of myself grows heavier.

I haven't found a way to reconcile my ambition with my obligations and qualifications. The principal of my elementary school kept urging my mother, who worked as an aide, to resume her education and become a teacher, for which she had unusual potential. My mother turned down the opportunity, because she believed it would take too much time from *her* children. Is that the answer for me?

It would have been easier if this had happened earlier, giving me the jolt I needed to prepare for the life I think of for myself, but for which I lack preparation. At thirty-three, with two young children, I am not in the ideal position to strike out for a new career. On the other hand, I was lucky the jolt came at all. Without it I would surely be less at sea now, but undoubtedly slip into middle age without knowing much about myself.

My "psychic" powers tell me something positive will come of my experience. On a national level the hostage crisis seems to have contributed little to a growth of awareness. On a personal level it has been my liberation. Barry has refrained from asking, "What do you want to be liberated *for*, Barbara?" I doubt that many men are so understanding. It is clearer than ever that I made the right choice, if that's how to put it; clearer than ever that we are blessed with exceptional children and an extended family that *is* important in contemporary life. The crisis has left me a little at a loss, but also grateful. That sounds confused; so am I.

When four hostage months had passed, I confided their most important insight to Barbara. "I see this situation as a lesson about ego and striving," I wrote from my basement room with Bob Ode and E-shut the Door. "I was really happy but didn't know it before I left for Iran. If only the clock could be turned back." That was easier observed than learned. I'm back to "ego and striving."

My moral was to spend more time doing what I knew to be most important. I'd had glimpses of the truly good life I would lead when I got out of the guarded rooms. Its central rule was not to say, "I'll take care of this little matter today so I can have tomorrow free," but to make time then and there for quiet hours with the children. I had been dashing about too much for the sake of *future* happiness—which would never come.

But I was off and running from the moment we drove up to Barbara's house, in Brooklyn, where the telephone was ringing. Proposals for this talk and that appearance, this interview in London and that award in Texas hardly stopped coming during the following months. Only I was to blame for accepting too many of them, but surely my belief that I had discovered a formula for the "optimum" way of spending time would have collapsed anyway.

Back from my idealization of American life to the real thing, I relearned that everything is a compromise—even this book, which I very much wanted to do, yet which took me away from the family many more months than I wanted to "sacrifice." I found I couldn't escape the "rat race" without withdrawing from worthy projects. Perhaps the only lesson I've learned is that prison can provide no overriding lesson for dealing with ordinary routine. Against the fantasy of my "new" life—which was going to be as pure and full of meaning as the leaf I plucked on the first day we were permitted outside—my return has been a disappointment. If anything, temptations to rush about on momentarily "urgent" matters have increased, making it even harder than before to focus on the important.

Much of the trouble came with the Niagara of undeserved publicity that deluged us. "My heart is so full of love and joy whenever I think of you and the children," I wrote to Barbara when release had become a real possibility. "All I want is to be with you once again. I hope I can skip the whole public relations aspect of the return and just settle down with you and the children into middle-class anonymity." But it would have taken a more resolute person than I to resist the current. Being imprisoned is essentially a passive experience unless one tries to escape. Although I tried to make clear that I wasn't the hero people wanted me to be, most Americans seemed determined to believe I had performed something admirable, *done* something worthy of extravagant praise. Scores of plaques mentioned my "devotion to Americanism," "strength of character," and "courage." The truth is that I was no hero, "unless," as Bob Ode put it, "there is a new definition of hero as being in the wrong place at the wrong time." I could only repeat that I did nothing in any way extraordinary. I am convinced that most Americans, including those who cheered me long and loud as a symbol of national virtues, would have behaved as well or better. The proof of this was that most hostages did; and we were a fairly ordinary collection of people. My own driving force came mostly from nothing more elevated than the instinct for survival and for not demeaning my people.

But the public wanted a hero, and the public is difficult to disappoint. Gatherings, dinners, school assemblies, television shows, and other events in my honor built one upon the other. Once one organization certified me a stalwart, a recommendation passed to the next and I was invited to yet another head table. As the ticker tape showered down on a Manhattan parade and the crowds shouted "B-A-R-R-Y, B-A-R-R-Y!" I tried to tell Barbara how escapist the picture of me was. "I don't want this, I want *us*," I said. "I want some reality about that misery; otherwise what possible good can come of it?"

Yet I couldn't often refuse honors and invitations. Who wouldn't be moved by the outpouring of affection from strangers all over the country; who would want to offend the good people who released it? The attention to us was partly an expression of an extraordinarily powerful desire to find a source of national pride and unity after the disappointments and dissensions of the Vietnam War, the apparent decline of American strength, and the humiliation of the hostage situation itself. After many years of starvation of the national esteem, a pent-up craving for good news was being released on us.

The good side of this was obvious: Some of the best American qualities—generosity, good fellowship, and uncalculating neighborliness—poured out together with the happiness for us. What Kate Koob called the "bath of love" in which we soaked for months contained something innocent in the best sense. The national rejoicing was confirmation of Americans' affection for America, of sincere happiness that we would again enjoy its blessings—of which I, the son of a poor immigrant, was doubly aware after living without them.

The bad side seemed equally obvious: The urge to pretend that we were as tough as cowboys and selfless as a crack squad of soldiers was one manifestation of unwillingness to face reality that tended to undermine thinking about Iran and preparation for a similar experience in the future. The remaking of the mostly drab and dreary four hundred and forty-four days with bright lights and glory went together with something approaching a fixation to declare an American "victory." A sign I saw in one of the parades read "U.S. 52, Iran 0." This expressed the wishful thinking of hundreds of people I talked to, most of whom resented my opinion that we hadn't *won*, or that I myself wasn't part of the proof of this. Surely our former guards in Tehran were also proclaiming victory, whipping themselves into a kind of mania. It seemed to me, however, that the entire episode was closer to defeat for both sides, which no amount of celebrating could transform into its opposite.

If it *was* a defeat, its major cause was misunderstanding. I could do nothing now to try to correct Iranian distortions of American reality, but the thought that I might be contributing to half-truths and myths that swirled around the American view of Iran was particularly disturbing. Here again the fireworks and congratulations tended to substitute for examination of what landed the United States in so much trouble in the first place. It was easier to celebrate, just as it had been easier to assume the Shah was in control.

The same kind of self-deception continues to pervade most American writing and broadcasting about Iran for the general public. It is understandable—and dangerous. By far the greatest attention is being given to the country's troubles, especially the instability and potential chaos of the new regime. Attempts to enforce Islamic laws, and resistance to this expressed by assassinations and bombings of leading revolutionary politicians, have made the major news stories. Executions and other forms of terror against the revolution's real and imagined opponents are presented as evidence that the new regime is more repressive than the Shah's. It would be abnormal to suggest that the revolution hasn't degenerated in many ways from its own idealism— as it showed signs of doing with its first steps to control the press; as almost all revolutions do that promise purity or paradise. Like so many previous revolutions, the Iranian one quickly squandered its opportunity to set an example of social progress without suffocation of dissent. By Western standards—my own standards—it is growing more odious daily. As I feared during my early days in captivity, editors I knew were persecuted, some thanks to meetings with me. They are a handful of thousands executed without proper trial, forced to flee the country, jailed, or hounded.

But I believe this is but one aspect of a complex situation in Iran. Despite our horror at the new brutality and misery, despite even growing disenchantment and disillusionment there, most Iranians still appear to support the radical clerics. The new regime's attempt to create a self-sufficient country, as free as possible from outside influences, is especially popular among the urban and rural poor— although not, of course, with the Iranians who have fled, nor with many of the middle class who have not. Despite the revolution's grave flaws and shortcomings, the majority probably prefer a Shi'ite state to the Shah's. They are combative, not defeatist—and enjoying a pride in Iran they have not known for decades.

Iranians remain Iranians, with cultural and social attitudes developed over thousands of years. Although future events are difficult to predict, the country will change in keeping with those fundamental attitudes, most of all deriving from Shi'ite Islam and its concept of social justice (which is not very different from the American one, despite great differences in methods and approach). Together with keeping track of the new regime's fumbles, jockeying for power among rival mullahs, and depressing violations of human rights, we ought to reflect on that.

I myself ought to reflect on why Iran so enamored me, whether it was a young man's infatuation with the first foreign country he was in. It's now obvious the country's politics are dismal and I no doubt gave that too little weight in my early years there, when I was charmed by the attraction of its "inner life." But how should this be measured in terms of Iran's great contributions, especially cultural, to civilization? I hope, one day, I'll strike a fair balance between the pluses and the minuses.

The principal lesson of the revolution and hostage crisis is yet unlearned. Revolutionary pressures are building in many Third World countries. Why does America, originally the most revolutionary and least imperialist of Western countries, take the brunt of their hatred and create opportunities for Soviet expansionism? Partly because we still believe our aid and presence can prop up unpopular leaders. When another "Iran" comes, we will have opened ourselves to the revolutionaries' revenge, because we will have supported the fatally vulnerable "strong man" they detest—all for expediency and against our long-range national interest.

*

Returning to the family has also been less the triumph than I had imagined. Worry about my relationship with the children was groundless. I am deeply grateful for the strong, easy rapport Ariana and I developed within days. Alexander is a gentle, loving, intelligent boy: all I wanted, without myself having "molded" him. But things are more difficult with Barbara, as I soon realized they had to be. She has changed considerably.

The catalyst was clearly her work in the domestic side of the crisis. Barbara's radio and television appearances were all the more remarkable in light of her previous shyness in public. In another sense, they were no surprise. I always knew how well she thought and spoke. Few of the hundreds of Americans I talked to in the first months home failed to mention how much and how well she did in her appearances. When I saw some of the tapes, I felt the praise was understated. Barbara was more than articulate and diplomatic: She showed an instinctive ability to get to the heart of matters under discussion, and a matching perception of Iranian attitudes.

I was proud of her. She never allowed her answers to descend to the level of "poor hostage wife talks about her imprisoned husband," but turned even silly questions to the point. In the aftermath she is troubled by not finding the challenging vocation she very much wants. Anyone who has been galvanized for one purpose as she was for that long is let down, of course. I love her and try to support her, but only she can make decisions about her own career.

Instead of walking away into a glorious sunset, we've entered the most difficult, potentially most constructive period of our friendship, which is underlining our personality differences. I am more romantic —or quixotic; she is more evenhanded, just. Her wanting more time for herself, which would require more help from me with the children, is no less than fair—but hard to put into practice. Should I skip seminars to bring the children home from school? This isn't how our society works yet, or how the family can be supported.

When we solve these problems, our marriage will be stronger than ever. Even on days when we appear to be pulling in independent directions, I am certain we will succeed. Survival in Iran would have been difficult without Barbara. After our shared ordeal, life would be an empty mockery without our commitment and trust. Our old ability to talk is returning; that is our method. The more I know of "the real Barbara," her desires as well as her abilities, the more deeply I respect her.

I mention the disappointments and difficulties because it is beyond me how to convey the joys. No one can appreciate daily life in a free, democratic country until he has been deprived of it. I never quite understood the profound affection for America, even in hard times, of émigrés from less-fortunate countries. Now I feel a bond with them, whatever our political differences.

Those who have survived a similar experience will understand this; those who haven't probably cannot, just as I couldn't before being captive. I don't know why one must lose things in order to cherish them. All the clichés are true, and when it comes to the most basic emotions, it's hard to speak in other ways. I am deeply grateful for the accident of my birth, deeply grateful to be home, deeply grateful to those who worked for my release. I cannot forget the eight who died. Otherwise, every day, with all its domestic uncertainty and with all my worry about our foreign policy, is a blessing. I love walking out of the apartment in the morning; I love returning in the evening.

INDEX